THE ESSAY AT THE LIMITS

THE ESSAY AT THE LIMITS

Poetics, Politics and Form

Edited by
Mario Aquilina

BLOOMSBURY ACADEMIC
LONDON • NEW YORK • OXFORD • NEW DELHI • SYDNEY

BLOOMSBURY ACADEMIC
Bloomsbury Publishing Plc
50 Bedford Square, London, WC1B 3DP, UK
1385 Broadway, New York, NY 10018, USA
29 Earlsfort Terrace, Dublin 2, Ireland

BLOOMSBURY, BLOOMSBURY ACADEMIC and the Diana logo are trademarks of
Bloomsbury Publishing Plc

First published in Great Britain 2021
This paperback edition published in 2022

Copyright © Mario Aquilina and contributors, 2021

Mario Aquilina and contributors have asserted their right under the Copyright,
Designs and Patents Act, 1988, to be identified as Author of this work.

Cover design: Jade Barnett
Cover image © Andrew Borg

All rights reserved. No part of this publication may be reproduced or
transmitted in any form or by any means, electronic or mechanical,
including photocopying, recording, or any information storage or retrieval
system, without prior permission in writing from the publishers.

Bloomsbury Publishing Plc does not have any control over, or responsibility for, any
third-party websites referred to or in this book. All internet addresses given in this
book were correct at the time of going to press. The author and publisher regret any
inconvenience caused if addresses have changed or sites have ceased to exist, but can
accept no responsibility for any such changes.

A catalogue record for this book is available from the British Library.

A catalog record for this book is available from the Library of Congress.

ISBN: HB: 978-1-3501-3448-5
PB: 978-1-3502-3537-3
ePDF: 978-1-3501-3449-2
eBook: 978-1-3501-3450-8

Typeset by Newgen KnowledgeWorks Pvt. Ltd., Chennai, India

To find out more about our authors and books visit www.bloomsbury.com
and sign up for our newsletters.

For Anita, Elias and Niamh

CONTENTS

List of Figures	x
Notes on Contributors	xi
Preface	xiv

Introduction
THINKING THE ESSAY AT THE LIMITS   1
   Mario Aquilina

Part I
THE ESSAY AND THE WORLD

Chapter 1
THE ESSAY AS PHENOMENOLOGY   23
   Erin Plunkett

Chapter 2
AN ESSAY ON THE POST-LITERARY   37
   James Corby

Chapter 3
BRIEF SCENES: ROLAND BARTHES AND THE ESSAY   49
   Neil Badmington

Chapter 4
THE 'SUBVERSIVE POSSIBILITIES' OF THE ESSAY FOR PUBLIC
INTELLECTUALS   63
   Nicole B. Wallack

Chapter 5
IS WRITING ALL OVER, OR JUST DISPERSED? DIGITAL ESSAYISM IN
TRINA, A DESIGN FICTION   77
   Joseph Tabbi

Part II
THE ESSAY AND THE SELF

Chapter 6
TONE AND THE ESSAY 97
    Ivan Callus

Chapter 7
WHAT THE PERIODICAL PRESS MADE POSSIBLE: WOMEN ESSAYISTS
IN THE EIGHTEENTH CENTURY 111
    Jenny Spinner

Chapter 8
OTHERNESS AND THE ESSAY IN THE PACIFIST WORK OF VERNON LEE 125
    Rachel Baldacchino

Chapter 9
MARGINS AND MARGINALITY: JEAN GENET AND THE QUEER ESSAY 137
    Aaron Aquilina

Chapter 10
THE ESSAY AND THE 'I': ELIOT WEINBERGER'S TRANSFORMATION OF
THE AUTHORIAL SELF 151
    Michael Askew

Part III
THE ESSAY, FORM AND THE ESSAYISTIC

Chapter 11
AT THE LIMITS OF *FIXITÉ*: THE ESSAY AND THE APHORISM 169
    R. Eric Tippin

Chapter 12
ASSAYING THE NOVEL 183
    Jason Childs

Chapter 13
WALLACE STEVENS, AUDRE LORDE AND THE QUEER
PERFORMATIVITY OF THE ESSAY 197
    Allen Durgin

Chapter 14
TRANSGRESSION AS TRANSCENDENCE: ESSAYISTIC POETICS IN
SELECTED WORKS BY DMITRI SHOSTAKOVICH AND JOSEPH VELLA   213
    Maria Frendo

Chapter 15
HERSEY, RESNAIS AND REPRESENTING HIROSHIMA: TOWARDS AN
ESSAYISTIC HISTORIOGRAPHY   229
    Bob Cowser Jr

Suggested Reading around *The Essay at the Limits*   243
Index   245

FIGURES

5.1 'She had gotten used to the live transcript, a curtain of text that dangled just beyond the brim of her hat during each session.' Voiceover 05:20, Slide 17 from *Trina: A Design Fiction* by Anne Burdick and Janet Sarbanes. © Anne Burdick and Janet Sarbanes, 2019. Reproduced with the permission of Anne Burdick and Janet Sarbanes 84

5.2 'Someone forwarded the first letter ever typed by Mark Twain.' Voiceover 12:20, Slide 38 from *Trina: A Design Fiction* by Anne Burdick and Janet Sarbanes. © Anne Burdick and Janet Sarbanes, 2019. Reproduced with the permission of Anne Burdick and Janet Sarbanes 86

5.3 'Concrete Poetry or Typewriter Activism?' Slide 49 from *Trina: A Design Fiction* by Anne Burdick and Janet Sarbanes. © Anne Burdick and Janet Sarbanes, 2019. Reproduced with the permission of Anne Burdick and Janet Sarbanes 88

5.4 'Trina rubbed her SkyEyes, disconnecting them from Humanitas Inc. She turned off her audio and walked away, through the creosote and out onto the dirt road.' Voiceover 19:00, Slide 57 from *Trina: A Design Fiction* by Anne Burdick and Janet Sarbanes. © Anne Burdick and Janet Sarbanes, 2019. Reproduced with the permission of Anne Burdick and Janet Sarbanes 89

CONTRIBUTORS

Aaron Aquilina is an associate lecturer with Lancaster University's Departments of English and Sociology as well as an Assistant Director with the former. He is also the founding and general editor of *antae*. Aquilina obtained his PhD in English in 2019, and his work focused on literature of/and the death penalty. He has varied research interests and has published on concepts of destiny (2016), indifference (2019), and the genre of the suicide note (2019).

Mario Aquilina is Senior Lecturer in English at the University of Malta. Author of *The Event of Style in Literature* (2014) – a theory of style through readings of Derrida, Blanchot, Gadamer and Celan – Aquilina has published and edited on topics like the essay, creative nonfiction, style, rhetoric, literary theory, electronic literature and Shakespeare.

Michael Askew is a postgraduate researcher at the University of East Anglia, UK. His PhD thesis, which he is currently writing, examines the contemporary lyric essay, and includes chapters on Annie Dillard, Anne Carson, Maggie Nelson and Claudia Rankine.

Neil Badmington is Professor of English Literature at Cardiff University, UK. He is the editor of the journal *Barthes Studies* and his books include *The Afterlives of Roland Barthes* (2016) and *Perpetual Movement: Alfred Hitchcock's Rope* (2021).

Rachel Baldacchino is Academic Coordinator of migrant integration projects within the Department of Inclusion and Access to Learning of the University of Malta. Her research interests are early twentieth century theories of empathy and non-violence with special focus on women's literature and the essayistic. Her most recent publication is 'Being in Borders: Empathy, Pacifist Resistance, Vernon Lee', in *Women and Political Theory: Vernon Lee and Radical Circles*. ed. Sophie Geoffroy (2017).

Ivan Callus is Professor of English at the University of Malta. He has published and edited widely in the areas of contemporary fiction, poststructuralist literary theory, and posthumanism. He is the General Co-Editor of *CounterText: A Journal of the Post-Literary*, launched with Edinburgh University Press in 2015, and a founding member of the Critical Posthumanism Research Network.

Jason Childs is a writer and scholar currently based in Berlin, Germany. His criticism has appeared in the *Sydney Review of Books and American Book Review*. He was a 2019–20 fellow of the Electronic Literature Organization and is an associate editor of *electronic book review*. He is also the co-editor, with Christy

Wampole, of *The Cambridge History of the American Essay* and, with Denise Gigante, of *The Cambridge History of the British Essay*, both forthcoming in 2022.

James Corby is Associate Professor and Head of the Department of English at the University of Malta. He is General Co-Editor of *CounterText* and a founding member of the Futures of Literature Network. He has published on literature, philosophy, performance and politics.

Bob Cowser Jr is Professor of English at St Lawrence University, where he teaches courses in film, non-fiction writing and American literature. His most recent book is the true crime memoir *Green Fields: Crime, Punishment, and a Boyhood Between*. He is also the author of the memoir *Dream Season* and *Scorekeeping: Essays from Home*, and edited the anthology *Why We're Here: New York Essayists on Living Upstate*. He has taught in France, England, Denmark and in state and federal prisons.

Allen Durgin is Course Director of Readings in Gender and Sexuality at Columbia University. His most recent essay, 'Baby with the Bathwater: The Queer Performativity of Eve Kosofsky Sedgwick', appeared in the twenty-fifth anniversary issue of *GLQ: A Journal of Lesbian and Gay Studies*.

Maria Frendo read for her PhD in English Literature at the University of Durham. She is Senior Lecturer at the University of Malta and a member of the editorial board of *CounterText*, a Literary Studies Journal published by Edinburgh University Press. Maria is also a fully qualified musician, and a Fellow of the London College of Music and Trinity College of Music, London. She is co-curator of the Joseph Vella Music Archive at Il-Ħaġar Museum, Victoria, Gozo.

Erin Plunkett is Lecturer in Philosophy and Religious Studies at the University of Hertfordshire, UK. Her research interests include Kierkegaard, phenomenology and poetics. She has analysed the relationship between style and philosophical thinking in her book, *A Philosophy of the Essay: Scepticism, Experience, and Style* (2018), and she is the editor of a forthcoming Jan Patočka Selected Edition.

Jenny Spinner is an essayist and Professor of English at Saint Joseph's University in Philadelphia, where she teaches creative nonfiction and journalism and serves as director of the Writing Center. Her scholarly work focuses specifically on women essayists. Her most recent book is *Of Women and the Essay: An Anthology from 1655 to 2000* (2018).

Joseph Tabbi, an American academic who currently works at the University of Bergen, Norway, has made significant contributions to the field of experimental, often essayistic fiction in both print and electronic media. In 1995 he co-founded, and is still Editor-in-Chief of the reputable scholarly journal, *Electronic Book Review*.

R. Eric Tippin is Assistant Professor of English at Palm Beach Atlantic University, USA. His research centres on the periodical essay in Britain at the end of the nineteenth and the beginning of the twentieth century. He has published on the essay as well as the work of Oscar Wilde and G. K. Chesterton, most recently in the journals *English Literature in Transition, 1880–1920* and *Religion & Literature*.

Nicole B. Wallack is the Director of the Undergraduate Writing Program and Senior Lecturer at Columbia University in the Department of English and Comparative Literature. Her research interests focus on writing studies, English education, American studies and teacher education. She has published on the essay and on practices of writing-based teaching. Her most recent book is *Crafting Presence: The American Essay and the Future of Writing Studies* (2017).

PREFACE

The seeds for this book were sown in the early stages of a conference on the essay held in Malta in April 2019, *The Essay: Present Histories, Present Futures*, which was intended to initiate and extend conversations among and across different traditions and contemporary schools of essay studies.

Having studied in Malta and the United Kingdom, and having worked for a number of years on theoretical approaches to literature, my interests in the essay initially centred on canonical English essayists like Woolf, Orwell, Hazlitt and Lamb as well as critical theory's investment in the form – Lukács, Adorno, Benjamin, Derrida, Blanchot and Barthes. However, I was also well aware that the essay has been an important form across the Atlantic for the best part of the last hundred years and is also currently flourishing in the United States, especially in terms of interest in the craft of the essay, its use as a pedagogic tool in college contexts and its participation in political and cultural debates. I hoped the conference would encourage a more sustained exchange of ideas across these different traditions in essay writing and essay studies.

The Essay at the Limits was conceived quite early in this process, and by the time the conference was held – gathering more than sixty essayists and scholars from all over the world – the book had already been contracted. What brought the sixteen contributors together was a willingness to think of the essay critically or, more specifically, to reflect on the theory, poetics, forms and politics of the essay, both in its history and its current moment. We felt that this kind of approach would complement the already well-established interest in the history and craft of the form.

I believe the book delivers on what it promised: the development and refinement of theoretical conceptions of the essay in ways that are of interest to students, scholars and essayists. The contributors think of the essay alongside literature, philosophy, critical theory and politics. They invite the reader to think about how the essay relates to the self, identity, gender and culture, and they dwell on aspects of form, tone, style and voice. They also make a case, primarily through the introductory chapter but also throughout the volume, for thinking of the essay as a form at the limits, constituted by a productive tension between the essay and the essayistic, that is, the essay as a genre and the essayistic as a mode that may or may not coincide with the genre.

What the book lacks, sadly, is a chapter by the late Ned Stuckey-French, a much loved and respected essayist and scholar, who supported my work around the essay with profoundly generous advice and encouragement despite never having met me in person. For this volume, Ned was drafting a chapter on what he termed 'the political possibilities of the essay in this moment' when he passed away in June

2019. He was looking at essays that are 'lyrical, innovative, wedded to the "truth", aware of the opportunities that come with the digital, seeking new audiences'. Ned, his work and his friendship are sadly missed, but I remain grateful for his support and enthusiasm for the book as well as for having introduced me to essayists who I now can count as friends.

Of course, I am grateful to many others. David Avital, at Bloomsbury, was the first to show a keen interest in the book. David expertly guided and accompanied me through the ideation, drafting, submission and the reviewing of the proposal. At Bloomsbury, I was also assisted by Lucy Brown, who I thank for her patient responses to my editorial queries; Katy Day, for dealing efficiently with contractual matters; and Ben Doyle. In Malta, I owe a debt of gratitude to Ivan Callus for being a generous interlocutor about the essay and other subjects; James Corby for his support and for facilitating sabbatical leave that helped in the early stages of this book; and all the contributors for their work on this volume.

Finally, I would like to thank Anita, Elias and Niamh, for their love and support and for giving me the space and time needed to finish the book, especially in the three months spent at home during a soft lockdown due to Covid-19.

1 May 2020, Siġġiewi, Malta

INTRODUCTION: THINKING THE ESSAY AT THE LIMITS

Mario Aquilina

Preamble

The essay is at the limits. Indeterminate, changeable and heterogeneous, it is marked by an appetite for the experimental, the transgressive and the tentative as well as an equally decisive pull towards tradition, the communal and the familiar. The essay is a private form with an eye on the reading public, or a public intervention tinged with personal experience. It is dynamic, daring to speculate and disobey while gathering and recollecting. It provokes and consoles, breaks the rules and retreats. It is both product and process: a product that foregrounds process, and a process that resists but ultimately settles, tentatively, as product.

The essay, as this book will show, flourishes in these productive tensions and has done so since its birth, irrespective of whether we locate it in Michel de Montaigne or in earlier figures like Plutarch, Seneca and several others whose writing we may sometimes read as genealogically relevant in alternative histories of the essay.[1] This introduction will seek to contextualize, explore and develop this thinking of the essay at the limits.[2] My aim is to elucidate and hopefully extend theoretical discussions of the essay while providing a conceptual framework for the other fifteen contributions in this volume, all of which, in their own ways, discuss the essay in relation to limits of different kinds.

The word 'limits' in the title may initially seem to be a counter-intuitive choice. As a noun, 'limits' carries the meaning of 'boundaries' or 'restrictions', and this begs the question of why one would aspire to write about the limits of the essay, the boundaries that circumscribe it or, put crudely, what the essay cannot do. However, as it will become clear both in this introduction and in the other chapters of the book, the 'limits of the essay' are not only productive in a definitional sense – without limits, something would be everything and hence nothing – but also crucial to understanding what is specific to the essay as a literary form. I argue that the essay is *at the limits* because it is constituted by an often paradoxical negotiation of limits, both formal and conceptual. Like other literary forms, the essay is made recognisable by its limits, but the essay negotiates these limits in specific and distinct ways, and this is important in understanding not only the essay but also that quality we call 'essayistic', which I will be discussing below.

As far as literary forms go, the essay may be said to be somewhat readable, often aiming at what Phillip Lopate describes as a 'conversational style of writing'.[3] In the words of Graham Good, it 'presupposes' a 'sympathetic reader'.[4] The essay establishes a relationship of trust and 'friendship' with the reader,[5] who is engaged by what Michael L. Hall calls a 'shared experience', an 'implied dialogue' or at least through a 'heuristic, cooperative exploration of a subject'.[6] 'You leave the essay', writes Sarah Levine, 'feeling as if you have met somebody'.[7] In short, the essay is a human form – fundamentally interested, as William Hazlitt puts it, in the 'mixed mass of human affairs',[8] whether trivial or vital, and it tends to be written in 'language capable of rendering and communicating observations'.[9]

However, these aspects of the essay – its being a human form interested in human matters, written in a conversational style and dependent on a readership that shares similar interests and concerns – sit side by side with its tentative and experimental tendencies that make it repeatedly reinvent itself in different contexts. Indeed, as we will have the opportunity to see below, the essay is often defined as transgressive and future oriented. It is thought of as a swerve from convention, an experimental attempt at the new and even as a form that, paradoxically, shows the impulse to move 'away from genre altogether, in the direction of formlessness'.[10] From these perspectives, which coexist in the history and theory of the essay with the characterization of the essay as a human and familiar form, the essay is marked more by the desire to stretch and transgress previously established limits than specific formal features, such as style, tone, structure, thematic concerns or rhetorical functions, which are generally more useful in defining other literary genres.[11]

The rest of this chapter attempts to expand on and think through the implications of these different conceptions of the essay.

The essay at limits, in theory

An observation to begin (or begin again) with is that it is striking how *essayistic* theories of the essay tend to be. It is also remarkable how *self-reflexive* essays tend to be. They are so already in Montaigne, who digresses from his ostensible topics repeatedly to reflect and theorize about the book of texts he names as *Essais*.[12] 'How often and perhaps how stupidly have I extended my book to make it speak for itself!' he declares.[13] For Montaigne, the essay is a project of the self, for the self and about the self, which means that the self-reflexivity of the form is both inescapable and a source of apprehension: 'For as for my excuse, that I ought to have more liberty in this than others, precisely because I write of myself and my writings as of my other actions, because my theme turns in upon itself – I do not know whether everyone will accept it.'[14] Not only, however, has this self-turning or turning toward the self or *itself* been accepted in the tradition of the essay, but it has been emulated to the point of becoming a staple of the essay. As Rachel

Blau DuPlessis writes in '*f*-Words: An Essay on the Essay': 'Essays tend to call the genre into question, as theory about genre also does',[15] and this happens not only in essays like hers or like Hilaire Belloc's 'An Essay upon Essays upon Essays', Katherine Fullerton Gerould's 'An Essay on Essays' and Michael Hamburger's 'An Essay on the Essay', but also in others in which the declared subject of the essayist (the one indicated in the title, that is) is not the essay.[16] Robert Atwan frames the issue of the essay's concern with itself slightly differently, preferring to focus on the perspective of those who write about the essay. More than other literary forms, he claims, the essay 'seems to demand' definition. It imposes an 'obligation to propose definitions', but, at the same time, 'anyone who has attempted to write about the essay knows how difficult the genre is to define' and thus cannot help but feel 'nervous'.[17]

This nervousness, for instance, is manifested in how frequently studies of the essay begin by renewing the perennial attempt on definition, as if doing so would still seas otherwise too treacherous to navigate. Such discussions may invoke, for instance, with varying degrees of depth and detail, the etymology of the word, 'essay', highlighting its Latin origins in the word *exegium* ('to weigh' or 'a weight'), its accrual of the meanings, 'to try', 'to attempt', in Romance languages and, following Montaigne, the metonymic sliding of the word '*essai*' in French from naming 'a trial' or 'an attempt' to naming a specific 'form of writing' inaugurated by Montaigne, *the essay*. Some will refer to this etymology and unearth there alternative definitional inflections. Consider André Belleau, who notes that the Latin verb *exigere* – from which the French, *essai*, derives – had a secondary meaning apart from 'to weigh': '*chasser hors d'un lieu*' ('to hunt or chase out of a place'). From here, Belleau notes, we get *essaim* ('swarm'), a popular form of *exagium*, which allows Belleau to essay his definition of the essay: '*L'essai n'est pas un pensée, une évaluation des idées; c'est un essaim d'idées-mots*' ('The essay is not a thought, an evaluation or weighting of ideas; it is a swarm of ideas-words').[18] 'A swarm of ideas-words' – no wonder defining the essay is problematic.

Another strategy of containment or domestication used for this unruly or feral form is to establish the limits – and, by implication, the *freedoms* – of the essay as an object of study by outlining its historical origins and genealogy. In other words: domestication by canonization. And this typically leads, as with Hazlitt, to identifying Montaigne as 'the first person who in his Essays led the way to this kind of writing among the moderns'.[19] Hazlitt's well-known passage about Montaigne in 'On the Periodical Essayists' is worth quoting at some length here because it outlines why Montaigne is often thought of as foundational of the form:

> The great merit of Montaigne then was, that he may be said to have been the first who had the courage to say as an author what he felt as a man. … He was, in the truest sense, a man of original mind, that is, he had the power of looking at things for himself, or as they really were, instead of blindly trusting to, and fondly repeated what others told him they were. … In taking up his pen he did not set up for a philosopher, wit, orator, or moralist, but he became all these

by merely daring to tell us whatever passed through his mind, in its naked simplicity and force, that he thought any ways worth communicating.[20]

For Hazlitt, Montaigne not only initiates the essay, giving it the direction that would be pursued by 'his imitators' – the individual, original and honest pursuit of truth communicated to his readers – but he also takes it to its limits by leaving 'little for his successors to achieve in the way of just and original speculation on human life'.[21] Montaigne did not say everything that can be said about human life, but Hazlitt argues that Montaigne's writing establishes stances and attitudes in how to observe human beings that other writers would subsequently emulate but not really extend.

Montaigne's seminal status is seldom questioned in histories of the essay, but the argument about how he shows the way for later essayists is often complicated by positing him in a dichotomy with Francis Bacon, whose *Essays, or Counsels Civil and Moral* (1597) closely follows the various editions of Montaigne's *Essais* – published between 1580 and 1595 – and anticipates John Florio's translation of Montaigne into English in 1603. Bacon is usually presented as a secondary foundational figure for the essay, secondary both in the sense of coming soon after Montaigne but also in terms of standing for a different conception of the form. G. Douglas Atkins, for instance, 'acknowledge[s] the fact and difference of Bacon's essays' and the 'important and crucial deviations from the Frenchman Montaigne'.[22] Montaigne's essays, with their focus on what Walter Pater terms 'experiences' rather than the 'fruits' of such experiences (more *process* than *product*),[23] are 'loose, exploratory and digressive'.[24] Bacon's essays 'appear more carefully crafted, more structurally integral, more shaped and formed'.[25] 'Even in its infancy', writes O. B. Hardison Jr, 'the essay shows its Protean heritage. … Being the first of their kind, [Montaigne's essays] ought to at least have become models for what followed. … They did not. Bacon's essays were inspired by Montaigne's, but are, if anything, anti-Montaignian.'[26]

Bacon's relatively 'formal, prescriptive and didactic' writing is typically presented as standing on the other end of the 'spectrum on which the essay has always played'.[27] Lopate frames these distinct characteristics in terms of the 'personal [or informal] essay' and 'the formal or Baconian essay', and he argues that 'the difference is one of degree' rather than absolute.[28] However, as Atkins suggests, the dichotomy at the generic origins of the essay is rarely conceived in neutral terms. It quickly morphs into a hierarchy of purity, with 'many … tempted to assign to Montaigne the essence of the essay and relegate Bacon not as derivative but as veering from the Frenchman's meandering way into something formal'.[29] Following this line of thought, then, Montaigne's essays can be made to show what an essay is meant to be, with Bacon's '*essays*' becoming misnomers, a foil against which the essay defines itself. Walter Murdoch, for instance, expresses this view when commenting on Bacon's style, which he sees as diverging significantly from Montaigne's conversational language: 'Bacon's bundles of wise saws are not essays – nobody ever talked like that'.[30]

This dichotomy at the origins, though, can be problematized. Bacon himself does not think of his essays as foundational of any genre. And significantly, when in an unpublished dedicatory letter to Prince Henry for the second edition of the *Essays* (1612) Bacon refers to his predecessors, he does not mention Montaigne. The 'brief notes' that he has 'called Essaies' have earlier origins: 'The word is late, but the thing is ancient; for Seneca's Epistles to Lucilius, if you mark them well, are but Essays; that is, dispersed meditations though conveyed in the form of epistles.'[31] Thus, Bacon distinguishes between the 'form' of Seneca's epistles and the essay as a 'thing', claiming that while the form of what he is doing is different from Seneca's letters, the thing itself is the same – the essay as 'dispersed meditations' (in hindsight, Bacon's description of his own work as 'dispersed' is curious given that Bacon would then often be pitted as the one who stands for structure and rigidity in the constructed duality with Montaigne).

Seneca's epistles, with their non-systematic, reflective and occasionally playful attempts at exploring general ideas about a range of topics from a personal perspective but within a wider conceptual framework, share many qualities that we often associate with the essay. Take, for instance, Seneca's Letter LVI, 'On Quiet and Study', which starts with Seneca locating himself in the very concrete and particular context of his 'lodgings right over a public bathhouse' and 'with a babel of noise going on all about' him.[32] Seneca gives his addressee, Lucilius, a detailed description of his personal experience of dealing with unsavoury noises such as when 'the strenuous types are doing their exercises, winging weight-laden hands about … grunting as they toil away'[33] and continues by surmising that what is really disturbing for a man is not so much external noise but 'his mind [being] in a ferment'.[34] 'It is this which needs to be set at peace', Seneca reflects, and then – often using aphoristic statements – he outlines several aspects of his Stoic philosophy including that: 'there is nothing so certain as the fact that the harmful consequences of inactivity are dissipated by activity' and that external noise 'will never break into our thinking when that thinking is good'.[35] Seneca's voice in this letter is lucid and assured, and like Montaigne would do so often, he develops his arguments by accumulating other classical voices, including Homer, Virgil and Apollonius. But the ending surprises us. If you have internal peace, 'voices never shake you out of yourself', he begins to conclude, before abruptly 'conced[ing]' that it is 'sometimes a lot simpler just to keep away from the din':[36]

> in fact it is the reason why I shall shortly be moving elsewhere. What I wanted was to give myself a test and some practice. Why should I need to suffer the torture any longer than I want to when Ulysses found so easy a remedy for his companions even against the Sirens?[37]

Seneca's swerve at the end undoes the previously outlined Stoic quest for inner peace through gentle wit and through admission of individual fallibility. Seneca, who was an important and acknowledged influence not only on Bacon but also on Montaigne,[38] justifies this abrupt change in tone by claiming that what he was doing was simply 'giv[ing] himself a test', a truly essayistic gesture if there is any.[39]

Definitional dichotomies and exclusions as well as narratives of origins are meant to establish a core for the essay as a genre. They seek to determine what a proper essay is, what the noun 'essay' properly refers to and what belongs to – *is a property of* – the essay as a form. However, these strategies of containment are particularly problematic for the essay, and one main reason is that the essay tends to be conceived as a form of 'veering'. Nicholas Royle, citing Montaigne and Theodor W. Adorno, thinks of 'the genre of the essay as *writing that goes off*'.[40] It veers in the sense that it is unmethodical and progresses in non-linear ways. And when an essayist follows the thoughts of another writer, Royle argues, he does so only pending a 'singular and perverse' departure.[41] By 'perverse', Royle does not simply mean 'morally' unacceptable (though that kind of swerve may happen in essayistic veering) but something generally counter-intuitive that goes against the acceptable or expected. He quotes Edward Said writing about 'late style' to explain further what veering in the essay may be: 'a nonharmonious, nonserene tension, and above all, a sort of deliberately unproductive productiveness going *against*'.[42]

In this context, the specific subject of the essay is not what is at stake in thinking of what the essay is or does. Indeed, the essay can be, has been, about anything and everything. 'The theme of an essay', as Cynthia Ozick puts it, 'can be anything under the sun.'[43] No list of topics reproduced here could ever hope to do justice to this variety, but even if I only limit myself to browsing essays of Charles Lamb, Virginia Woolf, Hazlitt, Annie Dillard and E. B. White – five essayists chosen purely on the basis of personal preference and their proximity on a book shelf adjacent to my writing desk – I can see that the subjects range from the purely abstract (time, unity, consciousness, separation, dreams) to the concrete (ears, moths, the railroad, old actors, a key, professions for women, footprints, a weasel, the South Sea House, old Mrs Grey), with all the shades, moods and tones imaginable in between (grief, humour, reminiscence, nostalgia, reflection, daydreaming, observation). I am tempted here to quote Jorge Luis Borges, who comes to mind as I struggle to recount this variety. I return to 'The Aleph' to reread the impressive and moving one-page list that Borges writes to represent 'the dizzying spectacles inside' the aleph,[44] one of the points in space that contain all points'.[45] I find there what seems like an adequate analogy to thinking of the heterogeneity of the essay: An Aleph is 'the place where, without admixture or confusion, all the places of the world, seen from every angle, coexist'.[46]

That essays can be about anything is a frequently mentioned characteristic of the essay, but this is hardly sufficient in understanding what is distinct and specific about the essay. I suggest returning to the notion of the swerve and the essay's peculiar relation, stance or attitude to the world. The essay may indeed recount and express every aspect of the familiar, but it tends to do so by swerving in some way. The essay has a knack for disturbing platitudes, questioning the accepted and rethinking the known. Hall traces what he calls the 'spirit of exploration' of the essay in its Renaissance roots: it is the '"idea" of discovery' and the essayists' response to this idea that marks the emergence of the genre.[47] The essay, Hall writes, is 'particularly suited to the examination of conventional wisdom, the exploration of received opinion, and the discovery of new ideas and insights' that allow 'the author to think freely outside the constraints of established authority and traditional rhetorical forms'.[48] As Elizabeth Hodges observes, the discovery of the new world makes it obvious that that which we previously thought was confined and contained, is potentially limitless.[49]

This 'spirit of exploration' persists in the essay. And the spirit of discovery, it must be said, is not only something that the essay embraces in its relation to the world but also something that the reader of essays comes to expect of the essay itself. The essay does not only recount an experience or a process of discovery that the essayist undergoes through the writing; it also demands an attunement to or propensity for discovery from the 'sympathetic reader'.[50] Again, random examples will have to suffice. Consider, for instance, David Foster Wallace's 'Consider the Lobster', which draws us in as a cultural and culinary analysis of a Maine Lobster Festival published in a magazine, *Gourmet*, where such pieces are what the reader would expect, but quickly turns into a disturbing consideration of the moral and philosophical dilemmas around cooking lobsters alive.[51] Or Hazlitt's 'On the Pleasure of Hating', which begins with the controversial position that a fundamental law of nature is 'hate': 'without something to hate, we should lose the very spring of thought and action'.[52] Or, as a third and final example, Samuel Johnson's 'The Solitude of the Country', which is much more rigid and structured in form than the essay by Hazlitt. Johnson's essay is not digressive but follows rhetorical models of arrangement to the extent that we can clearly identify the key stages of its argument against solitude on the way to a somewhat didactic and moralistic conclusion that presents the desire for solitude as a dereliction of duty assigned by Providence.[53] Hazlitt disliked Johnson's rigidity of form and style, which he compared to being 'upon stilts',[54] but Johnson too depends on a swerve in this essay as he begins with a socially acceptable idea at the time – the idealization of solitude – from which the essay will then veer:

> There has always prevailed among that part of mankind that addict their minds to speculation, a propensity to talk much of the delights of retirement: and some of the most pleasing compositions produced in every age contain descriptions of the peace and happiness of a country life.[55]

Apart from the swerve, one other useful way of thinking about the essayist's peculiar relation to the world is suggested by Réda Bensmaïa, who adopts Roland Barthes's term, 'recessive', to refer to the essayist's attitude towards one's past or one's ideas. One 'falls back, but … may also gain perspective thereby'.[56] The essay has a propensity to 'fall back'. Indeed, the intertextual and allusive qualities of the essay must surely be included in any poetics of the essay. William Gass writes that 'it is the words of others which most often bring the essay into being',[57] and he assures us that we 'are reading an excellent essay when' we find ourselves 'relishing the quotations as much as the text that contains them'.[58] For Lopate, who is thinking of Montaigne's essays, 'the essay sprang from quotation'.[59] Hazlitt, with his almost obsessive use of quotations from Shakespeare, is another case in point,[60] but this dependence on past essays, past books or what Lopate calls a 'shared literary culture' that nowadays extends beyond the literary into the realms of popular culture is a characteristic of most essays.[61] It is also what Rebecca Solnit seems to refer to when she thinks of the 'essayist's job' as 'gather[ing] up the shards or map[ping] them where they are, to find the pattern out there or make one with words about the disconnections and the mysteries'.[62]

The essay, then, gathers. It echoes. It falls back, recollects and organises. But it also reflects, inflects, deflects and dwells in doubt. It swerves, veers, gains insight or fails to do so. It questions, probes from different perspectives, shifts in tone, and it remains open to the future of thought, even when it is revisiting the past. It is in this sense that John Locke uses the term 'essay' for *Essay Concerning Human Understanding*, where 'essay' does not refer to 'spontaneous prose' but to 'a book where new ideas are proposed, an original interpretation of a controversial problem'.[63] As Jean Starobinski argues, the term 'essay' 'alerts the reader and makes him wait for a renewal of perspectives, or at least the statement of the fundamental principles from which a new idea will be possible.'[64]

This future orientation of the essay, its opening up of thinking, together with the possibility of speaking about anything, makes the essay resistant to restrictive limits. Indeed, the veering of the essay does not only happen *within* an essay. In other words, it is not only the internal digressive and unmethodical manoeuvres of the essayist or the conceptual departures from previous thinkers that are seen as constitutive of the genre. It is also each essay's tension with the limits of genre, tradition and accepted ideas. Its origins at the end of the sixteenth century (the narrative goes) involve a swerve from certainties and formal rigidity through an anti-rhetorical and anti-generic impulse. Stylistically, Hall explains, the foil is Ciceronianism, with its 'balanced clauses and studied formality' being 'overthrown' by Montaigne and Bacon, both of whom, despite their different styles and tones, share a fundamental scepticism with received authority and the rhetorical methods associated with it.[65] Along these lines, W. Wolfgang Holdheim describes Montaigne's essays as 'quite deliberately ... anti-genre, designed to flaunt the prescriptiveness in literary matters which had been inherited from a rationalistic rhetorical tradition'.[66] Montaigne's essays are a form of 'active deconstruction in the genuine sense: a clearing away of rubbish, of reified sedimentations so that issues may once again be laid bare in their concreteness'.[67] The veering in these texts then persists in 'the theory and practice of the essay'.[68]

Bensmaïa, in a frequently cited study theorizing Barthes's contribution to the essay as reflective text, discusses the swerving of the essay primarily in terms of genre or, more precisely, the essay's resistance to it.[69] For Bensmaïa, the essay is the 'other' to genre: it does not simply 'mix' genres, but 'complicates' them.[70] It is 'a-generic' or an 'anti-genre'.[71] This, Bensmaïa argues, explains why critics have been unable to define the essay; they are too concerned with identifying the 'rhetorical synthesis'[72] that would define a literary work's participation in genre, but with its incompletion, plurality, fragmentation and digressive nature,[73] the essay breeds 'chaos' rather than synthesis.[74] What actually returns in the essay, for Bensmaïa, is not authorial voice or style or the unity of an idea but diversity, and thus the essay's unity is 'unsubsumable' under notions of genre[75] and can only be expressed 'in the language of paradox'.[76]

This paradox at the heart of the essay needs to be reckoned with and it may be rephrased as follows: that which distances itself from the proper centre of the essay as a genre is that which does not veer enough, like Bacon's more formal essays or other writing in that tradition, such as Samuel Johnson's or Ralph Waldo Emerson's essays. Or, to unfurl the paradox differently: the more resistant to genre an essay is, the more properly an *essay* it is.

However, it seems to me that this paradox – while very appealing because it celebrates the infinitely inventive potential of the essay – requires nuancing and qualification. Bensmaïa uses the terms 'essay' and 'Barthesian Essay' interchangeably, revealing one issue with his theory of the essay as 'a-generic': he does not account for the essay when the essay does not do what he deems to be Barthesian things, for example, when it does not radically question the essayist as a 'subject of enunciation'.[77] In *Roland Barthes by Roland Barthes* and elsewhere, Barthes questions the 'American (or positivist, or disputatious …)' understanding of 'subjectivity' in terms of 'talking about oneself' and proposes instead a subjectivity 'deconstructed, taken apart, shifted without anchorage'.[78] Bensmaïa follows this and argues that 'at the origin of the work … is no longer Subject, identified and identical to itself, but the formal structure of the work'.[79] In other words, what anchors the essay is not the voice or the presence of the essayist, but decentred, fragmentary, intertextual and plural centres manifested in the formal (a-generic) qualities of the essay.[80] Bensmaïa sees his thinking as applicable to others beyond Barthes, notably also Montaigne, whose essays he reads not as 'the instrument for the expression of an Author's "ideas," nor as self-presence" of a Self' but in terms of a ' "resistance" to a spontaneous movement that can only be the repetition of outworn ideas, the refurbishing of already familiar sites, the culling of "stock phrases" and "images" '.[81] The essay, for Bensmaïa, is a space of encounter with and resistance against received language rather than a means of *self*-expression or *self*-exploration – if by 'self' we mean a unified presence, a constant entity that is or corresponds to a single human being. The essayist is aware of the '*debt to Rhetoric*' but tries to overcome it with a 'plethora of formal inventions', 'frenzy' and 'rage' against 'what has *already* been said, *already* formulated'.[82]

Bensmaïa's work is important in terms of outlining several insights that are central to post-structuralist theories of the essay, and the problematization of the self as subject would have to be confronted in any theory of the essay that reads not only Barthes but also Jacques Derrida, Maurice Blanchot, Michel Foucault, Gilles Deleuze and others working in the same tradition of literary theory and philosophy. However, we need to find a way of theorizing the essay without excluding the essay when it is more familiar than groundbreaking, when it leans more towards genre than the a-generic, when it constructs human presence rather than deconstructing it, or when it is more polemical than playful. And this, I believe, is even more urgent today, at a time when 'truth' is as much at stake as it has ever been. As Solnit suggests in her Introduction to *The Best American Essays 2019*, there is also a sense in which 'often the work an essay does is taxonomical'.[83] The essay, for Solnit, is 'a meeting ground'. It can be a form of 'gathering', a way of 'find[ing] the pattern out there or mak[ing] one with words'.[84] The essay, in other words, does not only deviate, disperse and digress. Even when it veers – indeed it often does – it also reflects, recounts and attempts to formulate shared and communal meanings. There is indirection, but there is also centring, and perhaps there cannot be one without the other.

Building on Bensmaïa, Claire de Obaldia also grapples with the paradox of the a-generic instincts in the essay, but she does so by focusing on the relationship between *genre* and *mode*. De Obaldia's argument appeals to the familiar dichotomy between Montaigne and Bacon, presenting their different approaches to the essay as 'two possible actualizations of the genre'.[85] For de Obaldia, in Bacon, the essay appears in its guise of a traditional *genre*, with conventional styles and structures being dominant. As opposed to this – but also stemming from it (de Obaldia's argument reveals an anachronism with Montaigne, so to speak, coming *after* Bacon) – de Obaldia thinks of Montaigne as representative of the 'essayistic' or the essay as a mode. Montaigne's essayistic writing, for de Obaldia, challenges the recuperative and centring instincts in Bacon's writing and it 'stretch[es itself] to its outermost limits beyond genre'. The 'radical … essayistic explosion of the genre' does not involve the complete overcoming of genre because the essayistic can only happen as long as the 'generic boundaries' are reaffirmed as a basis beyond which the stretching can happen.[86] However, despite this qualification, de Obaldia's work clearly foregrounds the essayistic essayists – from Montaigne to Borges, through Robert Musil, György Lukács, Adorno, Barthes and Derrida – who adopt the 'decentred' and ' "excessive" logic of the [essayistic] mode'.[87] In so doing, de Obaldia arguably relegates the 'genre' side of the dichotomy with 'mode' to a *secondary* status, not in the sense of it coming *after* the essayistic but in the sense of it serving primarily as a launching pad for the essay towards its essence in the essayistic (a potential in the genre actualised along a historical trajectory culminating in post-structuralist conceptions of the essay).

What I propose is modulating this slightly and thinking of the essay – to use a Derridean term (Derrida has been haunting this chapter) – as *always already* informed, constituted even, by an *irresolvable tension* of genre and mode. This involves thinking of the essay and the essayistic not as opposite ends in a spectrum along which different essays may be plotted at various points on a continuum (whether diachronic or synchronic) but as simultaneous forces (centripetal and centrifugal, if you will) that mark any essay and that determine the radical questioning of formal and conceptual limits that is paradoxically defining of the essay.

Before proceeding further, though, I want to be more specific in terms of what I mean by 'mode' and 'genre' in this discussion. Alastair Fowler distinguishes between *mode* and *genre* as follows: 'Genres have their own formal structures, whereas modes depend less explicitly on stance, motif, or occasional touches of rhetorical texturing'.[88] 'Genres', he explains, 'have a relatively circumscribed existence in space and time'[89] and they are 'limited by [their] rigid structural carapace', but mode, which 'corresponds to [an] attitude or stance' and is 'independent of particular contingent embodiments of it', is 'flexible, versatile, and susceptible to novel commixtures'.[90] This means that mode may outlive genre, and perhaps, we may add, it may even anticipate it. Building on Fowler, John Frow refines the terms further and he makes the term 'mode' work in an " 'adjectival' sense".[91] What this means is that for Frow, modes function as:

> qualifications or modifications of particular genres (*gothic* thriller, *pastoral* elegy, *satirical* sitcom) ... they specify thematic features and certain forms and modalities of speech, but not the formal structures or even the semiotic medium through which the text is to be realised.[92]

Thus, we may have, for instance, an *essayistic* film, an *essayistic* poem, an *essayistic* novel, an *essayistic* musical composition or even an *essayistic* digital video. In this context, the 'essayistic' would refer to what is often called the 'spirit' (if not the form of the essay): what Hall calls the 'spirit of exploration' and the 'exploration of received opinion';[93] or what Adorno terms the heretic impulse.[94] It may refer to the 'spirit of sceptical inquiry, daring experimentation and ironic play'.[95] Or else, to what Musil describes as the taking of a 'thing from many sides without wholly encompassing it'.[96] In other words, it is the essay's possibilitarian spirit lifted from specific formal requirements. It is 'this allure of beginning, this *inchoative* aspect of the essay' and the 'abundance of joyous energy' that comes with knowing that its 'scope is unlimited'.[97]

However, what complicates matters becomes clearer when we apply the mode in an adjectival sense as Fowler and Frow use it to the essay itself: an 'essayistic essay'. If the *essayistic* implies 'writing experimentally'[98] or the centrifugal and anti-generic possibilitarian (whether this is understood as a potential *within* the essay to try anything and write about anything or *between* one essay and the next) we are faced again by the paradox or the constitutive tension when approaching the essay as a genre.

We return to the etymology of *essai*, where we rediscover this tension. The dual or multiple meanings of both '*essai*' in French and 'essay' in English ('a short form of writing', 'an attempt' *and*, as a verb, to 'try') reveal the dual meaning of *essay* as both product and process. Claire de Obaldia says this of the word: 'We are left, then, with a term which is neither completely covered by the verbal (modal), etymological sense of "to essay", nor completely by the unifying generic utilization towards which it nevertheless gestures.'[99] Before de Obaldia, Good notes how this tension between the essay as process or attempt and the essay as product or genre already operates anachronistically in Montaigne's use of the term, in whom '*essai* ... hovers between the then established usage as "attempt" or "trial" and an anticipation of the generic usage' of the term.[100] This anachronism or, echoing de Obaldia, 'paradoxicality', puts the essay, suspends it rather, at the irresolvable limits of genre and mode.[101]

The essay being constituted around the limits of genre and mode may account for the recurring claims throughout literary history about the supposed deaths and rebirths of the essay. Exemplifying what he deems to be the inevitable death of genres when detached from the cultural and literary contexts that allowed them to flourish, Fowler claims that 'the use of the essay – a form reflecting the liberal attitude of uncommitted interest – began and ended with Humanism'.¹⁰² Michael Hamburger makes a similar point in a well-known 1965 essay in which he laments that 'the essay has been a dead genre' since G. K. Chesterton and Virginia Woolf because the individualism and the ability to saunter without design that are prerogatives of the 'spirit of essay-writing'¹⁰³ are frowned upon as 'shameless, egoistic and insolent' in contemporary society.¹⁰⁴ Within this context, what Hamburger saw as the loss of fortitude of the individual, authorial 'I' in the 1950s and 1960s would inevitably lead to the demise of the essay. It is fascinating to see, though, how seventy years earlier, in a witty 1894 essay, Agnes Repplier already expresses her suspicion of such recurrent claims about the many deaths, near-misses and returns of the essay. As an essayist, she writes, she may feel discouraged 'to be suddenly informed that [her] work is *in articulo mortis*'.¹⁰⁵ And yet, writing at a time when Woolf is still only twelve years old, she finds that the work of different essayists through time forms 'a linked chain, and … all are of service to the whole'. Thus, if one were to be free of prejudice in what to expect from essays, one would discover that 'the essay may die, but just now it possesses a lively encouraging vitality'.¹⁰⁶

Obituaries for the genre across its history (Hazlitt's claim that Montaigne's essays already take the form to its limits foreshadows such reasoning) are counterbalanced by celebratory pronouncements of rebirths and of being *in the time of* the essay. Robert Atwan, two years after founding *The Best American Essays* series in 1986, writes that 'essays are making a remarkable literary comeback,'¹⁰⁷ something he attributes to pollination by the 'same imaginative spirit as fiction and poetry' or, more specifically, the return of the 'personal essay' and the development of 'a prose that lives along the borders of fiction and poetry' and that blurs 'the boundaries of criticism, biography, and exposition'.¹⁰⁸ More recently, David Shields thinks of our time as the time of the essay and other essayistic forms of non-fiction, and he presents the essayistic in *Reality Hunger: A Manifesto* as an antidote to an 'unbearably artificial world', bringing the real back to reinvigorate the tired work of fiction. In 2019, Rebecca Solnit thinks about the largely political essays she selects for *The Best American Essays 2019* and writes that 'we live in an essayistic age'. For Solnit, the essay is far from a reflection of what Fowler saw as the 'uncommitted interest' that characterizes the essayist's attitude towards the world: 'in recent years some of the key transformations in the United States have proceeded in no small part by the arguments advanced in essays'.¹⁰⁹ At this particular moment in history characterized by fake news, post-truth politics and social media alienation, the essay, she insists, is a form of gathering and meaning-making that is 'passionately engaged, informed, and committed to ideals including accuracy and precision and fact and memory'.¹¹⁰

The essay, as these narratives of death, resilience and rebirth show, is always at the limits. Propelled by a tension between generic recollection and essayistic change, in constantly returning, the essay does not come back as the same thing but adapts itself to its moment in history. However, even when it changes, as Ozick puts it, 'the essay is a consistently recognizable and venerable – or call it ancient – form'.¹¹¹ This is the paradox of the essay, which would seek to be a genre that is most essayistic when it transgresses generic expectations. As O. B. Hardison Jr puts it, therefore: 'The essay is not a sensitive species on the point of extinction. It is tough, infinitely adaptable, and ubiquitous.'[112] And this adaptability and changeability is inherent to the essay and, paradoxically, at the root of its indefinability. It is 'a *real* Proteus – it changes into so many shapes so unlike the real one that it requires an act of faith to believe the shapes merely variations on a single underlying identity'.[113] Paul Heilker phrases the sentiment beautifully: 'the essay is kineticism incarnate – the embodiment of perpetual mobility, motion, and movement', something which becomes even more obvious when listing some of the tropes commonly associated with the essay or, more precisely, with the essayistic: 'the essay as motion/movement, as flying, slithering, flowing, journeying, walking, rambling, wandering, meandering, roaming, exploring, searching, seeking, venturing, following, tracking, hunting, and transgressing'.[114]

The rest of this book

As I come to the end of this Introduction, I cannot help but think that there is so much more to be said and done. For one, I have not provided a conclusive conclusion, settling rather on the essay and the essayistic in motion. Perhaps, this is appropriate for the argument that the essay, in dialectical and not easily resolvable ways, is a form that is constituted by and prospers from tensions around limits.

Many other things this introduction does not say are said by the other fifteen contributions to this volume, some of which are more essayistic and some more academic in style. Each of the individual chapters is contextualized and introduced in more detail in one of the three introductions to the three different parts of this volume, focusing on 'the essay and the world', 'the essay and the self' and 'the essay, form and the essayistic', respectively. As it will become clear in these chapters and essays, several lines of argument pursued in this introduction reappear with different inflections – indeed, my thinking of the essay here is also a response to the chapters I have had the privilege of reading and editing. However, as you, hopefully sympathetic reader, will discover, these contributions also address aspects of the essay which are barely or only very briefly mentioned here, including the essay's political and public functions; the essayistic in non-literary forms such as music, film and digital videos; and the relation between the essay and gender as well as identity and race. And in the essayistic spirit of the essay, what follows assays to break new ground in thinking about the essay while remaining firmly aware of and grounded in the essay tradition from which it inevitably proceeds.

Notes

1 For alternative genealogies of the essay, see John D'Agata, ed., *The Lost Origins of the Essay* (Minneapolis, MN: Graywolf Press, 2009) and Phillip Lopate, *The Art of the*

Personal Essay: An Anthology from the Classical Era to the Present (New York: Anchor Books, 1995), 5–39.
2. I am grateful to Ivan Callus, Nicole B. Wallack, Joseph Tabbi, Eric R. Tippin and Michael Askew for reading and commenting on an early draft of this chapter.
3. Phillip Lopate, 'What Happened to the Personal Essay?' *Against Joie de Vivre: Personal Essays* (New York: Simon & Schuster; 1989), 75–86 (79).
4. Graham Good, *The Observing Self: Rediscovering the Essay* (London: Routledge, 1988), 4.
5. Arthur Christopher Benson, 'From "The Art of the Essayist"', in Carl H. Klaus and Ned Stuckey-French (eds), *Essayists on the Essay: Montaigne to Our Time* (Iowa City: University of Iowa Press, 2012), 40–3 (40).
6. Michael L. Hall, 'The Emergence of the Essay and the Idea of Discovery', *Essays on the Essay: Redefining the Genre*, ed. Alexander J. Butrym (Athens: University of Georgia Press, 1989), 73–91 (82).
7. Sarah Levine, 'From "The Self on the Shelf"', in *Essayists on the Essay*, 159–66 (159).
8. William Hazlitt, 'On the Periodical Essayists', in *Lectures on the English Comic Writers* (London: Taylor and Hessey, 1819), 177–207 (177).
9. Good, *The Observing Self*, 4.
10. Ibid., 1.
11. See John Frow, *Genre, The New Critical Idiom*, 2nd edn (London: Routledge, 2015).
12. Making this point, Klaus gives the example of Montaigne, who 'repeatedly sought to describe it, explain it, justify it, celebrate it, and sometimes even denigrate it in digressive passages that can be found in 26 of his 107 essays' ('Toward a Collective Poetics of the Essay', in *Essayists on the Essay*, ed. Klaus and Stuckey-French, xv–xxvii (xv)).
13. Michel de Montaigne, 'Of Experience', in *The Complete Works of Montaigne*, trans. Donald Frame (Stanford, CA: Stanford University Press, 1957), 815–57 (818).
14. Ibid.
15. Rachel Blau DuPlessis, 'f-Words: An Essay on the Essay', *American Literature* 68, no. 1 (1996): 15–45 (23).
16. These three essays and others that can substantiate this point are anthologized in *Essayists on the Essay*, ed. Klaus and Stuckey-French.
17. Robert Atwan, 'Notes towards the Definition of an Essay', *River Teeth: A Journal of Nonfiction Narrative* 14, no. 1 (2012): 109–17 (109).
18. André Belleau, 'Petite essayistique', *Liberté* 25, no. 6 (December 1983): 7–10 (9). My translation.
19. Hazlitt, 'On the Periodical Essayists', 179.
20. Ibid., 179–80.
21. Ibid., 182.
22. G. Douglas Atkins, *Tracing the Essay: Through Experience to Truth* (Athens: University of Georgia Press, 2005), 42.
23. Walter Pater, *The Renaissance: Studies in Art and Poetry*, The 1893 Text, ed. Donald L. Hill (Berkeley: University of California Press, 1980), 188.
24. Good, *The Observing Self*, 45.
25. Atkins, *Tracing the Essay*, 43.
26. O. B. Hardison, Jr, 'Binding Proteus: An Essay on the Essay', in *Essays on the Essay*, ed. Alexander J. Butrym, 11–28 (14–15).
27. Atkins, *Tracing the Essay*, 56.
28. Phillip Lopate, 'Introduction', in *The Art of the Personal Essay*, xxiii–liv (xlvii).

29 Atkins, *Tracing the Essay*, 43.
30 Walter Murdoch, 'The Essay', in *Collected Essays* (Sydney: Angus and Robertson, 1945), 284–7 (286).
31 Francis Bacon, 'To the Most High and Excellent Prince, Henry, Prince of Wales, Duke of Cornwall, and Earl of Chester', as reproduced in Basil Montagu, 'Preface', in Francis Bacon, Alexander Spiers and Basil Montagu, *Bacon's Essays and Wisdom of the Ancients* (Boston: Little, Brown, and Company, 1884), i–xxix (xvi).
32 Seneca, 'Letter LVI', in *Letters from a Stoic (Epistulae Morales ad Lucilium)*, ed. and trans. Robin Campbell (1969, London: Penguin Classics, 2014), 112–18 (112).
33 Ibid.
34 Ibid., 115.
35 Ibid.
36 Ibid., 117.
37 Ibid., 118.
38 Montaigne writes about Seneca and Plutarch: 'The familiarity I have with these two authors, and the assistance they have lent to my age and to my book, wholly compiled of what I have borrowed from them' (Montaigne, 'Defense of Seneca and Plutarch', in *The Complete Works of Montaigne*, 545–9 (545)).
39 Seneca, 'Letter LVI', 118.
40 Nicholas Royle, *Veering: A Theory of Literature* (Edinburgh: Edinburgh University Press, 2012), 61.
41 Ibid., 63.
42 Edward Said, *On Late Style: Music and Literature against the Grain* (London: Bloomsbury, 2006), 7, as cited in Royle, *Veering*, 63.
43 Cynthia Ozick, 'Portrait of the Essay as a Warm Body', *Quarrel & Quandary: Essays* (New York: Vintage, 2001), 178–87 (181).
44 Jorge Luis Borges, 'The Aleph', in *Collected Fictions*, trans. Andrew Hurley (London: Penguin Books, 1998), 274–86 (283).
45 Ibid., 280.
46 Ibid., 281.
47 Hall, 'The Emergence of the Essay and the Idea of Discovery', 73.
48 Ibid., 78.
49 Elisabeth Hodges, *Urban Poetics in the French Renaissance* (Aldershot: Ashgate, 2008), 119.
50 Good, *The Observing Self*, 4.
51 David Foster Wallace, 'Consider the Lobster', *Gourmet*, August 2004, 50–64.
52 William Hazlitt, 'On the Pleasure of Hating', in Lopate, *The Art of the Personal Essay*, 189–98 (190).
53 Samuel Johnson, 'The Solitude of the Country', in Lopate, *The Art of the Personal Essay*, 141–4.
54 Hazlitt, 'On the Periodical Essayists', 135.
55 Johnson, 'The Solitude of the Country', 141.
56 Réda Bensmaïa, *The Barthes Effect: The Essay as Reflective Text*, trans. Pat Fedkiew (Minneapolis: University of Minnesota Press, 1987), 119.
57 William H. Gass, 'Emerson and the Essay', in *Habitations of the Word: Essays* (New York: Simon & Schuster, 1985), 9–49 (26).
58 Gass, 'Emerson and the Essay', 28.
59 Lopate, 'What Happened to the Personal Essay?', 80.

60 See Mario Aquilina, 'Echoing as Self-Fashioning in the Essay: Hazlitt's Quoting and Misquoting of Shakespeare', *Polysèmes: Revue d'études intertextuelles et intermédiales*, 20 (2018), DOI: 10.4000/polysemes.4262
61 Lopate, 'What Happened to the Personal Essay?', 80.
62 Rebecca Solnit, 'Introduction', in *The Best American Essays 2019*, ed. Rebecca Solnit, series ed. Robert Atwan (Boston: Mariner Books, Houghton Mifflin Harcourt, 2019), xvii–xxvii (xvii).
63 Jean Starobinski, 'From "Can One Define the Essay?" trans. Lindsey Scott, in *Essayists on the Essay*, ed. Klaus and Stuckey-French, 110–15 (111).
64 Ibid.
65 Hall, 'The Emergence of the Essay and the Idea of Discovery', 79.
66 W. Wolfgang Holdheim, 'Introduction: The Essay as Knowledge in Progress', in *The Hermeneutic Mode: Essays on Time in Literature and Literary Theory* (1931, Ithaca, NY: Cornell University Press, 1984), 19–32 (20).
67 Ibid., 21.
68 Royle, *Veering*, 63.
69 Bensmaïa, *The Barthes Effect*, 25.
70 Ibid., 92.
71 Ibid., 90.
72 Ibid., xxx.
73 Ibid., 4.
74 Ibid., 8.
75 Ibid., 11.
76 Ibid., 8.
77 Ibid., 51.
78 Roland Barthes, *Roland Barthes by Roland Barthes*, trans. Richard Howard (New York: Hill and Wang, 2010), 168.
79 Bensmaïa, *The Barthes Effect*, 52.
80 See Nicole B. Wallack, *Crafting Presence: The American Essay and the Future of Writing Studies* (Colorado: The University Press of Colorado, 2017) for an alternative discussion of 'presence' in the essay as a product of the essaysist's engagement with the paradoxes and uncertainties in their thinking and writing. For Wallack, 'presence' is a temporary stabilization of the presence of the writer in the text for the specific occasion of writing.
81 Bensmaïa, *The Barthes Effect*, 53.
82 Ibid., 54.
83 Solnit, 'Introduction', xviii.
84 Ibid., xvii.
85 Claire de Obaldia, *The Essayistic Spirit: Literature, Modern Criticism, and the Essay* (Oxford: Clarendon Press, 1995), 57.
86 Ibid., 58.
87 Ibid., 57.
88 Alastair Fowler, 'The Life and Death of Literary Forms', *New Literary History* 2, no. 2 (1971): 199–216 (202).
89 Fowler, 'The Life and Death of Literary Forms', 207.
90 Ibid., 214.
91 Frow, *Genre*, 71.
92 Ibid.
93 Hall, 'The Emergence of the Essay and the Idea of Discovery', 78.

94 See Theodor W. Adorno, 'The Essay as Form', trans. Bob Hullot-Kentor and Frederic Will, *New German Critique* 32 (Spring–Summer, 1984): 151–71.
95 John A. McCarthy, *Crossing Boundaries: A Theory of Essay Writing in German, 1680-1815* (Philadelphia: University of Pennsylvania Press, 1989), 58.
96 Robert Musil, *The Man without Qualities*, Volume 1, trans. Sophie Wilkins (New York: Vintage International, 1996), 270.
97 Starobinski, 'From "Can One Define the Essay?"', 113.
98 Max Bense, 'From "On the Essay and its Prose"', in *Essayists on the Essay*, 71–4 (71).
99 De Obaldia, *The Essayistic Spirit*, 29.
100 Good, *The Observing Self*, 28.
101 De Obaldia, *The Essayistic Spirit*, 29.
102 Fowler, 'The Life and Death of Literary Forms', 207.
103 Michael Hamburger, 'An Essay on the Essay' (1965), in *Essayists on the Essay*, 91–3.
104 Hamburger, 'An Essay on the Essay', 93.
105 Agnes Repplier, 'From "The Passing of the Essay"', in *Essayists on the Essay*, 32–5 (32).
106 Repplier, 'From "The Passing of the Essay"', 35.
107 Robert Atwan, 'Foreword', in *The Best American Essays 1988*, ed. Annie Dillard and Series ed. Robert Atwan (New York: Ticknor & Fields, 1988), ix–xi (ix).
108 Ibid., x.
109 Solnit, 'Introduction', xxiii.
110 Ibid., xxiv.
111 Ozick, 'Portrait of the Essay as a Warm Body', 181.
112 O. B. Hardison Jr, 'Binding Proteus', 11.
113 Ibid., 27.
114 Paul Heilker, *The Essay: Theory and Pedagogy for an Active Form* (Champaign, IL: National Council of Teachers of English, 1996), 169.

Part I

THE ESSAY AND THE WORLD

The contributors in Part I of the volume focus on the essay's relation to what we may loosely call the 'world'. They do so from different perspectives – philosophical, political and aesthetic – but they share an interest in refining our thinking of the essay as a form that seeks to understand, represent or participate in the world or aspects of the world 'out there'. In doing this, they tend to build on an intellectual tradition that thinks of the essay in terms of knowledge of the world and aesthetic form. They invite us to interrogate the ways in which the essay, as a form of thinking, navigates the limits and relations between the subjective and the objective in the quest for different kinds of 'truth'.

Thinking primarily alongside Theodor W. Adorno, but also other philosophers and theorists like René Descartes, David Hume, Edmund Husserl, Martin Heidegger, György Lukács and Stanley Cavell, Erin Plunkett presents the essay as a way of thinking rooted in experience. The essay is an attempt to describe and interrogate our mode of being in the world or 'the *how* of experience'. Plunkett argues that since Michel de Montaigne, the essay has been theorized in epistemological terms – the essay as 'an outgrowth of sceptical inquiry into the grounds of knowledge claims' – but the essay's peculiarity, which also gives it an advantage over other writing forms in philosophy, is that it has a 'phenomenal' relation to truth. Positioned 'between subjectivity and objectivity', the essay embodies 'the activity of subjects in the world'. It allows for thought that, in navigating a 'constellation' of concepts – rather than seeking their systematic and methodical abstraction – retains what Adorno calls the 'non-identity' of things, that is, the gap that relates but also separates things from each other.

Writing essayistically – in the sense of performing thought in writing – James Corby begins with the question, 'What is the relation between the essay and the post-literary?' It quickly becomes apparent for Corby that pursuing this question will be difficult because what may seem to unite the essay and the post-literary is also what makes them very hard to define: their open-endedness, their mutability and their future-orientedness. If writing about the essay is difficult, writing about the essay in relation to the post-literary is doubly so. However, basing himself on a close reading and explication of Lukács's writing on the essay – and also informed by post-Romantic poetics – Corby perseveres in exploring and elucidating the different nuances of the essay's relation to literature. The leading question then becomes whether the essay is really about 'that which it was supposed to be about' – its professed 'occasionalism' – whether the essay is an autotelic form – thus making it not only potentially *about* literature but (akin to) literature – or whether the essay should be understood in terms of a peculiar dialectic between these two possible ways of relating to the world.

The scope of Neil Badmington's contribution may initially seem to be narrower than Plunkett's and Corby's in that it proceeds from the question of why a specific writer, Roland Barthes, favoured the essay – or what he called 'brief scenes' – as a form. Badmington's meticulous reading of Barthes as an essayist shows how Barthes's essayism is ultimately an inherent part of his Saussure-inspired semiological project. Badmington discusses Barthes's *Elements of Semiology* and the short essay, 'The Kitchen of Meaning', in some detail, arguing that Barthes uses the essay in response to the challenge of dealing with the meaning of signs when 'meaning depends upon difference within a larger signifying system' and when the proliferation of meaning may become overwhelming and uncontrollable. In other words, for Badmington, the necessity of the essay as a form is traceable to our attempts to understand the world of signs. The implications of this insight, while arising from a reading of Barthes, are clearly relevant beyond him.

The essay's relation to the social, cultural and political sphere through the work of contemporary public intellectuals is the focus of Nicole B. Wallack's contribution. Beginning with a wide-ranging survey of the essay's thinking of its own relation to the world – a survey that discusses Montaigne, Francis Bacon, Virginia Woolf, George Orwell, W. E. B. Du Bois and James Baldwin, among others – Wallack then proceeds to inquire about the possibilities of the essay's intervention in a post-truth world. Kwame Anthony Appiah and Ta-Nehisi Coates provide Wallack with contemporary examples of how the public intellectual may use the essay to comment, critique and interpret the world for the public. Through the essay form, these public intellectuals modulate their voice as social commentators by introducing the vulnerability of personal experience – a risk that the essay encourages. At the same time, however, the form of the essay – with its provisionality and tentativeness – allows them to 'craft a truth into' a 'sharable … literary experience'.

The organization of the chapters into sections in this volume is an attempt to indicate the general direction of the contributors' arguments, but several chapters proceed in a 'state of flux', with essayistic dispersal being a guiding poetic as they explore the essay's limits in relation to the world, the self and form. Joseph Tabbi's chapter, which discusses digital essayism through an intricate and sustained reading of Anne Burdick's *TRINA: A Design Fiction*, is a case in point as it includes several observations that are particularly relevant to the essayistic and the essay form. However, what makes Tabbi's chapter relevant to the relation between the essay and the world is the way he thinks of the essayistic aesthetic of digital writing as almost a natural platform for the 'non-fictional, never fully narrativized and always contingent thought stream' that characterizes the essay. For Tabbi, digital essayism is not only a formal quality dependent on 'technological affordances' because technology affects our relation to the world. Quoting Nietzsche, he reminds us that 'our writing tools also are working on our thoughts', and in this respect it is important to reflect – as Tabbi does with Burdick – on the way digital essayism is informed by and resistant to social, institutional and political limits.

Chapter 1

THE ESSAY AS PHENOMENOLOGY

Erin Plunkett

As the title of this volume suggests, the essay invites, even demands, a questioning of limits: between 'science' and 'art'; subjectivity and objectivity; 'life' and 'living'. While the conceptual pairing of essay and limit tends to centre on a discussion of the essay's transgression of familiar generic or disciplinary boundaries, I read this overspilling of critical limits as a consequence of the essay's more fundamentally expansive character. Theodor W. Adorno describes the essay as an expression of 'intellectual freedom', an 'arena of intellectual experience' (*Schauplatz geistiger Erfahrung*) in which all 'objects are equally near the centre'.[1] What then is the basis of this intellectual freedom? What does the essay recover that is lost in other ways of thinking and writing?

Reading both within and outside the bounds of Adorno's thinking on this subject, I would like to develop the idea that the intellectual freedom of the essay issues from a rootedness in experience, an interest in describing as well as interrogating our mode of being in the world. It is lived experience that is, in the first instance, expansive, that transgresses the boundaries of subject and object, and that refuses to be resolved into a system. Adorno sets up a polemical framework in which the essay is contrasted with positivism, the scientific method, idealism, systematic philosophy and abstract speculation. I would like to suggest that in each of these approaches what is obscured, and what the essay is able to recover, is the structure of experience itself. Kierkegaard asks, in his aptly named *Concluding Unscientific Postscript to Philosophical Crumbs*: 'From what does pure thinking abstract? From existence, consequently from what it is supposed to explain.'[2] So the essay, in its 'methodically unmethodical' way, pushes back against 'pure thinking', against 'the system' – in order to recover and re-evaluate what eludes their grasp, or counts as mere 'crumbs'.

1. Form as philosophy

Umberto Eco has made the case for reading textual form as an 'epistemological metaphor', representing ways of thinking about the world.[3] In *The Open Work*, he contends that: 'In every century the way that artistic forms are structured reflects the way in which science or contemporary culture views reality.'[4] Beryl Lang has formulated readings of philosophical textual forms as indicative of epistemological and ethical commitments.[5] John Hollander has suggested, more generally, that textual forms may offer us metaphors for what our life is like.[6] Describing the works of Stanley Cavell, Hollander writes that 'the activities of philosophizing become synecdochic, metonymic, and generally parabolic for the activities of the rest of life itself.'[7] What these ideas have in common is a notion that forms of writing are indicative of ways of seeing and thinking, of inhabiting a world. To the extent that forms can be read in this way, they have a philosophical import, since they contribute to the investigation of what it is to be in a world, how truth is sought and decided upon, how writing can obscure or illuminate these considerations, and other matters of philosophical concern.

While it is not contentious within literary studies and critical theory to 'read' form as significant in its own right, it is rare to find such arguments within contemporary analytic philosophy, and philosophers have much to gain from a literary approach to texts. As Jonathan Lavery notes, 'opening up questions about genres of philosophy leads inexorably to questions about what philosophy *is*', about philosophy's understanding of itself.[8]

If forms of writing can be considered constructions of epistemological or metaphysical positions, they of necessity have something to say about what it is to experience a world, about how thought and world relate. This is especially true of the essay, since to follow Adorno (following Kierkegaard), it is the *how* of existence that is of interest to the essay and that the essay lays bare. How does the world open itself to human being in phenomenal experience? How does the presentation of the essayist relate to the way in which the world is experienced? These are what I take to be some of the central philosophical concerns of the essay as a form.[9]

The particular way in which the essay 'tells the truth about things' means that essayistic writing offers certain philosophical advantages over other forms, particularly in relation to the questions posed above.[10] In what follows, I will offer a reading of the essay as an interrogation of experience, first considering a sceptical reading of the essay, and ultimately combining Adorno's insights with a broadly phenomenological framework.

2. Scepticism

It is worthwhile to begin with a brief sketch of one of the primary ways in which the essay as a way of thinking the world has been understood. The most common philosophical reading of essays is that they engage in scepticism of a certain kind, that the stylistic features which mark essayistic writing – heterogeneity, discontinuity, circularity, reflexivity, open-endedness, a focus on particular experience – can be read as an outgrowth of sceptical enquiry into the grounds of knowledge claims or, more generally, as a metaphor for our necessarily provisional and uncertain relationship to what is.[11] While scepticism has many varieties, they are united by the notion that there is a disconnect between our thinking of the world and what the world is like in itself. The essay can therefore be read as an attempt to inscribe that essential difference and uncertainty into a form of writing. This sceptical reading of the essay has two main sources. The first is the historical fact of Michel de Montaigne's engagement with ancient Greek scepticism – specifically Pyrrhonism. The second is the more linguistically oriented post-structuralist critiques of knowledge that dominate theory in the latter third of the twentieth century.

Two of the most influential essay writers within the philosophical tradition, Montaigne and David Hume, are explicitly engaged with the Pyrrhonian tradition of Greek scepticism, and it makes sense to view their choice of essay writing through this lens. One can plausibly read the openness of the essay form, the rejection of closure, as a manifestation of the *aporia* and resulting suspension of judgement that the Pyrrhonian method was devised to generate.

But perhaps the more important aspect of Pyrrhonism for our purposes is not its aporetic nature but its response to aporia. Pyrrhonism has a pragmatic or therapeutic bent: absent the means to rigorously justify our beliefs about the world, we are left to turn our attention from the question of *knowing* to the task of living a good life. Sextus Empiricus, in his second-century tract *Outlines of Pyrrhonism*, presents the case that withholding judgement or refraining from positive beliefs issues in a state of *ataraxia*, or tranquillity.[12] The Pyrrhonian understanding of aporia does not result in nihilism or in the search for some more certain ground for knowledge, as is the case with most other varieties of scepticism. It instead involves coming to terms with a lack of certainty, orienting away from ungrounded speculation and towards existential realities.[13] For this reason, ancient scepticism has been deemed 'therapeutic': it releases us from the false idea that knowledge (of some kind) is what leads to human flourishing.[14]

Reading through the lens of Pyrrhonian scepticism, one can link the essay to a kind of epistemological modesty that is therapeutic in aim – both a limiting of the scope of knowledge and a limiting of the relevance of knowing as an approach to the world. In essayistic writings, the drive to *know* is put into a wider context of our possibilities of relating to the world, which include but are not limited to knowing. In this way, what it is to know is redefined. And the value of *knowing*, in relation to other ways in which the world is opened up to us, is also reassessed. The backdrop for this reassessment is a return to the experiential grounds out of which things can be known at all.

I have elsewhere characterized this turning using Stanley Cavell's phrase, 'from knowledge to acknowledgement', suggesting that the promise of the essay form, as influenced by the sceptical tradition, would be an acknowledgement of the conditions under which our relation to the world takes place.[15] Following Adorno, the form is an attempt to find a mode of communication that remains within the bounds of experience and brings to light the structure of our experience – rather than altering experience to make it fit the structure of conceptual thought. For Cavell, this is important because the tendency to ignore or actively reject our mode of being for a 'fantasy', philosophical or otherwise, is ever present.[16]

Whether one follows the sceptical line or not, essayistic writings can be read as bringing to light – through a variety of formal techniques – what Cavell calls 'the human conditions of knowledge and action'.[17] In giving our attention to these conditions, we at the same time are led to re-contextualize and re-evaluate our conception of what it is to 'know' or of what truth looks like. For all its critique of *knowledge*, the essay still aims to 'speak "the truth" about things'.[18]

Cavell himself does not elaborate on the 'human conditions of knowledge and action', though it is clear that for him our being-in-language is such a condition. 'Human conditions' denote something like our existential or phenomenological situation, our being in the world. In my own work, temporality, subjectivity and language are the conditions that I give the most attention to, though of course other conditions are important here, such as embodiment and social-historical environment (Adorno stresses the importance of the latter to experience).[19] Essayistic writing brings our attention to these conditions as relevant to whatever we want to call knowledge or understanding. Our particular mode of being becomes both frame and subject.

While sceptical philosophy inevitably involves some discussion of the grounds of knowledge, essayistic thinking is clear that these grounds are experiential, rather than rational or logical, and that attention must be called to these grounds as part of the process of understanding and orienting oneself in the world. In this emphasis on how it is to be in the world and on the manifestation of the world in experience, essaying as mode of philosophizing turns out to have more in common with phenomenology than scepticism proper, whether we think of scepticism as a kind of global doubt, as in postmodernism, or whether it takes the more Pyrrhonian form of epistemological modesty.

3. Subject and object in the essay

So how does the essay, in György Lukács's words, 'speak "the truth" about' things?[20] I will attempt to describe in greater detail the essay's relationship to *things* and to subjectivity in order to understand the particular truth of the essay and its philosophical advantages over other modes of writing. The first thing to clarify is that the reflection on experience in the essay is not a reflection on something that is first immediate and later skewed and distorted by concepts. Adorno sketches the contours of a form – a form of thinking as much as a form of writing – that is 'without scaffolding or edifice', that stands against either first principles or final principles, that rejects any species of totalizing thought – be it scientific or philosophical.[21] This may at first glance suggest that the particular mode of being that the essay tries to capture is itself immediate and intuitively given, not subject to any structuring principles. Experience understood in this sense would be something like the reception of pure sensory data, prior to the application of conceptual categories. But a chaos of undifferentiated sensation is precisely what experience cannot be since experience as such is never devoid of conceptual activity. Adorno[22] echoes Kant's famous dictum to this effect: 'thoughts without content are empty, intuitions without concepts are blind'.[23] Having an experience at all requires the organizing and unifying activities of consciousness, just as consciousness is only given content by its application to experience. This perhaps makes some sense of the way in which the essay is both resolutely subjective and object-oriented. The essay is poised between what Lukács calls the 'soul content of things', and the way in which soul itself is constituted by things 'out there'.[24]

If the essay begins with concepts already in play, already given meaning in concrete, mediated historical and cultural contexts, it is because experience is always already mediated by such concepts. The point is not to turn away from speculation in order to grasp the a-conceptual, the intuitive, the immediately given, but to plunge into the complexity of the given world and of 'intellectual experience, without simplifying it'.[25] The essay for this reason occupies itself with that which, in Lukács's words,

> has already been given form, or at least something that has already been there at some time in the past; hence it is part of the nature of the essay that it does not create new things from an empty nothingness but only orders those which were once alive.[26]

The concern with what is there, what has been there, sometimes manifests as a concern with a particular artwork, artefact or object, sometimes as a reflection on words written by others. The philosophical significance of this aspect of essayistic writing is that the essay is always already *in* a world, within historically and linguistically mediated experience.

This grounding in experience makes sense of another of Adorno's claims about the essay, that it constitutes a rejection of the scientific-positivistic conception of objectivity as neutrality, as 'an objectivity that is said to spring forth after the subtraction of the subject'.[27] The essay's relationship to the real relies on a more profound understanding of objectivity that includes the lived experience of subjects in relation to objects. 'The measure of such objectivity is not the verification of asserted theses', for this would be to take for granted that every kind of truth can and should be converted into a scientific truth; it is rather 'individual experience [*einzelmenschliche Erfahrung*], unified in hope and disillusion'.[28] Objects are made sense of through a particular here and now, and they reveal their truths, their different 'soul content' to use Lukács's terminology, through our multiple possible relations to them. These relations arise in the first place from our orientations within lived experience. Objects and their relationships to one another come into view through our own actions and aims – whether primitive aims such as eating and shelter or more sophisticated projects such as aesthetic contemplation or the forming of scientific hypotheses. A consequence of this is that the determination of objects remains open-ended. A precise definition or scientific description alone does not exhaust what an object is, and there is always more to an object than what is revealed through a particular aspect or project.

This interplay between subjective perspective and objective determination appears both in the 'occasional' nature of the essay – starting from what is already there – and in the characteristic use of multiple perspectives within a singular essay. Indeed, an essayist introduces multiple perspectives in the very act of taking up how others have thought about some object or idea. Montaigne most often begins his reflections in the form of a gloss on another writer, prompting his oft-quoted comment: '*on ne fait que nous entregloser*' (We do nothing but gloss one another).[29] Setting different points of view side by side in order to show the limited nature of any single view is a technique that can be seen in both Montaigne and Hume, and Montaigne reflects on this explicitly in his own writings. He writes in the *Apology for Raimond Sebond*: '*Les subjects ont divers lustres et diverses considerations*' (Any object can be seen in various lights from various points of view), and these '*subjects*' include the writer as the subject of the *Essais*.[30] Montaigne's writing technique is an attempt to present himself from as many angles or aspects as possible: '*Je me presente debout, et couché; le devant et le derriere; à droitte et à gauche; et en touts mes naturels plis*' (I describe myself standing up and lying down, from front and back, from right and left and with all my inborn complexities).[31] The *Essais* develop their texture by way of a treatment of multiple and sometimes incongruous perspectives. He writes: '*Tant y a que je me contredis bien à l'advanture, mais la verité, comme disoit Demades, je ne la contredy point*' (I may happen to contradict myself, but the truth, as Demades said, I never contradict).[32] It is apparent from this statement and from the *Essais* considered as a whole that Montaigne includes contradictions in his work precisely *for the sake of* truth – a truth which departs from a logical model and embraces a more experimental approach, even embracing error as a part of the mode of disclosure of the world.[33]

Hume uses contrasting perspectives to great effect in his empirical philosophy. His 1742 essay, 'Of the Standard of Taste', opens with a remark about the great variety of taste among individuals, which is 'too obvious not to have fallen under everyone's observation'.[34] But later in the essay, he offers the contrary and equally evident claim that there is in fact great unanimity of taste, within a specific cultural environment, regarding what works are worthy of continued praise and attention. Both statements are endorsed by common sense, and by treating the two as equally worthy, Hume offers a philosophical interrogation of and refinement of the mechanism of 'common sense', of how consensus works. Oscillating between the ways in which the same words are used in different senses is a significant feature of Hume's essay writing – one which shows his interest in the ambiguity that characterizes experience and ordinary language in contrast to the precise definitions or systematic general principles that characterize many contemporaneous philosophical accounts.

The heterogeneous or plural character of Montaigne and Hume's essays is in fact a recognizable feature of essayistic writing. While essays are undoubtedly tied to subjectivity, as in Montaigne's use of the first person and his reflection on his own experience, this subjectivity is problematized from the very start. Montaigne is explicit about his effort to preserve the *diversity* of his own perspectives, and he draws attention to the writing process itself as constitutive of identity, describing himself as 'consubstantial' with his essays.[35] Essays employ a range of voices or perspectives, regardless of whether the narrative voice is a singular 'I'. Crucially, there is no attempt to decide on a single perspective within the frame of an essay; in this way the essay is an epistemologically open rather than closed form. This 'polyphonic' quality of essayistic writing is philosophically rich and can be read in a number of ways.[36] For the purposes of this enquiry, the key lesson is that presenting a plurality of perspectives without deciding on one acknowledges different and irreducible ways of seeing a single object. This is in keeping with the essay's rootedness in experience, since to be experiencing is always to be within a specific perspective, a being there which is not the same as another's there or a there that I do not yet occupy, but which does not exclude other perspectives, nor other modes of encounter with the world. On the contrary, in ordinary experience, I constantly infer perspectives other than the one I currently occupy, for example, imagining that the box I see also has a back and sides, though I cannot presently see them, or projecting my own existence and the existence of things into the future. The multiplicity of perspectives in an essay points to the world as phenomenal in character, as capable of being manifested in myriad different aspects and modes to subjects in the world. This in turn denies the existence of an objective position that could be said to stand outside of any particular perspective and to encompass all aspects of an object, resulting in the ideal objects of mathematics and the sciences. The disclosure of objects is always subjective. So the determination of an object is never absolute and always open, as the essay is open.

Yet the essay speaks the truth about *things*, Lukács declares. The subjective dimension of the essay does not seem to be adequately accounted for by a sceptical frame, in which our position as subjects – determined by temporality, language, history and so on – means that we cannot know the world in a satisfactory way. Subjectivity, as our mode of being, is included not to eliminate the possibility of truth but rather to offer a more rigorous account of truth as the distinctive possibility of human being. In the essay, the truth of things is sought through careful attention to how some particular object or experience appears – which includes the subject (the writer) to whom it appears. But this description of phenomena, of what appears, is not thought separately from the essence or truth of things, as though the phenomena were *mere* appearance. While appearances can deceive – as the legacy of scepticism reveals – the phenomenal is nevertheless an opening to things. Further, it is a feature of *things* – not of subjects – that they are capable of appearing to consciousness. The world is *known* through its manifestation.

The essay's position between subjectivity and objectivity represents the phenomenal character of the world and thus suggests an alternative to the model of truth as conceptual precision, abstracted from lived experience. Truth becomes the activity of subjects in the world rather than something independent of subjectivity or history.

4. Two models of truth

The essay's interest in phenomenal experience contrasts most sharply with what Adorno, in an argument that strongly echoes Husserl's 1936 *Crisis in the European*

Sciences, calls the 'scientific' model of truth. Both Edmund Husserl and Adorno see such a model – epitomized by Cartesian 'method' – as reductive of lived experience – and Adorno makes the case that an essayistic approach to philosophy aims to recover what is lost in scientific consciousness.[37] Although the sciences presuppose that 'all knowledge can potentially be converted into science', 'the fact that this convertibility has remained a mere assertion and that living consciousness has never really been transformed into a scientific consciousness, points to [...] a qualitative difference.'[38] Adorno uses Proust as an example of a literary effort to 'salvage, or perhaps restore' what the 'man of experience' knows.[39] Because of Proust's emphasis on particular experience and his reflection on the process of presentation itself, he is able 'to express necessary and compelling perceptions about men and their social relations which science simply cannot match.'[40]

While Adorno uses 'science' in an equivocal way in this essay (indeed, he is aware of this and makes a case for it[41]), the difference between a view from within lived experience and a scientific (or philosophical) conception of the world is clear in Husserl's *Crisis* text. In the scientific framework, truth is recognized by exactness and objectivity – the latter implying universal applicability and the absence of the subjective perspective that characterizes lived experience.

> What constitutes 'exactness' [*Exaktheit*]? [It is] empirical measuring with increasing precision, but under the guidance of a world of idealities, or rather a world of certain particular ideal structures that can be correlated with given scales of measurement – such a world having been objectified in advance through idealization and construction.[42]

Husserl here describes the process by which the lived world is translated into scientific knowledge. What is real becomes what can be measured, with 'ideal structures' – or concepts – viewed as more precise iterations of ambiguous, variable subjective lived experience. Husserl describes the effect of this conversion with equal clarity. 'Here the original thinking [within lived experience] that genuinely gives meaning to this technical process and truth to the correct results ... is excluded.'[43]

The intimate relation of things to ourselves that is experienced in the lifeworld loses its sense of validity and significance when this experience itself comes to be viewed through idealized, conceptual structures. Husserl offers the example of a lived experience of warmth versus a physicist's atomic description of heat.[44] The various ways in which the world opens up to the embodied and culturally embedded subject lose their status as a knowledge, replaced by a model in which knowledge is something precise, measurable, and neutral – 'an objectivity that is said to spring forth after the subtraction of the subject'.[45]

In Adorno, the essay 'attempts to make reparation' for what is lost in the higher levels of abstraction represented by the scientific.[46] As I have argued above, it is not the case that lived experience is immediate and intuitive as opposed to the mediated abstractions of the sciences. Nor is it the case that such essential human abilities as abstraction or idealization are to be avoided. However, the essay does involve a wider conception of truth than that which is formulated in the sciences, one that does not rely on measurement and objectivity, and one that is not orientated towards prediction and control ('the control of nature and material production').[47] Adorno is clear that the structure of possibility within experience itself – one that we have reflected on in discussing the infinite determination of objects – is something that slips through the net of systematic thought, whether scientific or philosophical. The possibility of a different future or of 'transcendence vis-a-vis the frozen relations of production' is actually present in the open-ended, indeterminate or overdetermined structure of lived experience but is lost in the conversion of all truth into scientific truth, which for Adorno has the ultimate aim of making the future conform to what has been.[48] So an essayistic form of thinking, which stresses the many possible modes of encounter with the world and which keeps the living subject within the frame, is not only a better metaphor for what our life is like but also houses the potential to foster better ways of relating to the environment and to others. There is a utopian element hiding within the apparent modesty of the essay.

5. Adorno and non-identity

I have attempted to present the essay form as disclosive of our mode of being in the world – of those features of existence that are lost in scientific or philosophical schema. This basic thesis now requires some qualification. Adorno refers at several points in his essay on the essay to the 'non-identity' of a concept with its content, that is, the difference between the structure of conceptual thought and the structure of being. Is this not, finally, a sceptical gesture, and one that undermines the notion that the essay is capable of speaking the truth about *things*? The essay, Adorno claims, establishes itself as an 'arena of intellectual experience' instead of a conceptual system, and it does this because it does not assume that the structure of thinking and the structure of things are identical. This is clear in Adorno's criticism of Cartesian method. For Adorno, Descartes' assumption that an exhaustive treatment of things is possible relies on the determining 'in advance that the object in question can be fully grasped by the concepts that treat it; that nothing is left over that could not be anticipated by these concepts.'[49] Adorno charges both idealism and positivistic science with taking for granted that the world corresponds to our concepts of it, that nothing in principle is excluded from our ability to know and that there is no difference in kind between our conceptual schema and the structure of things. Despite the wane of both idealism and logical positivism, it remains a prevalent view in both philosophy and the sciences that the world is, in principle, knowable and presents no structural but only practical barriers to total knowledge.

But is Adorno, by contrast, offering a straightforward sceptical statement about our inability to know the world? Is the essay sceptical after all? This requires a more thorough investigation. The relevant questions seem to be: how does the essay express the truth of things without committing to the erroneous view that things conform to our conception of them? How can an essay present without distorting, while being aware that there is no neutral presentation? I will offer a reading of Adorno's answer to these questions before proposing a broader phenomenological reading.

For Adorno, the poetics of the essay – its style and its process, its means of development – turn out to be the key factor, since the 'essay becomes true in its progress'.[50] It is the essayist's reflection on language and presentation (*Darstellung*) that ends up making the essay form a suitable metaphor for what our lives are like. I have noted the essay does not abandon the conceptual, since experience is itself conceptual. Adorno adapts from Walter Benjamin the notion of a 'constellation' of concepts, as an alternative to the logic of a Hegelian dialectic of concepts.[51] In Adorno's terminology, concepts *contain* non-conceptual content – they name something that is not itself conceptual. This is what Adorno calls the 'irritating and dangerous elements of things' and what gives rise to the non-identity of concepts with what they describe.[52] Things are 'dangerous' because their determination is never definite; the fact that they always exceed any particular determination makes them unpredictable and resistant to control. The context in which Adorno's discussion of the non-identity of concepts arises is linguistic: 'All concepts are already implicitly concretized through the language in which they stand.'[53] This is perhaps more familiar territory than the corresponding ontological point.

The meaning of words or the ability to interpret what is said always outruns any fixed set of possibilities – whether an attempt to precisely define the scope of some word or an attempt to establish the criteria for a definitive reading of a text. The essay enters into this ambivalence, not in order to come to a more exact understanding of the concept, divorced from its concrete uses or possible meanings, but to 'force these meanings on further', to elaborate an understanding of the web of signification of which any concept is a part. This is what Hume attempts in his discussion of ordinary language surrounding moral and aesthetic taste. Adorno writes: 'Not less, but more than the process of defining, the essay urges the reciprocal interaction of its concepts in the process of intellectual experience.'[54] In a sense, it puts forward what is already there, but hidden, 'to grasp these concepts reflectively in the way that they are already unconsciously named in language'.[55] So Adorno is clear that objects outrun any of our concepts, though they are always seen through them.

Constellations of concepts, as opposed to the refinement of concepts through abstraction or idealization (the model of philosophical definition), aim to preserve the relations between things in experience – reflected in ordinary language use. In his illuminating article on the philosophical significance of 'constellations', Stewart Martin explains that the excess of meaning (or being) that is a feature of things is preserved in the essay's use of configurations of concepts: 'The essay involves the articulation of a relation of elements that is binding, but without being exhaustive or exclusive.'[56] An essay offers a reading, or readings, of the relation of things, but in its openness includes the possibility of other readings. This works to maintain the gap that is always present between our thinking of an object and the object itself – what Adorno calls their non-identity.

> The experience of non-identity, revealed in the failure of a concept to sufficiently identify the non-conceptual, informs a process whereby such an inadequate concept is combined with other concepts that attempt, from their different vantages, to conceptualize the nonconceptual; endeavouring to say, through their combination, what they could not say individually.[57]

Constellations thus 'negatively invoke a speculative experience of something beyond the choices that frame the present'.[58] It is precisely an essay's looseness with concepts, its tendency to multiply concepts or to use a concept ambivalently, that invokes non-conceptual content.

One might make the mistake of thinking that the indeterminacy of things is due to the very fact that they are determined *by subjects*, that their identity is nothing other than a progressive projection of meanings onto them. But the deeper point, and one the term non-identity strongly suggests, is that hiddenness is a feature of things themselves and forms a part of the way in which things are known. The manifestation of the world involves not only disclosure but an ongoing dialectic of concealment and unconcealment.[59] In other words, the essay's 'constellations' are not the projection of *any* arbitrary meaning on things, but instead enact the dialectic of experience, the way in which the world both opens up to and recedes from our efforts to know it. Writing the 'irritating' dimension of hiddenness or non-identity into the text, as the essay does, is not so much a sceptical gesture as it is a reflection of phenomenal experience.

Notes

1. Theodor W. Adorno, 'The Essay as Form', trans. Bob Hullot-Kentor and Frederic Will, *New German Critique* 32 (Spring–Summer, 1984): 151–71 (167).
2. Soren Kierkegaard, *Concluding Unscientific Postscript to Philosophical Fragments*, ed. and trans. Howard V. Hong and Edna H. Hong, Vol. 1 (Princeton, NJ: Princeton University Press, 1992), 328.
3. Umberto Eco, *The Open Work*, trans. Anna Cancogni (Cambridge, MA: Harvard University Press, 1989), 13.
4. Ibid.
5. Beryl Lang, *The Anatomy of Philosophical Style: Literary Philosophy and the Philosophy of Literature* (Oxford: Basil Blackwell Ltd, 1992). See also 'The Ethics of Style in Philosophical Discourse', in *Literary Form, Philosophical Content: Historical Studies of Philosophical Genres*, ed. Jonathan Lavery and Louis Groarke (Madison, NJ: Fairleigh Dickinson University Press, 2010), 219–34.
6. 'The ability to produce more compelling models of what our moral – and even what our epistemologically and metaphysically wondrous – life is like has given major novelists and great poets, in the same three and a half centuries since Descartes, a

disproportionate claim to human knowledge of the human.' (John Hollander, 'Stanley Cavell and *The Claim of Reason*', *Critical Inquiry* 6, no. 4 (1980): 575–88 (582)).

7   Hollander, 'Stanley Cavell', 586.
8   Jonathan Lavery, 'Philosophical Genres and Literary Forms: A Mildly Polemical Introduction', *Poetics Today* 28, no. 2 (2007): 171–89 (187).
9   For a rich and insightful treatment of the essay's philosophical import, see Claire de Obaldia, *The Essayistic Spirit: Literature, Modern Criticism, and the Essay* (Oxford: Clarendon Press, 1995), 99–145.
10 György Lukács, 'On the Nature and Form of the Essay', in *Soul and Form*, trans. Anna Bostock (Cambridge, MA: MIT Press [1910] 1974), 1–18.
11 Dagmar Barnouw, 'Skepticism as a Literary Mode: David Hume and Robert Musil', *MLN* 93, no. 5 (1978), 852–70; Frederic Brahami, *Le Travail du scepticisme: Montaigne, Bayle, Hume* (Paris: PUF, 2001); Graham Good, *The Observing Self: Rediscovering the Essay* (New York: Routledge, 1988); R. Lane Kauffman, 'The Skewed Path: Essaying as Unmethodical Method', in *Essays on the Essay: Redefining the Genre*, ed. A. J. Butrym (Athens: University of Georgia Press, 1989), 234–5; Richard H. Popkin, *The History of Scepticism from Erasmus to Spinoza* (Berkeley: University of California Press, 1979).
12 'As a shadow follows from a body' (Sextus Empiricus, *Outlines of Scepticism*, ed. and trans. Julia Annas and Jonathan Barnes (Cambridge: Cambridge University Press, 2000), 11 (1.12.29)) (the last three numbers are book, chapter, paragraph of any edition; this style is used in other notes as well).
13 Sextus suggests that, having suspended one's judgement about matters of speculation, one ought to live 'in accordance with everyday observances', including biological impulses such as thirst and hunger, cultural and societal conventions, and technical expertise or know-how (*Outlines of Scepticism*, 9. (1.11.4)).
14 'Principally, the Sceptic's view was that rather than guide us in the search for the knowledge that would enable us to live happy lives, philosophy should cure us of the disposition to believe that there is any such knowledge.' (Neil Gascoigne, *Scepticism* (Durham, NC: Acumen, 2002), 31).
15 Erin Plunkett, *A Philosophy of the Essay: Scepticism, Experience, and Style* (London: Bloomsbury, 2018).
16 Stanley Cavell, *The Claim of Reason: Wittgenstein, Skepticism, Morality and Tragedy* (New York: Oxford University Press, 1979), 216.
17 Ibid.
18 Lukács, 'On the Nature and Form of the Essay', 10.
19 'Merely individual experience, in which consciousness begins with what it nearest to it, is itself mediated by the all-encompassing experience of historical humanity' (Adorno, 'The Essay as Form', 158).
20 Lukács, 'On the Nature and Form of the Essay', 10.
21 Adorno, 'The Essay as Form', 161.
22 Ibid., 158.
23 Immanuel Kant, *Critique of Pure Reason*, trans. Norman Kemp Smith (London: Macmillan [1781] 1929), 93 (B75).
24 Lukács, 'On the Nature and Form of the Essay', 8.
25 Adorno, 'The Essay as Form', 161.
26 Lukács, 'On the Nature and Form of the Essay', 10.
27 Adorno, 'The Essay as Form', 153.
28 Ibid., 156.

29 Michel de Montaigne, *Les Essais*, ed. Jean Balsalmo, Michel Magnien and Catherine Magnien-Simonin (Paris: Gallimard, Bibliothèque de la Pléiade, 2007), 1115.
30 Montaigne, *Les Essais*, 616. The source of the English translation is Michel de Montaigne, *Essays*, trans. M.A. Screech (London: Penguin Classics, 2013), 226.
31 Montaigne, *Essais*, 989/Montaigne, *Essays*, 376.
32 Ibid., 845.
33 For more on Montaigne's essayism, see de Obaldia, 28–98; Terence Cave, *The Cornucopian Text: Problems of Writing in the French Renaissance* (Oxford: Oxford University Press, 1979); Sylvia Giocanti, *Penser l'irrésolution: Montaigne, Pascal, La Mothe Le Vayer* (Paris: Honoré Champion, 2001).
34 David Hume, 'Of the Standard of Taste', *Selected Essays* (Oxford: Oxford University Press, 1998, 2008), 133–54 (133).
35 '*Je n'ay pas plus faict mon livre que mon livre m'a faict. Livre consubstantiel à son autheur*' (I no more write my book than my book writes me. A book consubstantial with its author) (Montaigne, *Essais*, 703).
36 See Mikhail Bakhtin, *Problems of Dostoevsky's Poetics* (Minneapolis: University of Minnesota Press, 1984) 5–46. In the context of his criticism of the novel and of Dostoevsky's novels in particular, Bakhtin proposes the term 'polyphonic', where polyphony is 'a plurality' of 'equally valid consciousnesses' (6). The term signifies not just multiple voices within a text but the absence of any overarching judgement on those voices.
37 For a treatment of Adorno's discussion of Descartes' *Discourse on Method*, see de Obaldia, 115–20.
38 Adorno, 'The Essay as Form', 156.
39 Ibid.
40 Ibid.
41 '[The essay] uses equivocation neither out of slovenliness nor in ignorance of their proscription by science, but to clarify what usually remains obscure to the critique of equivocation and its mere discrimination of meanings: whenever a word means a variety of things, the differences are not entirely distinct, for the unity of the word points to some unity, no matter how hidden, in the thing itself' (Adorno, 'The Essay as Form', 169).
42 Edmund Husserl, *Crisis in the European Sciences* (Evanston, IL: Northwestern University Press, 1970), 34.
43 Ibid., 46. For an excellent gloss on the philosophical significance of this point, see Anita Williams, 'The Meaning of the Mathematical', in *Asubjective Phenomenology*, ed. Lubica Učnik, Ivan Chvatik and Anita Williams (Nordhausen: Verlag Traugott Bautz GmbH, 2018), 227–52 (231ff.).
44 Husserl, *Crisis in the European Sciences*, 36.
45 Adorno, 'The Essay as Form', 153.
46 Ibid., 159.
47 Ibid., 157.
48 Ibid.
49 Ibid., 169. See also the discussion of this passage in de Obaldia, 116.
50 Adorno, 'The Essay as Form', 161.
51 See Stewart Martin, 'Adorno's Conception of the Form of Philosophy', *Diacritics* 36, no. 1 (2006), 48–62.
52 Ibid., 160.
53 Ibid.

54 Ibid.
55 Ibid.
56 Martin, 'Adorno's Conception of the Form of Philosophy', 56.
57 Ibid., 50.
58 Simon Jarvis, *Adorno: A Critical Introduction* (Cambridge: Polity, 1998), 230, quoted in Martin, 'Adorno's Conception of the Form of Philosophy', 54.
59 Heidegger's term for truth is *aletheia*, literally 'unconcealment' or 'unhiddenness' (Martin Heidegger, *Being and Time*, trans. Joan Staumbaugh (Albany: State University of New York Press, 1996). The term ἀλήθεια is taken from ancient Greek philosophy.

Chapter 2

AN ESSAY ON THE POST-LITERARY

James Corby

> That mysterious literary essence known as essayism which pervades all literature.
> – Anon., *Saturday Review* (1887)

It was immediately clear to me that if I were to write an essay on the essay, its focus should be on the relation of the essay to 'the post-literary'. Perhaps intuitively, I sensed that there is considerable fertile crossover between the essay and the post-literary and that the two phenomena could be brought together in a fruitful dialogue – something that, to my knowledge, has not hitherto been staged explicitly. Beyond that intuition, I was also struck by a particular similarity between the essay as genre and the post-literary, namely that they are both rather slippery, nebulous terms. Admittedly, that's not an awful lot to go on when deciding on an essay topic. And whereas writers and critics have long tried to define, or at least refine, what an essay actually is, the post-literary, as well as being difficult to pin down, has the added disadvantage of being a new and relatively unknown term, one around which critical positioning is just starting to take shape. But though the post-literary may not (yet) be common critical currency, it does, I believe, name a contemporary literary reality with which it is important to come to terms.

By way of context, I should say that it is this contemporary literary reality that I try to explore in my capacity as co-general editor of the journal *CounterText*, the subtitle of which is 'A Journal for the Study of the Post-Literary'. The premise of the journal is that literature as it has traditionally been understood is experiencing a period of accelerated change and that the literary has spilt over the established genres and forms of literature and flowed into new domains in ways not yet readily or widely recognized as 'literary'. The term 'the post-literary' was adopted in order to name, in an intentionally broad and unrestrictive way, this contemporary devolved space of the literary, encompassing everything from literature as it is popularly and traditionally understood, to new cultural manifestations and artefacts that might (yet) have some claim on the literary. My co-editor, Ivan Callus, and I posited the idea that the literary might be gradually moving away from 'literature' because while the 'literary impulse', whatever that is,[1] remains powerful and urgent, literature – again, popularly and traditionally conceived – perhaps no longer possesses the flexibility and the affordances to accommodate satisfactorily all of the dynamic exigencies of the contemporary literary impulse. It's a provocative idea, and as I rehearse here now in this abbreviated way I can hear the chorus of dissent that it is likely to prompt. But the idea that literature is experiencing a kind of exhaustion is not in itself a new idea. John Barth's 'The Literature of Exhaustion'[2] comes immediately to mind, of course, as does Alvin Kernan's dramatically titled book *The Death of Literature*.[3] More recently, one might also think of David Shields's *Reality Hunger*[4] or, perhaps more obliquely, the myriad of books that have been published over the past decade bemoaning the decline of the relevance of the humanities in universities and in public life. Meanwhile, though, new forms of expression have emerged, often thanks to digital technologies and the way those technologies are rapidly reconfiguring social interaction, offering new, vital, relatively unrestricted spaces and opportunities that the literary impulse can occupy and transform. The consequence of this is what might be considered new appearances of the literary *beyond* 'literature', perhaps not yet fully identified and understood as such – 'countertextual' works or cultural productions that stretch our understanding of literature, requiring us to rethink, again, the question of literature and the literary. The post-literary would include all of this, from contemporary literary enervation, to occasions of countertextual revitalization.

In naming a literary reality that is in a constant state of becoming, therefore, the post-literary is necessarily conceived of as open-ended and future-oriented. Which, of course, imposes an immediate challenge to any attempt to discuss the post-literary in relation to *something else*. And discuss it in relation to something else is precisely what I would have to do if I were to write a piece called 'An Essay on the Post-Literary' that would feature in a book about the essay. Of course, in this context, the essay as genre is a very particular 'something else', not least because it seems to share the post-literary's qualities of mutability, open-endedness and relative indefinability. That, as I've indicated, was the similarity that initially struck me. Not that that makes things any easier – once those similarities are acknowledged what more can be said without imposing definition? The more I thought about it, the more I began to doubt the viability of the topic, despite feeling compelled by it. To write an essay discussing just the post-literary would be more straightforward (though I tend to see any critical writing on the post-literary as, inevitably, an *essay* – as in 'assay', an attempt or challenge – on a topic that, for the reasons I have given, ultimately escapes determination). To write an essay *about* a form of writing notoriously resistant to definition – the essay – *and* the post-literary is altogether more of a challenge. And to complicate matters further, I've recently come to suspect that we should consider the possibility that the literary in one form or another has not only overspilt traditional forms of literature into new cultural spaces, but has increasingly come to occupy all aspects of social, civic and political life in an unprecedented way.[5] Whether we are narrativizing our lives on social media, or responding in an increasingly affective, rather than logical or moral, manner to politicians' competing and often patently fabricated stories, the contemporary moment seems to be that of a deeply aesthetic turn that draws significantly from affordances once associated with literature as a distinct discourse. It's a complicated argument, which I cannot unpack here, and it may at face value seem a preposterous notion, but what else is the age of post-truth if not an age of supreme fiction? So, the post-literary predicament may encompass all of this too. These cumulated considerations threaten to render 'the post-literary' an impossibly unwieldy subject to tackle in an essay on the essay.

But, as tends to be the way, I proposed the seemingly inevitable topic – An Essay on the Post-Literary – and put off my concerns about actually writing the chapter till another day. Till this day, as it turns out, when I find myself wishing I had offered to write about something less intractable and elusive. A host of alternative topics now come effortlessly to mind to compound my regret. Perhaps the most appealing of them would be 'An Essay on the Literary'. I could review the fraught relationship of the essay to literature – it has, for instance, often been treated merely as a secondary form[6] with literary pretensions (a sort of literature *in potentia*[7]) – and then perhaps I could develop the idea that the *essay is an essay* (as in 'assay') on the literary. In other words, I could point out that while the essay is always typically *on* or *about* something, it is never entirely subordinate to its object – it has a life of its own, a degree of autonomy that may, if it is sufficiently pronounced, lay claim to literature. The *essaying* of the essay would thereby multiply satisfyingly, particularly in the case of essays *on* literature: an essay on a literary work puts that work to the test in some way – it assays it, as is its critical function – and in so doing, in its execution, it *attempts* and *accomplishes* the literary in its own right, bestowing upon itself an artistic value that can stand independently of the persuasiveness or otherwise of its treatment of its object.

That would have made for a neat argument. But perhaps too neat – and not particularly original. György Lukács's letter to Leo Popper, published in 1910 in the book *Soul and Form* as an essay called 'On the Nature and Form of the Essay', famously explores the essay's possible claims to itself being considered a work of art.[8] He notes that 'it has been argued that the essay can be stylistically of equal value to a work of the imagination', though he insists that even if one grants it the status of a work of art, that does not in itself deny its particularity, and indeed his stated aim is 'to try and define the essay as strictly as is possible, precisely by describing it as an art form'.[9] One might imagine that Lukács will claim that while an essay might ostensibly be *on* or *about* something, the quality of the language in a great essay rises to the level of literature, thus claiming for itself a formal value that can be weighed separately from the value of its content – if one were to permit that rather problematic form/content distinction. And, indeed, early on in his essay, Lukács seems to be heading in this direction when he points out that we still read essays the truth claims of which we are no longer convinced by. He writes:

> Our view, our appreciation of classical tragedy is quite different today, is it not, from Lessing's in the *Dramaturgy*; Winckelmann's Greeks seem strange, almost incomprehensible to us, and soon we may feel the same about Burckhardt's Renaissance. And yet we read them: why?[10]

We might expect the answer to be: we read them for their literary quality, for the beauty of their language. For their style, in other words, which renders the essay 'literary'. As Claire de Obaldia points out:

> The literary attribute that most immediately comes to mind when thinking about the essay and/or of essay-relatives is a certain concern with style. The essay, no matter what form it chooses to appear in, is considered to be literary first and foremost by virtue of being well or elegantly written.[11]

But that is not Lukács's position at all. Indeed, he writes: 'I believe that the aspect of "being well written" has been too one-sidedly emphasized in this context.'[12] As Michael Holzman puts it in an article on Lukács: 'Style alone ... does not constitute art.'[13] Indeed, Lukács suggests that attempts to identify the essay as literature, whether by dint of style or some other supposedly literary attribute, only serve to obscure what is particular about the essay:

> Let us not, therefore, speak of the essay's similarities with works of literary imagination, but of what divides it from them. Let any resemblance serve here merely as a background against which the differences stand out all the more sharply.[14]

So what, for Lukács, is the principal value of the essay, the value that remains even after its arguments, analyses and perspectives are no longer found to be compelling and after the quality of its language has been considered? However Lukács answers this is likely to place the essay somewhere between a discourse primarily focused on content (paradigmatically 'science', which 'offers us facts and the relationship between facts') and a form of work whose principal value is typically associated with its form (paradigmatically 'art', which, Lukács says rather mysteriously, 'offers us souls and destinies').[15] Given his claim that he wishes to understand the essay as an art form, it is likely that Lukács will argue that although it occupies a position somewhere between the two ideals of science and art, it is more closely affiliated with the latter, but perhaps in a distinctly singular way. One might recall the thought that Ulrich has in Robert Musil's *The Man without Qualities* (written decades after Lukács's essay), when Ulrich wonders to himself:

> A man who wants the truth becomes a scholar; a man who wants to give free play to his subjectivity may become a writer; but what should a man do who wants something in between?[16]

The answer presented by Musil is that such a man should pursue '*essayismus*' or 'essayism', which is 'the inner hovering life' that exists 'between religion and knowledge, between example and doctrine, between *amor intellectualis* and poetry'.[17] Essayism would, broadly, seem to be Lukács's answer too, though his position isn't absolutely clear. The best reconstruction I could give is that although essays often have a named focus, an object, whether that is a work of art or some aspect of daily life, this is only secondary to their primary value, which is the 'expression of human temperament', of 'experiences' understood as 'intellectuality, conceptuality as sensed experience, as immediate reality, as spontaneous principle of existence; the world-view in its undisguised purity as an event of the soul, as the motive force of life'.[18] Lukács thinks of this, quoting Matthew Arnold, as '*criticism of life*', which 'represents the ultimate relationships between man and destiny and world'.[19] This would seem to position the essay as essentially ironic, and it is precisely that irony that conveys 'a world-view, a standpoint, an attitude'.[20] This might seem incidental to the object that is being considered, but understanding the essay form in this way reveals the object – the essay's apparent focus, the particular prompt or occasion from which the essay flows – to be always incidental to the essay's aptitude for expressing life as it is lived in the modern world. Somewhat obscurely, Lukács invites us to understand this in terms of a relationship between 'the problem of destiny' and 'the problem of form', where 'destiny' is understood as that which 'lifts things outside the world of things, accentuating the essential ones and eliminating the inessential'.[21] Poetry 'receives' its form 'from destiny', but in essays 'form *becomes* destiny, it is the destiny-creating principle'.[22] In poetry and other artworks, form springs, as of necessity, as though destined, from life, whereas in the essay life emerges from the consideration of forms, and from the (essayistic) form that those considerations take. Art creates from nothing, whereas the essay works with already existing order, even if it orders that form anew. The essayist will often write about works of art because they provide ready-made forms for contemplation – they constitute orderings of the world ripe for consideration – but they are not essential to the essay. The essayist could just as well focus on any 'immediate sensual expression of life', reading 'reality' into and out of 'every such experience'.[23] The successful essay might, therefore, focus on a particular object, but what it really finds is 'life'.[24] 'Lukács's essayists', Holzman concludes, 'are the mystics of everyday life'.[25]

This reading works well with part of Lukács's essay but is complicated by the fact that when, in 1911, he translated it from the Hungarian to German he rewrote it quite extensively.[26] The reworked essay retains the mystical claims about the essay, but in the second half Lukács sets out a quite new argument asserting that the essay is a fragmentary forerunner of a system to come. The essayist is, in Lukács's words, 'delivered from the relative, the inessential, by the force of judgement of the idea he has glimpsed'.[27] The value of the essay lies not in the judgement itself, which is always 'provisional and occasional',[28] but in the 'process of judging that it embodies'.[29] In a way that is indicative of the shift of focus in the reworked version of the essay, he interprets this judging as a 'longing' for its systematic fulfilment. The essay is positioned as a 'John the Baptist' for the aesthetician.[30] Lukács writes:

> The essay can calmly and proudly set its fragmentariness against the petty completeness of scientific exactitude or impressionist freshness; but its pure fulfilment, its most vigorous accomplishment becomes powerless once the great aesthetic comes.[31]

It seems clear that, for Lukács, the essay was never really about that which it was supposed to be about. What it *is* really about, for Lukács, depends on which version of his essay you give preference to, with the 1910 version 'arguing for the essay as a unique art form, as philosophical poetry, and the second version … stressing the essay as a forerunner of a systematic aesthetics'.[32] In both cases, though, what constitutes the essay's claim to being art is that it is 'an autonomous and integral giving-of-form to an autonomous and complete life'.[33] What is vital, in other words, is 'the gesture, the sovereignty of its attitude', the manner of its judging rather than its actual judgement.[34] This is quite fascinating, because if we accept this, the essay's assay on the literary, its claim to be literature, even if literature here is understood only broadly as a written art form, where art is understood as primarily autotelic, can be understood as conditional upon a characteristic of the essay that has long thought to distinguish it from literature, namely its occasionalism, the fact that it is *on* or *about* something other than 'itself'. T. S. Eliot articulates this view in his 1923 essay, 'The Function of Criticism'. He assumes that it is 'axiomatic that a creation, a work of art, is autotelic', whereas 'criticism, by definition, is *about* something other than itself' – 'there is no equation'.[35] Lukács seems to bring the critical function of the essay closer to the condition of art by dialectically overcoming this opposition, suggesting, in effect, that the essay's aboutness provides the conditions for its ultimate self-directedness. For Lukács, then, the essay is not subordinate to its object, but it is dependent upon it insofar as it affords it the occasion for an ironic articulation of itself as an ultimately autotelic – that is, in this context, literary – discourse. As de Obaldia puts it, quoting Lukács, 'Irony prevails in the fact that as well as being accidental, inessential, this relationship between the essay and its object is also "profound and necessary".[36] In the final analysis, then, 'the essay is always its own object'.[37]

Like Claire de Obaldia, the critic Geoffrey Hartman sees in this position a debt to early German Romanticism, remarking that 'Lukács, of course, inherited this enlarged concept of irony from the German Romantics'. He then goes on to make the following assertion:

> The essay form is a secret relative of the Romantic 'fragment': it acknowledges occasionalism, stays within it, yet removes from accident and contingency that taint of gratuitousness which the mind is always tempted to deny or else to mystify.[38]

The fragment was a privileged form of expression for the early German Romantics because it was seen as constituting a single formal expression of completion and incompletion, determinacy and indeterminacy, finitude and infinitude. As Philippe Lacoue-Labarthe and Jean-Luc Nancy put it in *The Literary Absolute*, 'the fragment combines completion and incompletion within itself, or one may say, in an even more complex manner, it both completes and incompletes the dialectic of completion and incompletion'.[39] Elsewhere they describe 'its completion as the incompletion of its infinity'.[40] The fragment is complete in itself and yet this completion is its incompleteness; it is not, as Novalis points out, merely 'unfinished': 'That which is imperfect appears most tolerably as a fragment – and thus this form of communication is to be recommended above that which as a whole is not yet finished.'[41]

In this way the fragment leads the reader to a beyond that both is and is not itself, though it does not do so in any determinate manner. Rather, it presents us with the possibility of endless possible combinations in a manner that points to an underlying unity that the reader is unable to grasp directly. In Maurice Blanchot's words, the fragment 'does not realise the whole, but signifies it by suspending it, even breaking it'.[42] The fragment is therefore disruptive and anti-systematic, gesturing beyond itself in an essentially ironic procedure. Theodor W. Adorno, in his essay 'The Essay as Form', written largely in response to Lukács, also notes the modern essay's debt to the romantic fragment. He writes:

> If the essay opposes, aesthetically, the mean-spirited method whose sole concern is not to leave anything out, it is following an epistemological impulse. The romantic conception of the fragment as a construction that is not complete but rather progresses onward into the infinite through self-reflection champions this anti-idealist motive in the midst of Idealism.[43]

'The essay', he writes, 'incorporates the antisystematic impulse into its own way of proceeding and introduces concepts unceremoniously, "immediately", just as it receives them.'[44] It 'abandons the royal road to the origins, which leads only to what is most derivative – Being, the ideology that duplicates what already exists'.[45] 'Discontinuity is essential to the essay', he remarks.[46]

So, yes, back to my regret – perhaps I could have taken all this material, explored it further, and put together a solid enough chapter called 'An Essay on the Literary'. After all, if we're going to talk about the nature of the literary the early German Romantics seem unavoidable, and thanks to Adorno, Hartman, de Obaldia, Brian Lennon[47] and others, who explicitly link the essay to German Romanticism by way of the fragment, I would have had my cue. I could have explored the well-worn – but still compelling – argument that literature as we understand it today emerges from that late-eighteenth-century milieu. I could have examined Maurice Blanchot's idea that it was in the pages of *The Athenaeum*, the journal produced by the Schlegel brothers between 1798 and 1800, which published some of the most important fragmentary romantic writing, that 'Literature … suddenly becomes conscious of itself, manifests itself, and, in this manifestation, has no other task or trait than to declare itself'.[48] It is at this moment that literary writing breaks away from the world and received ideas about reality, when it rejects its subordination to representation, when, in other words, it is no longer primarily *on* or *about* something in the world, and becomes its own question – a move that is itself essentially disruptive and anti-systematic. As Blanchot puts it in 'Literature and the Right to Death': 'Let us suppose that literature begins at the moment when literature becomes a question.'[49] 'Literature contemplates itself in revolution, it finds its justification in revolution.'[50] Blanchot quotes Hegel to suggest that literature's emergence to itself is 'that moment when "life endures death and maintains itself in it" … This is the "question that seeks to pose itself in literature, the "question" that is its essence".⁵¹ The death or revolution that literature emerges from is, I think, the rejection of 'the given' as the ordering authority in any creative act, even when that 'given' is a received idea about what constitutes literature. Literature, thus conceived, might nominally still be *on* or *about* this, that, or the other, but only incidentally to an essentially recursive and self-interrogating move that challenges and transforms what it is that it – that is, literature – is taken to be.

In this regard too, then, the literary and the essay appear to be similar – they are implicitly (and perhaps primarily, in terms of what signally identifies them) *about* something other than what they seem explicitly to be about. And yet both require the occasion and opportunity of their explicit *aboutness* in order to be addressed to the implicit *aboutness* that elevates them to the level of art. That is to say that their autotelicity is dependent upon their occasionalism, or, to coin a word, their *allotelicity*. They are both, in essence, therefore, auto-hetero-logical in a way that could be understood as redeeming the anonymously authored epigraph to this chapter, which names 'essayism' as 'that mysterious literary essence … which pervades all literature', if essayism is taken to name, in an exemplary fashion, the procedure of mounting an unscripted, autotelic, self-challenging manoeuvre by recruiting, in a particular way, inessential particulars. As Robert Atwan puts it, reversing the usual marginalization of the essay in relation to literature: 'Is the essay literature? Perhaps the question to ask is: can literature exist without it?'⁵²

Of crucial importance here, however – and it is something that any 'Essay on the Literary' would have to negotiate carefully – is the degree to which a work's allotelicity – its relationship to its explicit, objective, aboutness – is subordinate to its implicit, subjective, autotelicity. Early German Romanticism, for instance, was fiercely criticized by Hegel and, later, Carl Schmitt, for propagating an occasionalism radically disinterested in the objective particularity that constitutes an artwork's explicit aboutness, being consumed instead by a passion for subjective generality attested to by the artwork's implicit aboutness. Hegel criticizes this as art's 'self-transcendence',⁵³ which he sees as structurally religious – specifically Christian – and as marking a certain end of art as an organon of truth. In the *Aesthetics*, for instance, he writes:

> At the stage of romantic art the spirit knows that its truth does not consist in its immersion in corporeality; on the contrary, it only becomes sure of its truth by withdrawing from the external into its own intimacy with itself and positing external reality as an existence inadequate to itself.⁵⁴

The romantic artwork's external appearance, its objectivity, its explicit aboutness, therefore, is utterly incidental and contingent. Structurally necessary but of no *particular* interest, it constitutes merely the *occasion* for the recursive self-interrogation of 'art' or 'literature' into which it dissolves. The romantic work's apparent allotelicity serves merely a slave-like function, serving art's autologic, quasi-religious self-exaltation. This triumph of subjective artistic autonomy, so derided by Hegel, is what Lacoue-Labarthe and Nancy would later call 'the literary absolute'.

I would suggest that it is broadly this Romantic paradigm that became, and has remained, the dominant artistic ideal in modernity, the trajectory of which charts the gradual move away from referentiality and representation towards abstraction and self-knowing irony, privileging work that asserts its autonomy. Think, for instance, of James Joyce's *Finnegans Wake*, Kazimir Malevich's *Black Circle*, or John Cage's *4'33* as extreme examples of this tendency to radically subordinate any explicit aboutness to an implicit aboutness. And in a far more subtle way this tendency informs the contemporary distinction between literary fiction and popular fiction – these categorizations are eminently debatable, of course, but generally the former might be thought of as manifesting an artistic autotelicity lacking in the latter.

Given its self-promoting and self-aggrandizing impulse, which treats anything external to it as, at best, subordinate and contingent, it was perhaps inevitable that, given the opportunity, the expression of this unbounded subjective productivity released by Romanticism would not remain limited to 'art', but would seek expression in all aspects of lived experience. The line of descent connecting romanticism with fascism, and the aestheticization of politics more generally, is well known, so I probably wouldn't rehearse that position in any detail in 'An Essay on the Literary'. Instead, I would limit myself to a brief reflection on the views of Carl Schmitt, the German jurist, political theorist and vociferous critic of Romanticism's readiness to co-opt any occasion (any explicit putative aboutness) to its own ends (its implicit aboutness). Schmitt, for instance, writes:

> Romanticism transposed intellectual productivity into the domain of the aesthetic, into art and art criticism; and then, on the basis of the aesthetic, it comprehended all other domains [...] Released from all shackles, art seems to expand immeasurably. An absolutization of art is proclaimed. A universal art is demanded, and everything that is intellectual, religion, the Church, the nation, and the state, flows into the stream that has its source in the new center, the aesthetic.[55]

Romanticism, Schmitt argues, reduces the world and everything in it simply as potential opportunities to exercise the poetic imagination:

> For the romantic achievement, the external world and historical reality are of interest only insofar as they can be – to use that expression from Novalis – the beginning of a novel. The given fact is not objectively considered in a political, historical, legal, or moral context. On the contrary, it is the object of an aesthetic and emotional interest, something with which the romantic enthusiasm catches fire.[56]

'Every concrete point of the external world', he goes on, 'can be the "elastic point"': in other words, the beginning of the romantic novel, the *occasio* for the adventure, the point of departure for the fanciful game.'⁵⁷ This assessment leads Schmitt to characterize Romanticism as 'subjectified occasionalism',⁵⁸ with the 'consummation of romanticism'⁵⁹ being a 'political romanticism' where 'the state is a work of art'.⁶⁰

And so the literary, as theorized by the German Romantics, overspills the bounds of 'literature', traditionally and popularly conceived, colonizing all spheres of human activity, constituting … a radically expanded field of the literary. Ah … that sounds familiar. It sounds a lot, in fact, like 'the post-literary' as I outlined it at the start of these notes towards 'An Essay on the Post-Literary'….

On reflection, then, 'An Essay on the Literary' would not have been the easier option after all. It would have delivered me to the thorny issue of the post-literary in any case. And what then? Well, given what I have said, I think I would have to start the 'Essay on the Post-Literary' from the premise that the post-literary contemporary offers little cause for complacency, and even less for celebration. I could then perhaps argue that today the type of intervention most likely to *counter* the post-literary effectively, regardless of whether the intervention is literary or political, would perhaps be essentially essayistic – and by this I mean open-ended, discontinuous, anti-systematic, and, above all, occasionalist, but occasionalist in a manner very different from romantic occasionalism. In the occasionalism of the essay autotelicity and allotelicity tend to be more fully dialectical. Essayism, to co-opt Musil's term, carefully engages the specificity of its object, working closely with its being, crucially allowing a subjective autotelicity to emerge in a way that doesn't require the subordination of the object. Above all, therefore, the essay names a procedure of occasionalist intervention, a particular way of assaying an occasion. *Occasio*, it now occurs to me, is the Latin name for Caerus, or Kairos, the personification of opportunity and favourable moments. More broadly, the term *kairos* names what Antonio Calcagno calls the 'strategic time to act'.⁶¹ These moments must be perceived and acted upon, and thus 'both subject and *kairos* must work together in order to bring about the intervention that will give us events'.⁶² The disruptiveness of *kairos* is often contrasted with the continuous linearity of *chronos*, but the two are in fact inextricably linked – just as, I imagine, countertexts and the post-literary are. As Giorgio Agamben points out: 'Kairos … does not have another time at its disposal; in other words, what we take hold of when we seize *kairos* is not another time, but a contracted and abridged *chronos* … *kairos* is nothing more than seized *chronos*.'⁶³ And perhaps only when the implications of this are fully realized will there be 'An Essay on the Post-Literary'.

Notes

1 I have a go at answering this in: James Corby, 'The Ancient Quarrel between Performance and Literature?', *Performance Philosophy* 1 (2015): 36–50.
2 John Barth, 'The Literature of Exhaustion' (1967), in *The Friday Book: Essays and Other Non-Fiction* (London: Johns Hopkins University Press, 1984), 62–76.
3 Alvin Kernan, *The Death of Literature* (New Haven, CT: Yale University Press, 1990).

4   David Shields, *Reality Hunger* (London: Penguin Books, 2010).
5   James Corby, 'The Post-Literary, Post-Truth, and Modernity', *CounterText* 5, no. 1 (2019): 33–69.
6   E. B. White, writing in 1979, comments: 'The essayist, unlike the novelist, the poet, and the playwright, must be content in his self-imposed role of second-class citizen' (White, *Essays of E. B. White* (New York: Harper Perennial Modern Classics, 1999), ix–x). This idea is later developed by G. Douglas Atkins in a chapter titled 'Irony or Sneakiness: On the Essay's Second-Class Citizenship' (Atkins, *Tracing the Essay: Through Experience to Truth* (Athens: University of Georgia Press, 2005), 9–25).
7   Alastair Fowler, *Kinds of Literature: An Introduction to the Theory of Genres and Modes* (Cambridge, MA: Harvard University Press, 1982). See also Claire de Obaldia, *The Essayistic Spirit: Literature, Modern Criticism, and the Essay* (New York: Oxford University Press, 1996), 1–64.
8   György Lukács, *Soul and Form* [1911], trans. Anna Bostock (Cambridge, MA: MIT Press, 1974).
9   Ibid., 2.
10 Ibid.
11 De Obaldia, *The Essayistic Spirit*, 8.
12 Lukács, *Soul and Form*, 2.
13 Michael Holzman, '"Writing," Criticism, Lukacs, and the One', *Criticism* 24, no. 4 (1982): 362–78 (365).
14 Lukács, *Soul and Form*, 2.
15 Ibid., 3.
16 Robert Musil, *The Man without Qualities* [1943], trans. S. Wilkins (London: Picador, 1995), 274.
17 Ibid., 273.
18 Lukács, *Soul and Form*, 7.
19 Ibid., 5.
20 Ibid., 8.
21 Ibid., 7.
22 Ibid., 7.
23 Ibid., 8.
24 Ibid., 12.
25 Holzman, '"Writing," Criticism, Lukacs, and the One', 371.
26 Ibid., 375–7.
27 Lukács, *Soul and Form*, 16.
28 Ibid., 17.
29 Ibid., 18.
30 Ibid., 16.
31 Ibid., 17.
32 Andrew Arato and Paul Breines, *The Young Lukács and the Origins of Western Marxism* (New York: Seabury Press, 1979), 34.
33 Lukács, *Soul and Form*, 18.
34 Ibid., 18.
35 T. S. Eliot, 'The Function of Criticism', in *Selected Essays* (London: Faber and Faber, 1932, enlarged edition in 1934), 23–34 (30).
36 De Obaldia, *The Essayistic Spirit*, 107.
37 Ibid., 100.

38 Geoffrey H. Hartman, *Criticism in the Wilderness: The Study of Literature Today* (New Haven, CT: Yale University Press, 1980), 193–4.
39 Philippe Lacoue-Labarthe and Jean-Luc Nancy, *The Literary Absolute* [1978], trans. P. Barnard and C. Lester (Albany: State University of New York Press, 1988), 50.
40 Lacoue-Labarthe and Nancy, *The Literary Absolute*, 44.
41 Novalis, *Philosophical Writings*, trans. M. Mahony Stoljar (Albany: State University of New York Press, 1997), 81.
42 Maurice Blanchot, *The Infinite Conversation*, trans. S. Hanson (Minneapolis: University of Minnesota Press, 1993), 353.
43 Theodor W. Adorno, *Notes to Literature: Volume One*, trans. S. Weber Nicholsen (New York: Columbia University Press, 1991), 16.
44 Ibid., 12.
45 Ibid., 11.
46 Adorno, *Notes to Literature*, 16.
47 Brian Lennon, 'The Essay in Theory', *Diacritics* 38, no. 3 (2008): 71–92.
48 Blanchot, *The Infinite Conversation*, 354.
49 Maurice Blanchot, *The Work of Fire*, trans. C. Mandell (Stanford, CA: Stanford University Press, 1995), 300.
50 Ibid., 321.
51 Ibid., 321–2.
52 Robert Atwan, 'Essayism', *The Iowa Review* 25, no. 2 (1995): 6–14 (13).
53 G. W. F. Hegel, *Aesthetics: Lectures on Fine Art*, Vol. 1, trans. T. M. Knox (Oxford: Oxford University Press, 1988), 607.
54 Hegel, *Aesthetics*, Vol. 1, 518.
55 Carl Schmitt, *Political Romanticism* [1919, 1925], trans. G. Oakes (Cambridge, MA: MIT Press: 1986), 15.
56 Ibid., 84.
57 Ibid., 98.
58 Ibid., 17, 18.
59 Ibid., 93.
60 Ibid., 125.
61 Antonio Calcagno, *Badiou and Derrida: Politics, Events and their Time* (London: Continuum, 2007), 98.
62 Calcagno, *Badiou and Derrida*, 101.
63 Giorgio Agamben, *The Time That Remains: A Commentary on the Letter to the Romans* [2000] (Stanford, CA: Stanford University Press, 2005), 69.

Chapter 3

BRIEF SCENES: ROLAND BARTHES AND THE ESSAY

Neil Badmington

'I am an essayist.' So declared Roland Barthes in a brief text of just three paragraphs published in *Les Nouvelles littéraires* in February 1979.[1] He had said something similar in his inaugural lecture at the Collège de France around two years earlier:

> I should probably begin with a consideration of the reasons which have led the Collège de France to receive a fellow of doubtful nature, whose every attribute is somehow challenged by its opposite. For though my career has been academic, I am without the usual qualification for entrance into that career. And though it is true that I long wished to inscribe my work within the field of science – literary, lexicological, and sociological – I must admit that I have produced only essays, an ambiguous genre in which analysis vies with writing.[2]

I have produced only essays. There is, particularly if the emphasis falls upon '*only*', something self-effacing, something disingenuous about this statement – a statement made in a lecture which formally marked Barthes's entrance to one of the most prestigious academic institutions of all. And yet, it seems to me that there is also something in the statement. Barthes published books – yes, obviously – but these were often collections of previously published essays.[3] Alternatively, the volumes were composed of short bursts of text – 'discontinuous writings, fragments, miniatures, paragraphs with titles', in Barthes's own words.[4] His books, as Susan Sontag once remarked, 'tend to be multiples of short forms rather than "real" books'.[5]

Barthes was an essayist, then, and there is nothing remotely original about describing him in this way. But why did he favour the form? Why was Barthes so consistently committed to the essay, to what he once called, referring to the mode of *Mythologies*, 'brief scenes'?[6] This question has not been asked enough or answered in an entirely satisfactory way. Barthes the essayist is a familiar formulation, and the pull of positivism might tempt us simply to place him in a tradition of French *essayistes* stretching back to Michel de Montaigne. Barthes, from that perspective, produced essays because he had read essays, because writing is a matter of lineage and tradition, because form follows history and nation. Alternatively, someone in search of an extremely quick and easy answer to my question about Barthes's embrace of the essay might turn to biography, to the fact that Barthes's work contains many references to his tendency to become bored rather easily.[7] In this monadic light, the essay is perfect for Barthes because it enables a flitting and floating that keeps boredom at bay. But how dull, how timid, how boring a conclusion. We can do better, I think, than turning either to 'the author, his person, his history, his tastes, his passions' or to mere literary tradition in order to address Barthes's commitment to brief scenes.[8] With this in mind, I want in what follows to address Barthes's essayism more specifically and theoretically than has tended to be the case in scholarship to date.

1. Semiology and 'the very history of the modern world'

'I had just read Saussure'. This, I think, is the most significant phrase in the whole of Barthes's work; it marks, to take a phrase from Jean-Claude Milner, 'the revelation of the Sign'.[9] The statement occurs near the beginning of a preface that Barthes wrote in 1970 to mark the republication of *Mythologies*.[10] The book had first appeared in 1957, and it had established Barthes's reputation as a cultural critic.[11] Having been introduced to Saussurean linguistics by Algirdas Greimas in Alexandria in 1949 or 1950, Barthes embraced the description of semiology that occurs in a famous passage of Saussure's *Course in General Linguistics*:[12]

> A science that studies the life of signs within society is conceivable; it would be a part of social psychology and consequently of general psychology; I shall call it semiology …. Semiology would show what constitutes signs, what laws govern them. Since the science does not yet exist, no one can say what it would be; but it has a right to existence, a place staked out in advance.[13]

These lines are never quoted in *Mythologies*, and Saussure's name is mentioned explicitly on just a handful of occasions in the book. The debt is clear – particularly in the long theoretical essay entitled 'Myth Today' that acts as a coda – but the debt is downplayed. (Tiphaine Samoyault has pointed out, in fact, that five notes explicitly naming Saussure were deleted by Barthes as he prepared 'Myth Today' for publication.)[14]

In 1964, however, Barthes published two texts that were much more open about the influence of Saussure upon his attempt to bring into existence the science of semiology imagined in the *Course in General Linguistics*: a very short essay titled 'The Kitchen of Meaning' and *Elements of Semiology*. I want to turn to these publications, especially the former, because I think that their discussion of signs illuminates Barthes's commitment to the essay as a form.

Elements of Semiology appeared initially as a long piece in the journal *Communications* in 1964. According to Umberto Eco, Barthes never meant for these pages to appear in book form, but they were published as a separate volume by Seuil in 1965; an English translation followed in 1967, which is rather early for Barthes in English.[15] The text opens with the following statement:

> In his *Course in General Linguistics*, first published in 1916, Saussure postulated the existence of a general science of signs, or Semiology, of which linguistics would form only one part. Semiology therefore aims to take in any system of signs, whatever their substance and limits; images, gestures, musical sounds, objects, and the complex associations of all these, which form the content of ritual, convention or public entertainment: these constitute, if not languages, at least systems of signification. There is no doubt that the development of mass communications confers particular relevance today upon the vast field of signifying media, just when the success of disciplines such as linguistics, information theory, formal logic and structural anthropology provide semantic analysis with new instruments. There is at present a kind of demand for semiology, stemming not from the fads of a few scholars, but from the very history of the modern world.[16]

Two moments in this passage strike me as particularly relevant in the present context. First, Barthes refers to what he calls 'the vast field of signifying media' and the impact of 'mass communications'. *Vast*, *mass* – these are terms of scale and sweep, of daunting size. I will set this vastness alongside Barthes's brief scenes later in this essay. Second, Barthes's allusion to the situation in which he was writing is followed by a reference to how 'the very history of the world' has given rise to 'a kind of demand for semiology'. Cause and effect; demand and response: semiology is a reaction. In fact, if we set *Elements of Semiology* in context by opening the volume of Barthes's complete works which covers this period in his life, we find related texts in which he is trying to respond to this very demand for semiology, trying to bring Saussure's speculative science of signs into existence and into the academy. The courses at the École pratique des hautes études in Paris in 1962–3 and 1963–4, for instance – Barthes's very first at the institution – are on 'contemporary systems of signification' and turn their attention to the 'still prospective' and 'little applied' method of semiology.[17] The published summary of the first course of 1962–3 makes it clear that the work undertaken in the classroom was laying the foundations for the book that we now know as *Elements of Semiology*; Barthes even uses the phrase at one point to describe the work undertaken in the second part of the course.[18]

2. *The kitchen of meaning*

In the same volume of Barthes's *Oeuvres complètes*, we also find a text that is, to my mind, one of the most significant pieces of writing from this stage of Barthes's career. It has received little critical attention, even when the renaissance of Roland Barthes that has occurred in recent years has invited us to revisit all aspects of Barthes's work with fresh eyes. The text in question is a short essay titled 'The

Kitchen of Meaning', which first appeared in *Le Nouvel Observateur* in December 1964. It opens in the following manner:

> A garment, an automobile, a dish of cooked food, a gesture, a film, a piece of music, an advertising image, a piece of furniture, a newspaper headline – these indeed appear to be heterogeneous objects.
>
> What might they have in common? This at least: all are signs. When I walk through the streets – or through life – and encounter these objects, I apply to all of them, if need be without realizing it, one and the same activity, which is that of a certain *reading*: modern man, urban man, spends his time reading. He reads, first of all and above all, images, gestures, behaviors: this car tells me the social status of its owner, this garment tells me quite precisely the degree of its wearer's conformism or eccentricity, this *apéritif* (whiskey, Pernod, or white wine and cassis) reveals my host's lifestyle.[19]

We are surrounded by meaning; we spend our days interpreting sign after sign – even if, as Barthes notes, we do not necessarily realize what we are doing. These signs come in radically different forms, too: food, clothing, music, advertising and so on. If Saussure was only really interested in speech, the semiology that he imagined in the *Course in General Linguistics* understands that words are not the only things to bear meaning.

What follows from this recognition? What next for the one who has noticed that all of these things are signs? Barthes explains in his next paragraph: 'All these "readings" are too important in our life, they imply too many social, moral, ideological values, not to attempt to account for them by systematic reflection: it is this reflection which, at least for the moment, we call *semiology*.'[20] But the 'systematic reflection' of semiology, Barthes acknowledges, is a tricky business. For one thing, he writes: 'The world is full of signs, but these signs do not all have the fine simplicity of the letters of the alphabet, of highway signs, or of military uniforms: they are infinitely more complex.'[21] The eager semiologist needs the vocabulary and the capacity to reflect upon signs which take forms that fox easy analysis; reading the world involves stepping outside convenient interpretive parameters. If meaning is golden, as Barthes would propose some years later in *S/Z*, it is also quicksilver.[22]

There is, moreover, the problem that Barthes had identified in *Mythologies* in 1957. As he puts it in 'The Kitchen of Meaning':

> To decipher the world's signs always means to struggle with a certain innocence of objects. We all understand our language so 'naturally' that it never occurs to us that it is an extremely complicated system, one anything but 'natural' in its signs and rules: in the same way, it requires an incessant shock of observation in order to deal with the content of messages but with their making: in short, the semiologist, like the linguist, must enter the 'kitchen of meaning'.[23]

In the very next paragraph, Barthes identifies a further challenge for the semiologist. It is, from my perspective in the present essay, the most pressing issue facing the discipline:

This is a tremendous undertaking. Why? Because a meaning can never be analyzed in an isolated fashion. If I establish that blue jeans are the sign of a certain adolescent dandyism, or the *pot-au-feu* photographed by a luxury magazine that of a rather theatrical rusticity, and if I even multiply these equivalences in order to constitute lists of signs resembling the columns of a dictionary, I shall have discovered nothing at all. *The signs are constituted by differences.*[24]

Meaning does not exist in isolation; signs are constituted by differences. The debt to Saussure is particularly clear here – above all the Saussure of the chapter in the *Course in General Linguistics* titled 'Linguistic Value', where we read that 'in language there are only differences *without positive terms*'.[25] What is also clear, beyond the motivating trace of Saussure, is the monumental task facing semiology, which Barthes is, of course, attempting to bring into existence here and elsewhere in his writings from the period. Meaning cannot be analysed in an isolated fashion because, following Saussure, meaning depends upon difference within a larger signifying system. When the semiologist's gaze falls upon a single sign – a pair of blue jeans, perhaps, to take Barthes's example – they have to recognize that this particular sign circulates alongside other signs, from which it differs and is thus made meaningful. Jeans mean what they mean because they are not a pair of pin-striped trousers, a pencil skirt and so on. At the same time, those same jeans could gain some of their resonance from being paired with a worn leather jacket and not a starched shirt and silk tie. (These are close to clichés, of course, but I think that, even now, they nonetheless ring true.) Meaning depends upon difference, not reference or inherence – and difference within a larger signifying system. Little wonder that Barthes ends 'The Kitchen of Meaning' by referring to how 'the tasks of semiology are constantly enlarging'.[26] The problem, in short, is that 'the world is full of signs'.

What is to be done? How is a critic to proceed once they have, in the wake of Saussure and semiology, realized that 'meaning can never be studied in an isolated fashion'? If the world is full of signs, if signs are more than merely words, and if meaning is the domain of criticism, what on earth do we do?[27] If, as Barthes puts it, 'there is at present a kind of demand for semiology', what form should the response to this demand take? The essay comes gradually into view.

3. An exemption from meaning

Towards the end of his life, Barthes repeatedly articulated a desire for what he called 'an exemption from meaning'. The possibility flickers briefly in 'The Death of the Author' in 1967, occupies a section of *Empire of Signs* three years later, and then finds itself summarized in *Roland Barthes by Roland Barthes* in 1975:

> Evidently he dreams of a world which would be *exempt from meaning* (as one is from military service). This began with *Writing Degree Zero*, in which is imagined 'the absence of every sign'; subsequently, a thousand affirmations incidental to this dream (apropos of the avant-garde text, of Japan, of music,

of the alexandrine, etc.). … Yet for him, it is not a question of recovering a pre-meaning, an origin of the world, of life, of facts, anterior to meaning, but rather to imagine a post-meaning: one must traverse, as though the length of an initiatic way, the whole meaning, in order to be able to extenuate it, to exempt it.[28]

This desire for an exemption from meaning – for a liberatory 'state of *a-language*' – is perfectly understandable, I think, in the light of what semiology reveals and requires.[29] 'The world is full of signs', Barthes realizes – and those signs never stop signifying. Everyday life involves encountering meaning after meaning, whether we like it or not: this is what it means to move through a culture's 'webs of significance', as Clifford Geertz called them.[30] The symbolic deluge is unending: the 'utopia of a lifting of signs' is precisely that.[31]

So much so, in fact, that on 11 March 1978, Barthes made a rather desperate announcement: 'I am trapped by language', he declared during a discussion of 'laudatory adjectives' at the Collège de France.[32] Two weeks later, in the same venue, he took a longer and less gloomy view:

> All my life long, I've been living this back-and-forth: caught up between the exaltation of language [*jouissance* taken in its drive] [→ whence: my writing, my speaking are glued to my social being, since I publish and I teach] and the desire, the great desire for a respite from language, for a suspension, an exemption.[33]

These statements were made during Barthes's course on the Neutral, in which he pursued ways to baffle or suspend conventional binary thinking. But the desire for a complete exemption from meaning is, of course, a fantasy – a dream, precisely. Death provides a release from the empire of signs, of course, but it is a little drastic as a response. Fortunately, there is another way in which Barthes responds to the demands of semiology, to the realization that the world is full of signs: he writes essays.

4. Opening a dossier

Theodor W. Adorno once noted that the essay, as a form, does not 'strive for closed, deductive or inductive, construction'.[34] It 'refuses to believe as though it had deduced its object and had exhausted the topic', he proposed, and it 'gently defies … absolute certainty'.[35] The essay, he concludes, 'does not begin with Adam and Eve but with what it wants to discuss; it says what is at issue and stops where it feels itself complete – not where nothing is left to say'.[36] Much divides Adorno from Barthes, but much in these moments from Adorno's 'The Essay as Form' illuminates Barthes's commitment to brief scenes. In Adorno's words we find a direction – a form – for the critic who has realized that 'the world is full of signs' and that these signs twinkle within a constellation of differences.

In *The Barthes Effect: The Essay as Reflective Text*, Réda Bensmaïa notes that Barthes the essayist 'refuses any idea of mastery' in his short bursts of writing.[37]

'The *form of the Barthesian essay* can be neither *monumental nor finished*', he proposes.[38] He is absolutely right, I think, but I am not convinced that his book – one of the few sustained attempts to discuss Barthes and the essay form – ever really asks *why* this is the case, why the Barthesian essay resists mastery and monument. (We could perhaps invoke Montaigne's insistence that the essay is tentative and anti-systemic, but this fails to address the specificity of Barthes the essayist.[39])

It seems to me, in the absence of such investigations, that one of the implications of semiology as a discipline is that the work of the critic responding to meaning – the semiologist – can never be over. Meaning keeps on coming, keeps on going, and signs cannot be studied in isolation. In this light, writing lengthy, weighty, time-consuming, monumental texts would simply be the wrong way to go: such forms are too slow, too clumsy, too heavy on their feet to respond adequately to the world (the world which is 'full of signs'). Essays, by way of contrast, are more responsive, more adept at responding. In a passing remark in a late text on Proust, Barthes proposes that 'the real question of any Essay' is 'What is it? What does it mean?'[40] He does not dwell on the point, but I want to linger and add that, yes, this is 'the real question of any Essay' – and specifically of the essay as a form – because 'What is it? What does it mean?' takes us into the realm of semiology and thus the recognition that 'the world is full of signs'. The 'demand for semiology', as Barthes calls it in 'The Kitchen of Meaning', is, I think, a demand for the essay.

It is important, however, to stress a difference and a distance from the self-centred tradition of essay-writing that unfolds from Montaigne's 'I am myself the substance of my book'.[41] Barthes's later essays are certainly autobiographical at times – just as his more explicitly autobiographical compositions are essayistic – but it seems to me that the essays are prompted first and foremost by signs, by meaning, rather than by a self with founding desires.[42] The Barthesian brief scene comes from a world that is 'full of signs', not an individual who sings in plenitude.[43]

It is perhaps a little surprising, then, to read Barthes claiming, in conversation with Raymond Bellour in 1970, that he 'generally do[es] not much like the word "essay" when it's applied to critical work'.[44] Can this be the Barthes who called himself an essayist? Yes, it can, because of what Barthes adds in parentheses immediately after stating that he is not fond of the term 'essay'. His full statement, which I cut short for essayistic effect at the beginning of this paragraph, reads as follows: 'I generally do not much like the word "essay" when it's applied to critical work (when the essay then appears to be a falsely prudent way of being scientific)'. Those two final words are crucial here if we are to understand Barthes's reservations about the essay as a form. If an essay, in asking itself 'What is it? What does it mean?', aspires to be science, to tell truth, it is not to be trusted. No one who has grasped Saussure's basic point about meaning, particularly in the light of Derrida's rereading of the *Course in General Linguistics*, could be taken in by closure.[45] This, I think, is why Barthes, having articulated his uncertainty about the term 'essay', immediately adds the following: 'I can accept the word if it is understood as "to essay a language or an object, a text": one tries out a language as one tries on a garment; the better the fit, i.e., the further it goes, the happier one is.'[46] *The better the fit; the further it goes.* Essaying is not about reaching an end point, a perfect fit.

Something similar is at work when Barthes finds himself delivering long lectures in his courses at the Collège de France in his final years. Even in speech, that is to say, and even when facing an audience of hundreds at the nation's most elevated academic institution, Barthes is an essayist. I referred to his inaugural lecture at the Collège at the very beginning of my investigation, when I quoted his self-effacing remark about having 'produced only essays'. That lecture was delivered in the first week of January 1977, and Barthes proceeded, after calling himself 'a fellow of doubtful nature', to call for, or promise, a form of teaching that would not be magisterial or in the service of power and the transmission of knowledge, but which would instead be about, in his words, 'loosening, baffling, or at the very least ... lightening this power'.[47] 'There is', he noted in his closing remarks:

> an age at which we teach what we know. Then comes another age at which we teach what we do not know; this is called *research*. Now perhaps comes the age of another experience: that of *unlearning*, of yielding to the unforeseeable change which forgetting imposes on the sedimentation of knowledges, cultures, and beliefs we have traversed.[48]

What might this new form of teaching look like? Barthes sketches a brief scenario:

> I am increasingly convinced, both in writing and in teaching, that the fundamental operation of this loosening method is, if one writes, fragmentation, and, if one teaches, digression, or, to put it in a precisely ambiguous word, *excursion*. I should therefore like the speaking and the listening that will be interwoven here to resemble the comings and goings of a child playing beside his mother, leaving her, returning to bring her a pebble, a piece of string, and thereby tracing around a calm centre a whole locus of play within which the pebble, the string come to matter less than the enthusiastic giving of them.[49]

If this is the theory, we see what things look like in practice less than a week later, when, on 12 January 1977, Barthes begins the first of his courses at the Collège – *How to Live Together*. In the first session, Barthes reminds his audience of how, in his inaugural lecture five days earlier, he had proposed undertaking each year 'a research inquiry from a fantasy'.[50] On 19 January, he explains in more detail how he will be working, how he will present his research within the institution. 'From now on', he stated, 'this lecture course must consent to take the form of a series of discontinuous units: traits'.[51] He has, he explains, been gathering his materials for the course on index cards; this was his habitual way of working for most of his writing life. But how to organize these discontinuous traits, these pebbles and pieces of string? How to order these brief scenes for public presentation? If writing in fragments is easy to imagine, what, Barthes asks, would *speaking* in fragments involve?[52] His solution, he explains, has been to gather the different traits together and arrange them alphabetically for presentation: anachoresis, animals, Athos and so on. 'This method of the traits', he concludes, 'is clearly bound up with a certain politics ...: a politics that seeks to deconstruct metalanguage'.[53]

It is also implicitly a politics of the essay. As *How to Live Together* unfolds, Barthes often refers to how, with the turn to each new trait, he is merely 'opening a dossier'. In the very last session of the course, he reflects on what he has been doing for several months in the lecture theatre, in the name of research. Beneath the title 'BUT WHAT ABOUT METHOD?', he states the following: 'We're not following a path; we're presenting our findings as we go along.'[54] And then, in a short section titled 'To Open a Dossier', he adds:

> I have said repeatedly (in relation to virtually every figure): 'I'm merely opening a dossier'. Opening a dossier: encyclopedic act *par excellence*. Diderot opened all the dossiers of his age. But at that time the act was effective, since knowledge could be mastered – if not by a single man (as in the time of Aristotle or Leibniz) then at least by a team. ≠ Today: no longer possible to acquire an exhaustive knowledge; knowledge is now wholly pluralized, diffracted across discrete languages. The encyclopedic act is no longer possible.[55]

Isn't this the essayist at work in the lecture theatre? Isn't this the semiologist who has realized that 'the world is full of signs' responding to this realization in how he proceeds in the classroom? Opening a dossier … and then opening another when the need arises, when something else comes into view and demands the attention of the critic who recognizes that we are in 'the kitchen of meaning'. Opening without closing. Speaking in fragments. Essaying.

5. The risk

There is a risk, of course – a risk raised by the decision to teach openly in this way or to write essays which make no claim to mastery. The risk is that you are seen as a dilettante, a lightweight, a butterfly.

This, more or less, is how Pierre Bourdieu viewed Roland Barthes. Clearly wanting something more scientific and monumental, Bourdieu wrote, in *Homo Academicus*, the following lines:

> Roland Barthes represents the peak of the class of essayists, who, having nothing to oppose to the forces of the field, are condemned, in order to exist, or subsist, to float with the tides of the external or internal forces which wrack the milieu, notably through journalism. He calls to mind the image of a Théophile Gautier whom a contemporary described as 'a spirit floating on every breeze, quivering at every touch, able to absorb every impression and to retransmit it in turn, but needing to be set in motion by a neighbouring spirit, always eager to borrow a watchword, which so many others would then come to seek from him'.[56]

For Bourdieu, Barthes the essayist lacks scientific rigour: he floats or flits from topic to topic, following fashion after fashion. There is insufficient substance, authority, weight. (Bourdieu launches his attack, notably, not in an essay, but in a book that runs to nearly 350 pages.)

'I am an essayist', declares Barthes. I favour brief scenes. I merely open dossiers. I drift. And in doing so, I face the wrath of critics like Bourdieu who want *Homo academicus* to bring authority to bear upon an obedient world. The risk is there, certainly; such is the way of the profession. But the reader of Roland Barthes is in a position to see that, when it comes to the kitchen of meaning, when it comes to signs, the real risk is believing that the work can be over, that rigour can be scientific, that authority is within reach. Brief scenes are the order of the day for the one who grasps the full implications of seeing that 'the world is full of signs'.

Barthes is not, of course, the only critic who enlists the essay in response to entering 'the kitchen of meaning'. His essayistic engagement with the empire of signs informs the work of Umberto Eco, Susan Sontag, Gilbert Adair, Marjorie Garber, Rosalind Coward and Peter Conrad, among others.[57] Each of these cultural critics has, in different ways, crafted brief scenes that acknowledge how 'a meaning can never be studied in an isolated fashion' while at once reading whatever of significance passes into view. But if Barthes could not have become 'Barthes' without Saussure, those who have written in Barthes's wake could not, I think, have followed quite the same path without his devotion to the sign, his spells in the kitchen of meaning, his open dossiers, his pebbles, his pieces of string, his brief scenes.

Notes

1 Roland Barthes, 'An Extremely Brutal Context', in *The Grain of the Voice: Interviews 1962-1980*, trans. Linda Coverdale (Berkeley: University of California Press, 1991), 319-20 (319).
2 Roland Barthes, 'Lecture: In Inauguration of the Chair of Literary Semiology, Collège de France, January 7, 1977', trans. Richard Howard, *Oxford Literary Review* 4, no. 1 (1979): 31-44 (31).
3 *Mythologies* is the most famous example here, but we might also consider Barthes's very first book, *Writing Degree Zero*. See Roland Barthes, *Mythologies*, rev. edn, ed. Annette Lavers, trans. Annette Lavers and Siân Reynolds (London: Vintage, 2009) and *Writing Degree Zero*, trans. Annette Lavers and Colin Smith (London: Jonathan Cape, 1967). Barthes actually called the latter book an 'essay' in 1967; see his 'Conversation on a Scientific Poem', in *The Grain of Voice*, 63-7 (63).
4 Roland Barthes, 'Twenty Key Words for Roland Barthes', in *The Grain of the Voice*, 205-32 (209).
5 Susan Sontag, 'Writing Itself: On Roland Barthes', in *Where the Stress Falls: Essays* (London: Vintage, 2003), 63-88 (69).
6 Roland Barthes, *Roland Barthes by Roland Barthes*, trans. Richard Howard (London: Papermac, 1995), 93.
7 See, for instance, 'The Play of the Kaleidoscope', in *The Grain of the Voice*, 198-204 (199); 'An Interview with Jacques Chancel (Radioscopie)', in *'Simply a Particular Contemporary': Interviews, 1970-79*, trans. Chris Turner (London and

New York: Seagull Books, 2015), 45–81 (73–4); and Barthes, *Roland Barthes by Roland Barthes*, 24. I have discussed boredom in Barthes at greater length in chapter 5 of *The Afterlives of Roland Barthes* (London and New York: Bloomsbury, 2016), 83–108.
8   Roland Barthes, 'The Death of the Author', in *The Rustle of Language*, trans. Richard Howard (Oxford: Blackwell, 1986), 49–55 (50).
9   Jean-Claude Milner uses the phrase 'la révélation du Signe' (the revelation of the Sign) on numerous occasions in *Le Pas philosophique de Roland Barthes* (Lagrasse: Éditions Verdier, 2003). See, above all, Part III of the book.
10 Barthes, *Mythologies*, xvii.
11 I have discussed the impact of *Mythologies* upon Barthes's reputation in my introduction to the 2009 Vintage translation of the volume (ix–xiv). See also chapter 2 of Andy Stafford's excellent *Roland Barthes: Phenomenon and Myth: An Intellectual Biography* (Edinburgh: Edinburgh University Press, 1997).
12 Tiphaine Samoyault explains how Greimas introduced Barthes to Saussure's work in *Roland Barthes: Biographie* (Paris: Seuil, 2015), 235. See also Marie Gil, *Roland Barthes: Au lieu de la vie* (Paris: Flammarion, 2012), 175 and Louis-Jean Calvet, *Roland Barthes: A Biography*, trans. Sarah Wykes (Bloomington: Indiana University Press, 1995), 94.
13 Ferdinand de Saussure, *Course in General Linguistics*, ed. Charles Bally, Albert Sechehaye and Albert Reidlinger, trans. Wade Baskin (London: Fontana, 1974), 16.
14 Samoyault, *Roland Barthes*, 329.
15 Eco's claim is reported in Samoyault, *Roland Barthes*, 415. For an excellent account of Barthes's gradual appearance in English translation from 1958 onwards, see Calum Gardner, *Poetry & Barthes: Anglophone Responses 1970–2000* (Liverpool: Liverpool University Press, 2018), 4–9.
16 Roland Barthes, *Elements of Semiology*, trans. Annette Lavers and Colin Smith (New York: Hill and Wang, 1973), 9.
17 For the summaries of the two courses, see Roland Barthes, 'Inventaire des systèmes contemporains de signification: systèmes d'objets (vêtement, nourriture, logement)' and 'Inventaire des systèmes de signification contemporains', in *Oeuvres complètes*, rev edn, ed. Éric Marty, 5 vols (Paris: Seuil, 2002), Vol. 2, 253–4 and 613–34, respectively. The quotations are taken from the former text (253). While some of Barthes's teaching materials have been published in recent years, these early courses at the École remain unavailable; all that we have are their official summaries, which were prepared by Barthes himself. For a full list of Barthes's courses at the École, see Lucy O'Meara, *Roland Barthes at the Collège de France* (Liverpool: Liverpool University Press, 2012), 205.
18 Barthes, 'Inventaire des systèmes contemporains de signification: systèmes d'objets (vêtement, nourriture, logement)', 253.
19 Roland Barthes, 'The Kitchen of Meaning', in *The Semiotic Challenge*, trans. Richard Howard (Berkeley: University of California Press, 1994), 157–9 (157). As a rendering of the original French title of 'La Cuisine du sens', 'The Kitchen of Meaning' is not inaccurate, but it should be remembered that the French term 'cuisine' can refer both to the room in which food is prepared *and* to the act of preparation itself.
20 Barthes, 'Kitchen of Meaning', 157–8. Italics in original.
21 Ibid., 158.
22 Roland Barthes, *S/Z*, trans. Richard Miller (Oxford: Blackwell, 1990), 9.
23 Barthes, 'Kitchen of Meaning', 158. Elsewhere on the same page of the essay, Barthes notes that 'most of the time, we take [signs] for "natural" information'. The way in

which meaning becomes naturalized into myth is one of the central issues addressed in *Mythologies*, of course. As Barthes wrote in his original preface to the book in 1957:

> The starting point of these reflections was usually a feeling of impatience at the sight of the "naturalness" with which newspapers, art and common sense constantly dress up a reality which, even though it is the one we live in, is undoubtedly determined by history. In short, in the account given of our contemporary circumstances, I resented seeing Nature and History confused at every turn. (xix)

24 Barthes, 'Kitchen of Meaning', 158–9. Emphasis in original.
25 Saussure, *Course in General Linguistics*, 120.
26 Barthes, 'Kitchen of Meaning', 159.
27 Ibid., 158.
28 Barthes, *Roland Barthes*, 87. Italics in original. For the earlier references, see 'The Death of the Author', 54 and *Empire of Signs*, trans. Richard Howard (New York: Hill and Wang, 1982), 73–6.
29 Barthes, *Empire of Signs*, 75.
30 Clifford Geertz, *The Interpretation of Cultures: Selected Essays* (New York: Basic Books, 1973), 5.
31 Roland Barthes, 'Roland Barthes Versus Received Ideas', in *The Grain of the Voice*, 188–95 (195).
32 Roland Barthes, *The Neutral: Lecture Course at the Collège de France (1977–1978)*, ed. Thomas Clerc, trans. Rosalind E. Krauss and Denis Hollier (New York: Columbia University Press, 2005), 57.
33 Barthes, *The Neutral*, 93. I have modified the published English translation here, for it seems to me that 'jouissance' has been discussed widely enough in anglophone contexts by now for the term to be left 'in French' in English.
34 Theodor W. Adorno, 'The Essay as Form', trans. Bob Hullot-Kentor and Frederic Will, *New German Critique* 32 (1984): 151–71 (158).
35 Adorno, 'The Essay as Form', 164, 161.
36 Ibid., 152.
37 Réda Bensmaïa, *The Barthes Effect: The Essay as Reflective Text*, trans. Pat Fedkiew (Minneapolis: University of Minnesota Press, 1987), 31.
38 Ibid., 18.
39 Michel de Montaigne, *Essays*, trans. J. M. Cohen (Harmondsworth: Penguin, 1958), 358.
40 Roland Barthes, 'Longtemps, je me suis couché de bonne heure…', in *The Rustle of Language*, 277–90 (278).
41 Montaigne, *Essays*, 23.
42 Éric Marty sums things up perfectly when he observes that Barthes 'profoundly reorient[ed] his journey through the notion of pleasure, through first-person writing, through the use of the novelistic or of autobiographical elements' during the 1970s. Éric Marty, *Roland Barthes, la littérature et le droit à la mort* (Paris: Seuil, 2010), 10. My translation. For examples of Barthes's essayistic autobiographical texts, see, for instance, *Roland Barthes by Roland Barthes* and the posthumously published *Incidents*, trans. Teresa Lavender Fagan (London: Seagull Books, 2010).
43 In his *Essayism* (London: Fitzcarraldo Editions, 2017), Brian Dillon offers a Barthes-inflected celebration of essays as 'responses to the world of things and books and pictures and places and memories' (35).

44 Roland Barthes, 'On *S/Z* and *Empire of Signs*', in *The Grain of the Voice*, 68–87 (78).
45 See, above all, the chapter titled 'Linguistics and Grammatology' in Jacques Derrida, *Of Grammatology*, trans. Gayatri Chakravorty Spivak (Baltimore, MD: Johns Hopkins University Press, 1976), 27–73.
46 Barthes, 'On *S/Z* and *Empire of Signs*', 78. Translation modified.
47 Barthes, 'Lecture', 42.
48 Ibid., 43-4. Italics in original.
49 Ibid., 42-3.
50 Roland Barthes, *How to Live Together: Novelistic Simulations of Some Everyday Spaces*, trans. Kate Briggs (New York: Columbia University Press, 2013), 4.
51 Barthes, *How to Live Together*, 19.
52 Ibid., 20.
53 Ibid.
54 Ibid., 133.
55 Ibid., 135.
56 Pierre Bourdieu, *Homo Academicus*, trans. Peter Collier (Stanford, CA: Stanford University Press, 1988), xxii. In *Roland Barthes at the Collège de France*, Lucy O'Meara points out that Bourdieu's own inaugural lecture at the Collège de France in 1982 insisted upon 'rigorous science' instead of essayism (34). For an English translation of the latter text, see Pierre Bourdieu, 'A Lecture on the Lecture', in *In Other Words: Essays Towards a Reflexive Sociology*, trans. Matthew Adamson (Stanford, CA: Stanford University Press, 1990), 177–98.
57 See, for instance, Umberto Eco, *Travels in Hyperreality: Essays*, trans. William Weaver (New York: Harcourt Brace Jovanovich, 1986); Sontag, *Where the Stress Falls*; Gilbert Adair, *Myths & Memories* (London: Fontana, 1986); Marjorie Garber, *Symptoms of Culture* (London: Penguin, 1999); Rosalind Coward, *Female Desire* (London: Paladin, 1984); and Peter Conrad, *Mythomania: Tales of Our Times, from Apple to Isis* (London: Thames and Hudson, 2016).

Chapter 4

THE 'SUBVERSIVE POSSIBILITIES' OF THE ESSAY FOR PUBLIC INTELLECTUALS

Nicole B. Wallack

Virginia Woolf depicts in 'The Modern Essay' the animating force – psychological and intellectual – that draws essayists to their work when she claims that 'the art of writing has for backbone some fierce attachment to an idea'.[1] Essayists should be preoccupied with the strength, flexibility and beauty of their ideas; after all, in essays ideas tend to be on full display. And yet, even compelling ideas will not hold an essay upright if they are not grounded in truths. Writers since Michel de Montaigne have sought in the essay a literary praxis to discover and examine truths about the worlds in which they live, in their own guise, and often for an unspecified public – or perhaps none at all. In 'Of Practice', Montaigne offers a disclaimer for his essays: 'What I write here is not my teaching, but my study; it is not a lesson for others, but for me. And yet it should not be held against me if I publish what I write. What is useful to me may also by accident be useful to another.'[2] That Montaigne's readers would encounter both a truth and an idea about it that is 'useful ... by accident', has been simultaneously a point of pride and contention for essayists from his own generation onwards.

It is possible to hear a clear echo of Montaigne's defence of self-inquiry and representation in Virginia Woolf's conclusion to *A Room of One's Own:* 'I find myself saying ... that it is much more important to be oneself than anything else. Do not dream of influencing other people ... Think of things in themselves.'[3] Woolf does not forbid the women writers she imagines in her audience from changing the world, but reassures them that their presence in the world as writers will be change enough. Even so, Woolf's revolutionary argument in this extended essay is also couched within a disclaimer; she writes that her remarks should be understood as 'an opinion upon a minor point – a woman must have money and a room of her own if she is to write fiction'.[4] Woolf cannot offer more, she claims, because 'when a subject is highly controversial – and any question about sex is that – one cannot hope to tell the truth. One can only show how one came to hold whatever opinion one does hold. One can only give one's audience the chance of drawing their own conclusions as they observe the limitations, the prejudices, the idiosyncrasies of the speaker'.[5] Truths cannot be 'told' – that is, not transmitted to readers fully formed – but readers can evaluate the writer's ethos and method. Unlike Montaigne, Woolf does not forswear her role as a teacher, but she refuses the mantel of expert; instead, she invites us to track the peculiar particulars of her logic and language, authority and trustworthiness. Woolf reminds us that readers judge ideas, but only as an extension of the writer's presence.

Francis Bacon voices none of Montaigne's or Woolf's reservations regarding his role as counsellor and expert. He notes with distaste in 'Of Wisdom for a Man's Self', 'men that are great lovers of themselves, waste the public... It is a poor centre of a man's actions, himself. It is right earth.'[6] So as not to 'waste the public', some essayists have sought to make their publics more aware of the troubles of their times. Writing in 1946, George Orwell defines in political terms the stakes of wasting his public: 'What I have most wanted ... is to make political writing into an art. My starting point is always a feeling of partisanship, a sense of injustice... I write it because there is some lie that I want to expose, some fact to which I want to draw attention, and my initial concern is to get a hearing.'[7] It is surprising, perhaps, to hear Orwell, late in a career that had already brought him acclaim and influence, judge his work a success only if his literary capacities ensure that the wrongs he detects 'get a hearing' from readers.

Orwell depended creatively on identifying a clear political or ethical exigence for his reviews, essays and novels; this orientation was shared among other essayists in his era including Randolph Bourne, Virginia Woolf, E. B. White and James Baldwin. Entrusting one's *literary* reputation to writing essays that foreground social commentary was a subversive choice in the early twentieth century, when the essay was still primarily associated with the 'genteel tradition' of Charles Lamb. In the post-war period, essayists found in *The Atlantic Monthly, Harper's Magazine* and *The Partisan Review*, among many other journals, had opportunities to situate themselves in their historical and cultural contexts.

Essayists in the second half of the twentieth century flourished as they embraced the freedom to speak as themselves, and many did so as a form of political or social protest, as Ellen Joeres[8] and Brian Norman have noted.[9] Norman argues that writers working in the protest essay tradition – W. E. B. Du Bois, Emma Goldman, James Baldwin and June Jordan – found in the essay 'a form uniquely able to bring experiences of exclusion and particular cultural practices into direct conversation with universalist beliefs and utterances about equality, especially on the national level'.[10] Essayists have always constructed their experiences in order to highlight the truths they reveal for themselves and for others, welcome or not. Twenty-first-century public intellectuals depend upon and resist productively the idea that their own experiences can provide 'evidence' for collective experience itself. Instead, essayists like Kwame Anthony Appiah and Ta-Nehisi Coates dramatize the transmogrifying power of turning experiences into ideas to share with their reading publics. In the process they enact what John Duffy has characterized as the central rhetorical virtue of *phronesis*, 'the wisdom of knowing which [writerly] choices to make ... and in which situations'.[11] After 2016, when 'post-truth' became the *Oxford English Dictionary*'s 'word of the year', public intellectuals need the essay as a genre and practice to sustain the civic and literary values of truth-telling, and the essay needs public intellectuals who play this role due to the expertise they have garnered through their research in academic and public spheres.

1. Essaying the limits of thinking

It is axiomatic among essayists that all subject matter can reward thinking. Susan Sontag suggests that the essay's topical expansiveness accounts in part for the genre's longevity since Montaigne's and Bacon's eras: 'It is not only that the essay could be about anything. It usually was. The good health of essay writing depends on writers continuing to address eccentric subjects.'[12] For these 'eccentric subjects' to warrant readers' attention, essayists also need to exercise their singular power 'to convert the world and everything in it to a species of thinking'.[13] For Sontag, thinking – or 'consciousness' as she often calls it – is not an activity, but a locus of investigation around which a writing life could be organized, since it is both singular and social. As A. O. Scott notes, for Sontag 'consciousness inheres in a single person's private, incommunicable experience, but it also lives in groups, in cultures and populations and historical epochs. Its closest synonym is thought, which similarly dwells both within the walls of a solitary skull and out in the collective sphere'.[14] Contemporary writers who take to the genre, whether as a full-time occupation or as an extension of other pursuits, need to solve the ethical, political and aesthetic problems of how they titrate the individual and collective dimensions of their thinking. When essayists inquire and reflect on an urgent problem shared by other people, and attempt to address it by virtue of their demonstrable expertise on the subject, they assume the role of 'public intellectuals'. It is worth exploring, then, not only what the audience for essays gains from the work of public intellectuals, but what these writers can make or do (or unmake and undo) only in essays.

Generations of intellectuals in the United States, for example, have delved into the legacy of slavery and the ongoing effects of systemic racism to gauge the depth and breadth of the tragedy and to propose actions for citizens, lawmakers and the state itself. Among American writers, W. E. B. Du Bois's essays remain a touchstone for examining these issues. In his own time, Du Bois had enjoyed a meteoric rise as an academic historian; he was the first African American to graduate from Harvard's doctoral program and later, he was the first Black scholar to present at the American Historical Association.

In 1897, Du Bois entered into larger American conversations about the civic and political impediments facing Black citizens when he published his essay in *Atlantic Monthly*, 'Strivings of the Negro People'. Du Bois defines in this essay the dilemma of 'double consciousness' for all Black Americans in the thirty years after the conclusion to the Civil War: 'One feels his two-ness, – an American, a Negro; two souls, two thoughts, two unreconciled strivings; two warring ideals in one dark body, whose dogged strength alone keeps it from being torn asunder. The history of the American Negro is the history of this strife.'[15] In four, short pages Du Bois names the social and psychological costs of living with the strife created by double consciousness: 'The freedman has not yet found in freedom his promised land.'[16] Only in an essay could Du Bois draw on all of the following as evidence: a painful memory from his own childhood, a callous quip from a white acquaintance ('they say, I know an excellent colored man in my town'),[17] Rousseau's ideals for liberty, the Fifteenth Amendment to the Constitution, the Ku Klux Klan, popular American music and 'fairytales', which had been created by Black and indigenous people. Ultimately, 'Strivings of the Negro People', reworked, would provide the centrepiece of his most well-known book, *The Souls of Black Folk*, a collection of essays that would secure Du Bois's place as one of the most influential American intellectuals both on and off the page. Du Bois exemplifies the complex role of the public intellectual for others who take on the role regardless of their professional affiliations.

2. *The roles of public intellectuals*

Interest in the concept of the public intellectual both as an academic or disciplinary specialist, which has been attributed to Russell Jacoby,[18] has increased in Europe and the United States in the digital age; researchers across disciplines have theorized, troubled, defended and reframed it, sometimes as a proxy for the value of thinking itself, or the value of academics and higher education, writ large. Edward Said[19] and Henry A. Giroux[20] have explicated the social – and specifically political – importance of the intellectual who chooses 'publicly to raise embarrassing questions, to confront orthodoxy and dogma (rather than produce them), to be someone who cannot easily be co-opted by governments or corporations, and whose *raison d'être* is to represent all those people and issues that are routinely forgotten or swept under the rug'.[21] Said identifies four characteristics public intellectuals require to take these risks – courage, scepticism, autonomy and selflessness. To raise the 'embarrassing questions' Said imagines, Giroux argues that intellectuals need to write 'in a language that is accessible without sacrificing theoretical rigor'.[22] As Giroux explains, to pursue these dual goals, intellectuals must '[commit] to language as a site of experimentation, power, struggle, and hope in the interests of building democratic social movements that are both inspired and informed'.[23] It is not lost on Said or Giroux that the stakes are high, especially for academics: those who can make their ideas comprehensible, 'accessible' and compelling to a wider audience demonstrate the continued need and value of institutions of higher learning for the public good.

Scholars who cast their gaze outwards find themselves in a time and media environment that favours search-friendly content, which means that they must telegraph their ideological leanings to potential publics in an effort to garner attention in what used to be the 'marketplace of ideas', but in the twenty-first century has been recast as 'the Ideas Industry'.[24] Daniel Drezner, an international politics scholar and *Washington Post* columnist, suggests that this competition can compromise intellectuals' integrity and cause public intellectuals to devolve into 'thought leaders': 'A thought leader is an intellectual evangelist. Thought leaders develop their own singular lens to explain the world, and then proselytize that worldview to anyone within earshot'.[25] By contrast, 'public intellectuals know enough about many things to be able to point out intellectual charlatans'.[26] While thought leaders and public intellectuals both 'truck, barter, and exchange in the world of ideas'[27] and individuals may tack between these two positions over the course of a career, thought leaders are currently most in demand.

In Drezner's formulation, a 'thought leader' would not write essays; they traffic in certainties, confidently delivered. A public intellectual would write an essay to articulate an insight or truth that could be tested or overturned. The public intellectual needs what Brian Dillon identifies as 'the conflict inside the essay as form: it aspires to express the quintessence or crux of its matter, thus to a sort of polishing integrity, and it wants at the same time to insist that its purview is partial, that being incomplete is a value in itself, for it better reflects the brave and curious but faltering nature of the writing mind'.[28] The promise of partiality – in all senses of the word – commits essayists primarily to 'see with precision' (as Virginia Woolf tells us) the materials or experiences they shape into evidence for their ideas.[29]

Some public intellectuals, such as Slavoj Žižek, make uncertainty and conflict their writing's primary purpose:

> My obsession … is how a certain rule, slogan or practice which may appear to open up the space for new freedom, emancipation, nonetheless can be misused or has potentially dangerous consequences. Usually people say a philosopher when you are confused should bring clarity. I say no! We think we see things clearly in daily life; I long to confuse things.[30]

Žižek, then, could be said to work in an anarchic essayistic mode – heightening rather than resolving tensions and conflicts – as a matter of principle, or even as an ethical commitment. Žižek's insistence that he will use his knowledge to instruct readers about the errors underlying our truths could be said to simply enact Ralph Waldo Emerson's dictum in his essay, 'Circles', that we 'unsettle all things'.[31] More typically, scholars write essays to minimize confusion and uncertainty, but some find that their ideas are too challenging to engage the publics they most want to reach.

Reflecting on the ten-year anniversary of her groundbreaking book on mass incarceration in the United States, *The New Jim Crow*, Michelle Alexander, the American civil rights activist and lawyer, remembers the doubt she felt as she researched and wrote her book in the years leading up to the election of Barack Obama: 'Few people wanted to hear the message I felt desperate to convey: Despite appearances, our nation remains trapped in a cycle of racial reform, backlash and re-formation of systems of racial and social control.'[32] Even scholars working on subject matter that ought to resound with a broad public can struggle to 'get a hearing' in Orwell's terms. It is no surprise, then, that intellectuals such as Alexander first circulate their ideas in essays for publications drawing smaller readerships. Before *The New Jim Crow* garnered international attention, Alexander contributed essays on the same material to the progressive journals, *The Nation*,[33] *Sojourner's*[34] and *The American Prospect*.[35]

In her 2010 essay, 'Obama's Drug War', Alexander warns that the president of the Unites States' initiatives to defund drug prosecutions, while fiscally and rhetorically appealing, would not change the more fundamental problems faced by people of colour who continued to be arrested and incarcerated at disproportionately higher rates. She argues that the government and public across the political spectrum must be willing to examine the root causes of the incarceration crisis:

> This moment of opportunity … will inevitably fail to produce large-scale change in the absence of a large-scale movement – one that seeks to dismantle not only the system of mass incarceration and the drug war apparatus but also the habits of mind that allow us to view poor people of color trapped in ghettos as 'others', unworthy of our collective care and concern.[36]

In essays, scholars bridge the worlds of the academy and the public sphere, and prompt readers to test their own deeply held convictions for a short time. The public intellectual uses the essay itself as both a provocation and invitation for readers to explore issues that they might not be willing or able to engage at length.

Drezner suggests that 'successful' public intellectuals are more likely to gain the confidence of readers in a wider sphere, if they are willing 'to acknowledge fallibility'.[37] By 'successful' intellectuals, Drezner means those who continually 'embrace the need for greater self-reflection; they seek out and understand criticism without it leading to paralysis. They learn to balance the twin intellectual impulses of play and piety'.[38] Quintessentially, essayists embrace contradictions and uncertainties within their texts, and largely are allergic to pieties. The genre gives public intellectuals licence to ask questions of themselves, express emotions and doubts and acknowledge that their singular understanding is partial or flawed.

For public intellectuals inside and outside the academy, the essay is the genre that underscores 'the importance of language and communication as a theoretical practice [which] is derived, in large part, from their critical and subversive possibilities'.[39] In the twenty-first century, the essay remains among the most ubiquitous of many genres across media that intellectuals choose for this public-facing work. An essay, as Graham Good reminds us, 'is an act of personal witness. The essay is at once the *in*scription of a self and the *de*scription of an object [or phenomenon]'.[40] It is a negotiation and reciprocal process of discovery between a writer and their materials: 'The heart of the essay as a form is this moment of characterization, of recognition, figuration, where the self finds a pattern in the world and the world finds a pattern in the self.'[41] Essays may be works of lasting merit, but they are subversive in how they foreground the temporary, contingent and negotiated nature of our understandings of ourselves and our experiences of the world.

When well-known public intellectuals publish essays, they are likely to 'get a hearing' for their ideas about social problems that are complex, tenacious and painful to acknowledge and difficult to address. Kwame Anthony Appiah and

Ta-Nehisi Coates – acclaimed writers whose essays are widely recognized and circulated – unsettle in their essays common-sense truths about identity and the ongoing effects of systemic racism. They exemplify how the essay as a form does justice to (and with) their expertise for myriad publics of readers. By making small semantic shifts in his own subject position, Appiah invites readers to stand with him as he explores the problems that arise when any of us chooses to speak as a representative of our identity categories. Ta-Nehisi Coates subverts readers' expectations for which publics are addressed in an essay written as 'open letter.' As public intellectuals, Appiah and Coates subvert any expectation that their readings of the world are comprehensive and final, enjoining more people to think their way through our precarious and precious times in essays.

3. *Kwame Anthony Appiah changes the subject*

Intellectual eclecticism may be a hallmark of essayists, but they also have a 'hidden nerve' as André Aciman has called it, 'something irreducibly theirs, which stirs their prose and makes it tick and turn this way or that, and identifies them, like a signature, though it lurks far deeper than their style.'[42] A nerve in an intact body is hidden and stimulated by agents beyond it – a passive metaphor to describe the way writers inhabit their work. By contrast, the essays of philosopher and public intellectual, Kwame Anthony Appiah, are pulled centripetally to a concern so pervasive that it is not so much a 'nerve' as a 'nervous system.' In every essay, speech, novel and academic monograph, Appiah seeks to explain and trouble our truths about *identity*. There hardly could be a more essayistic concern for a public intellectual to take on, given that the essay is the genre in which a writer is expected to represent themselves in 'the singular first person', as Scott Russell Sanders has called it.[43] Appiah crafts an essaying presence for himself that is both visible and elusive. He challenges readers' attachments to our identities and argues that they can limit our agency, and cause us to misread others.

Appiah sets the stage in his op-ed for *The New York Times*, 'Go Ahead, Speak for Yourself', with a seemingly simple question: 'What does it signify when people use this now ubiquitous formula ("As a such-and-such, I…) to affix an identity to an observation?'[44] He answers it simply but not simplistically: 'Typically, it's an assertion of authority. As a member of this or that social group, I have experiences that lend my remarks special weight.'[45] We exercise authority when we refer to identities as warrants for our political or social preferences, practices and beliefs. We identify ourselves also to anticipate how other people may perceive us at moments of contact: when a police officer stops us with or without obvious cause, when we answer questions on a school form about our family members, or when we choose to include our preferred pronouns on an email signature.

For the first half of this essay, Appiah reiterates the central findings about identity drawn from his books (*The Lies That Bind: Rethinking Identity*);[46] essays, such as 'The Politics of Identity',[47] 'The Democratic Spirit'[48] and 'Bending towards Justice';[49] and major speeches, including his presidential address for the Modern

Language Association, 'Boundaries of Culture'.[50] Appiah frequently foregrounds a pragmatic dimension of his scholarly identity: 'I am a philosopher by profession. And if there is anything that a philosopher can usefully do for the rest of human kind, it is to try to clarify our thinking about issues that matter.'[51] As Jahan Ramazani notes in his introductory essay for the special volume of *New Literary History* in honour of Appiah's oeuvre, for Appiah 'social identities can play vital roles in our lives, maybe especially once demystified by the clarity, self-reflexivity, and analytic precision of philosophical thinking'.[52] Ramazani elevates not only the stakes of Appiah's work, but also of his method – especially his 'self-reflexivity'.

Appiah's own identity associations are not a primary focus of his academic and public-facing essays; and yet, it is the rare essay in which he does not both name and implicate himself explicitly as a person whose intersecting identities – national, racial, scholarly, political, literary, sexual – orient without determining his ideas. The second half of Appiah's op-ed, 'Go Ahead, Speak for Yourself', begins with a 'caveat auditor: Let the listener beware. Representing an identity is usually volunteer work, but sometimes the representative is conjured into being'.[53] As an illustration, he references his first-hand experiences of being a British-born, Ghanian American, married gay man:[54]

> Because people's experiences vary so much, the 'as a' move is always in peril of presumption. When I was a student at the University of Cambridge in the 1970s, gay men were *très chic*: You couldn't have a serious party without some of us scattered around like throw pillows. Do my experiences entitle me to speak for a queer farmworker who is coming of age in Emmett, Idaho? Nobody appointed me head gay.[55]

Appiah follows this moment of reflection and instruction, complete with a bit of irreverent humour, by subsuming his own position as an individual gay man within a larger, social group. He does not speak *for* other gay men, but his disclosure increases the likelihood that readers will hear him addressing us (yes, he's looking at you): 'If someone is advocating policies for gay men to adopt, or for others to adopt toward gay men, what matters, surely, isn't whether the person is gay but whether the policies are sensible. As a gay man, you could oppose same-sex marriage … or advocate same-sex marriage.'[56] For a moment, Appiah invites readers to step away from the position of an abstract 'someone' making or responding to policies that affect gay men; he creates space for us to try on (for just a few words' worth of time) the guise of the 'you' he addresses – the gay man whose stance on same-sex marriage should not be assumed.

That Appiah would be able to offer persuasive arguments and careful reasoning about the tricky concept of identity is not a surprise. Unexpectedly, Appiah unsettles readers' status within the essay itself. We may begin the essay passively giving him a 'hearing', but Appiah blurs the boundaries of his own identity in the text, which gives readers room to assume his subject position. In this essay, Appiah enjoins his readers to try using the phrase, 'speaking for myself' as an exercise not in autonomy or disclosure, but in precision and political efficacy. In his 2006 essay,

'The Politics of Identity', Appiah notes, 'not all political claims made in the name of group identity are primarily claims for recognition'; often they are claims for specific actions (e.g. gaining the right to vote or marry).[57] Appiah prompts each of us also to reflect on the cost to truth-telling we inflict when we insist that other people speak or act primarily out of their affiliation with their identities. Appiah has returned repeatedly to a challenge offered by the literary critic and theorist, Gayatri Spivak, in 'Questions of Multi Culturalism': 'the question "Who should speak" is less crucial than "Who will listen?"'[58] As an essayist, Appiah creates an occasion for his readers to practise listening, both to ourselves and to those whose identities and ideas differ profoundly from our own.

4. Ta-Nehisi Coates shows his work

W. E. B. Du Bois's 1897 essay 'Strivings of the Negro People' begins: 'Between me and the other world there is ever an unasked question ... How does it feel to be a problem?'[59] One hundred and eighteen years later, Ta-Nehisi Coates's book-length, National Book Award-winning essay, *Between the World and Me*, answers Du Bois's question with renewed exigence. Intellectuals from the academy, like Michelle Alexander (law) and Kwame Anthony Appiah (philosophy and literature), provide both data and analytical frameworks to 'unsettle' our thinking about social inequities and to offer alternatives to limiting beliefs. As an essayist, Coates animates the experience of living as a Black man and as a father to a son. In answer to Du Bois's question, and as an update to James Baldwin's 1962 essay, 'A Letter to My Nephew', Coates writes an open letter that explains to his son, Samori, then fifteen years old, how Black people continue to be understood as 'problems' in the minds and actions of 'those who believe they are white'.[60]

This phrase, which works as a refrain through the essay, is a slight reshaping of a similar phrase, 'because they think they are white', from James Baldwin's essay for *Essence* magazine in 1984, 'On Being "White" ... and Other Lies.'[61] In this essay, Baldwin traces the underlying conceptual deceits that European settlers in the Americas had to promote about themselves, indigenous people and enslaved people in order to construct whiteness as an identity category: 'America became white – the people who, as they claim, "settled" the country became white – because of the necessity of denying the Black presence, and justifying the Black subjugation. No community can be based on such a principle – or, in other words, no community can be established on so genocidal a lie.'[62] Baldwin accounts for the unstable founding assumptions of American identity and emphasizes that thinking is an action. People 'who think they are white' do so as a matter of choice and teach whiteness to future generations. By Coates's time, the action has changed from 'thinking' to 'believing,' from toxic logic to faith. Writing a public letter to his son, Coates does not seek to test that belief (he does not feel as if he can or should), but uses the phrase to explain the threat to his body, his person, as a Black man.

The first section of the book appeared as 'Letter to My Son' in the *Atlantic*. In this section, Coates recounts the traumatizing lessons he learned navigating the daily precarity of life as a young man in his Baltimore neighbourhood and school. He describes how he readied himself to attend Howard University as a history major, 'toting a new and different history, myth really, which inverted all the stories of the people who believed themselves to be white',[63] so that he could find heroic arcs, narratives of redemption in suffering and intrinsic nobility in being Black. His professors thwarted his desire for this corrective; similarly, Coates refuses his son and his readers the comfort of a clearly uplifting narrative of his own life.

Coates allies himself intellectually with Baldwin as he explains why the price for some people's identification as white requires lifelong psychic and bodily violence for Black people. He denies his readers any solutions, comforts, or obvious next steps for himself or his son, while honouring the binding beauty of existential struggle:

> They made us into a race. We made ourselves into a people…. None of us were 'black people.' We were individuals, and when we died there was nothing. Always remember that Trayvon Martin was a boy, that Tamir Rice was a particular boy, that Jordan Davis was a boy like you. … It is terrible to see our particular beauty, Samori, because then you see the scope of the loss. But you must push even further. You must see that this loss is mandated by the history of your country, by the Dream of living white.[64]

As a journalist, student of history and storyteller, Coates might be expected to circle back to the questions of racial justice that have been an explicit part of the public conversation in the United States since the Civil War. The art of the essay, as practised by Coates, reveals his 'fierce attachment' to this idea of ceaseless struggle for himself, for his son and for all Black people because 'those who believe they are white' cannot awaken from that Dream that reads race as the definitive identity category.

In staging this essay as a letter, Coates unsettles his publics – those who will and will not, can and cannot claim to identify with his experiences. Coates requires us to read over Samori's shoulder how his father learned first-hand to fear bodily injury and erasure. As James Baldwin observes in 'Stranger in the Village', 'people are trapped in history, and history is trapped in them';[65] history is one of the traps that Coates reveals in this essay; he also demonstrates how history traps people in and with their anger and fear.

In the final section of the essay, Coates asks Samori to recall a frightening episode they had shared, years before, when a middle-aged white woman shoved Samori on an escalator at a movie theatre in Manhattan. In response, Coates defends his small son in language, 'hot with the all of the moment and all of my history'.[66] In the primarily verbal confrontation that follows, a white man tells Coates, 'I could have you arrested!' Coates explains that he would not have cared what happened next for his own sake, but he stops himself: 'I remembered someone standing of to the side there, bearing witness to more fury than he had ever seen from me – you.'[67] Coates reflects that he has recounted this episode often, 'not out of bravado, but out of a need for absolution'; he tells the story, not to alleviate shame, but because he regrets putting his son in harm's way while trying to defend him.[68] The danger Coates regrets is both bodily and psychic – Samori could have been injured in the crowd and he could have lost his father to jail had he been arrested. Most profoundly, Coates underscores the trauma of witnessing racist violence in words and deeds.

Edward Said has suggested that public intellectuals serve many functions, but primarily they must exercise their faculty for 'representing, embodying, articulating a message, a view, and attitude, philosophy or opinion to, as well as for a public'.[69] Public intellectuals must represent the *facts* of a crisis that even those most immediately affected do not have language to name. In Said's formulation, the intellectual does not tell their story or present their facts to shore up their own reputation or security in their professions, but to resist dominant narratives, images, ideas and understandings of phenomena shaping their own times.

At the root of the ancient Doric Greek word for 'idea' is the concept of '*idein*' (to see). As a public intellectual, Coates reconstructs his experiences in his own past, and in the life he has shared with his son as a way to see it newly. For Coates, the essay's textual body holds – if it cannot protect – the facts of our histories, the facts of our suffering, the facts of our emotions as well as the wisdom not to turn those facts into dangerous despair or delusion.

5. On the need for public intellectuals

If public intellectuals need the essay, it is reasonable to ask whether the essay needs public intellectuals – after all, there is no shortage of people with opinions, ideas, and expertise in the world, or in sites to circulate them. The philosopher of rhetoric, Steven Mallioux, has identified four rhetorical functions of what he calls 'the hybrid intellectual, the academic who goes public with his or her thinking… [namely] translator, commentator, inventor, and metacritic'.[70] Translators provide the public with accessible language for work within disciplines, show 'immediate application to social issues' and provide insight into the 'speculative thought and practice philosophy' within the fields; commentators analyse and provide 'specific critiques and general explanatory models of society and its culture'; inventors 'not only respond critically to existing understandings, but present alternative ways of thought'; and metacritics synthesize and 'comment on the rhetorical work of the translators, commentators, and inventors'.[71] Mailloux's categories can help identify the cultural work intellectuals accomplish in their essays.

In Mailloux's taxonomy, Appiah could be said to function as both translator and commentator. Coates assumes the responsibilities of a commentator and inventor. Seeing essayists as inventors in Mailloux's sense has to do with their power to invent a unique method for representing and *re*-reading the world in which we live. In essays, public intellectuals could compromise their standing as commentators or meta-critics when they share personal memories or strong emotions. And yet, without this material, these writers would be unable to distil a large amorphous truth into a small, potent one. Essays require the public intellectual to show up in the world as an individual: embodied, connected to others and vulnerable; in their work, they craft a truth into a literary experience that is sharable, but not universal. Intellectuals risk overreach when they entrust figurative, elliptical and declarative language to represent and *test* their truths in essays. Scholarship and prestige cannot ensure that anyone 'gets a hearing', but in a post-truth age, public intellectuals have a special responsibility to acknowledge the limits, affordances and power of their own expertise.

Notes

1. Virginia Woolf, 'The Modern Essay', in *The Common Reader, First Series*, ed. Andrew McNeillie (London: Harcourt, 1986), 211–22 (221).
2. Michel de Montaigne, 'Of Practice', in *The Complete Essays of Montaigne*, trans. Donald M. Frame (Stanford, CA: Stanford University Press, 1968), 267–75 (273).
3. Virginia Woolf, *A Room of One's Own* (London: Harcourt Brace, 1929), 111.
4. Ibid., 4.
5. Ibid.
6. Francis Bacon, *Essayes; or, Counsels Civill & Morall* (London: J. M. Dent, 1897), 85–7 (85).
7. George Orwell, *A Collection of Essays* (San Diego, CA: Mariner Books, 1970), 315.
8. Ruth-Ellen B. Joeres and Elizabeth Mittman, *The Politics of the Essay: Feminist Perspectives* (Bloomington: Indiana University Press, 1993).
9. Brian Norman, *The American Protest Essay and National Belonging: Addressing Division* (Albany: State University of New York Press, 2007).
10. Ibid., 155.
11. John Duffy, *Provocations of Virtue: Rhetoric, Ethics, and the Teaching of Writing* (Logan: Utah State University Press, 2019), 122.
12. Susan Sontag, 'Introduction', in *The Best American Essays 1992*, ed. Susan Sontag, series ed. Robert Atwan (New York: Ticknor & Fields, 1992), xiii–xix (xv).
13. Ibid., xviii.
14. A. O. Scott, 'How Susan Sontag Taught Me to Think', *The New York Times Magazine*, 8 October 2019, https://www.nytimes.com/interactive/2019/10/08/magazine/susan-sontag.html
15. W. E. B. Du Bois, 'Strivings of the Negro People', *Atlantic Monthly*, August 1897, 194–8.
16. Ibid., 195.
17. Ibid., 194.
18. Russell Jacoby, *The Last Intellectuals* (New York: Basic Books, 1987).
19. Edward W. Said, *Representations of the Intellectual: The 1993 Reith Lectures* (New York: Vintage, 1996). See also Edward W. Said, 'The Public Role of Writers and Intellectuals', in *The Public Intellectual*, ed. Helen Small (Oxford: Wiley-Blackwell, 2002), 19–39.
20. Henry A. Giroux, 'Public Intellectuals, the Politics of Clarity, and the Crisis of Language', *Counterpoints* 400 (2012): 99–115.
21. Said, *Representations of the Intellectual*, 11.
22. Giroux, 'Public Intellectuals, the Politics of Clarity, and the Crisis of Language', 101.

23 Ibid.
24 Daniel Drezner, *The Ideas Industry: How Pessimists, Partisans, and Plutocrats Are Transforming the Marketplace of Ideas* (New York: Oxford University Press, 2017), 13.
25 Ibid., 9.
26 Ibid.
27 Ibid.
28 Brian Dillon, *Essayism: On Form, Feeling, and Nonfiction* (New York: New York Review Books, 2018), 17.
29 Woolf, 'The Modern Essay', 221.
30 Mike Bulajewski and Slavoj Žižek, 'Getting a Grip on Slavoj Žižek (with Slavoj Žižek)', *JSTOR Daily*, 27 June 2018, np. https://daily.jstor.org/getting-a-grip-on-slavoj-zizek-with-slavoj-zizek/.
31 Ralph Waldo Emerson, 'Circles', in *Essays of Ralph Waldo Emerson* (New York: A.S. Barnes, 1940), 102–9 (108).
32 Michelle Alexander, 'Opinion | The Injustice of This Moment Is Not an "Aberration"', *The New York Times*, 17 January 2020, https://www.nytimes.com/2020/01/17/opinion/sunday/michelle-alexander-new-jim-crow.html.
33 Michelle Alexander, 'Obama's Drug War', *The Nation* 291, no. 26 (27 December 2010): 25–7.
34 Michelle Alexander, 'Cruel and Unequal', *Sojourners Magazine* 40, no. 2, February 2011, 16–19.
35 Michelle Alexander, 'The New Jim Crow', *The American Prospect* 22, no. 1 (2011): A19–21.
36 Alexander, 'Obama's Drug War', 27.
37 Drezner, *The Ideas Industry*, 248.
38 Ibid., 249.
39 Giroux, 'Public Intellectuals, the Politics of Clarity, and the Crisis of Language', 114.
40 Graham Good, *The Observing Self: Rediscovering the Essay* (London: Routledge & Kegan Paul, 1988), 23.
41 Ibid.
42 Andre Aciman, 'Writers on Writing: A Literary Pilgrim Progresses to the Past', *The New York Times*, 28 August 2000, https://www.nytimes.com/2000/08/28/arts/writers-on-writing-a-literary-pilgrim-progresses-to-the-past.html
43 Scott Russell Sanders, 'The Singular First Person', *The Sewanee Review* 96, no. 4 (1988): 658–72.
44 Kwame Anthony Appiah, 'Opinion | Go Ahead, Speak for Yourself', *The New York Times*, 10 August 2018, https://www.nytimes.com/2018/08/10/opinion/sunday/speak-for-yourself.html
45 Ibid.
46 Kwame Anthony Appiah, *The Lies That Bind: Rethinking Identity* (New York: Liveright, 2018).
47 Kwame Anthony Appiah, 'The Politics of Identity', *Daedalus* 135, no. 4 (2006): 15–22.
48 Kwame Anthony Appiah, 'The Democratic Spirit', *Daedalus* 142, no. 2 (2013): 209–21.
49 Kwame Anthony Appiah, 'Bending towards Justice', *Journal of Human Development* 9, no. 3 (2008): 343–55.
50 Kwame Anthony Appiah, 'Presidential Address 2017 – Boundaries of Culture', *PMLA* 132, no. 3 (2017): 513–25.
51 Kwame Anthony Appiah, 'The Politics of Culture, the Politics of Identity' (Toronto: Royal Ontario Museum, 2008), 6, as quoted in Jahan Ramazani, 'Appiah's Identities: An Introduction', *New Literary History* 49, no. 2 (2018): v–xxxix (vi).

52 Jahan Ramazani, 'Appiah's Identities: An Introduction', *New Literary History* 49, no. 2 (2018): v–xxxix (xx).
53 Appiah, 'Opinion | Go Ahead, Speak for Yourself'.
54 Appiah, 'Kwame Anthony Appiah | Official Site of Author, Lecturer Kwame Anthony Appiah', accessed 24 April 2020, http://appiah.net/.
55 Ibid.
56 Appiah, 'Opinion | Go Ahead, Speak for Yourself'.
57 Appiah, 'The Politics of Identity', 20.
58 Gayatri Chakravorty Spivak and Sneja Gunew, 'Questions of Multiculturalism', in *The Post-Colonial Critic: Interviews, Strategies, Dialogues*, ed. Sarah Harasym (New York: Routledge, 1990), 59–66 (59).
59 Du Bois, 'Strivings of the Negro People', 194.
60 Ta-Nehisi Coates, 'Letter to My Son', *The Atlantic Monthly*, 1 September 2015, 82–91 (83).
61 James Baldwin, 'On Being "White"… and Other Lies', *Essence*, April 1984, 90–2.
62 Ibid., 92.
63 Coates, 'Letter to My Son', 88.
64 Ibid., 88–9.
65 James Baldwin, 'Stranger in the Village', in *The Price of the Ticket: Collected Nonfiction 1948–1985* (New York: St. Martin's, 1985), 79–90 (81).
66 Coates, 'Letter to My Son', 91.
67 Ibid.
68 Ibid.
69 Said, *Representations of the Intellectual*, 11.
70 Steven Mailloux, 'Thinking in Public with Rhetoric', *Philosophy & Rhetoric* 39, no. 2 (2006): 140–6 (145).
71 Ibid.

Chapter 5

IS WRITING ALL OVER, OR JUST DISPERSED? DIGITAL ESSAYISM IN *TRINA, A DESIGN FICTION*

Joseph Tabbi

1. Introduction

Literature, etymologically 'things made from letters', is Robert Coover's starting point in a 2018 essay that does not forecast so much as inhabit 'The End of Literature'.[1] This essay by Coover, like his overall career and lifework, exemplifies a kind of writing that is 'all over' – in the double sense of being finished but also dispersing, even as the printed word itself is displaced into and reconfigured within digital media. Indeed, there is today an emerging recognition that computation and a universalized digitization might be regarded not as a displacement of writing so much as its continuation and expansion. As Serge Bouchardon and Victor Petit have argued, 'the computer is a multi-faceted and complex machine which has at least one very clear consequence: the extension of the domain of writing, in the same way as our possibilities for calculation have been enhanced and multiplied.'[2] Indeed, if we are able to revisit, resituate and *extend* our understanding of generic terms like novel, narrative, poem and (not least) the digitally inscribed *essay*, we might approach digitization not as a prospective 'end' of literary production but its renewal: continuous with the same long history of 'practices developed in Mesopotamia five millennia ago'.[3]

Once we recognize the 'overall' extension of writing's domain, we might also discern a longer, more loosely structured minor tradition whose exemplars are more essayistic than narrative; neither novels nor poetry so much as *poiesis*: a 'making' that extends to the materiality of one's vocal, print, and/or digital delivery.[4] The renewal of literature, arguably, its *novelty* is affiliated not so much with the nineteenth-century realist novel or more structured experiments in literary modernism as it is with earlier, epical thought streams. These might include, in literature's earliest formulations, non-fiction narratives such as *Gilgamesh* (the first work treated in Steven Moore's definitive and notably *Alternative* history of the novel); and literature's ongoing modernity can be seen to have originated well before the turn of the twentieth century.[5] Predating Oscar Wilde, Ezra Pound, T. S.

Eliot, James Joyce and Gertrude Stein (each of whom contributed canonical essays both within and outside their creative work), we might locate an earlier, looser and institutionally more diverse modernism in Francis Bacon's sixteenth-century 'Dispersed Meditations' or the eighteenth-century essays that Samuel Johnson (in his *Dictionary*) characterized as a 'loose sally of the mind; an irregular indigested piece; not a regularly and orderly composition'.[6] One source of the literary greatness of American Transcendentalism, to name a distinctively less than literary anticipation of later dispersals, is that it too avoids disciplinary strictures or clearly set generic configurations. The beliefs of its leading lights 'were often in a state of flux' and without a 'specific program or common cause'.[7] Essayistic works like Henry David Thoreau's *Walden* and Ralph Waldo Emerson's *Nature* can be best 'viewed as a cluster of motifs rather than a fixed form'.[8]

In all instances, from Michel de Montaigne to Francis Bacon, Samuel Johnson in London and the Transcendentalists in Boston to the transatlantic literary modernists, it is the non-fictional, never fully narrativized and always contingent *thought stream* that has prominence. And for this reason, insofar as the reader is encouraged for extended stretches to participate (and partake) in the author's generative thought, the essay is better suited to the collaborative tenor and dispersed connectivity in digital writing. Indeed, as we shall soon see, it is *that* particular disciplin*ary* structure – the study of post-digital literature within the humanities – that is at present undergoing a thorough questioning within academic institutions, by creative writers and designers no less than literary scholars.

The example I have chosen is a collaborative fiction, *Trina: A Design Fiction*, by Anne Burdick and Janet Sarbanes that was designed to be 'experienced through three different media forms: a live performance comprised of a slide show, a reading, and electronic music (played live or recorded)';[9] a published book; and a *Trina* presentation with voice-overs.[10] The work also sets out self-consciously 'to investigate the future of humanities research and to question the worlds made possible by the use of emerging technologies for reading and writing'.[11] And one way for literary scholars to understand (and embrace) the emerging *Digital Humanities* is by observing how both the essay and the digital transgress and possibly reset the institutional and medial limits of print practices.

2. Essay writing and/as human science

The rambling and wandering associated with the essay, we might now observe, was only partially constrained by print and codex formats during the Gutenberg parenthesis. And the naming of the essay as such during this five-hundred-year period is yet another act of containment, and constraint. Consistent with the rise of Enlightenment rationalism and extension of both geographic and scientific exploration, depictions of our humanity came to depend on material forms distinct from nature and animal being: in *letters* that could be stabilized and reprinted, through *numerical identifiers* that could render the external world calculable along with much in our minds, also: hence, our present economization of likes and dislikes, frequencies of sites visited and pathways traversed, friends contacted and those avoided or deleted, and so on. At the same time, for any who stop for a moment to *reflect* on such enumerations, in both our everyday lives and distributed photographs, video recordings and geographical locations, we are as often confronted with limits, absences and silences as we are with delineated knowledge. The same holds for any 'digital' depiction that implies an infinity of states between the zero and the one, however that is designated, or inscribed materially in punch cards, keyboards or silicon chips. As Friedrich Kittler more precisely noted in his 1992 essay, 'There Is No Software', between the million transistor cells of any highly connected computer system, there will be 'some million to the power of two interactions' already taking place. 'There is electron diffusion, there is quantum-mechanical tunnelling all over the chip.'[12]

It is precisely in this liminal space, in the exploration of what is left out and lost in our digital rationalizations and disciplinary locations, where we can anticipate an essayistic aesthetic for literary arts in today's digital media. The constructed *persistence* of our moment-to-moment, day-to-day pathways and encounters are only partially knowable; their enumeration and textual documentation constrains our individuated lifeworlds, bringing events and our recorded reflections into the same sphere of accessibility, comparative evaluation and accountability as scientific observation. A difference, however, needs to be noted: where scientific knowledge is accepted because it is both shared and *falsifiable*, much of our digitized knowledge is proprietary (and hence, unavailable to observation and collective questioning, testing and experimentation).[13] In such cases, we would better describe our present technological lifeworlds as pseudo-scientific, because without sharing the terms and basis of our knowledge, and with few opportunities publicly to question what we know, no rational consensus is available. Or to phrase it differently, any society that would ground itself in rationalism must needs be *communicative*, insofar as its reasons are expressed and enforced in and through language.

With this important qualification in mind, we can begin to observe a continuity throughout the modern era of scientific descriptions of our human nature. Rather than posit an objective world outside of our own communicative spheres, the world we share – as rational (and ethical) beings – is available to us by virtue of our sensual, linguistic and conceptual capacities. And this necessarily tentative, falsifiable and communicative availability – with all its inherent uncertainties and errant linguistic formulations – in turn allows us to understand 'the impact of essay writing on early modern human science'.[14] As Emiliano Ferrari notes in an article on 'Essay Writing and Human Science',

> Montaigne speaks of 'science humaine' (II, 12, *passim*) and Bacon of 'human knowledge' or 'humanity' (which follows the knowledge of nature and God). Through these expressions, they refer to the study of human nature.[15]

This convergence of the human with the scientific, arguably, is a foundation of what we would now term the *humanities*, which were at least nominally an institutional location where the arts and sciences could cohabit and communicate. For Anne Burdick and Janet Sarbanes in *Trina*, such essayistic, born digital modalities are channelled quite differently within a public sphere that uncomfortably incorporates business, military and educational concerns.¹⁶ Presented in their co-authored design fiction as Humanitas, Inc, this enterprise offers a reasonable, and quite realistic account of our present trans-humanist, corporate communities. At the same time, if we are ready with Burdick and Sarbanes to combine in our research and writing elements of programming, visuals and design *along with* printed matter, we stand a chance of both recognizing and countering instrumental tendencies in today's Humanities – and maintaining the critical inquiry and intersubjective community that has also been part of the literary humanities. Indeed, I will be arguing that Burdick's and Sarbane's work might be said in the present era to have advanced a 'digital essayism' that self-consciously integrates *Trina: A Design Fiction* with similarly ranging explorations from the period before print – as well as practices alongside and always separate from mainstream modernisms and contemporary literary humanities. Which is to say: all over the literary landscape.

3. *The essay as an expanse of current knowledge*

> In this unusual show-and-tell (PechaKucha meets La Jetée), the audience follows Trina, an unemployed literary scholar who creates virtual 'n-dimensional knowledge objects' alone in her RV in the desert. Through Trina's augmented eyes we see the software-mediated daily life within which the mystery of a cryptic, typewritten document unfolds.
>
> Anne Burdick (project description for a practice-based PhD, of which *Trina: A Design Fiction* is a part)

The phrase 'All Over Writing' that will describe this counter-history is one that Anne Burdick, Ewan Branda and I chose for a panel we had put together at a HASTAC conference of 2009, celebrating a fourth iteration of our collaborative literary project, *ebr* (www.electronicbookreview.com). Burdick herself points out that she 'originally launched *Trina* to take up a challenge'¹⁷ that she and her co-authors made in a landmark 2012 collection, titled *Digital_Humanities*:

> Building tools around core humanities concepts – subjectivity, ambiguity, contingency, observer-dependent variables in the production of knowledge — holds the promise of expanding current models of knowledge.¹⁸

And not only concepts and models, but the materiality of their designation so that the underscore in the collection title, *Digital_Humanities*, might convey – as much as anything written in the book – how any relation between digital arts, literature and the humanities must needs be a thing 'made from letters' (to again cite Coover, and not for the last time).[19] Burdick's and Sarbanes's *Trina: A Design Fiction* asks us to look at letters similarly – as objects in themselves as much as they are signifiers. Indeed, the re-emergence in digital writing of the idea of the signifier as a material object can disrupt, in a radical way, the thinking of the essay – and its seamless integration into both fictions and graphic designations – as a conduit for human wandering and reflection (though the so-called 'lyric essay' in print has been known to play with these aspects too).

The character Trina is an employee of Humanitas, Inc.[20] Her situation coheres with that of Burdick herself, who produced this work as a mid-career 'dissertation' with commentaries and continuations by selected 'outside readers'.[21] The conflation of author and character, whose name is embedded in that of the purported concrete poet, Doctrina Fortior, situates Burdick's and Sarbanes's fiction within the reflexivities and self-aware recursions of postmodern literary practice.[22] So too does the initial release of *Trina* to an at once expert and external audience with the potential of accessing other audiences in diverse fields (of design research, technology development, photography, media theory, film and literary studies). Indeed, the focus on self-expression within a circumscribed academic but also engaged field can be cited as another continuity with the essayism of Bacon, Montaigne and Transcendentalist anticipations of – and deviations from – the modern. While both are similarly situated in an emerging humanist discourse, the direct address among compeers better enacts the essay's personal nature, while at the same time increasing our awareness of the many ways our persons are situated and formed by institutions. That these institutions in turn can themselves be reformed, and differently formulated (as Emerson, for example, argued in 'Self-Reliance' and his 'Divinity School Address'), is consistent with the idea of incompletion and inconclusiveness that are definitional for the essay.

The Transcendentalist model is particularly relevant insofar as Emerson, for example, marks the emergence of an expressive, agential self with our capacity to distance ourselves from conventional articulations – and not least the religious conventions of his own time. This does not mean that Emerson rejects religion or embraces apostasy – though there were plenty enough dogmatic Unitarians who accused him of just that. Notoriously, the Reverend Dean Palfrey is cited by Henry Wadsworth Longfellow as having said that what in the Address 'was not folly was impiety!' Longfellow himself, by contrast, like the majority of his contemporaries found Emerson's claims 'after all' to be 'only a stout *humanitarian* discourse; in which Christ and Goethe were mentioned together as great philosophers'.[23] Longfellow could accept without dogmatic quibbles the conventional faith in Jesus as a bearer of God's power and will – although such transcendence is felt, Emerson posits, in moments of ecstasy that, though rare, are available equally to all. His argument is not so much with the channelling of our individual beliefs, as it is with belief's reduction to doctrines and procedures, 'idioms of language and the figures of rhetoric' wherein we 'but half express ourselves, and are ashamed of that divine idea which each of us represents'.[24]

But a still more radical position, one that takes Emerson beyond the '*humanitarian* discourse' cited by Longfellow, is not so much stated outright in

'Self-Reliance' as it is suggested and felt in a recurrent stream that runs all through Emerson's exposition. This is the suggestion that our human selfhood is immanent and not wholly possessed in our individual, spiritual being. As he says in the essay, 'Circles', our self-reliance is largely cultural (not self-produced), and the 'present order of things' is attained in large part through a recognition that 'all nature is the rapid efflux of goodness executing and organizing itself'.

> The things which are dear to men at this hour are so on account of the ideas which have emerged on their mental horizon, and which cause the present order of things, as a tree bears its apples. A new degree of culture would instantly revolutionize the entire system of human pursuits.[25]

More than a humanist self-reliance, a degree of self-*organization* inheres in 'nature' and extends beyond our human agency or awareness, even as 'the minds of men' are capable, by our own human nature, of extending beyond 'the present order of things'. Rather than affirming the individuation of human agency, Emerson is here asking his readers (and congregational listeners in the 'Divinity School Address') to recognize and participate in larger and more consequential processes. His 'entire system of human pursuits' is closer to what we might now term *autopoiesis*, a continuous and changeable *making* that is *distributed* 'in the minds of men' (in Emerson's time – Burdick's cognitive redistribution and expansion of 'current models of knowledge' is gender-neutral). Such an autopoietic fashioning is always larger than any individual consciousness, and uncontainable within any given set of intellectual classifications. The expanding knowledge base takes shape *within and among* the collectivity of individuals and our interactions with the natural world – which engage a much broader range of cognition and sensuality than mere consciousness.

We begin to see, in Emerson and throughout modern literary history, that the essay could never have emerged without institutions; but neither can the institutionalized form settle into fixed conventions, genres or static visualizations. And once this determinedly minority tradition of the essay is recognized, the potential becomes apparent for its renewal (and re-centring) in the digital era.

4. Digital Humanitas, Inc

Such an essayistic aesthetic, I would suggest, is enacted in the multimodal flow of visual images and voice-overs in a 'design fiction' such as *Trina*. There, on nearly every screen or page we find an unchanging background image of the desert setting for the main character's mobile home and workplace. We also have, imposed on (and occasionally overtaking) this conventional background, photographs and animated drawings of the van's sitting, dining and sleeping areas as well as projections of digital sites that connect with, and collectively constitute the 'Commons' where Trina conducts her research. This sphere would not exist, nor would it be accessible were in not for technological affordances supplied and interactive communities supported by Trina's employer. Yet the setting for Humanitas itself is never visualized in Burdick's sequence of images; and the one (and only) character's position within that organization is precarious, isolated and at a distance. And neither does Trina let herself be distracted (not for long) by an occasional 'boom of guns from the nearby marine base' (00:30, Vimeo video).

Following one of Burdick's and Sarbane's models, PechaKucha – the 2003 Tokyo-based installation of twenty images that are each projected with voice-overs for twenty seconds – we are invited to read the text (or listen to Burdick's voice-over in the Vimeo version) while viewing and deciphering each image.[26] In one photo, Trina's feet can be seen resting on a hammock outside the van, along with a tea cup (just one; the tea is brewed with a bag on a string), cans in the shelves, unpacked groceries in the kitchenette, sneakers on the van's floor.

> Like other out-of-work literary scholars, Trina was able to eke out a living performing human intelligence tasks for Humanitas. She knew the information she tracked down could get people killed – there was no other possible use for it – and sometimes she let herself think about that, though most of the time she didn't. (00:43, Vimeo video)

The humanities themselves, Burdick suggests, are looking out for, and finding channels of communication that are larger than academia (even as Emerson, for his part addressed the still robust, but in retrospect diminishing New England Unitarian establishment). We might even note a certain faith-based rationale for Trina's 'trade-off' between an economic precarity and her present freedom from the constraints of a nine-to-five office job. There is also a conceptual trade-off between this character's freewheeling isolation and an imagined ability to access an informational 'cloud' – as if this were itself a kind of public sphere:

> Workers with security clearance, like Trina, were required to sync up their implants with the agency's proprietary software. The tradeoff seemed worth it – after all, Humanitas gave her access to the cloud. And without the cloud, there was no Commons. (01:09, Vimeo video)

The public sphere has been an admittedly precarious, largely imagined but at the same time necessary ground for a robust and participatory democracy, even as literacy was and remains (with added internet facility) necessary to our individualized performance as citizens and employees. Yet such a field of communication, when it is broadcast, received or projected onto the nation-state or (of late) an emerging 'global' society, is demonstrably notional and its power dependent on a widely held, and shared faith. At the national level, we can still (almost) recognize the 'imagined communities' described by Benedict Anderson in the mid-1980s, although the outsourcing of decisions once in the hands of elected officials to transnational corporate concerns has created a disconnect between one's situation as a voting citizen and the actual decision making (about political no less than economic and cultural matters).[27] Robin Murray, at the start of the

FIGURE 5.1 'She had gotten used to the live transcript, a curtain of text that dangled just beyond the brim of her hat during each session.' Voiceover 05:20, Slide 17 from *Trina: A Design Fiction* by Anne Burdick and Janet Sarbanes. © Anne Burdick and Janet Sarbanes, 2019. Reproduced with the permission of Anne Burdick and Janet Sarbanes.

1990s, already showed 'how the twentieth-century state was based on what could be called a Fordist model of administration – centralised, standardised, large-scale, and vertically organised. "Schools, dinners, desks and uniforms could all be produced and purchased as if for the army." '[28] One such outsourcing of 'expertise' would be the literary humanities, and more generally the orientation of literacies, didactics and the kind of 'imagined community' that the education system facilitates. Or once did. This transformation of a public sphere into a militarized zone (administering goods 'as if for the army') is worth bearing in mind, when we observe Trina's departure from her own occupation as a humanities researcher with the phrase (the last one she will circulate through the digital Commons): '[I] AM ... AS ... AN ... ARMI' (slide 59, slide show).

5. The end of literature?

The *Trina* story, as Burdick notes in a preface, 'considers the perils and potentials of bringing nascent digital technologies and cyberinfrastructures together with the critical and interpretive practices that are central to the humanities'.[29] Embodying essayist practice no less than narrative structures, *Trina* is a story of second thoughts about our professional and personal commitment to the official world that systematically obscures its own medial supports. Essayism in our present era, arguably, is trans-institutional (as it often was before) as well as multimodal (as it is now, more radically than it was in the time when epic – and epochal – narratives were carried from person to person and voice to voice in regions reached via horses, carriages, running messengers and sea vessels): the idea of the signifier as a material object in the digital essay could either facilitate or disrupt, in a radical way, the thinking of the essay as a conduit for human wandering and reflection.

The 2018 essay on 'The End of Literature' is not the first time that Robert Coover has sounded a death knell for the literary. He is known, if not notorious, for his 1991 *New York Times* essay, 'The End of Books'.[30] Back then it was the emergence of experimental, born digital hypertext that signalled this end, but just eight years later Coover was already lamenting the passing of this post-print 'golden age' of stand-alone computer access prior to the internet.[31] Back then, at the start of the end of print books, practitioners might have assumed that hypertext, for all its interactivity, could still be situated (like the book itself) in a privileged space apart from visual, sonic and affective realms. By 2018, a work like *Trina* could instead inhabit 'this 3-D installation we call the modern world'.[32] Ours is a world not opening out to possibility, but rather enclosing all elements – image, text, sound and touch – in 'its root deep either/or operations', a situation that Coover identifies with the Sophists of old, for whom knowledge was reducible (and known exclusively) to power and rationality, and communication was instrumental not – as might often have happened during that earlier period of hypertext idealism – intersubjective or interactive.[33]

Still more troubling, from a literary perspective, is the loss of sustained attention that comes with the universalization of online readings, writings and viewings whose haphazard links and distractions disrupt and disorient more often than not. Even the wandering, essayistic practice of sustained and pleasurable attention requires a self-conscious separation of the literary work from our ordinary, everyday encounters. The early experiments in hypertext could achieve this, and so can films and YouTube clips that allow one to scan the self-generated commentary of the Commons, while watching and listening (and perhaps adding comments of one's own). Part I of Burdick's and Sarbanes's design fiction can be viewed on Vimeo, and a number of sustained presentations to date have been performed in public. But it remains to be determined, whether or how our integrated, visual and textual essays and fictions (such as this one) will be presented and experienced online, and disengaged from a digital environment that fosters, for the most part, rather more joyless and compulsive reading and viewing habits.

For Burdick and Sarbanes in the book version of *Trina*, reading is itself a primary concern and theme. Our awareness of how we read and write – materially, and differently in different media – is itself the narrative, as our co-authors explore cognitive and affective capacities that are brought to bear on our worldly habitus and our (self-)understanding. 'In writing by hand', Trina notes (citing Kittler, as it happens), 'the eye must constantly watch the written line … and only that. It must

FIGURE 5.2 'Someone forwarded the first letter ever typed by Mark Twain.' Voiceover 12:20, Slide 38 from *Trina: A Design Fiction* by Anne Burdick and Janet Sarbanes. © Anne Burdick and Janet Sarbanes, 2019. Reproduced with the permission of Anne Burdick and Janet Sarbanes.

attend to the creation of each sign'[34] (slide 02, slide show). In reading Burdick's and Sarbanes's compilation that is presented as both a book and slide show, our eyes (and our ears and our positioned bodies) are more widely engaged than they might have been in the time of Nietzsche and Mark Twain – both of whom sensed a change that the typewriter was bringing to their own literary practice. And we are undergoing a similar transformation today, at the end of (print) literature.

The message Trina types signals a multiplication of identities, in which her own fingertips create a multitudinous '"I", who AM … AS … AN … ARMI' (slide 59, slide show). Trina in her isolation, and in her position working for Humanitas, Inc., keeps most of her research secret – though she does find time to post messages within 'the ghostly wordscape of The Commons' (00:20, Vimeo video), and read messages that reach her from other subscribers. Most satisfying is the culminating occasion when Trina sends out her own document, whose content could cause her to lose her security clearance:

> When she was done, she released her document into The Commons, watching as the spindles adjusted to the latest addition.

She sat back, waiting for the moon to rise. Listening to the sounds of the desert and the network … (15:00, Vimeo video)

The visualization of the spindles, multicoloured but momentarily inactive in the dead of night in the desert (slide 47, slide show), is reimagined a few slides later, with Trina's lit-up fingers casting her message upwards, and the responding messages showing below the spindles as a series of posts (slide 50, slide show), ripostes, supporting and contradicting documents gathered instantly, more or less. Whether or not the rise of images, texts and voices will be more significant than that of the moon is left unanswered.

6. An armi of me (multiplied)

I would like to follow more closely the military analogy – which is more than metaphorical if we look closely (as Burdick and Sarbanes do) at the machinery of a controlled and increasingly official consciousness. It is a framework that turns out to be particularly inhospitable to the essayistic exploration that Burdick's Trina enacts, even as she unveils the alternative, open access and often feminist pre-histories of these very corporate and computational spheres. Indeed, by bringing to the fore infrastructural realities that could either advance or frustrate the minor tradition of the literary essay, we could well be observing a set of institutional norms within and against which a digital essayism could find its place as *the* literary tradition for our time.

Thomas Pynchon in *Gravity's Rainbow* (1973) has his paranoid narratorial persona observe that the typed orders from bureaucrats in London offices might have sent more young men to death than any wartime general. And few today would disagree with Nietzsche's observation on the typewriter – as his own sight and mental capacities were diminishing – that: 'Our writing tools also are working on our thoughts.'[35] The Remington brothers divided up their attention similarly: the elder, Philo (born 1916, died 1983), ran the manufacture 'of firearms and typewriters in Ilion, New York, along with his brother Eliphalet III, who oversaw the typewriter division' (04:00, Vimeo video). There could scarcely be a more apt or focused concurrence than this of the official worlds – the military and the reproducibly typewritten – that Burdick and Sarbanes engage and (through Trina) reject.

The documentation we find in Burdick's and Sarbanes's design fiction, as of the present writing, exceeds that of Wikipedia – whose entry for Philo is a stub.[36] Neither is there an entry in Wikipedia for Eliphalet III, an absence that Burdick and Sarabanes fill in with a mix of fictitious and factual characters. Eliphalet is paired with a fictitious secretary named Ida Wayne, who is said to have suggested instead of QWERTY a typewriter layout that would have spelled PEACE. It is Ida, too, who gives birth out of wedlock to Doctrina Fortiori, whose concrete poetry is consistent with the lettrist aesthetic and orientation that is Burdick's, Sarbanes's (and Coover's, and Chris Marker's) theme.[37]

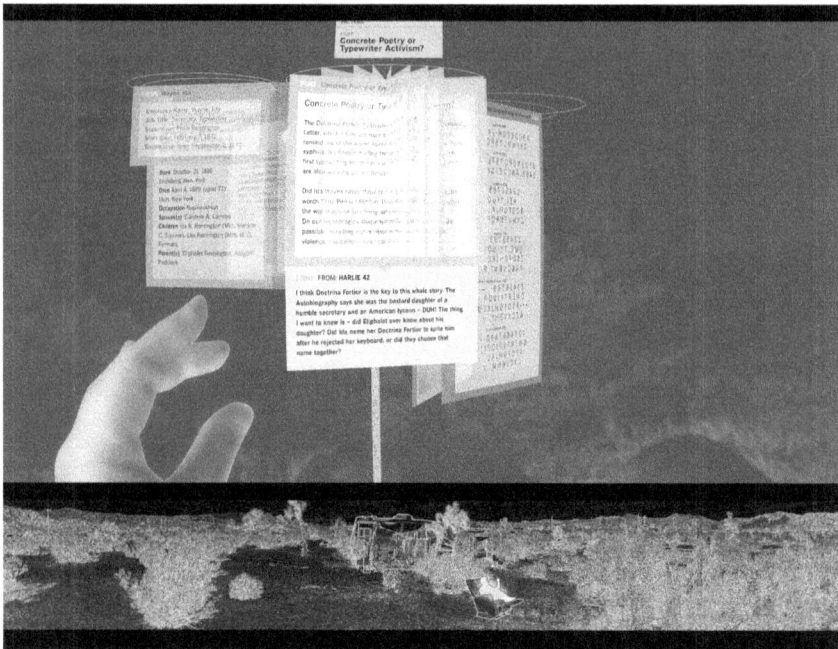

FIGURE 5.3 'Concrete Poetry or Typewriter Activism?' Slide 49 from *Trina: A Design Fiction* by Anne Burdick and Janet Sarbanes. © Anne Burdick and Janet Sarbanes, 2019. Reproduced with the permission of Anne Burdick and Janet Sarbanes.

As men were sent to war, women began to occupy offices, as Trina learns from a 'private note' sent to her over The Commons (17:00, Vimeo video). We are told that, 'in the late 1800s, the typist was seen as the ultimate liberated woman. Even though women were cheap labour, their "dainty fingers" gave them independence' (17:05, Vimeo video). Burdick and Sarbanes, like so many others whose careers emerged alongside digital advances, most likely learned from N. Katherine Hayles's *My Mother Was a Computer* about the introduction of women into the official world.[38] ('Computer' was the name given in the 1930s and 1940s to a clerical labourer, usually a woman, who did calculations.) The machinery, and later digital technologies that (as Donna Haraway similarly noted) did much to facilitate women's entry into the modern workforce, arguably reinforcing the Sophistry and instrumental nature of work that was neither managerial nor physically labour-intensive.

All along, Trina 'knew the information she tracked down' for Humanitas 'got people killed – there was no other possible use for it' (00:40, Vimeo video).

What is compelling about the presentation as a whole is its quiet, mostly non-verbal infusion into our Sophist culture of aesthetic features where the reception of beauty can impart a sense of aliveness to the reader: all that is literally touching (to the reader's eyes, ears, and senses) and the objective being of words. A living

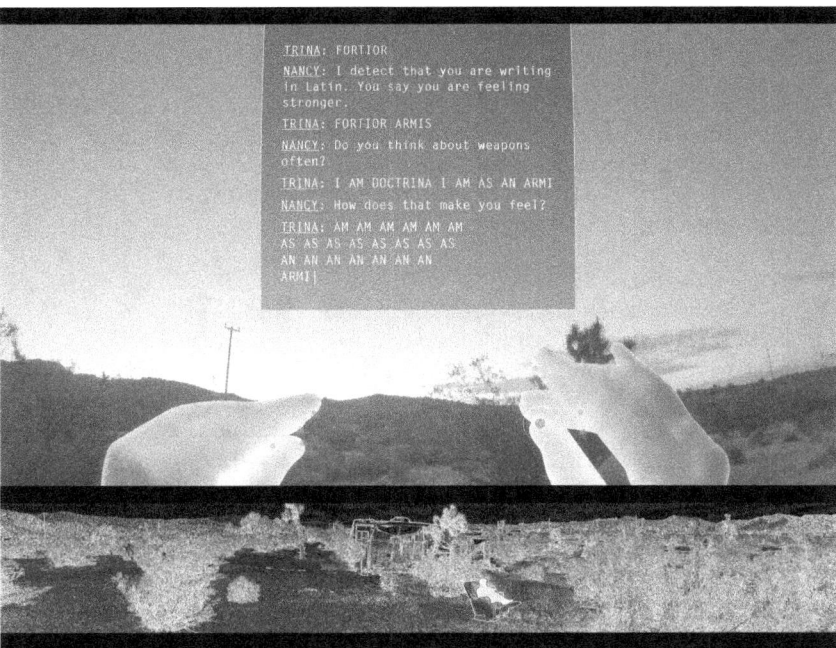

FIGURE 5.4 'Trina rubbed her SkyEyes, disconnecting them from Humanitas Inc. She turned off her audio and walked away, through the creosote and out onto the dirt road.' Voiceover 19:00, Slide 57 from *Trina: A Design Fiction* by Anne Burdick and Janet Sarbanes. © Anne Burdick and Janet Sarbanes, 2019. Reproduced with the permission of Anne Burdick and Janet Sarbanes.

poetics that engages equally all elements that a computational field has to offer while requiring (quite rightly) a focused, concentrated period of attention. That, after all, was the term Robert Musil devised for his own essayistic (and never finished) narrative: a '*lebendiges Denken*' (living thinking), whose settled conclusion could only coincide with an author's own passing. A design fiction that represents, enacts and is informed by a digital 'Commons'; a narrative structure whose realism is more cognitive than outwardly descriptive; an attentiveness more ranging than focused; and an ongoing-ness that does not rest in a definitive 'edition' – no more than Montaigne's collection of essays, which were continually revised and expanded: these are qualities we might expect to observe in a digital essayism appropriate to the present.

Notes

1 Robert Coover, 'The End of Literature', *American Scholar*, 4 September 2018, https://theamericanscholar.org/the-end-of-literature/

2   Serge Bouchardon and Victor Petit, 'Digital Writing: Philosophical and Pedagogical Issues', *electronic book review*, 6 October 2019, https://doi.org/10.7273/xkjp-rk21
3   Bouchardon and Petit, 'Digital Writing'.
4   Citing Joan Retallack's *The Poethical Wager* (Berkeley: University of California Press, 2003), Jason Childs in this volume explores a similar essayistic turn (or, perhaps, a definitive 'swerve') in contemporary literary practice.
5   Steven Moore, *The Novel: An Alternative History: Beginnings to 1600* (New York: Continuum, 2010).
6   Samuel Johnson, 'Essay', in *A Dictionary of the English Language … in 2 Volumes* (London: W. Strahan, 1755).
7   Lawrence Buell, *Literary Transcendentalism: Style and Vision in the American Renaissance* (Ithaca, NY: Cornell University Press, 1973), 3. That's partly because the literary cohort in the United States was composed largely of pastors and transcontinental explorers who were concerned not so much with literary genres as with a wider, more interactive communicability: 'the conversation, the essay, the sermon, the literary travelogue or excursion, the catalogue, the diary, and the autobiography' (3).
8   Buell, *Literary Transcendentalism*, 17. Emerson's break with his Unitarian profession clearly influenced the less disciplinary (if no less disciplined) essayism that he brought to American Literature. The essayist historian James Marcus notes that Emerson 'was said to have a deep and entrancing baritone. A voice like that works directly on our nervous system' and may have been 'helpful on the lecture circuit because so much of what Emerson had to say to his rural audiences was close to incomprehensible' (James Marcus, 'Channeling Emerson', *American Scholar*, 2 December 2019, https://theamericanscholar.org/channeling-emerson/). Given that the link from any given sentence to the next can be elusive in Emerson, he too can be said to have drawn on an oral literary tradition that was still active in his own, as yet only partially print era.
9   Burdick set out the 'three different media forms' in the preface to an unpaginated print edition of *Trina* that was circulated privately to the initial readers.
10 Anne Burdick and Janet Sarbanes, *Trina: A Design Fiction*, Vimeo video, 21:00, http://micromegameta.net/trina/, accessed 10 March 2020. References to this video will be noted as (Vimeo video) in parenthesis in text.
11 Burdick summarizes her mix of critical and design writing in her online description of *Trina: A Design Fiction*, https://vimeo.com/294304334/75c4c04773, accessed 10 March 2020.
12 Friedrich A. Kittler, 'There Is No Software', in *Literature, Media, Information Systems: Essays*, ed. John Johnston (Amsterdam: G + B Arts International, 1997), 147–55 (155).
13 The deviation from conventional (and credible) scientific practice was also noted by Kittler. In 'There Is No Software', he marks the start of this anti-scientific practice with Microsoft's foundational decision not to make their operational software available for circulation, and potential development by a scientific community: the programmed 'layers which, like modern media technologies in general, have been explicitly contrived to evade perception' (Kittler, 'There Is No Software', 148). Since then, scholarly communities have made some tentative moves toward Open Access. But it's not at all assured that the democratic and open promise of the internet will be protected politically and advanced in practice – any more than the 'public sphere' advocated by Kittler's contemporary, Jürgen Habermas, could sustain itself without

14 Emiliano Ferrari, '"A Knowledge Broken": Essay Writing and Human Science in Montaigne and Bacon', *Montaigne Studies* 28 (2016): 211–21 (214).
15 Ibid. Ferrari's quotations of Montaigne are from *Les Essais*, ed. Pierre Villey (Paris: PUF/Quadrige, 2004). Ferrari is also citing from *Francis Bacon: The Major Works*, ed. Brian Vickers (Oxford: Oxford University Press, 2008).
16 The book credits attribute authorship thus: 'Story by Anne Burdick and Janet Sarbanes; Design by Anne Burdick'. As Burdick explained to me, the interfaces are hers but the story concepts and texts (both in the images and in the narration) are co-authored.
17 Anne Burdick, Johanna Drucker, Peter Lunenfeld, Todd Presner and Jeffrey Schnapp, *Digital_Humanities* (Cambridge, MA: MIT Press, 2012), 104.
18 Ibid.
19 Coover, 'The End of Literature'.
20 Burdick articulated her purposes in a privately circulated document titled, 'Reading Trina'. There, she asked her colleagues not for peer review, but instead for more critical, subjective interpretation through close reading. Part of the originality of the piece, then, was its re-conception of the humanities in part through their own mechanisms of assessment.
21 Designated readers for the project included Jeffrey Schnapp, Joseph Tabbi, Jessica Pressman, Denise Gonzales-Crisp, Daniela Rosner, Whitney Trettien, Thomas Lee, Jentery Sayers, Lori Emerson, Ahmed Ansari, Johanna Drucker, Holly Willis and Sascha Pohflepp.
22 The poet's name derives from *Doctrina Fortior Armis*, which is Latin for 'the pen is mightier than the sword'. In Burdick's and Sarbanes's fiction, 'PRSN: Fortior, Doctrina' is said to be a reclusive, Left Bank acquaintance of Gertrude Stein and Alice B. Toklas, 'though nothing survives of her poetry' (slide 16, slide show). Because Fortior's experiments with typography were never published, or archived, this figure's actuality is debated by members of the NewFangled Machines Group of 'amateur typewriter historians' (09:30, Vimeo video). The group, in turn is itself named after Mark Twain's first ever typed document, a letter to his brother: 'I AM TRYING T TO GET THE HANG OF THIS NEW F FANGLED WRITING MACING, BUT AM NOT MAKING A SHINING SUCCESS OF IT' (slide 38, slide show).
23 Henry Wadsworth Longfellow, 'Letter Dated 28 July 1838 to Clara Crowninshield', in *The Letters of Henry Wadsworth Longfellow*, ed. Andrew Hilen, Vol. 2 (Cambridge, MA: The Belknap Press of Harvard University Press. 1966), 86–7 (87).
24 Ralph Waldo Emerson, 'Self-Reliance', in *Selections from Ralph Waldo Emerson: An Organic Anthology*, ed. Stephen E. Whicher (Boston: Houghton Mifflin, 1957), 147–68 (148).
25 Ralph Waldo Emerson, 'Circles', in *Selections from Ralph Waldo Emerson*, 168–78 (172).
26 'PechaKucha Night was devised in Tokyo in February 2003 as an event for young designers to meet, network and show their work in public. It has turned into a massive celebration, with events happening in over 1,000 cities around the world' (see 'PechaKucha', accessed 5 March 2020, https://www.pechakucha.com/about).
27 Benedict Anderson, *Imagined Communities: Reflections on the Origin and Spread of Nationalism* (London: Verso, 1983).

28 Mary Kaldor, *Soundings* 72, 'Democracy and Brexit' (2019): 17–30 (21), https://www.lwbooks.co.uk/soundings/72/brexit-and-democracy, accessed 12 December 2020. The quote in the quote is from Robin Murray, 'Life After Henry (Ford)', *Marxism Today*, October 1988, 8–13, as cited by Kaldor.
29 August 2018 (unpaginated preface to *Trina: A Design Fiction*). See printed book pdf, http://micromegameta.net/trina/.
30 Robert Coover, 'The End of Books', *New York Times Book Review*, 21 June 1992, 23–5.
31 Robert Coover, 'Literary Hypertext: The Passing of the Golden Age', *Feed Magazine*, 10 February 2000, np.
32 Coover, 'The End of Literature'.
33 Ibid.
34 Kittler, for his part is citing Richard Herbertz quoting 'Angelo Beyerlen, the royal stenographer of Württemberg and the first typewriter dealer of the Reich'. (Friedrich A. Kittler, *Gramophone, Film, Typewriter*, trans. Geoffrey Winthrop-Young and Michael Wutz (Stanford, CA: Stanford University Press, 1999), 203.)
35 Nietzsche is cited by Burdick and Sarbanes (slide 46, slide show).
36 Accessed 6 October 2019.
37 The director of La Jetée, one of the models for Burdick's and Sarbanes's Design Fiction, was born Christian François Bouche-Villeneuve. His professional surname was inspired by the magic marker.
38 N. Katherine Hayles, *My Mother Was A Computer: Digital Subjects and Literary Texts* (Chicago: University of Chicago Press, 2005).

Part II

THE ESSAY AND THE SELF

In 'The Decay of Essay Writing', Woolf claims that the modern popularity of the essay is due to 'the fact that its proper use is to express one's personal peculiarities'. For instance, Montaigne, she writes in an eponymous essay, is the 'master' of the genre precisely because his essays are 'an attempt to communicate a soul', a way of 'talking of oneself, following one's own vagaries, giving the whole map, weight, colour, and circumference of the soul in its confusion, its variety, its imperfection'. Of Hazlitt, she writes that 'his essays are emphatically himself', while also noting in 'The Modern Essay' that 'what [Max] Beerbohm gave was, of course, himself.' Woolf's insights into the relationship between the essay and the self are much subtler than these decontextualized pronouncements may suggest. More than simply an expression of the self (the essay is the man) she thinks of the essay as a 'thin … veil' through which we can see the essayist, but a veil nonetheless. Beerbohm, for example, 'has brought personality … so consciously and purely that we do not know whether there is any relation between Max the essayist and Mr. Beerbohm the man'. More than the man himself, what 'permeates every word that he writes' is actually 'the spirit of personality'.

This sense of human presence in the essay, the idea that the essay is in some ways an expression or modulation or veiling of personality or identity, the ways in which voice, point of view, style and publication affordances construct or problematize the sense of self in the essay are some of the central concerns discussed by the contributors in this part of the volume.

Ivan Callus sets the tone for this section with a wide-ranging, reflective piece on tone in the essay or, more precisely, on its elusiveness in criticism. How can tone, he asks, be 'so *present* in what we read as we are reading it' while at the same time being so 'hard to seize and settle upon'? Callus tries to answer this question by looking at a selection of British writers from the seventeenth century onwards – Samuel Johnson, Alexander Pope, Joseph Addison, Jonathan Swift, Matthew Arnold and Brian Dillon. These are essayists in whose work, for different reasons, tone is a crucial concern, but he also considers the insights of twentieth-century theorists like Maurice Blanchot, Jacques Derrida and Jacques Rancière, who write about 'literature' more than the essay specifically, but who more often than not use the essay to do so. The outcome is a playful but rigorous discussion of the recognizability of tone in the essay, its affinities with voice, its use in political discourse and, ultimately, its resistance to criticism.

Tone and voice, as Callus notes, are also dependent on context, and this is something that Jenny Spinner discusses in detail in her chapter on women periodical essayists. Indeed, as Spinner puts it, 'as much as the essay celebrates interiority, it also relies on interaction with a world beyond oneself …, and eighteenth century women often found that world closed off to them.' Spinner queries the thinking of the essay as an expression of self by showing that for women essayists – she focuses on the eighteenth century, but her argument is extendable to other centuries – it is never as simple as that. Taking various examples from a range of women essayists and writers – Judith Sargent Murray, Lady Mary Wortley Montagu, Eliza Haywood, Charlotte Lennox and Mary Wollstonecraft among others – Spinner shows how the publication contexts and conventions in the eighteenth-century periodical essay allowed women writers to use rhetorical devices (such as literary personae that do not require revealing their private identity) that circumvent while not necessarily overcoming gender-based limits for essay writing at the time. Ultimately, 'male writers still dominated and controlled the conversation about women … and it is imperative to read the work eighteenth century women essayists in that context.'

Rachel Baldacchino's chapter introduces another layer to the discussion of the self in the essay by focusing on the essay as a meeting point between self and other. Baldacchino identifies the thinking of the essay in terms of its primarily 'antirhetorical', possibilitarian spirit and in terms of an 'essayistic space of non-coercive tact, a space of radical empathy or radical otherness' as the dominant conception of the essay. From this viewpoint, the essay does not seek to persuade or to argue but to entertain or accompany the reader. Against this, Baldacchino proposes thinking of the potential of what she calls the essay 'of demand', that is, the persuasive essay, 'a practice of otherness rooted in the rhetorical tradition'. By discussing a number of pacifist essays by Vernon Lee, Baldacchino shows how the essay can engage the other through styles that are not propelled by the wandering self but by a self that desires to engage the other persuasively.

Aaron Aquilina and Michael Askew, in their respective chapters, take the discussion of the self in the essay in a somewhat different direction, showing what may be loosely described as the deconstructionist impulse to problematize the idea of a stable self with a corresponding stable voice in the essay. Aquilina focuses on the queer essay, which, following David Lazar, he thinks of in terms of its gender/genre dissolution. There he finds a fragmentary form full of 'broken voices' that, analogously to 'queer subjectivity', manifests a 'fragmentary "I"'. Through a close reading of selected essays by Jean Genet – chosen as representative of the tendencies and potentialities of the queer essay – Aquilina discusses the queer essay as a form of resistance to the idea of the essay as 'self-disclosure' and 'self-seeking' and to the idea of 'voice' as the manifestation of the individual being at the heart of the essay.

The questioning of voice as a conduit for the essayist's self is also central to Askew's chapter on Eliot Weinberger's 'literary essays', which Askew reads as a 'direct challenge to the prominence of the essayistic "I"'. The essay, Askew reminds us, 'has historically been, quite literally, self-centred', but what happens when the essay projects 'no opinions, no commentaries, no personal pronouns, no first-hand accounts or personal experiences'? What happens, in other words, when it is neither personal nor argumentative, as in Weinberger's essays? To answer this question, Askew focuses on voice, which, following Amy Bonnaffons, Askew thinks about in terms of a 'speaker' that transcends the 'boundaries of the … historical self'.

Chapter 6

TONE AND THE ESSAY

Ivan Callus

Around the theme of tone and the essay, what is an essay to do for tone?

A deliberated tone is a strained one. Effortless poise is what the essay, or at least a certain tradition of it, is after. To think of performing tone would be to have it contrived. Squarer and safer, then, to look at what literary criticism – and studies on the essay specifically – might have had to say about tone. 'Not very much', it turns out, might be the answer. This is perplexing. On and off the page the wrong tone can really rile, so schooling in how to know or strike a better one would be a fine thing. Tone, however, is writing's most untutored attribute. If criticism has ample studies on style, but, curiously, far fewer on tone, it might be because there is something to tone that eludes, disarms or even undoes analysis. Ask to be directed to a standard study on tone and even those people trusted to be expansive will hesitate. Tone, so *present* in what we read as we are reading it, is what it is hard to seize and settle upon. It is what criticism underreads. To overstate the case, tone mutes criticism. In view of what tone is about this is rather odd and not a little ironic.

Why would tone be elusive, awkward for criticism? Wouldn't criticism be piqued, exercised by tone's inscrutability? Not necessarily: as Jacques Derrida confirms, 'The attention to tone, which is not just style, seems rather rare. ... Tone has been little studied for itself, if we suppose that is possible or has ever been done.'[1] The intractability of tone to critical inquiry and its import for the tradition of the essay, itself elusive to characterization, motivates this chapter, which unfortunately does not have the space to study the implications of Derrida's brief but tantalizing references to 'timbre'.[2] The *Oxford English Dictionary* (*OED*) and its definitions supervene: squarer, safer. Or actually, *no*. It is instructive to go, first, to Samuel Johnson's *Dictionary of the English Language*. How, back in 1755, did Johnson explain 'tone'? Practised in many genres, he is surely someone to set us right. Except he doesn't, not quite. Here is how he defines 'tone'.

TONE. n.s [*ton* Fr. *tonus* Lat.]

1. Note; found.
    Sounds called *tones* are never equal. *Bacon's Nat. Hift.*
    The ftrength of a tone or found makes a difference in the loudnefs or foftnefs, but not in the *tone*.   *Bacon's Nat. Hist.*
    > In their motions harmony divine
    > So fmooths her charming *tones*, that God's own ear
    > Liftens delighted.   *Milton's Par. Loft, b, v.*
2. Accent; found of the voice.
    > Palamon replies
    > Eager his *tone*, and ardent were his eyes.   *Dryden.*
3. A whine; a mournful cry.
    > Made children, with your *tones*, to run for't
    > As bad as bloody-bones, or Lunsford.   *Hudibras*, iii
4. A particular of affected sound in fpeakig.
5. Elafticity; power of extenfion and contraction.
    Drinking too great quantities of this decoction may weaken the *tone* of the ftomach.   *Arbuthnot*.[3]

This is not what might have been hoped for. The dominant understanding of tone offered in Johnson's definition is more allied to what David Crystal was exploring when he wrote *The English Tone of Voice* more than forty years ago, in a mode of inquiry that has since been much expanded in phonetics, stylistics and linguistics more generally.[4] Here the more appropriate intertext might feature Johnson's own essays, of which it is routinely said that they are, 'in tone and subject matter ... both lengthier and more serious than [their] popular ancestor in the genre', namely those in Joseph Addison and Richard Steele's the *Spectator*. Wikipedia, which is routine enough, says so.[5] But as with the *Dictionary*, the leads on tone that emerge from Johnson's writing veer from what might be expected. He will report of 'the Admirable [James] Crichton', the sixteenth-century polymath, that 'once hearing an oration of an hour, he would repeat it exactly, and in the recital follow the speaker through all his variety of tone and gesticulation'.[6] Meanwhile in *The Lives of the Poets* there is a reference to Jonathan Swift's voice being 'sharp and high-toned, rather than harmonious'.[7] This is interesting enough but not revealing about tone in *writing*. Johnson, poet, lexicographer, essayist and critic, speaks neither directly nor regularly about tone and its rhetorics as it would be understood today, though an exploration of how he himself handles it might make for compelling study.

Indeed: what is said about Johnson's tone by those who sought the wit and weight of his conversation and its pitch of aphoristic raillery? James Boswell's *The Life of Samuel Johnson* is the obvious source. Johnson's tone is there described as having been, on different occasions, 'subdued', 'gentle', 'low and earnest', 'solemn but quiet', 'decisive', 'high', 'loud', 'angry', 'fervid' and having 'animation'.[8] On another occasion, Boswell reports that it was marked by 'conciliating courtesy'.[9] Once, after Johnson is seen saying, 'I have known what it was to LOSE A WIFE.—It had almost broke my heart', his tone is described as having been 'solemn, tender, faultering'.[10] Again, it is all about conversation, though there are two occasions when Boswell's observations on his subject's tone carries marginally more detail. The first has Boswell referring to one episode in which David Garrick perfectly mimicked 'the tone and air of Johnson'.[11] In the second, he reports Johnson uttering – in a 'strong determined' tone, Boswell takes the trouble to specify – 'an apophthegm, at which many will start'. This is where he sets down one of Johnson's most quotable lines, 'Patriotism is the last refuge of a scoundrel.'[12]

Two points seem noteworthy. The first is that 'tone', 'air' can be so identifying that they can recognizably be bodied forth in another's performance of them ('By their tone shall you know them …'). Here is scope for parody and pastiche. Tone can be both what is most proper as well as something that can be worn, or affected. It is hardly necessary to point out the many analogies with those areas of literary theory that acknowledge *style*'s individualizing force (rephrasing Buffon to say, 'Tone is the man,' does seem irresistible) – as well as the potential for impersonation or parody. The second point concerns the quotable quickness with which an accomplished essayist will turn to the aphoristic, an 'apophthegm', in speech as well as in writing … (*Here, motivating the ellipsis, comes my first parenthesis, one of a number across this essay's length. The earlier resolution to play it safe is tedious. At the risk of repeatedly striking a wrong tone in what follows, indulgence of these parentheses is claimed through what Montaigne said about his essayistic method in 'On Three Kinds of Social Intercourse'. 'I can turn over the leaves of this book or that, a bit at a time without order or design. Sometimes my mind wanders off, at others I walk to and fro, noting down and dictating these whims of mine.*'[13] *Montaigne is being disingenuous. There is method in this desultoriness. The parentheses here will hopefully have some level of perceptible method of their own. Their thrust is not merely to disturb a correct tone or a consistent voice.*)

There is ample scope for the aphoristic in the heroic couplet, integral to so much of Alexander Pope's work and certainly to 'An Essay on Criticism': a *verse* essay from 'the age of prose and reason' (as Matthew Arnold had it) that is as practised a performance of tone as any in eighteenth-century literature, to which decorum is famously vital.[14] But in that metacritical space there is no direct mention of any question of tone. (*Parenthesis 2. Surely it is possible to speak about tone and its challenges for criticism without actually mentioning the word. Rancière's* Mute Speech, *which does explore tone though the word is mentioned infrequently, is interesting in this respect, as indicated later.*) 'An Essay on Criticism' is published in the same year, 1711, as a series of essays in the *Spectator* by Joseph Addison, on 'True Wit' and 'False Wit'. Tellingly, Addison expresses unease when one person arrogates to themselves another's tone. 'Nay some carry the Notion of Wit so far, as to ascribe it even to external Mimickry; and to look upon a Man as an ingenious Person, that can resemble the Tone, Posture, or Face of another,' he writes.[15] Clearly these eighteenth-century essayists and poets are unsettled by imitation (Pope's *The Dunciad* abominates it), though Johnson is interestingly nuanced, aware of the complexities:

> As not every instance of similitude can be considered as a proof of imitation, so not every imitation ought to be stigmatized as plagiarism. The adoption of a noble sentiment, or the insertion of a borrowed ornament, may sometimes display so much judgment as will almost compensate for invention: and an inferior genius may, without any imputation of servility, pursue the path of the ancients, provided he declines to tread in their footsteps.[16]

Here is openness to tone of a different kind. It is the Johnsonian ability to see that there can be other tones, *shades*, to a circumstance, making more prismatic perception appropriate. This itself underlines the ability – the *propensity* – to discern and convey the sense of multiple or unregarded facets to a question that is integral to the finest traditions of the essay, both when it is being contrarian or allowing itself, to use Brian Dillon's word in *Essayism*, 'sententiousness'.[17] (*Parenthesis 3. The urge of the essayist to come up with counter-intuitive perspectives can be tiresome sometimes, as can its opposite motivation to be n'er so well expressing what oft was thought by everyone else.*)

That nothing very specific is said about tone by these poets and essayists who are the eighteenth-century masters of it reconfirms a pattern. In the *Dunciad*, for instance, Pope refers to tone once, disparagingly and again in relation to utterance, not composition: 'Then mount the clerks, and in one lazy tone / Through the long, heavy, painful page drawl on.'[18] In that masterpiece of tone, 'A Modest Proposal', Swift never refers to tone.[19] That would have undone his text. The pattern suggests that it does not set the right tone to talk of tone – which makes *this* essay, which speaks of little else, a gaucherie. The safer definitional issues might, against that, offer some reassurance. Here, taken from the *OED* (the move is timelier now), are aspects to tone's definitions that Johnson does not address:

> A particular style in discourse or writing, which expresses the person's sentiment or reveals his character; also *spec.* in literary criticism, an author's attitude to his subject matter or audience; the distinctive mood created by this.
>
> A state or temper of mind; mood, disposition.
>
> A special or characteristic style or tendency of thought, feeling, behaviour, etc.; spirit, character, tenor; *esp.* the general or prevailing state of morals or manners in a society or community.[20]

The thought arises that Johnson would not have featured these senses because the term did not already bear them in his time. Addison, Swift, Pope: they could not have invoked tone in our sense because that denotation was not then current, though tone's finer elaborations certainly were. This appears to be borne out by that wonderful resource in the *OED*: complementing its etymological work, its examples of pioneering usage. The earliest example given for the senses of 'tone' provided in the *OED* entry is from 1641 in Robert Naunton's *Fragmenta Regalia*: 'As the toan of his house, & the ebbe of his fortune then stood.'[21] Fascinatingly, most of the other indicative uses post-date the compilation of Johnson's *Dictionary*.[22] Consequently the understanding of tone as the modulating conveyance of attitude is quite modern. And fascinatingly, the modern meaning of tone settles just before the modern meaning of the word 'literature' emerges. Johnson's *Dictionary* carries none of our contemporary understanding of the word. 'Literature' is defined as 'learning, ſkill in letters'. The gloss for letters is, similarly, 'learning'. As Derrida has argued, our contemporary sense of literature only starts to emerge in the eighteenth century.[23] 'Tone' and 'literature', in their present senses, are young terms.

In the present, meanwhile, the *OED*'s definitions prime the theme of 'tone and the essay' interestingly. To consider the theme in the most general sense without a specifying grounding in one body of work and of its particular inflections is to ask about the sentiment, character, attitude, mood, temper and disposition of the essay as a whole, in its disembodied, abstract, notional sense, as if that were frameable. Besides, the essay has infinite variety and is liable to disingenuousness. The same author can shift their tone's (and tones') peculiarity not only across platforms (it has been shown how Richard Steele did this across the *Tatler* and the *Spectator*),[24] but also within the same piece, in recursive and remodulating moves.[25] And how might all this be different if the focus fell on tone not in the essay but rather, for instance, in the elegy? Would the tonal range in that case come, so to speak, preloaded and anticipated? Is it not a particular kind of tone that is expected in an elegy? Possibly – though the thought might be a little inattentive to how genre, mode, form, might be reconceived and recast.

More relevant here are the implications arising from the essay's coextensiveness *and* play with the temper of personality and the affect of persona. The essay is a genre whose tradition and rationale upholds the attitudinizing it potentiates, bears and sometimes dissimulates. To consider this capacitive potential of the essay and its unbounded hospitality to the personal and its pluralities, while also exploring tone, which is coextensive with attitude or sentiment, temper or mood, spirit or disposition, is to presuppose that extending critical attention to the question of 'tone and the essay' is to open up for renewed and rawer inquiry those larger questions about persona and the implied author, intention and affect, reception and interpretation, hermeneutics and phenomenology that might lead any critic to blanch. It is to rethink the histories of literary criticism to see how their repertoires on tone vary. But it can be supposed that whatever the approach, the essay can continue to be thought of as the genre-principle, the capacity field for expression of attitude (the essay's emergence with Montaigne and its consolidation in the eighteenth century – in other words, with modernity's greater scope for individuality and property – is no historical accident). The irruptions of tone, as the projection or apprehending of a writerly stance, whether real or dissimulated, seals the realization of that space.

In turn, this instigates thought about the political essay, since the talk *is* of attitude and disposition and hence of individual, essayistic takes on politics' generality-transforming agency. Ahead of considering this, some mention of three areas of reference concerning tone is needed. The first concerns specialist lexicons, dictionaries of literary terms that confirm the association between attitude and tone. Some of them helpfully quote passages and characterize their tone. One, for instance, quotes Marvell's 'To His Coy Mistress' and Herrick's 'To the Virgins, to Make Much of Time', saying they both handle the traditional carpe diem theme, but noting the 'passionate entreaty' of the former and the 'gentle persuasion' of the latter.[26] This again exposes how in trying to convey the tone of a piece, adjectives and adjectival phrases, with accompanying quotation, are what criticism typically deploys, in expectation that what they thereby characterize is consensually perceptible. What to make, however, of the possibility that broadly consensual understanding of the tone of a piece can fail to cohere? What is left of tone when the reader doesn't get it, or when readers disagree on its subtle inflections in the text? (*Parenthesis 4. What is at issue exactly, if one critic who is certainly not tone-deaf says of an essay that it has, say, 'a brassy tone' and another, not tone-deaf either, says that's not the way it comes across, not at all?*) (*Parenthesis 5. Is that phrase, 'tone-deaf literary critic', a contradiction in terms?*) And what is a text reduced to when its stance and tone are misread?

The stakes emerge when consulting *The Princeton Encyclopedia of Poetry and Poetics*. Tone may be taken, 'somewhat intangibly, as a quality of the text as a whole, or of a significant part of it'. But it can suggest 'a personal attitude, whether that of the author or of an implied speaker within the text'. I. A. Richards's *Practical Criticism*, the entry recalls, equated tone with the author's 'sense of how he stands towards those he is addressing'.[27] Rereading Richards on how tone's modulations can be miscued by the author and misapprehended by the reader is indeed fascinating. *Practical Criticism* is driven by awareness of that challenge to criticism and interpretation. And readers have their own tones in *reception*. They might not converge in regarding the tone discerned by another reader or critic, or ascribable to an author, character or text as determining or even recognizable. (*Parenthesis 6. Consider* Hamlet *as an allegory, a drama, of tonal disequilibrium. The Prince is wayward and changeable, the constructions put upon his inconsistent tone unsteadying to himself and the Danish court. The many tonal shifts across the conversations, apparitions, soliloquies and contestations are, quite literally, murderous. Outside the play the interpretations of Hamlet's character and the irresolvable questions they hinge on appear overdetermined by those tonal shifts and, in turn, the critical (dis)positions thereto.*) (*Parenthesis 7. Consider the person of whom it can be said that they unfailingly strike the right tone. It's unnatural. The supremely well-adjusted person who always strikes the right tone is, frankly, a creep.*)

This cues the second area of reference. It takes in canonical works of literary criticism (like Richards's) to rediscover what, *if anything*, they say of tone. Lack of space means entire shelves of relevant titles, not to mention various *explication de texte* methodologies, stylistics and more are bracketed here. Instead, the reference will return to W. K. Wimsatt and Monroe C. Beardsley. Since tone has been defined in the ways seen, their essays on the intentional and affective fallacies carry a distinct relevance if misapprehension of or overinvestment in the tone of a text is at issue. Of the two, 'The Affective Fallacy' is the more relevant, referencing tone in the midst of disdain for the kind of critic whose disposition is too visibly the enthusiast's:

Affective theory has often less a scientific view of literature than a prerogative – that of the soul adventuring among masterpieces, the contagious teacher, the poetic radiator, a magnetic rhapsodic Ion, a Saintsbury, Quiller-Couch, a William Lyon Phelps. … 'To be quite frank,' says Anatole France, 'the critic ought to say: "Gentlemen, I am going to speak about myself apropos of Shakespeare, apropos of Racine. …"' The sincerity of the critic becomes an issue, as for the intentionalist the sincerity of the poet.[28]

The tone of this mode of criticism, from which disaffiliation is urged despite its enchantments, is not difficult to perceive. It is the same tone Eliot deplored in his essay 'The Perfect Critic': the impressionistic tone, against which he would position an ethic of impersonality.[29] Yet the strongest countering understanding of tone is locatable in Maurice Blanchot's essay, 'The Essential Solitude':

> When we admire the tone of a work, when we respond to its tone as to its most authentic aspect, what are we referring to? Not to style, or to the interest and virtues of the language, but to this silence precisely, this vigorous force by which the writer, having been deprived of himself, having renounced himself, has in this effacement nevertheless maintained the authority of a certain power: the power decisively to be still, so that in this silence what speaks without beginning or end might take on form, coherence, and sense.
>
> The tone is not the writer's voice, but the intimacy of the silence he imposes upon the word. This implies that the silence is still *his* – what remains of him in the discretion that sets him aside. The tone makes great writers, but perhaps the work is indifferent to what makes them great.

This is quite different to conventional understandings of tone. The word, thereby, is re-lexicalized. From which, once that logic is countenanced, certain implications do follow.

> The writer we call classic – at least in France – sacrifices within himself the idiom which is proper to him, but he does so in order to give voice to the universal. … Then literature has the glorious solitude of reason ….
>
> When to write is to discover the interminable, the writer who enters this region does not leave himself behind in order to approach the universal. … The third person substituting for the 'I': such is the solitude that comes to the writer on account of the work. It does not denote objective disinterestedness, creative detachment. … The third person is myself become no one, my interlocutor turned alien; it is my no longer being able, where I am, to address myself and the inability of whoever addresses me to say 'I'; it is his not being himself.[30]

This reframes the semantics of tone. Not temper, disposition, stance; rather, the renunciative principle acting on attitude. It is that principle realized. It connects with the lead question to this essay, 'Around the theme of tone and the essay, what is an essay to do for tone?', which is shown up by Blanchot's perspective. Tone and doing: each is inscrutable to the other.

To clarify: it is not being urged that Blanchot's understanding of tone is necessarily the one to carry forward. What it counters is too entrenched to displace. In *Mute Speech*, for instance, Rancière quotes Charles Batteux's 1761 *A Course of the Belles Lettres* in support of a point he is making: 'The tone, or key, of the discourse is determined by the particular state and situation the writer is in at the time of writing'.[31] Countering this in turn while commenting on the *Phaedrus*, Rancière has the following observation on tone:

> Writing ... is the regime for the utterance of speech that undoes the order that this hierarchy establishes among the 'logical' capacities of beings. It undoes any ordered principle that might allow for the incarnation of the community of the *logos*. It introduces a radical dissonance in the communal symphony as Plato understands it, namely, as a harmony between the modes of *doing*, *being*, and *saying*. There are three elements in this harmony: the *occupations* of the citizens ...; their *ethos* ...; and the communal *nomos* – the *nomos* that is not only the law but also the community's *air*, its spirit in the sense of a fundamental tone, a rhythm vital to each and all.[32]

If writing is inherently political, bringing in a different tone to the pre-existing tone and 'air', the implications for the essayistic's retoning of the *nomos* are appreciable. This point is considered later, in order to consider here the third plane and refer to what essayists have themselves had to say about tone and the essay. In the space available, one book must suffice. It will be Brian Dillon's *Essayism*. It is revealing about how an essayist might perceive tone and articulate that perception.

Dillon defines essayism at the start of his book. Essayism is 'not the practice merely of the form, but an attitude to the form – to its spirit of adventure and its unfinished nature – and towards much else'.[33] He adds later that 'essayism is tentative and hypothetical, and yet it is also a habit of thinking, writing and living that has definite boundaries', imparting to him 'the sense of a genre suspended between its impulse to hazard or adventure and to achieved form, aesthetic integrity'.[34] The pun on *hazard* contrasts interestingly with the acknowledgement that 'sententiousness is one of the aspects of essayism'.[35] Tone is thereby open to both whimsy and pedagogical direction.

It is revealing to witness Dillon describing the tone of other writers. At one point, Susan Sontag is seen noting in her early diaries, which Dillon describes as having a 'brittle and ambitious' tone, that she's taken Hannah Arendt as a 'model' for the '"noble" tone she wants to adopt in some pieces'.[36] In regard to Cyril Connolly, he bids us to 'observe the tone'.[37] Elsewhere he notes that 'Connolly's tone is unthinkable today'.[38] (The remark could not have been made had not the 'air' of the *nomos*, then and now, not been available to confident apprehending.) He describes it as 'genuinely dismal, aspirantly aesthetic, knowingly parodic'.[39] Throughout, the lead resource characterizing tone appears to be the adjectival phrase (as indicated above, this is the case in other writing, not only Dillon's). The suspicion is that the more distinctively turned that adjectival phrasing is, the more persuasive the identifications can be believed to be. If the phrase is accompanied by the aphoristic, or at least a rounded statement, the seeming incontrovertibility of judgement is enhanced. In Sebald, for instance, Dillon observes 'a hallucinatory tone and mode of attention that was so intense it threatened always to undo itself'.[40] The qualities thus pointed out are assumed to thereby be established. Nomination suffices for ostension, suffices for proof. It is, it has to be said, a strange assumption.

But perhaps Dillon's most interesting passage about tone is the following: 'When I cannot find the right tone and tenor in my writing, when it seems that a measure of control is wanting, or rather a kind of control that might well lead me to a place where I can relinquish the same, I turn to the essays of Elizabeth Hardwick.'[41] Dillon follows this with a brief appreciation of Hardwick's prose. It is dependent on long quotation, leaving little space for Dillon's own analysis. After another quotation from Hardwick, he simply adds, 'Here/there are the outlines of the Hardwick I love'.[42] When he does attempt to more forensically characterize how this dynamic works, noting 'vexing repetitions and sly inversions', or observing canny comma placement, the result is competent enough even if it cannot lay claim to practical criticism's procedures.[43] Of course, it's not meant to. The use of copious quotation depends on trusting that the accumulation of textual selection will carry the argument. It's all very immediately felt and deeply charged, but what it comes down to is him saying, in another instance of his method, 'Listen for a spell to Hardwick as she describes …' – and another long quotation follows.[44] One sympathizes, but surely the point is rather that one might not.

Which brings the argument back round to politics. There not sympathizing, not compromising, is all part of the theatre. Here it is good to remember that Blanchot, the essayist who spoke as he did on tone and silence, retreated to a regime of reclusiveness. Yet he came out of it to co-write with Dionys Mascolo and Jean Schuster the Manifesto of the 121. This was the declaration signed by 121 French writers and intellectuals to protest the Algerian War. Clearly there are times when a different and *present* tone is needed.[45] And for an earlier example of tone's work in an essay on changing times, a well-known passage in Matthew Arnold's 'The Function of Criticism at the Present Time' still carries point and charge. Arnold has been discussing Edmund Burke's reconsideration in the essay 'Thoughts on French Affairs' of his long aversion to what the French Revolution enabled. Arnold pays Burke the tribute of saying, 'Burke is so great because, almost alone in England, he brings thought to bear upon politics, he saturates politics with thought. … His greatness is that he lived in … the world of ideas, not the world of catchwords and party habits'. And then, he says this:

> That return of Burke upon himself has always seemed to me one of the finest things in English literature, or indeed in any literature. That is what I call living by ideas: when one side of a question has long had your earnest support, when all your feelings are engaged, when you hear all round you no language but one, when your party talks this language like a steam-engine and can imagine no other, – still to be able to think, still to be irresistibly carried, if so it be, by the

current of thought to the opposite side of the question, and, like Balaam, to be unable to speak anything *but what the Lord has put in your mouth*. I know nothing more striking, and I must add that I know nothing more un-English.

For the Englishman in general is like my friend the Member of Parliament, and believes, point-blank, that for a thing to be an anomaly is absolutely no objection to it whatever.[46]

Arnold saying that 'That return of Burke upon himself might just be one of the finest things in English literature' might itself be one of the finest things in the English essay and in English criticism. It has a tone of generosity that offsets other occasions when Arnold might come across as a touch priggish.

The difficulty is that this kind of statement cannot overcome the doubts arising from any characterization of tone remaining vulnerable. As Derrida has it, 'A tone's distinctive signs are difficult to isolate, if they even exist in complete purity, which I doubt, above all in a written discourse.'[47] It all goes back to the problem of tone even being intersubjectively recognizable. So in the face of those difficulties what is there to say, in the end, about tone and the essay, the latter itself famously intractable to characterization? Nothing very clinching. To expect otherwise would go against what Rod Mengham notes in Montaigne and the essay's engendering: the 'allergic resistance to the conclusive, the legislative, the incontrovertible', the avoidance of 'the shape, texture, weight and odour of the Great Thought'.[48] So instead, a list of less-than-great thoughts. Seven quick points, then. They're tentative, 'without order or design' (as Montaigne had it), partly recapitulative of the above and partly anticipative of what could follow in a longer study.

1. This has not been a piece conventionalized to the form of a book chapter, but it is not thereby an essay either. It may have essayistic characteristics, but that is another thing entirely.
2. The essay is what everybody in the humanities fancies themselves credentialled to comment on. It's their stock in trade. Tone, meanwhile, is what everybody in and outside the humanities interprets every day in some form, but what very few dare to properly analyse. There is wisdom in desisting.
3. It would be possible to reconsider the relative merits of literary criticism's various schools and approaches on the basis of how much they have or haven't done on the question of tone, and on their amenability to doing more.
4. A phenomenology of tone would be a fine thing to explore. Or would it have to be a phenomenology of tone perception? Neither seems probable.[49]
5. Commentaries on the essay can tend to characterize it as tentative and unsystematic (as other chapters in this volume attest). This sometimes feels rather like the essay's propaganda about itself. What is noticeable about great essays is that for the most part they have remarkable discipline and admirable cohesion. It comes off as a different kind of rigour, abetted by tone's cohering. That *is* system, though of a different kind. And yet there is the essay's genius, too, for *anti-system*, for the tonal shifts confounding critique to present a

particularized challenge articulated by Derrida in regard to writing more generally: 'By what is a tone marked, a change or rupture of tone? And how do you recognize a tonal difference within the same corpus? What traits are to be trusted for analysing this, what signposting [*signalization*] neither stylistic, nor rhetorical, nor evidently thematic or semantic?'[50]

6. 'Around the theme of tone and the essay, what is an essay to do for tone?' Tone is not supposed to do anything, as Blanchot's and Rancière's observations have shown. Tone should rather just 'write itself', to use a phrase of Dillon's in relation to 'the "guiding metaphor"' for an essay, 'the figure unfolding and fulfilling its promise'.[51] But it remains hard to dispel thought on tone's crafting.

7. The worst kind of tone? Quite possibly archness of tone, which quite possibly again works worse effects on the essay than on other genres. (*Final parenthesis: parenthesizing can be as arch as it may be cogent; there is no second guessing the tones of reception, which may find it apt or, conversely, anomalous.*)

Just the one inconclusive line then, in the inevitability of unresolved relation. Tone and the essay: together, they're just too much.

Notes

1 Jacques Derrida, 'Of an Apocalyptic Tone Recently Adopted in Philosophy' [1981], trans. John P. Leavey, Jr, *Oxford Literary Review* 6, no. 2 (1984): 3–37 (6).
2 See Derrida, 'Of an Apocalyptic Tone', 7, 9. For related reflections on timbre, see also 36–7 of the introduction by Peter Fenves to the volume in which Derrida's essay was subsequently collected: 'Introduction: The Topicality of Tone', in *Raising the Tone of Philosophy: Late Essays by Immanuel Kant, Transformative Critique by Jacques Derrida* (Baltimore, MD: Johns Hopkins University Press, 1999), 1–48. In the volume, Derrida's essay appears as 'Of a Newly Arisen Apocalyptic Tone in Philosophy', 117–71. The translation remains Leavey's: see 168–9 for his note on the difference between versions.
3 Samuel Johnson, 'Tone', *A Dictionary of the English Language … in 2 volumes* (London: W. Strahan, 1755).
4 David Crystal, *The English Tone of Voice: Essays in Intonation, Prosody and Paralanguage* (London: Edward Arnold, 1975).
5 'The Rambler', *Wikipedia*, 28 January 2020, https://en.wikipedia.org/wiki/The_Rambler.
6 Samuel Johnson, *The Yale Edition of the Works of Samuel Johnson*, Vol. 2, *The Idler and The Adventurer*, ed. W. J. Bate, J. M. Bullitt and L. F. Powell (New Haven, CT: Yale University Press, 1963), 402, 404 (orig. *The Adventurer*, No. 81, 14 August 1753).
7 Samuel Johnson, *The Lives of the Poets: A Selection*, ed. Roger Lonsdale and John Mullan (Oxford: Oxford University Press, 2009), 342.
8 James Boswell, *The Life of Samuel Johnson*, ed. David Womersley (London: Penguin, [1791] 2008).
9 Ibid., 706.
10 Ibid., 688.
11 Ibid., 437.
12 Ibid., 448.

13 Michel de Montaigne, 'On Three Kinds of Social Intercourse', in *The Complete Essays*, ed. and trans. M. A. Screech (London: Penguin, 2003), 922–34 (933).
14 Matthew Arnold, 'The Study of Poetry', in *Essays in Criticism: Second Series* (London: Macmillan, 1913), 1–55 (41). See also Alexander Pope, 'An Essay on Criticism', in *The Poems of Alexander Pope*, ed. John Butt (London: Routledge, 1989), 143–68.
15 Joseph Addison, 'No. 62, Friday, May 11, 1711', in Joseph Addison and Richard Steele, *The Spectator*, ed. Donald F. Bond, 5 vols (Oxford: Clarendon Press, 1965), Vol. 1, 263–70 (265).
16 Samuel Johnson, *The Yale Edition of the Works of Samuel Johnson*, Vol. 4, *The Rambler*, ed. W. J. Bate and Albrecht B. Strauss (New Haven, CT: Yale University Press, 1969), 401 (orig. *The Rambler*, No. 143, 30 July 1751).
17 Brian Dillon, *Essayism* (London: Fitzcarraldo, 2017), 78.
18 Alexander Pope, 'The Dunciad: In Four Books' [1742–3], *The Poems of Alexander Pope*, ed. John Butt (London: Routledge, 1989), 750 (Book 2, verses 387–8).
19 Jonathan Swift, 'A Modest Proposal for preventing the Children of Poor People from being a Burthen to their Parents or the Country, and for making them Beneficial to the Public', in *Jonathan Swift*, The Oxford Authors, ed. Angus Ross and David Woolley (Oxford: Oxford University Press, 1984), 492–99.
20 *Oxford English Dictionary*, 'Tone', Oxford: Oxford University Press, 2020. See 'III: Senses relating to temper, style, or spirit', No. 9.
21 Ibid. The quotation from Naunton is the first listed in the section referred to.
22 The two exceptions are Viscount's Bolingbroke admission in a letter to Pope that 'The strange situation I am in, and the melancholly state of public affairs … drag the mind down, by perpetual interruptions, from a philosophical tone or temper,' and Lord Chesterfield's injunction to 'Take the tone of the company that you are in, and do not pretend to give it.' See Ibid., 'III: Senses relating to temper, style, or spirit', No. 8 and No. 9.
23 See Jacques Derrida, 'Demeure', in Maurice Blanchot/Jacques Derrida, *The Instant of My Death/Demeure*, trans. Elizabeth Rottenberg (Stanford, CA: Stanford University Press, 2000), 13–103 (20ff.).
24 See Louis T. Milic, 'Tone in Steele's *Tatler*', in *Newsletters to Newspapers: Eighteenth-Century Journalism*, ed. D. H. Bond and W. Reynolds McLeod (Morgantown: School of Journalism, West Virginia University, 1977), 33–45.
25 For further reflections on this theme, see Phillip Lopate, 'Introduction', in *The Art of the Personal Essay: An Anthology from the Classical Era to the Present* (New York: Anchor Books, 1994), xxiii–liv.
26 Karl Beckson and Arthur Ganz, *Literary Terms: A Dictionary*, 3rd edn (London: André Deutsch, 1990), 282–3.
27 *The Princeton Encyclopedia of Poetry and Poetics*, ed. Roland Greene, Stephen Cushman and others (Princeton, NJ: Princeton University Press, 2012), 1141–2; see also I. A. Richards, *Practical Criticism: A Study of Literary Judgement*, ed. John Constable (London: Routledge, [1929] 2017).
28 W. K. Wimsatt, Jr, and M. C. Beardsley, 'The Affective Fallacy', *The Sewanee Review* 57, no. 1 (1949): 31–45 (41).
29 See T. S. Eliot, *The Sacred Wood: Essays on Poetry and Criticism* (London: Faber and Faber, [1920] 1997), 1–13.
30 Maurice Blanchot, 'The Essential Solitude', in *The Space of Literature* [1955], trans. Ann Smock (Lincoln: University of Nebraska Press, 1982), 19–34 (27–8).

31 Jacques Rancière, *Mute Speech: Literature, Critical Theory, and Politics*, trans. James Swenson (New York: Columbia University Press, 2011), 45.
32 Ibid., 95.
33 Dillon, *Essayism*, 20.
34 Ibid., 21.
35 Ibid., 78.
36 Ibid., 96, 99.
37 Ibid., 57.
38 Ibid., 61.
39 Ibid., 57.
40 Ibid., 119.
41 Ibid., 47.
42 Ibid., 48.
43 Ibid., 52–3.
44 Ibid., 51.
45 See Kevin Hart, 'Foreword: The Friendship of the No', in Maurice Blanchot, *Political Writings 1953–1993*, trans. Zakir Paul (New York: Fordham University Press, 2010), xi–xxix.
46 Matthew Arnold, 'The Function of Criticism at the Present Time', in *Selected Prose* (Harmondsworth: Penguin, 1982), 130–57 (140).
47 Derrida, 'Of an Apocalyptic Tone', 6.
48 Rod Mengham, *Grimspound and Inhabiting Art* (Manchester: Carcanet, 2018), 200–1.
49 Or, conversely, the possibilities can already be glimpsed in contrasting turn-of-the-century studies like Douglas Hofstadter's *Le Ton beau de Marot: In Praise of the Music of Language* (New York: Basic Books, 1997); and Norman D. Cook's *Tone of Voice and Mind: The connections between intonation, emotion, cognition, and consciousness* (Amsterdam: John Benjamins, 2002).
50 Derrida, 'Of an Apocalyptic Tone', 6.
51 Dillon, *Essayism*, 104–5.

Chapter 7

WHAT THE PERIODICAL PRESS MADE POSSIBLE: WOMEN ESSAYISTS IN THE EIGHTEENTH CENTURY

Jenny Spinner

In 1939, editor Louis Wann heralded his revised edition of *Century Readings in the English Essay* as the most comprehensive single-volume anthology of essays ever published.[1] It was not only the scope of Wann's book that set it apart from other anthologies of the essay but also its attention to the development of the periodical essay, situated in a lengthy introduction to the book that spanned biblical, Greek and Latin origins through the early twentieth century. The eighteenth-century periodical essayists whom Wann includes – notably, Richard Steele (1672–1729) and Joseph Addison (1672–1719) – are all men, however, and the same men who would nearly always represent the eighteenth-century periodical essay in future historical surveys of the essay. While considerably slimmer and narrower in purpose, Carl H. Klaus and Ned Stuckey-French's *Essayists on the Essay: Montaigne to Our Time* (2012)[2] is a characteristic example of contemporary handling of the periodical essay that reflects the continued marginalization of both the periodical form and the absence of female writers. Addison and Samuel Johnson (1709–1784) – and an essay by William Hazlitt *about* the periodical essayists – are included in Klaus and Stuckey-French's book, but no women from that time period.

The fact that women have been left out of even the sparest attempts at including the periodical essay in histories of the essay is a matter of both deliberate and unintentional oversight, rooted in sexism, and it is an oversight that extends to nearly the whole of the essay canon. But the glossing over of the eighteenth-century periodical essay in histories of the essay is more complex. One of the reasons may be that, at least on the surface, the periodical essay seems so un-essayistic. Many of its prominent features – pseudonyms, invented personae, fictionalized observations and experiences presented as evidence in arguments about morals and manners – contradict popular conventions of the genre that have guided the form, mostly intact, from its early beginnings in the sixteenth century to the present time. Typically comprised of one long letter or a patchwork of letters to an invented editor from invented correspondents, even the format of the periodical itself presents challenges to scholars and editors searching for accessible, archetypal excerpts to offer to contemporary readers. Yet, the eighteenth-century essay occupies a significant moment in the essay's history and, for that reason alone, demands its inclusion. In the periodical, epistolary, travel and even poem essays of the day, writers from Eliza Haywood (1693–1756) to Alexander Pope (1688–1744) stretched the boundaries of what we now understand are, even insist upon as, key features of the essay, no matter which branch it occupies on the form's many-branched tree: explorations of the mind, some level of allegiance to fact and a sense of a real person behind the words. What makes inclusion of the eighteenth-century essay so essential to any study of the essay is the fact that it pushed and pulled at the genre's boundaries, sometimes both at once. And what makes it so essential to a rewriting of the essay's history to include the women it has long left out is that in pushing and pulling at these boundaries, the eighteenth-century essay created publishing opportunities for women essayists that had not been open to them in the past. In fact, the eighteenth century ushered in a contradiction of limitations and freedoms for the woman essayist that helped cement her place in the essay's history.

Prior to the eighteenth century, essayists like Michel de Montaigne (1533–1592), Francis Bacon (1561–1626), Sir William Cornwallis (1579–1614) and Abraham Cowley (1618–1667), to name just a few of the genre's significant contributors to date, first published their essays in books rather than as stand-alone pieces in periodicals. This was an enterprise requiring resources that even the most educated men of means, let alone women, did not have. Yet Margaret Cavendish (1623–1673), who had both the finances and the gumption to try her hand at Montaigne's brand of essay writing, defied the odds, all the while inviting criticism and censure for doing so. In the century that followed Cavendish's 1655 publication of *The World's Olio*, publishing limits of the essay in prior centuries gave way to new contexts, primarily by way of the eighteenth century's newly established newspapers and magazines. While few periodicals existed before the eighteenth century, by the year 1800, more than 2,500 titles had come and gone.[3] In his comprehensive history of the English periodical, Walter Graham points out that the eighteenth-century periodical attracted novice and struggling writers who 'seized the opportunity offered by the increasing numbers of newspapers, magazines, and reviews, and the consequent multiplication of readers'.[4] Significantly, the periodical served as an important repository for a new generation of women who were recognized for their value not only as members of the reading public but also as writers to help fill the pages of this glut of periodicals.

With the 1580 publication of his first volume of *Essais*, Montaigne had pushed the idea of a real person behind the essay, turning his words, however deliberate and stylized, into whispers in his readers' ears. In 'Of Smells', he writes: 'The close kisses of youth, savory, greedy, and sticky, once used to adhere to [my mustache] and stay there for several hours after.'[5] In 'Of Repentance': 'I speak the truth, not my fill of it, but as much as I dare speak, and I dare to do so a little more as I grow old.'[6] To read Montaigne was to know Montaigne, and to know him on a variety of subjects, from liars to cannibals. But the eighteenth century rejected, for both men and women, the type of authorial intimacy that marked Montaigne's work. Instead, the periodical essay employed a variety of techniques – primarily pseudonyms and literary personae – that functioned as rhetorical masks, allowing authors to move about and within the print culture without revealing too much of their private selves. It is women who most benefitted from this literary masquerade. In previous centuries, they had struggled to replicate Montaigne's personal voice – it was not their place, as women, to speak so freely of themselves, as themselves. They could do now do so behind these masks.

Significantly, though, an essay without an essayist – disguised as she was by pseudonyms and/or spread about a collection of personae – confounds our notion of what an essay is and can be, especially in our own time in which the essay invites a multiplicity of authentic (or at least authentically crafted) voices to speak genuinely from their multiplicity of lived experiences. In contrast, eighteenth-century essayists generally wrote not as or of themselves but from behind the props of invented characters whose genders were less tied to that of their authors and more to the purpose of their periodicals and the demographic of their readers. Addison and Steele, authors of two of the earliest and most influential periodicals of the century in both England and America, featured the characters of Isaac Bickerstaff (*The Tatler*) and Mr. Spectator (*The Spectator*) in their essays. In America, Benjamin Franklin (1707–1790) wrote as Silence Dogood for the *New-England Courant*; Washington Irving (1783–1859), as Jonathan Oldstyle for the New York *Morning Chronicle*. As they were for their male counterparts, invented characters were a popular device for women essayists as well, if not an essential one. Frances Brooke (1724–1789) appeared as Miss Mary Singleton for *The Old Maid*; Charlotte Lennox (1729? –1804) as The Trifler for *The Lady's Museum*; and American Judith Sargent Murray (1751–1820) as The Gleaner for her *Massachusetts Magazine* column of the same name. Haywood, perhaps the century's most well-known woman periodical essayist from this period, then and now, opted for a club of personae in *The Female Spectator*. Haywood's club of characters was similar to those made popular in earlier periodicals such as the *Weekly Review of the Affairs of France* by Daniel Defoe (1660–1731), and Addison and Steele's *Tatler* and *Spectator*. The difference was that Haywood's club was composed entirely of women: Mira, a happily married woman; Euphrosine, a beautiful young virgin; an unnamed widow; and the Female Spectator herself. Margaret Ezell points out that contemporary scholars tend to reduce the use of pseudonyms to evidence of women writers' 'intimidation' and to 'cast a pitying glance on the practice of using pseudonyms'.[7] But in an age in which the motives of the woman writer remained suspect, these pseudonyms and personae gave women essayists access to a literary marketplace that they may not otherwise have had.

Murray's persona, The Gleaner, is one example of how a woman essayist assumed an alternative gender as a fictive character in order to present views that were risky for a woman author to own outright. Over the course of three volumes, the intellectual Gleaner, quite radical for his time in his advocacy for women's rights and education, offers his perspective on topics ranging from female equality to federalism to friendship. In a surprising twist, though, Murray reveals in the concluding column of *The Gleaner* that Constantia, a female persona she had used in another column, is actually the author behind The Gleaner. Constantia explains to the reader that she posed as The Gleaner because of 'the indifference, not to say contempt, with which female productions are regarded'.[8] In some sense, Murray needed The Gleaner to authorize and ensure acceptance of her public voice. Nina Baym argues that 'in so using a man's voice, [Murray] was not ceding the territory of significant discourse to men or to male impersonators. Rather ... she was effectively distancing print discourse from a clearly assignable gender through successive convolution.'[9] Fortunately, because such convolutions were already normalized conventions in periodical essays, women like Murray were freer to participate in the genre.

The reliance on invented personae, anecdotes and other fictional techniques in eighteenth-century periodicals coincides with the rise of the novel in the period. Women writers were increasingly drawn to – and indeed guided to – the novel as a genre particularly suitable for women. Popular opinion held that 'ladies and novels belong together', a sentiment not always meant as a compliment.[10] Spun in its best light, this viewpoint suggested that women were 'superior in imagination and fancy', in its worst, that women were incapable of the intelligent, rational thought often associated with non-fiction discourse.[11] The domestic novels that so many eighteenth-century women wrote offered a compromise in that, according to Nancy Armstrong, they 'provided a way of talking about conflict and contradictions within the socio-economic sphere while remaining remote from that world'.[12] But while fiction writers 'could fall back on the myth of the creative muse for which they were merely instruments', essayists were left to represent their own ideas and thoughts without the label of *fiction* to serve as a buffer, not only in terms of an author's rationale for writing but also the readers' acceptance of that rationale in the way they responded to and consumed texts.[13] In that vein, the periodical essay's embrace of fictional elements gave women writers unprecedented opportunity to successfully participate in a genre that had been relatively closed off to them. While it might be easy to dismiss the fictional elements in eighteenth-century periodical essays as aberrations in the genre's long history, the heteroglossic layering found in women's essays during this time reveals a truth every much as real as non-fiction prose created under less restrictive circumstances.

The invented letter was one popular technique they employed. Fortunately, the letter was already familiar and approved territory for women. As Virginia Woolf later wrote, looking back at a rich history of women engaged in letter-writing, 'the art of letter-writing is often the art of essay-writing in disguise ... such as it was, it was an art that a woman could practice without unsexing herself.'[14] A woman who wrote letters betrayed no social conventions, at least in the act of composition, for letter-writing, considered practical and unpresumptuous, belonged in woman's domain. Ruth Perry notes: 'Letters were the one sort of writing women were supposed to do well. Literate women wrote letters even in the days when they put pen to paper for no other reason, and so the public was ready to buy volumes of letters published under a woman's name.'[15] In addition to the letters found in periodicals, collections of letters enjoyed enormous popularity in the eighteenth century. Two years before her death, Lady Mary Wortley Montagu (1689–1762) presented her collection to an English clergyman, telling him in an enclosed note that the letters should 'be dispos'd of as he thinks proper'.[16] In bequeathing her letters to another, Montagu avoided the presumptuous act of publishing them herself. That she did not get rid of them herself also indicates she hoped they would be published. Readers enjoyed this common trope anyway, the idea that they were being given a glimpse into a private life that was never intended for them, even if it likely was.

The successful efforts of eighteenth-century essayists like Murray and Montagu to ensure their literary success again illustrates the restrictive freedoms that women essayists from this period had to navigate. In writing as in life, the eighteenth-century woman was expected to reflect the virtues that defined her place in and domination of the feminine sphere. Already the wings of the Angel in the House that Woolf would reference two centuries later in 'Profession for Women' were rustling about the woman writer, demanding domestic excellence, purity and self-sacrifice.[17] In the context of an ideology so restrictive that Woolf would say the only solution was to kill that angel, the most successful women essayists in the eighteenth century managed both to entertain and to tap into this higher calling that was foisted upon them. For instance, the essays of Lady Mary Chudleigh (1656–1710), particularly her *Essays upon Several Subjects in Prose and Verse* (1710), offer mostly didactic musings on such abstractions as death, fear, grief, self-love and friendship; yet, Chudleigh's voice in these essays is strong and engaging. Anna Laetita Barbauld (1743–1825) also authored several notable essays collected in *Miscellaneous Pieces in Prose* (1773), which she published with her brother John Aikin.

Still, Woolf's Angel persisted. In the new heyday of the periodical, which offered essayists instant gratification from timely publication, any incentive beyond that satisfaction – fame or fortune or even 'domestic and private' goals, in the spirit of Montaigne – proved tricky, especially for women.[18] Many women attempted to circumnavigate a break in the social code by divorcing themselves from a share in the profits, stressing purer motivations for writing.[19] In that regard, the woman writer found acceptance in literary society long before the professional woman writer who *needed* her profits. By publishing under either a male or female pseudonym, many women could also distance themselves from the business of writing. For example, as Robert Halsband notes, Montagu often used a pseudonym to spurn 'the vulgarity and commercial taint of practicing the trade of authorship'– an essential move because Montagu was not only a woman but also an aristocrat.[20] For women essayists, nowhere is the attempt to cater to ideological demands more apparent than in the opening numbers of their periodicals and in the prefatory pages of their books. While both male and female writers commonly explained their motivations for writing in these spaces, women largely honoured their prescribed roles as women here, nearly always addressing their own virtue as well as the moral intent of their works. This strategy, not always or even necessarily disingenuous, was designed to garner public approval, if not forgiveness, for any presumption brought on by the act of publishing, not to mention the unfeminine desire to achieve fortune and/or notoriety through that publication. In the presumably male editor's advertisement to Montagu's posthumous collection *Letters Of the Right Honourable Lady M---y W---y M---e: Written, during her Travels in Europe, Asia and Africa* (1763), the editor presents Montagu's letters to the public as a monument to her memory – an acceptable plea for prosperity given that it is offered second-hand – and, more notably, as a model of virtue for women who read it: 'As to those female readers, who read for improvement, and think their beauty an insipid thing, if it is not seasoned by intellectual charms, they will find in these Letters what they seek for, and will behold in their author, an ornament and model to their sex.'[21]

It is Haywood's introduction to her readers, however, which presents the deepest complexities, even as it seems, like Montagu's advertisement, to follow most closely the accepted practice of the day, highlighting the potential of the writing to serve as a moral guide for women readers. Notably, Haywood's periodical, *The Female Spectator* (1744–6), is thought to be the first periodical written by a woman for women. In the first issue, Haywood, writing as the Female Spectator, introduces herself to her readers as an older woman and one who, in her youth, had 'run through as many scenes of vanity and folly as the greatest coquet of them all'.[22] Because of these experiences, 'added to a genius tolerably extensive, and an education more liberal than is ordinarily allowed to persons of my sex', Haywood writes that her essays might be 'both useful and entertaining to the public'.[23] While Haywood's stated intention sounds similar to that of the *Tatler* or *Spectator* or any number of extant periodicals, it differs from them in one crucial way: Haywood was a woman writing for other women, and, moreover, one who confessed to having strayed from the ideal. The growing conservatism marching eighteenth-century England towards the Victorian Age made it impossible for Haywood, once a popular writer of amatory fiction, to be anything other than a voice of moral authority in her essays. At least on the surface, that is precisely what she was.

While women's essays during this period reflect the tensions their authors must have felt as a result of the demands of a patriarchal society and the possibility of censure from critics and readers who had the power to ensure, or deny, success, there are admissions of literary ambitions as well. For example, Hester Lynch Thrale Piozzi (1741–1821) hopes that her wish to make public the private reflections based on her travel journals is not perceived as 'too daring'.[24] She also states that the primary purpose of her reflections, unlike that attached to Montagu's letters, is to amuse, not to instruct. Lennox promises to do both, to be 'as witty as I can, as humorous as I can, as moral as I can, and upon the whole as entertaining as I can'.[25] Significantly, Brooke says that she knowingly adds her own work to 'the present glut of essay papers' because she *must* write: 'it may seem an odd attempt in a woman, to think of adding to the number; but as most of them, like summer insects, just make their appearance, and are gone, I see no reason why I may not buzz amongst them a little'.[26] For Mary Wollstonecraft (1759–1797), not surprisingly, the act of writing, and in particular, writing about oneself, is not only a compulsion but a right: 'A person has a right ... when amused by a witty or interesting egotist, to talk of himself when he can win our attention by acquiring our affection.'[27]

The 'Preface to the Reader' that appears in Murray's *The Gleaner* (1798) demonstrates Murray's struggle to balance society's rationale for her writing with her own and emblematizes the rhetorical ping-ponging found in the prefaces of so many women writers in the eighteenth century. While Murray, in her opening remarks, humbly excuses herself from any promise of moral instruction, insisting that she is incapable of influencing anyone 'whose understandings have passed the age of adolescence,' she still admits a desire to be useful: 'nor will I deny a pleasing hope plays about my heart, suggesting a possibility of my becoming in some small degree beneficial to those young people, who, just entering the career of life, may turn, with all the endearing ardour of youthful enthusiasm, to a *New Book,* to an *American Author*.'[28] That appeal to her American readers' nationalism softens the bolder, and certainly less feminine, intent of her writing, to which she also freely admits: 'My desires are, I am free to own, aspiring – perhaps presumptuously so. I would be distinguished and respected by my contemporaries; I would be continued in grateful remembrance when I make my exit; and I would descend with celebrity to posterity.'[29] At the end of her preface, Murray also admits a desire to make money from the venture, hoping that her writing will bring her fame and fortune.[30] Yet again, though, Murray ties her quest for financial gain to virtue, softening any lack of femininity associated with such a desire with a carefully placed reference to the infant daughter she says she desires to support.[31]

Like Murray, some women found acceptance for their work by emphasizing their maternity and/or their femininity, embracing and sometimes even exploiting the very limitations imposed upon them. Wollstonecraft, for instance, did not write under a pseudonym when she published *Letters Written during a Short Residence in Sweden, Norway, and Denmark* (1796), but her prose was certainly affected by the period's pervading ideologies regarding women and the subsequent fallout from her prior writings in which she argued against them. The letters in Wollstonecraft's book – addressed to Gilbert Imlay, Wollstonecraft's estranged lover and father of her child – chronicle her journey through Scandinavia. By then Wollstonecraft was well known – both celebrated and despised – for her revolutionary ideas about the necessary equality between men and women that she had outlined in *A Vindication of the Rights of Women* (1792). According to Mary Heng, by the time Wollstonecraft reached Scandinavia, she recognized that her 'social position and political ostracism placed constraints upon her rhetorical power'.[32] So, Wollstonecraft deliberately buried her feminist philosophies in 'observations about flowers and household details',[33] emphasizing her femininity, particularly her maternity, in order to return public sentiment to her favour. Wollstonecraft-the-social-critic never completely disappears from the book, but she is often brushed aside in favour of Wollstonecraft-the-astute traveller-and-mother. In 'Letter XIX', an essay essentially about capital punishment, Wollstonecraft interrupts her narrative with a self-derisive exclamation – 'Still harping on the same subject, you will exclaim – How can I avoid it, when most of the struggles of an eventful life have been occasioned by the oppressed state of my sex' – before returning to 'the straight road of observation.'[34] Heng contends that Wollstonecraft's strategy was a success for the book won 'grudging praise from [Wollstonecraft's] critics' and 'became a well-thumbed favorite for Wordsworth, Coleridge and Shelley'; stylistically, too, it 'sowed the seed for the Romantic period.'[35] By the end of the eighteenth century, professional women writers like Wollstonecraft had made some strides towards acceptance, even if they had to manipulate that acceptance through various rhetorical strategies, as Wollstonecraft did. Their success was also due in large part to the efforts of the Bluestockings, a group of well-known women writers, among them Elizabeth Robinson Montagu (1720–1800), Hester Chapone (1727–1801), Fanny Burney (1752–1840), Elizabeth Carter (1716–1806), Catherine Talbot (1721–1770) and Hannah More (1745–1833), all of whom were heralded for their virtue as much as their intellect. These women 'brought into public notice the idea that respectable women could study, write, and publish'[36] – as long as they remained respectable.

Indeed, with a handful of exceptions, the essays of women from this period present views about gender roles similar to those promoted in mainstream periodicals and magazines, largely dominated by men. For example, in 'The Trifler Number II,' Lennox argues for the return of female influence over men by way of 'prudence' and 'reserve' in women.[37] In short, The Trifler suggests that the permissiveness of British society makes it difficult for women to wield power over men: 'It has been observed, that there is no country in the world where women enjoy so much liberty as in England, and none where their sway is so little acknowledged.'[38] In Haywood's periodical, the Female Trifler often witnesses poor decisions and judgement on the part of women, and calls them out for this behavior. In one such scene, she observes a woman wearing a 'mischief-making' extended hoop skirt who becomes tangled up in a flock of sheep, causing an enormous ruckus in the street.[39] The Female Trifler bemoans the fact that such bad decisions – in this case, vainly adhering to a ridiculous fashion trend – make all women look bad. She ends the essay with a plea for better judgement: 'Let us all then endeavor to follow nature as closely as we can, even in the things which seem least to merit consideration… and I am very sure we shall be in no danger of incurring the censure of the world, for having a *bad taste*.'[40]

But as much as Haywood's later periodical essays do seem to cater to a more conservative age, they also betray glimpses of a writer whose rhetorical strategies countered the acceptable, and the expected. In fact, the Female Spectator's introduction of herself also highlights one of the ways in which women writers of periodical essays adapted the periodical essay to their own project, even if such moves were so subtle as to be barely distinguishable from the writings of their male counterparts. For example, unlike male-authored periodicals, which typically marginalized women's voices, presenting them as evidence of women's follies or including them only in service to the voices of the male editors, *The Female Spectator* offered its female readers the perspective of a community of voices who shared in the authority of advice-giving. Lennox does this as well in the *The Lady's Museum*, where multiple voices offer various perspectives in the components that make up the periodical, including The Trifler essays, a serial novella, poems and unconventional lessons in geography, history and philosophy. While the topics of this collective are all suitable to feminine readers, they operate, as Kathryn

Shevelow notes, 'not as the directives or criticism of an authoritative persona or persona-group' but from a 'collection of various different types of expression'.[41]

In reality, whether representing one voice or a collective, women had little authority in the world, at least beyond the domestic world that had been assigned to them. That left them little room to move freely between private and public spheres as their male counterparts did. As much as the essay genre celebrates interiority, it also relies on interaction with a world beyond oneself (even if only by way of wide reading and education), and eighteenth-century women often found that world closed off to them. Three important exceptions are the travel letters of Montagu (*The Turkish Embassy Letters,* 1763), Piozzi (*Observations and Reflections Made in the Course of a Journey through France, Italy, and Germany,* 1789) and Wollstonecraft (*Letters Written in Sweden, Norway and Denmark,* 1796), not only for their occupation of spaces outside the home but also for their documentation of travel in a century in which women were discouraged from doing so. Women who did travel were expected to do so in the company of male chaperones. But the fact that they were merely along for the ride also gave them a freedom that men traveling on commission or patronage or some other duty did not have. As Jan Robinson contends in her study of women travellers, free from such restrictions, women could 'afford to be more discursive, more impressionable, more *ordinary*'[42] than their male counterparts. In that sense, travel essays allowed women to take hold of the essay in ways other literary forms did not. Indeed, the voices of these women travellers betray an intimacy not found in the essays of the periodical writer, or even, for that matter, in travel writings by men of the period.

Outside of travel essays, though, women had difficulty moving freely about public spaces. For the periodical writer, the most significant of such spaces was the coffeehouse, where, as Baym notes, 'the typical essayist picked up his tattle and did his spectating'.[43] Since 1652, when a former Turkish slave had opened the first establishment in London, the coffeehouse had become a London institution. George Carver explains: 'It was here that the bulk of what were middle-class readers was to be found, for the most part, deep in the discussion not of a commercial idealism, not of commonplace details of personal business, but of the social, intellectual, and moral movements of time.'[44] Earlier periodicals such as the *Coffee-House Mercury* (1690) and *Humours of the Coffee-House* (1707), as well as the *Tatler,* relied on the coffee house not only as a symbolic setting that epitomized and centralized (male) London life but also as a real source of material and a place to be hawked to patrons who shared the various periodicals to which the establishment subscribed. Each coffee house attracted a different clientele, but one consistent factor was that women, especially respectable women, rarely participated in coffeehouse life. As a whole, Helen Berry explains, 'custom militated against women speaking in public places, or exhibiting studious habits by reading periodicals on their own in coffee house'.[45] In order to gather material then for their own work, many women periodical essayists turned to the one place where they already had access: their own feminine sphere. While women essayists at this time did not write exclusively about this sphere – Montagu authored a political periodical titled *The Nonsense of Common-Sense* (1737–8) – they did seem to understand marketplace demands and the fact that readers were far more interested in, and accepting of, commentary on the domestic and social activities of women than on their intellectual or travel pursuits.

Well into the eighteenth century, periodical essayists were pre-occupied with the same argument that had occupied intellectuals for four centuries: the 'woman question'. Addison and Steele vigorously engaged in this debate about the proper role for a woman, what she was made of, capable of and meant to do, and they used a receptive audience of new women readers to peddle their perspectives. In 1711, two years after the publication of the first issue of the *Tatler*, in which Steele had promised to offer 'entertainment to the fair sex',[46] he reveals a more serious purpose in his role as editor of the *Spectator*. He writes that because women 'compose half the world, and are by the just complaisance and gallantry of our nation the more powerful part of our people', he will dedicate a significant portion of his periodical to helping 'lead the young through all the becoming duties of virginity, marriage, and widowhood'.[47] Shevelow calls the didacticism in periodicals like Addison and Steele's 'double-edged', oscillating between two rhetorical levels of persuasion at work, one that is 'overt', the other, 'covert'.[48] Shevelow's argument is significant not only to our understanding of the multiple forces that influenced how women *read* periodicals but also how they *wrote* them. Certainly, such learned responses directly and indirectly influenced women's decisions as writers as well, shaping the private and public knowledge they were able and willing to access and expose.

In 'Of Essay Writing', eighteenth-century philosopher David Hume celebrates the essay as a bridge between the learned and conversable worlds, the latter of which he posits as the domain of women. A learned intellectual but one who values imagination and emotion, characteristics increasingly associated with women, Hume portrays himself in this essay as a 'Kind of Resident or Ambassador from the Dominions of Learning to those of Conversation'.[49] For him, 'the great Defect of the last Age' has been the 'Separation of the Learned from the conversible [*sic*] World', and he thus encourages women to 'accustom themselves a little more to Books of all Kinds' in order to improve the quality and nature of conversation, which he argues provides material to the world of learning.[50] To some extent, the periodical of the age meant to do just that: to make public the private conversation of women, and in the process, to reform it. Many male writers, believing as Hume did, denigrated women's conversation as 'tattling'. Shevelow contends that male 'idle conversation' was deemed respectable, even important; its feminine equivalent was considered trivial, perhaps vicious. Men met in public, women in private. Men 'conversed', women 'tattled'.[51]

Be that as it may, tattling by and about women sold periodicals and gave women an opportunity to write from a sphere that they knew better than anyone else. Historically, male writers still dominated and controlled the conversation about women, as well as the spaces in which it took place, and it is imperative to read the works of eighteenth-century women essayists in that context. But it is also important to read their works against that context, to understand how they navigated various gender and genre demands in order to publish essays. Ultimately, the essays by women from this period illustrate how they were able to turn limitations into advantages in the quest to be seen and heard as writers. That alone makes it worth taking notice of the eighteenth-century essay, its place in the history of the essay and, perhaps most significantly of all, the inclusion of women in that history, who have too long absent from it. It is hard to imagine our so-called 'golden age of women essayists' without this earlier century in which women worked so hard amid so many restrictions to say as much as they did.[52]

Notes

1. Louis Wann, ed., *Century Readings in the English Essay*, rev. ed. (New York: Appleton-Century-Crofts, 1939), ix.
2. Carl H. Klaus and Ned Stuckey-French, ed., *Essayists on the Essay: Montaigne to Our Time* (Iowa City: University of Iowa Press, 2012).
3. James E. Tierney, 'The Study of the Eighteenth-Century British Periodical: Problems and Progress,' *Papers of the Bibliographical Society of America* 69 (1975), 165–86 (183).
4. Walter Graham, *English Literary Periodicals* (New York: T. Nelson & Sons, 1930), 14.
5. Michel de Montaigne, 'Of Smells', in *The Complete Essays of Montaigne*, trans. Donald M. Frame (Stanford, CA: Stanford University Press, 1958), 228–9 (228).
6. Montaigne, 'Of Repentance', in *The Complete Essays of Montaigne*, 610–21 (611).
7. Margaret Ezell, *Writing Women's Literary History* (Baltimore, MD: Johns Hopkins, 1993), 35.
8. Judith Sargent Murray, *The Gleaner* (Schenectady, NY: Union College Press, [1798] 1992), 804.
9. Nina Baym, 'Introduction', in Judith Sargent Murray, *The Gleaner* (Schenectady, NY: Union College Press, 1992), i–xx (xiii).
10. Jane Spencer, *The Rise of the Woman Novelist: From Aphra Behn to Jane Austen* (Oxford: Blackwell, 1986), 4.
11. Robert Halsband, 'Women and Literature in 18th Century England,' in *Woman in the 18th Century and Other Essays*, ed. Paul Fritz and Richard Morton (Toronto: Samuel Stevens Hakkert, 1976) 55–71 (64).
12. Nancy Armstrong, 'The Rise of Feminine Authority in the Novel', *Novel: A Forum on Fiction* 15, no. 2 (1982): 127–45 (133).
13. Shirley Marchalonis, 'Women Writers and the Assumption of Authority: The *Atlantic Monthly*, 1857–1898,' in *In Her Own Voice*, ed. Sherry Lee Linkon (New York: Garland Publishing, 1997), 3–26 (9).
14. Virginia Woolf, 'Dorothy Osborne's Letters', in *The Second Common Reader*, ed. Andrew McNeillie (San Diego, CA: Harcourt, 1986), 59–66 (60–1).
15. Ruth Perry, *Women, Letters, and the Novel* (New York: AMS, 1980), 68.
16. Robert Halsband, 'Introduction to Volume I', in *The Complete Letters of Lady Mary Wortley Montagu*, ed. Robert Halsband, Vol. 1 (Oxford: Clarendon Press, 1965), xiii–xxi (xvii).
17. Virginia Woolf, 'Professions for Women', in *The Death of the Moth and Other Essays* (San Diego, CA: Harcourt Brace, 1970), 235–42.
18. Montaigne, *The Complete Essays of Montaigne*, 2.
19. In his 'Note to the Reader,' Montaigne writes: 'This book was written in good faith, reader. It warns you from the outset that in it I have set myself no goal but a domestic

and private one. I have no thought of serving you or my own glory' (*The Complete Essays of Montaigne*, 2).
20. Robert Halsband, 'Introduction', in *Lady Mary Wortley Montagu: Essays and Poems and* Simplicity, *a Comedy*, ed. Robert Halsband and Isobel Grundy (Oxford: Oxford University Press, 1976), 3–5 (3).
21. Lady Mary Wortley Montagu, *Letters of the Right Honourable Lady M-y W-y M-e*, Vol. 1 (London: T. Becket, 1763).
22. Eliza Haywood, *The Female Spectator*, 7th ed., Vol. 1 (London: H. Gardner, 1771), 2.
23. Ibid., 3.
24. Hester Lynch Thrale Piozzi, *Observations and Reflections Made in the Course of a Journey through France, Italy, and Germany*, Vol. 1 (London: A. Strahan and T. Cadell, 1789), iv.
25. Charlotte Lennox, *The Lady's Museum*, Vol. 1 (London: J. Newbery and J. Coote, 1760), 1.
26. Frances Brooke, *The Old Maid*, rev. ed. (London: A. Millar, 1764), 1.
27. Mary Wollstonecraft, *Letters Written During a Short Residence in Sweden, Norway, and Denmark* (London: J. Johnson, 1796).
28. Murray, *The Gleaner*, 14.
29. Ibid.
30. Ibid.
31. 'I am solicitous to obtain an establishment in the bosom of virtue – I would advance my claim to the sweetly soothing strains of just applause; and I would secure for myself; and for my infant daughter, (should our future exigencies require it) thy amity and thy patronage' (ibid.).
32. Mary Heng, 'Tell Them No Lies: Reconstructed Truth in Wollstonecraft's *A Short Residence in Sweden*', *The Journal of Narrative Technique* 28, no. 3 (1998): 366–87 (367).
33. Ibid., 380.
34. Mary Wollstonecraft, 'Letter XIX', in *Letters Written During a Short Residence in Sweden, Norway, and Denmark* (London, 1796), 207–18.
35. Heng, 'Tell Them No Lies,' 383–4.
36. Sylvia Harcstark Myers, *The Bluestocking Circle: Women, Friendship, and the Life of the Mind in Eighteenth-Century England* (Oxford: Clarendon Press, 1990), 11.
37. Charlotte Lennox, 'The Trifler Number II', in *The Lady's Museum*, Vol. 1 (82–161): 84.
38. Ibid., 82.
39. Eliza Haywood, *The Female Spectator*, 7th edn, Vol. 3 (London: H. Gardner, 1771), 161.
40. Ibid., 162.
41. Kathryn Shevelow, *Women and Print Culture: The Construction of Femininity in the Early Periodical* (London: Routledge, 1989), 182.
42. Jan Robinson, ed., *Unsuitable for Ladies: An Anthology of Women Travellers* (Oxford: Oxford University Press, 1994), xii.
43. Nina Baym, 'Introduction', in Judith Sargent Murray, *The Gleaner* (Schenectady, NY: Union College Press, 1992), i–xx (xii–xiii).
44. George Carver, ed. *Periodical Essays of the Eighteenth Century*, Essay Index Reprint Series (Freeport, NY: Books for Libraries Press, 1970), xxi.
45. Helen Berry, ' "Nice and Curious Questions": Coffee Houses and the Representation of Women in John Dunton's *Athenian Mercury*,' *The Seventeenth Century* 12, no. 2 (1997): 257–76 (261).

46 Richard Steele, 'No. 1, Tuesday, April 12, 1709', *The Tatler*, Vol. 1. (London: J. Johnson, 1808), 11–18 (12).
47 Richard Steele, 'No. 4, Monday, March 5, 1711', *The Spectator* (London: J. Johnson, 1806), 21–7 (26).
48 Kathryn Shevelow, 'Fathers and Daughters: Women as Readers of the *Tatler*', in *Gender and Reading: Essays on Readers, Texts, and Contexts*, ed. Elizabeth A. Flynn and Patrocinio P. Schweickart (Baltimore, MD: Johns Hopkins University Press, 1986), 107–23 (108).
49 David Hume, 'Of Essay Writing', in *Essays: Moral, Political, and Literary*, ed. Eugene F. Miller, rev. ed. (Indianapolis, IN: Liberty Classics, 1985), 533–7 (535).
50 Ibid., 534.
51 Kathryn Shevelow, *Women and Print Culture: The Construction of Femininity in the Early Periodical* (London: Routledge, 1989), 97.
52 Cheryl Strayed and Benjamin Moser, 'Is This a Golden Age for Women Essayists?' *New York Times Sunday Book Review*, 12 October 2014, 27.

Chapter 8

OTHERNESS AND THE ESSAY IN THE PACIFIST WORK OF VERNON LEE

Rachel Baldacchino

The essay is often linked to the lack of an elevated standpoint, the generation of circularity, digression, doubt, a sense of trial, incompleteness and provisionality, what Robert Musil identifies as its possibilitarian spirit.[1] When writing is about the essay, it is often about endless possibility, the proliferation of capability. The references here are endless and their nature familiar, perhaps too familiar. So the essay is not one voice but 'differences, polarities, and oppositions'.[2]

It is not a linear path but a circuit marked by 'interruptions, detours, returns, blocked exits, mishaps and serendipity',[3] and knows no endpoint but is 'a form of vagrancy, open to accident, and none too sure of its destination'.[4] The essay defers endpoint by 'sauntering from one topic to the next'.[5] It pursues a position but sooner or later abandons and leaves us with a sense of having witnessed not so much the event of a 'unifying concept' but its appearance and subsequent scattering.[6] The essayistic possibilitarian may be described as an undular moving back and forth – 'the essay must lap us about', writes Virginia Woolf.[7] It may also be described as a will to error. Hence we often speak of the essayistic as 'accident'. Walter Pater, for example, calls the essay a 'dexterous availing oneself of accident and circumstance'.[8] Claire de Obaldia says the essay finds and founds itself 'by accident', by 'losing the thread', by 'randomness'.[9] And Michel Foucault calls the essayistic will to error, accident and hesitation, 'the game of truth', a 'test' by which one laps about constant change.[10] If it ever hints at 'authority or authenticity', we expect the essay to quickly buffer 'all responsibility with regard to what is after all only "tried out"' and closer to the '"as if"' of fiction'.[11] The essayistic pull to doubt is what G. Douglas Atkins, drawing on John Keats, calls the 'negative capability' of the possibilitarian, which means that beyond the pleasures of essayistic sways, laps and saunters, is the heart of the matter – the commitment to ever stay with uncertainty and therefore ever puncture truth.

All these elements of essayistic style constitute what David Russell calls the essay's deliberate opposition to violence by means of which 'the practice of non-coercive tact' can take place.[12] Russell's concept of tact encapsulates all faces of the essayistic possibilitarian that, taken together, become the stylistic ways in which the essay engages with conflict without resort to head-on collision. The tactful essay then, to Russell, makes use of elements of 'possibilitarian' style to package conflict within non-persuasive, non-argumentative rhetoric that prioritizes sensuous experience – what Woolf called 'a basking, with every faculty alert in the sun of pleasure'.[13] Conflict is engaged with transitionally, allowing for it to appear and disappear depending on the aptitudes of subjective readerly disposition. The tactful essay, according to Russell, does conflict by lending itself to the 'liberalism of overhearing'.[14] This means that the essayistic space offers 'interesting objects for contemplation' but not 'propositions to the understanding' that follow in the manner of rhetoric understood as stating your case and proving it.[15] The essayistic space of propositions seeks to drive home a point whereas the one that overhears gives 'somebody something they might use'.[16]

According to this line of thought, self and other meet better this way. Theorists of the essay such as Catherine Anne Wiley and Atkins, in fact, have called this essayistic space of non-coercive tact, a space of radical empathy or radical otherness.[17] The argument here is that when the reader is not being cornered into the confines of one voice, trajectory or argument, they are in a better place to enter into what Wiley describes as 'a space in which a kind of radical empathy takes place'.[18] According to Wiley, this experience of radical empathy comes to be because 'the readers' psyche is invaded, widened, and sensitized' only gently, fluidly and 'by imperceptible degrees'.[19] The reader of the essay becomes truly receptive 'to the presence of the other within the self' and 'the self within the other' if the textual experience is sensuous and subtle, and certainly not by the poundings of persuasion.[20]

So what happens to an essay when it takes all elements of possibilitarian style and just about turns them upside down? What happens to the essayistic space when it does not stray afield, when it does not wander? What happens when it is driven by an agenda and when it seeks a position within a controversy? Does it then violate the possibility of a radical empathy or a radical otherness? In other words, does an essay which seeks above all else to persuade compromise the relational space? The tools for thinking about these questions are scattered if not unavailable because essay theory largely distils from the Montaignian, antirhetorical essay. It trains us to unpack the politics of style of an essay that builds on pleasure, personality and play but leaves us little with which to push the boundaries of an essayistic space that operates the politics of persuasion. We have cultivated measured patience for the essayistic as a space of 'glimpses, suggestions', 'delightful half-apprehensions' and 'hints of the innermost reason in things, the full knowledge of which is held in reserve'.[21] We are equipped to trace an essay's 'ambulatory and fragmentary' prose to find where its invisible structures sublimate into ethical gestures.[22] But we are critically uneasy with essays of 'tight rhetorical composition' and 'factual arguments'.[23] So much so that we find ourselves firmly attached to a moral continuum of thinking about the essayistic ideal as a neutral space of delay and divergence.

Between the essay of fragments, 'dialogical circularity and polyphonic play' as a virtual space of non-violence and the essay of aims and persuasions is what

I call here the essay of demand – a practice of otherness rooted in the rhetorical tradition.[24] 'Demand', understood in the Romanic sense, is as an authoritative command for obedience that operates hierarchically. The Latin origins of demand, *dēmandāre*, however, are anchored in trust.[25] To demand in this sense is to entrust 'responsibility to a person or an organization for something valued or important'.[26] The passing of trust to another person or community initiates where one's limits of action have been reached and the other must be called upon to step in. It is the passing of responsibility to an other deemed to be within a better sphere of action. Rhetorics of persuasion or argumentative closure hereby become vehicles of care for the other.

The early twentieth century saw if not the birth of the essay of demand its unprecedented proliferation. This came about as a direct response to heightened military tensions in Europe after the Boer War when organized pacifist campaigning was largely centred around textual communities of resistance in which the pacifist essay played a pivotal role.[27] By the outbreak of the First World War, the European Peace Movement consisted of up to 190 peace societies that generated twenty-four periodicals in ten different languages mostly operating the essayistic. This is also when author and pacifist activist Vernon Lee's (1856–1935) essayism took a pronounced political turn. During this period, Lee, a prominent essayist within decadent and aesthetic movements of the fin de siècle, responded to the urgent demands of conflict by means of persistent public intellectual activity particularly in the form of essayistic contributions to the pacifist cause. Much of Lee's early work (1880–90) – art historical essays, philosophical dialogues, fantastic tales, imaginary portraits and novels – carries the stamp of aestheticism. But from the 1890s through to the First World War, Lee travelled in England meeting socialist and radical leaders, observing working conditions and the life of social movements and wrote on economics, politics and international affairs. This saw her passage from aesthete, woman of letters and recluse of the British expat community of Fiesole in Tuscany to active writing agent of global pacifist movements. In the years preceding the First World War, Lee wrote against the Boer War, the Italo-Turkish War and the Balkan War and translated work by fellow pacifists based in other countries. In 1911, she joined a group of European intellectuals who formally opposed the British invasion of Agadir and went on to form the Union of Democratic Control (UDC). At this point, Lee's mastery of the essay[28] resulted in a steady presence in newspapers and periodicals with liberal and pacifist leanings that were the most efficient infrastructure for the mass circulation of pacifist politics.[29] The essay's concise and analytical framework fit the urgency of the pacifist agenda and ensured the rapid dissemination of ideas in as many public spheres as possible.

Lee's essays on war are firmly rooted in the demands of the UDC, one of the largest pacifist organizations of the First World War.[30] The broad-ranging scope of the essayistic community that grew around the UDC was to generate 'discussion of the causes of war and means of its avoidance in the future'.[31] Beyond this, however, the writing was anchored around the demand for a lasting peace settlement. Lee's essays on war forgo stylistics of roaming and confession, circulation, lyricism or intimate account to hone in on lobbying the British government for a post-war settlement based on four cardinal points: first, that any transfer of land can only take place if it has the approval of the population concerned; second, that Great Britain always needs the Parliament's approval before signing treaties, undertakings or any other form of arrangements; third, that its foreign policy should not aim at establishing power for the Allies but at international agreements for peace; and fourth, that the country should propose a drastic reduction of armaments of all belligerent powers through the nationalization of manufacture and the control of the exportation of arms.[32]

The demand for a lasting peace settlement is the core 'idea' that travels through Lee's essays on war. It is the 'very life blood, at once the occasion' and the driving force of the text.[33] Ideas, as Atkins explains, have a different life in the essay than they do in fiction or poetry.[34] While in fiction or poetry, the idea is generally present indirectly and transcends the text by means of, say, storyline, character or metaphor, in the essay it occupies centre stage. It never transcends its function as an idea and therefore never transcends the text. Indeed, in 'The Modern Essay', Woolf also suggests that what the essay lacks in space, time and narrative plot, it gains in the urgent cultivation of attachment to an idea.[35] The attachment to the demand for a lasting peace settlement steeps Lee's essayistic space in urgency, charge and requirement. It binds the essay to the historical impulse that George Orwell had described as the desire 'to see things as they are, to find out true facts and store them up for the use of posterity'.[36]

In essay theory this generally qualifies as harbouring 'a narrative of aims'.[37] It is a dabbling with the binaries of conflict and a veering towards the erudite article that pretends 'everything is clear, that its argument is unassailable, that there are no soggy patches, no illicit references' and 'no illegitimate connections'.[38] If as an essayist, I am 'giving you my insights in the form of an argument', then 'I am trying to persuade you, trying to use my linguistic power in order to change your views.'[39] This side of the essayistic, as Kuisma Korhonen puts it, 'has so often been connected with violence' and is the principal reason why Lee's essays on war, and the pacifist essay in general, are inaccessible and understudied.[40]

At this point, it is reasonable to mention that critical scholarship is slowly starting to show interest in the essay as a site of 'political and ethical prises de position'.[41] I have encountered loose acknowledgements of the valuable forms of the essay that flourish amid conglomerations of people who feel that truth is being obscured, 'but that the public would support them if only they knew the facts'.[42] Russell, for example, argues that the essay is the literary form that tempered 'the strident cords of Victorian political controversy' and responded 'to the period's mounting social pressures' of 'urbanization, industrialization, population growth and political reform'.[43] Réda Bensmaïa locates the rise of the essay during the inter-war period of the twentieth century in the need to generate spaces of 'common purpose and mutual cooperation' that sustained a sense of community.[44] And to Korhonen, the essay typically grows with the need to 'bridge the different sectors of a fragmented society' and 'to return to the foundations of our ethical and aesthetic beliefs'.[45]

Despite these nods to 'other' forms of the essay that sprout when communities are fragmented, change is ripe and truth is at stake, there is little to go by to 'save' the essayistic style of demand. If we measure by most available reflections on essayistic practice, the pacifist essay continues to fail for meddling with position and thereby sinking in the pitfalls of dogma and authoritarianism that tainted the newspaper article in periods of heightened political tension. Consider, for example, Cynthia Ozick's category 'genuine' essay versus the 'poetaster' or 'fake' essay.[46] Ozick's genuine essay reflects and gives insight on the interior life, is 'closer in kind to poetry' and 'rarely' has 'polemical, or sociopolitical use'.[47] On her side of the 'fake' is the essay that is less concerned with 'language', 'mood' and 'temperament' and engages with issues of the moment, thereby taking 'temporary advantage of social heat'.[48] The main consequence of such hierarchies of essayistic style is critical infatuation with the essay as personification of the secret self and critical confusion about any other manifestation of the essayistic, particularly if it shows remote signs of political agenda and overt demand.

To consider the life of demand in the essayistic space, I take off from Vernon Lee's 'Après la mêlée' ('After the Battle'), published in the *New Statesman* in 1915.[49] 'Après la mêlée' takes issue with Romain Rolland's calls for a peace settlement anchored in 'human sympathy'.[50] In his 'Au-dessus de la mêlée' ('Above the Battle'), also published in 1915, Rolland calls for communities of workers and thinkers to rise 'above the battle' and come together around 'the calming influence' of a 'wide human sympathy' to 'build higher and stronger … the walls of that city wherein the souls of the whole world may assemble'.[51] In 'Above the Battle', Rolland anchors his vision of an interconnected world in the belief that people harbour an indestructible instinct towards communion, what Rolland was also known to refer to as the 'oceanic feeling'.[52] Rolland's hopes for sustainable relational practices across borders emanate from what he explains as 'the feeling of the 'eternal' (which can very well be not eternal, but simply without perceptible limits, and like oceanic, as it were)'.[53]

Lee is known to have cherished a deep respect for Rolland's work and was apparently 'deeply moved' by Rolland's articles in the *Journal de Genève*.[54] So much so that in 1915, Lee wrote to Swedish feminist writer and journalist Ellen Key, proposing Romain Rolland for the Nobel Prize in Literature as 'the only man above the struggle'.[55] It is evident, however, that in 'Après la mêlée', Lee takes marked distance from Rolland's call to 'the calming influence' of a 'wide human sympathy' by theorizing what it means to relate to the world in psychological terms. The essay draws on Lee's understanding of the perceptible limits of sympathy to demonstrate that there is no such thing as an archaic mode of understanding that one taps into, that brings people together. 'There remains', she writes in 'Après la mêlée', 'another question: not merely *au-dessus* (where M. Rolland has soared in seraphic solitude), but *après* the universal scuffle, butchery, devastation and accompanying scientific and literary billingsgate'.[56] Lee's approach to what happens 'après the universal scuffle', in other words, her approach to collaboration post-conflict in 'Après la mêlée', dissects the limits of human sympathy by turning to 'the process of Association' and how this process, which lies 'at the bottom of all our mental operations', determines how we relate with the world.[57] The essay builds a case for the problem of sympathy, first by describing the mental process of association that interferes with our perception of unfamiliar others and, second, by drawing on two anecdotes to demonstrate the workings of association. Association is 'the investing of one object, having characteristics of its own, with the characteristics of some other object: the pushing aside, in short, of reality to make room for the fictions of imagination or memory'.[58] It is the reason why, particularly in times of extreme violence, people show limited capacity for surpassing personal standpoint and sympathizing with the unfamiliar other.

The two anecdotes of 'Après la mêlée' are the story of an old relative of Lee's and the story of a Belgian refugee of war. The old relative refuses to walk or drive along one road because her dog had perished there. The Belgian refugee plays Bach and Beethoven but 'will not hear of playing Strauss or even Brahms' because in his mind they are associated 'with the idea German, modern German' and with that idea 'is inextricably associated a change of pulse, a flush, a rising of gorge, a blaze of eye and contraction of muscle, a flood and flame of loathing and of wrath'.[59] Both examples, argues Lee, are 'cases of subjective' and 'of emotional association' and both demonstrate how people struggle to set aside their inner and emotional associations.[60] This in turn impacts their subsequent relationship to others and demonstrates that states of otherness are overlaid and limited by personal configurations and the social, political and cultural forces of place and time. The anecdotes brought in to demonstrate the mental processes of associations broaden the debate around sympathy. They illustrate the inextricable association between other things, happenings and people with 'our inner states, passions or moods' and with changes in the 'brain, nerves, heart and other viscera' and how these changes are an integral part of how individuals and communities relate to the world, particularly in times of escalating conflict.[61]

Based on this argument, Lee demands another relational stance for philosophies of peace and indirectly also another relational style for the essay. 'Après la mêlée' appeals for a relational model based not on sympathy but on the distancing gesture of learning to calibrate between 'objective' and 'subjective association', which allows 'things and happenings irrespective of ourselves' to emerge from 'the fluctuating, warm, violent chaos' of subjective desire.[62] In the essay *Proteus*, this process is described as a nurtured habit of weighing between 'ourself' which is 'what we feel … moods, passions, efforts, hope and fear, liking and disliking' and 'the not-ourself', which is 'other persons as well as other things'.[63] 'Après la mêlée' imagines the process as a form of unveiling, a lifting off of Maya's veil over 'the network of our own temporary and accidental, individual or collective, but always inner and emotional associations'.[64]

Where 'Après la mêlée' deals with describing association, its language, mood, temperament, stringent structure and heavy syntax serve the argument. The anecdotes afford a degree of humour and hint at the personality behind the essay, but we are never made to forget they are there to serve the case on the problem of sympathy. These are stylistic choices that stage non-violent relationality in the distance afforded by rhetorics of persuasion, argumentation and demand, and which also necessarily challenge the position of the essayistic possibilitarian as the only harbinger of non-violent tact.

The problem of sympathy versus the case for calibration that Lee raises in 'Après la mêlée' runs through several of her essays on war where it remains a site of conflict. 'As regards intensification and enlargement of sympathy', Lee writes in the essayistic notes to her war drama *Satan the Waster* (1918), 'that has doubtless taken place towards those fighting on one's own side', but 'it is more than counterbalanced by the addition of anger and vindictiveness' towards the enemy.[65] On the other hand, in 'War the Grave of All Good' (1915), Lee finds value in symbolic acts of togetherness, in hushing 'our hopes of victory and desire for vengeance' and sitting 'quiet and decent, as in a dark church where you feel your neighbour's presence without seeing it'.[66] Ultimately, however, she argues that progress requires something more than 'brotherly understanding'.[67] 'War the Grave of All Good' articulates this 'something more' as 'that great virtue', which 'enables men to see themselves and others dispassionately' and 'without which there is no room for the highest activity and imagination and sympathy which puts us in another's place'.[68]

Another site of conflict in Lee's essays on war is posed by the difficult demand of naming the unnamable – 'the idea German, modern German'. The essays on war repeatedly 'name' the German other as does, for example, 'Bismarck Towers' published in the *New Statesman* in 1915.[69] 'Bismarck Towers' warns the Allies against the pursuit of divisive militarism that only serves to extend the violent legacy of Bismarck that the Allies claim they are out to destroy. The essay turns Bismarck's Towers into a universal symbol of divisive politics that must be countered by a 'delicate, sympathetic perception' that embraces the 'anxiety' of getting 'inside a German's skin' and thinking 'a German's thoughts'.[70] Similarly, in 'The Lines of Anglo-German Agreement' (1910), Lee invites British radicals to 'step in imagination on to the German side' and consider the 'dangers threatening Germany on the part of England'.[71] This naming practice serves all aspects of the original demand – the attachment to an ideal of peace born of an inclusive and lasting settlement. But it also recovers the name of the other from exclusion. It honours, at least symbolically, the demand of the excluded other and in so doing invades 'imaginary spaces that provoke actual violence.'[72]

To Atkins, such sites of tension hover above an essay's attachment to an idea and play a crucial role. Korhonen similarly suggests reading through the closed confines and linearity of the propositional argument, 'which will always remain insufficient' and reaching 'the horizon towards which the author's thinking is moving'.[73] This means moving through 'words or propositions' towards where the larger structures of significance, 'thematizations and hermeneutical circles are trying to cover up some rupture'.[74] Both Atkins and Korhonen suggest that if we look closely, rhetorics of persuasion are necessarily accompanied by a sense of split afforded by historical context but also by the impartibility and communicability of language. Korohnen further argues that locating this rupture or tension within the essay of argumentative closure would mean locating its potential as a site of ethical encounter.

The tension that clouds an argument signals what Byung-Chul Han calls 'the negativity of the Other', which may allow us to begin articulating the nature of this ethical encounter.[75] Han argues that the language that names the unnamable 'interrupts the Same'.[76] In this sense, the essayistic tension wrought by arguments of a binary nature and the repetition of the name of the excluded other are sources of interruption that hold the potential of becoming a transformative force in the essay of demand. Lee's essays on war demonstrate an exacting loyalty to the sharp corners of the demand for a lasting and inclusive settlement. The tension ensuing from the inescapable confines of an argument is not allowed to dissipate in say stylistic techniques, which allow for a sensuous experience of embodied connection, the creation of symbolic space in which self and other dissipate. Outside this dynamic of struggle in which 'a negative other' interrupts the hegemony of 'the same', no insight is possible. The struggle at the site of conflict, that place where the negativity of the other's name and demand seep through, is thereby open to expansion, intensification, to becoming something else.

This is an important claim for the rhetoric of persuasion and argumentative closure as vehicles of care. In one of the most illuminating definitions of care available to me, Maurice Hamington describes it as the 'complex intertwining' of caring habits, caring knowledge and caring imagination.[77] Under caring knowledge, Hamington places processes which, like the coming together of an argument or the contours of persuasion, lead to insight or understanding. Understanding fuels our practices of interaction: the caring habits. It also fuels our capacity to understand situations beyond our immediate experience: the caring imagination. If we use 'insight' for Hamington's 'understanding', we may better capture the essence of the transformation being described here. Insight, writes Han, 'in an empathic sense is also transformative. It produces a new state of consciousness.'[78] Engaged with as insights that hold the power to move our sense of being in the world, the rhetoric of persuasion does not simply deliver an argument for logical understanding, and political demands are not just acts of public speech. In this manner, Hamington's 'caring knowledge' or Han's 'insight' or Lee's 'demand' may perform more than the linear movement from problem to solution. Knowledge, insight or argument may act transformatively by placing the parties concerned 'in an entirely different state of being'.[79] Viewed as such, the paradigm of rhetoric may also bind with the caring ethos.

The essayistic space that harbours difficult demands is a space which recreates what Hannah Arendt in *On Revolution* calls that 'worldly space between men where political matters and the whole realm of human affairs are located'.[80] Arendt calls this space, a space of 'distance' and a space that is bound by a 'talkative and argumentative interest in the world'.[81] It is a space that is bound by the 'wearisome processes of persuasion, negotiation, and compromise, which are the processes of law and politics'.[82] There are many moments in Lee's essays on war where the rhetoric of persuasion is given pride of place, where the reader is invited out of the bloodshed into something 'more methodically thought out and more prosaically set forth'.[83] This space of prosaic method is a worldly space where political matters take centre stage, where language is oriented towards argument, critique and counter-critique and asks us to re-evaluate what a productive state of otherness incorporates. In this space, individuals take responsibility for each other in terms of negotiation, persuasion, dissuasion, argument, comparison, demand, statement or claim. The discursive sociality of an essay built around these elements constitutes a strong form of attachment that Arendt calls a space of 'sheer human togetherness' where life is 'with others and neither for or against them'.[84]

So as ineffective as the pacifist essay was at drawing widespread validation, deterring the course of aggressive post-war settlements and subsequent escalations of violence, it challenged official accounts of truth in ways that must be recognized as a key contribution not only to wartime culture, and not only 'to the development of global organization after 1914', but also to how we may come to think of the ethical life of the argument in the essayistic space.[85] To overlook this form of the essay for being concerned with the public rather than the personal self, for forming part of an argumentative sociality rather than a contemplative one and for its attachment to an idea is to inhibit the essayistic possibilitarian. To maintain that polemical intent necessarily subordinates style to the treatment of an argument and therefore violates expectations of essayistic style, long held to be fluidity, proliferation of capability and focus on the secret self, is to deny more overtly political forms of the essay access to life on the back-benches of literary scholarship – on many fronts, a serious loss.

Notes

1 Robert Musil, *A Man without Qualities: A Sort of Introduction and Pseudo Reality Prevails*, Vol. 1 (New York: Vintage, 1996), 10.
2 G. Douglas Atkins, *On the Familiar Essay: Challenging Academic Orthodoxies* (New York: Palgrave Macmillan, 2009), 34.
3 Atkins, *On the Familiar Essay*, 54–5.
4 David Russell, 'A Literary History of Tact: Sociability, Aesthetic Liberalism and the Essay Form in Nineteenth-Century Britain' (PhD diss., Princeton University, Princeton, New Jersey, 2011), 105.
5 Claire de Obaldia, *The Essayistic Spirit: Literature, Modern Criticism, and the Essay* (Oxford: Clarendon Press, 1996), 2.
6 Ibid., 25.
7 Virginia Woolf, 'The Modern Essay', in *The Common Reader, First Series*, ed. Andrew McNeillie (London: Harcourt, 1986), 211–22 (216).
8 Walter Pater, *Appreciations: With an Essay on Style* (London: Macmillan, 1910), 115.
9 De Obaldia, *The Essayistic Spirit*, 2.
10 Michel Foucault, *The History of Sexuality: The Use of Pleasure* (London: Penguin, 1998), 9.
11 De Obaldia, *The Essayistic Spirit*, 2–3.
12 Russell, 'A Literary History of Tact', xii.
13 Woolf, 'The Modern Essay', 223.
14 Russell, 'A Literary History of Tact', 36.
15 Ibid.

16 Ibid.
17 See Catherine Anne Wiley, '"Warming me like a Cordial": the Ethos of the Body in Vernon Lee's Aesthetics', in *Vernon Lee: Decadence, Ethics, Aesthetics*, Palgrave Studies in Nineteenth Century Writing and Culture, ed. Catherine Maxwell and Patricia Pulham (New York: Palgrave Macmillan, 2006), 59; and Atkins, *On the Familiar Essay*, 153.
18 Wiley, '"Warming me like a Cordial": The Ethos of the Body in Vernon Lee's Aesthetics', 59.
19 Ibid.
20 Ibid.
21 Walter Pater, *The Works of Walter Pater Volume 5: Appreciations: With an Essay on Style* (Cambridge: Cambridge University Press, 2011).
22 De Obaldia, *The Essayistic Spirit*, 2.
23 Kuisma Korhonen, *Textual Friendship: The Essay as Impossible Encounter from Plato And Montaigne To Levinas And Derrida* (New York: Humanity Books, 2006), 31.
24 Korhonen, *Textual Friendship*, 21.
25 *Oxford English Dictionary*, s.v. 'demand, v.', 8 November 2019, [www.oed.com/view/Entry/49582]
26 *Oxford English Dictionary*, s.v. 'entrust, v.', 8 November 2019, [www.oed.com/view/Entry/63012]
27 Notable pacifist essayists of the First World War are Jane Addams, Emily Greene Balch, Mary Sheepshanks, Alice Hamilton, Clara Zetkin, Roxa Luxembourg, Helena Swanwick, Bertrand Russell, Romain Rolland, Alfred Hermann Fried, Norman Angell and Henri La Fontaine.
28 Throughout the seventy-nine years of her life, Vernon Lee published widely and in various genres but considered herself primarily an essayist. In her introduction to the novella *Ottilie*, she explains how the essay allowed her to run along 'the beaten roads of history' and 'be tied up in the narrow little stable of fact', but also how it allowed her to work with 'a certain half imaginative perception of the past', as well with 'a certain love of character and incident and description' and 'a certain tendency to weave fancies about realities' that she associated with fiction writing. (Vernon Lee, *Ottilie: An Eighteenth Century Idyl* (London: T. Fisher Unwin, 1883), 8). Her early essays were predominantly art historical essays on Ancient Greece, the Middle Ages and the Renaissance. These essays are driven by an eagerness to bring to art-historical criticism a style of writing that is guided by the sensory faculties rather than the language of theory and methodology. Eventually, through her essays on empathy, Lee also became one of the first British authors to mobilise the concept of *Einfühlung*, 'feeling into', that emerged in late nineteenth-century German aesthetics to define our relationship with aesthetic objects.
29 Vernon Lee's essays on war were published in *The Nation*, the *New Statesman*, *Jus Suffragii*, *The Westminster Gazette* and the *Labour Leader* between 1910 and 1918. *The Nation* was a staunchly pacifist literary and political weekly, which later merged with the prestigious literary weekly *Athenaeum* to become *The Nation and Athenaeum*. By the outbreak of war, it was an established pacifist institution involved in the dissemination of translations of European pacifist texts. It published authors of diverse radical and liberal leanings, such as prominent member of the UDC, H. N. Brailsford, the economist, J. A. Hobson, Labour Party member, Harold Laski and most members of the Bloomsbury Group. The *New Statesman* was not strictly speaking a pacifist institution. It was founded by the Fabian Society in 1913 to publish research

in Fabian areas of interest such as the eradication of poverty and the establishment of a modern political economy based on equal pay and the welfare state. When the First World War broke out, the *New Statesman* published pacifist opinion but was mostly a site of conflicting views. *Jus Suffragii* (from Latin 'the right of suffrage') was a monthly journal of the International Woman Suffrage Alliance published in English and French. *The Westminster Gazette* was a London-based liberal weekly. *Labour Leader*, also a London-based weekly, ran until 1987. During the First World War, it was published by the National Labour Press Limited that was run by the Independent Labour Party, which was the pacifist faction of the Labour Party.

30 The advocates of the UDC were politicians and pressure groups lobbying their cause across ranks of government, as well as non-combatant artists, writers and intellectuals running a complex propaganda campaign on various social, political and cultural platforms.
31 Vernon Lee, *Peace with Honour: Controversial Notes on the Settlement* (London: Union of Democratic Control, 1915), note on book cover.
32 The four cardinal points of the UDC are published on the opening pages of all of the organization's publications, such as Lee's *Peace with Honour* (1915).
33 Atkins, *The Familiar Essay*, 31.
34 Ibid., 34.
35 Woolf, 'The Modern Essay', 223.
36 George Orwell, *The Collected Essays, Journalism and Letters of George Orwell Volume II: My Country Right or Left 1940–1943*, ed. Sonia Orwell and Ian Angus (Penguin: Middlesex, 1971), 316.
37 Russell, 'A Literary History of Tact', 77.
38 William H. Gass, *Habitations of the Word* (New York: Simon & Schuster, 1985), 26.
39 Korhonen, *Textual Friendship*, 25.
40 Ibid., 21.
41 Réda Bensmaïa, *The Barthes Effect: The Essay as Reflective Text* (Minneapolis: University of Minnesota Press, 1987), xiv.
42 George Orwell, 'Introduction to British Pamphleteers 1' (1948) as cited in Ralph S. Pomeroy, '"To Push the World": Orwell and the Rhetoric of Pamphleteering', *Rhetoric Society Quarterly* 17, no. 4 (1987): 365–412 (391).
43 Russell, 'A Literary History of Tact', iii.
44 Bensmaïa, *The Barthes Effect*, xiv.
45 Korhonen, *Textual Friendship*, 34.
46 Cynthia Ozick, 'She: Portrait of the Essay as a Warm Body', in *Essayists on the Essay: Montaigne to Our Time*, ed. Carl H. Klaus and Ned Stuckey-French (Iowa City: University of Iowa Press, 2012), 151–8 (151).
47 Ibid.
48 Ibid.
49 Vernon Lee, 'Après la mêlée', The *New Statesman*, 19 June 1915, 249–51.
50 Romain Rolland, *Au-dessus de la mêlée* (Paris: Paul Ollendorf, 1915).
51 Romain Rolland, *Above the Battle* (Chicago: The Open Court Publishing Company, 1916), 52.
52 Romain Rolland gives the most definite description of the oceanic feeling in a letter to Sigmund Freud of 5 December 1927. Cited in William B. Parsons, *The Enigma of the Oceanic Feeling: Revisioning the Psychoanalytic Theory of Mysticism* (New York: Oxford University Press, 1999), 173–4.
53 Ibid.

54 Vineta Colby, *Vernon Lee: A Literary Biography* (Charlottesville: University of Virginia Press, 2003), 299. Lee also dedicated one of her most important pacifist texts, *The Ballet of the Nations* (1915), to Rolland.
55 Ibid.
56 Lee, 'Après la mêlée,' 249.
57 Ibid., 250.
58 Vernon Lee, *Juvenilia, Being a Second Series of Essays on Sundry Aesthetical Questions* (London: T. Fisher Unwin, 1887), 45.
59 Lee, 'Après la mêlée,' 250.
60 Ibid., 250–1.
61 Ibid., 250.
62 Ibid.
63 Vernon Lee, *Proteus: Or the Future of Intelligence* (London: Kegan Paul, 1925), 13.
64 Lee, 'Après la mêlée,' 251.
65 Vernon Lee, *Satan the Waster: A Philosophic War Trilogy with Notes and Introduction* (London: John Lane, 1920), xix.
66 Vernon Lee, 'War the Grave of All Good', *The Labour Leader XII*, 28 October 1915, 3.
67 Ibid.
68 Ibid.
69 Vernon Lee, 'Bismarck Towers', *New Statesman*, 20 February 1915, 481–3.
70 Ibid., 482.
71 Vernon Lee, 'The Lines of Anglo-German Agreement', *The Nation* suppl. 1–2, 10 September 1910, 838–9.
72 Byung-Chul Han, *The Expulsion of the Other* (Cambridge: Polity Press, 2018).
73 Korhonen, *Textual Friendship*, 43.
74 Ibid., 69.
75 Han, *The Expulsion of the Other*, 2.
76 Ibid., 4.
77 Maurice Hamington, *Embodied Care: Jane Addams, Maurice Merleau-Ponty, and Feminist Ethics* (Urbana: University of Illinois Press, 2004), 12.
78 Han, *The Expulsion of the Other*, 4.
79 Ibid.
80 Hannah Arendt, *On Revolution* (London: Penguin Books, 1990), 86–7.
81 Ibid.
82 Ibid.
83 Lee, *Satan the Waster*, xvii.
84 Hannah Arendt, *The Human Condition* (Chicago: University of Chicago Press, 1998), 180.
85 Grace Brockington, 'Translating Peace: Pacifist Publishing and the Transmission of Foreign Texts', in *Publishing in the First World War*, ed. Mary Hammond and Shafquat Towheed (New York: Palgrave Macmillan, 2007), 55.

Chapter 9

MARGINS AND MARGINALITY: JEAN GENET AND THE QUEER ESSAY

Aaron Aquilina

In opening up the idea of the 'queer essay', one must, in a manner quite conventional and not very queer at all, begin by defining what is meant by the term. Quickly, however, any attempt at defining the 'queer essay' reveals itself not only as difficult because of the term's invisibility throughout the essay's tradition, but also self-contradictory, for to define the queer would be to limit or even eradicate its very queerness. This chapter thus aims to address this taxonomic term, taking Jean Genet's essays as primary examples, while leaving open the possibility of queering the act of taxonomization itself.

Let us then begin with taxonomy, which emerges as rather crucial if the categorization of 'queer essay' is indeed a speciation of the essay in a manner similar to how 'the homosexual [is now considered] a species'.[1] In, for instance, Tracey Chevalier's *Encyclopedia of the Essay* – here taken as an exemplary attempt of division and classification – the term 'queer essay' evades any sort of dedicated entry. Perhaps aptly so, we are left to suppose that it lies instead somewhere 'in between' those 'subjects that must obviously have entries, and those that must obviously not',[2] and thus assume that our present term lies cryptically hidden somewhere beneath, or perhaps even beyond, Graham Good's 'four main categories of the essay – formal, national, individual, [and] periodical'.[3] As is made abundantly clear in the *Encyclopedia*, these four can be split up indefinitely: there are American essays, autobiographical essays, critical essays, familiar essays, film essays, historical essays, humorous essays, journalistic essays, medical essays, review essays, philosophical and religious essays, satiric essays, essays that are chapters, ones that are character sketches, memoirs, dialogues, letters, sermons, diary entries or newspaper columns, and essays that disappear into apothegms and aphorisms. I am leaving out many, but – and especially when one takes Chevalier's compendium as reflective of numerous traditional and canonical theories of the essay – there is, categorically, no such thing as 'queer essay'.

Context, however, should not be ignored. Had the *Encyclopedia* (and other attempts like it) been published today, more than two decades on, an entry on the queer essay would very likely be ineluctable, especially in the wake of recent research carried out by thinkers such as David Lazar, Rachel Blau DuPlessis or Nancy Mairs. As such, Chevalier's omission may be considered as one more historical than absolute. Nonetheless, and despite the inevitable institutionalization of the queer through academic research, the queer's status as that which is slippery, always between borders, remains unlocatable even in such totalizing works, and thus, even if included, would always be absent by its very nature. Even when successfully considering the queer, one necessarily fails.

With the queer essay's failure to appear *as such* – and the concept of 'failure' shall be returned to later – we begin to have at hand a sketched yet negative definition of the queer essay, one already echoing contemporary discussions around queer subjectivity: it must not be generic; it must not have form; it belongs neither to a single individual nor to one nation; it belongs to no period and has no history. It is not visible, not discussed and is nowhere to be found, neither on the public pulpit nor in one's private papers. As Genet remarks, 'no tradition comes to the aid of the pederast, or bequeaths him a system of references – except by omissions.'[4] The species of the queer essay, therefore, is not even to be considered a species – and perhaps nor would it want to be.[5]

Of course, this is not to say that there has been no contemporary intervention in understanding the conceptual links, ones seemingly intrinsic, drawn between queerness and the essay. At the forefront of this is Lazar's (now well-known) 'Queering the Essay', in which he digs into the genus, genre and gender of the essay as that which resists 'distinctions, discrete categories … and subdivision'.[6] He writes:

> Genre is a category after all. So is gender. And the gender category difficult to characterize by normative standards is queer. The genre category difficult or impossible to characterize, the essay, is also queer. The essay is the queer genre. … [Moreover,] queer theory defines queer as a continuing instability in gender relations that undermines the traditional binary of gender, replacing it with indeterminate, transgressive desires. The desire of the essay is to transgress genre.[7]

Indeed, the difficulties of defining the 'queer essay' rest on both pegs, encompassing not only the necessary elusiveness of a concept such as queerness, but also the looseness and transgressions of the essay form itself.

These are not unrelated; understanding the essay as that which undermines genre simultaneously paves the way towards a queer perspective of the essay. Among other writers who view the essay as similarly resistant to both generic and gendered categorization – such as DuPlessis and Mairs (these noted also by Lazar), or Roland Barthes, Heather Hewitt, Christine Ozick and perhaps even Michel de Montaigne himself – one may name Brian Blanchfield, whose essay 'On Housesitting', in *Proxies*, parallels the problematics of the essay form as ones related to the self beyond gender, the structural boundaries of which one may temporarily inhabit but never fully possess. Through residing within borders that can only be transitory, Blanchfield suggests, one could meditate 'a rather comprehensive queer literary history'.[8] After all, 'in housesitting, you have an established normalcy to play at, an established normalcy to play against', where 'your transitory identity ... wanders the premises with you: ... a tidy, socioeconomic parallel of queer desire in the twentieth and twenty-first centuries.'[9] In line with Lazar, who comments on how 'one of the first uses of genre suggests a person who is impossible to characterize',[10] here Blanchfield too forwards the indeterminate, transgressive self (of the essayistic) against the self understood as dissectible specimen, where 'housesitting, like playing house, is identity rehearsal', and where 'you're writing an other there onto the self here'.[11]

The fact that the essay's queer mode of resistance to classification – of both its own form and gestures as well as those of its persona – is being noted only now (that is, from the mid-1990s on) is surprising to say the least; one would think that the link between the queer and the essayistic would have been made earlier considering how the essay's resistance and indefinability has often enough been acknowledged as constitutive touchstone of the essay. It would be erroneous to think, however, that these present ideas are ones without precedent; indeed, it is only through several thinkers of the essay who shall here be brought in to bear on this discussion that the queer essay can be thought of at all. It may thus be fruitful to address the historical invisibility of the queer essay the other way around: that is, by seeing the existence of the queer essay as unlocatable not because it is nowhere, but because it is everywhere. We may, in fact, have long thought about the queer essay.

Indeed, if 'the essay is ... usually perceived as marginal to other literary genres',[12] then the queer essay must be what is at the margins of marginality itself, for the genre of the essay, viewed in this way, has always already been queer, a true oddity as described by Theodor W. Adorno.[13] The category of queer essay might not exist, then, because all essays are queer.

This idea, in my opinion, deserves extended interrogation that I can here only briefly dwell on before adding to it a subtle, yet important, caveat. Suffice it to say that, aside from Adorno, Lazar and the other writers mentioned above, much has been said about the generic oddity of the essay. As DuPlessis writes, 'the nature of the essay asks one to resist categories, starting with itself';[14] as Réda Bensmaïa explains, the essay can be understood as 'a moment of writing *before* the genre, before genericness – or as the matrix of generic possibilities'.[15] With Thomas Harrison, we may note that what is shared by diverse essayistic styles is a resistance towards a 'fixed, established, and authoritative literary method', and that this 'open, self-seeking form ... tends to be antigeneric. The essay rejects a fixed perspective and lens'.[16] This strand of commentary could be quoted indefinitely, but here I will end it with Claire de Obaldia's observation that 'the one commonly accepted fact about the essay is that indeterminacy is germane to its essence'.[17]

Here is, then, the essay as indeterminacy par excellence, as genre without genre – that is, following Lazar, without gender. Or, rather, the essay as the matrix and simultaneous opening (transgression) of all genres/genders. In short, this is the essay as queer, always at (and resisting) the margins. It is important that this marginality is not then understood as its defining – and circumscriptive – feature, as for instance G. Douglas Atkins believes. The marginal is not the essential, and the indeterminate nature of the essay is not to be understood as merely its role as '*via media*' – where, 'on a spectrum involving fiction, philosophy, and the essay, the essay would occupy a middle position' – which would consequently only uphold the essay's generic ties and limitations.[18] When the essay's ambiguity becomes what makes it 'distinctive' (or genre-normative), it fails to be ambiguous, and the queer is subsumed back into the taxonomic and dimorphic boundaries that its queerness allows it to escape.[19] Atkins's view of the essay as 'embodied truth' ('Do we *truly* need a *true* sex?' Foucault would rebut) reduces the essay to a third genre/gender that confesses (and thus categorizes) itself as such, rather than allowing it its space beyond generic boundaries.[20] This is why, writes Adorno, 'the law of the innermost form of the essay is heresy. By transgressing the orthodoxy of thought, something becomes visible in the object which it is orthodoxy's secret purpose to keep invisible.'[21]

The reader will by now have noticed a paradox already evident in this exploratory line of thought, and here is the caveat mentioned earlier. The claim that the essay, as a form, is intrinsically queer in its transgression of generic borderlines is exceedingly defensible. However, it is here argued that such a way of thinking designates the 'queer essay' as simply a synonym for 'essay', where 'queer essay' becomes mere tautology and thus renders the queer invisible once more. In this manner, any examination of the queer essay would involve an examination of *all* essays. The question thus becomes whether there are any essays that exhibit any impulses, or potentialities, that highlight the essay's 'germane' indeterminacy while offering alternative conceptions of thinking the self, its voice(s) and the trials of the essay form itself.

Before getting to such essays, let us briefly continue our negative taxonomy. Here, 'queer essay' is not necessarily analogous to the 'coming out' essay, and nor does it only refer to essays that are either written by queer authors or which exclusively deal with issues of sexual identity politics. If 'discussions of sexual behaviour' have traditionally 'depended on the structural symmetry … based on a logic of limits, margins, borders, and boundaries', then it is those essays which test and transgress such borders that might be usefully examined, through the term 'queer', in their marginal position both within and without the tradition of the essay itself.[22] If, as Adorno writes, 'luck and play are essential to the essay', then essays that play with such borders might, luckily for us or not, marginalize the essential itself.[23] Keeping in mind, then, a Foucauldian understanding of the term 'homosexuality' – that is, as that which 'take[s] place in a "marginal" space that exists beyond the boundaries', and which underlines 'a space of greater freedom – where "freedom" means … the ability to create oneself' – in what ways might subjectivity, with its ever-essential 'I', be both read and queered through the marginal essay?[24]

For the purposes of answering this question, I turn to Genet's essays, which are here taken not as representative of the essay (as a historical genre in its entirety) but of the tendencies and potentialities of the queer essay. Most of Genet's writings may at first glance be said to fit snugly into Good's characterizations of the essay: non-fictional prose between one and fifty pages, provisional rather than systematic, addressed to the general rather than academic reader, and reflective of the author's particular personality.[25] Indeed, Genet's essays might generally be called 'personal essays', what Phillip Lopate describes as a subset of the informal essay with '"an intimate style, some autobiographical content or interest, and an urbane conversational manner"', and which 'tends to put the writer's "I" … more at center stage'.[26] On this idea of self-disclosure and 'self-seeking', however – one quite opposed to (Foucauldian, queer) self-creation – we find in Genet, in line with contemporaneous post-structuralist thought, a certain resistance, one striking at the idea that, 'at heart, the essay is the voice of the individual'.[27] We shall return to this soon.

Genet's essay 'What Remains of a Rembrandt Torn into Little Squares All the Same Size and Shot Down the Toilet' does not only discuss the 'methodical disintegration' of identity, but does so with its own language dissolving.[28] The essay (or, more accurately, essay*s*) is (*are*) two seemingly unrelated pieces merged into one, with each page vertically divided into two columns bearing their respective, seemingly unrelated thoughts. This is especially apposite when considering that Genet's primary meditation through these pieces (pieces quite literally, in the sense of fragments) is the divide between subject and object, self and Other, and its perpetual state of decomposition.

The essay on the left presents Genet on a train, locking eyes with a stranger whose features and unkempt appearance he finds revolting, but with whom Genet nonetheless deeply identifies.[29] This leads him to contemplate the universal sameness of humankind, 'a sort of universal identity with all men' which induces in the narrator neither affection nor tenderness but only a pitiless disgust (*WRR*, 92A). The essay to its right, italicized, similarly deals with gazing and perception – this in specific relation to Rembrandt's self-portraits and those of his lover Hendrickje Stoffels – and is significantly shorter than the first, ending just as the other Genet, that of the left-hand essay, proclaims: 'Let's go on' (*WRR*, 99A).

Despite the common themes – barely connected as they are – the two fragment-essays differ drastically not only in content but also in tone. The voice of the first essay, serious and contemplative, interrupts ('I did not suspect – but that's not true, I knew it obscurely'), contradicts ('No! It didn't happen so quickly, and not in that order'), doubts and clarifies itself ('I wrote that sentence first, but I corrected it'), at times breaking down completely ('What was it, then, that had flowed out of my body – I fl… – and what part of the traveller flowed out of his body?') (*WRR*, 91–94A). That of the second essay, on the other hand, is much more self-assured, suave, playful and at times purposefully puerile, talking of the 'beefy Dutchman' Rembrandt or of the large ass on 'The Jewish Bride' (*WRR*, 94B, 92B).

There is a lot to be said of this disjuncture and disarray, but I shall here be focusing on the composition of the essay in tandem with the multiplicity of voices that suggest a de-composition (un-writing, un-making) of the 'I' – what I here understand as one of the main efforts of what one may call the queer essay.

In terms of composition, Genet's essay is challenging. One might already be familiar with this kind of unconventional formatting through, for example,

Jacques Derrida's much better known 'Living On', despite Genet's essay having been written roughly ten years prior.[30] It frustrates the typical Western instinct of going from left to right and presents the reader with the immediate difficulty, usually left unpresented, of how to *start* reading. Even when finishing one side and moving back up to start the next, the disjointed themes and voices rebuff any attempt at seamless unification. As noted earlier, the incredible flexibility and adaptability of the essay, open to digression, symbiosis and fragmentation, has often been remarked upon, and is what leads Good to write that, historically, the 'initial impulse' of the essay 'was [to move] away from genre altogether, in the direction of formlessness'.[31] However, this 'supposed formlessness', according to Lopate, 'is more a strategy to disarm the reader with the appearance of unstudied spontaneity than a reality of composition'.[32] György Lukács, in fact, would say that this uniqueness of form within the genre of the essay is at core an attempt at re-ordering, claiming that it 'is part of the nature of the essay that it does not create new things from an empty nothingness but only orders those that were once alive'; the essay, then, 'does not form something new out of formlessness' but rather '*defines the limits* of the immaterial' through form – that is, not a fictional life created from aesthetic abstraction (Lukács uses the example of poetry) but rather a natural life re-organized and re-represented through the essayistic.[33]

While Lukács's definition of form is the broader one – the textual and essayistic incarnation of life rather than deliberate format, layout or presentation – these three writers on the essay allow us to frame our question of composition as follows: is Genet's formlessness studied and feigned, designed to re-order and circumscribe life and put forward a particular interpretation of it, or is it a unique manifestation of the mutability of the essay and the inherent disorganization of, and resistance to, life's categories – and the category of life itself? In other words, is it life given a new form, or is it a new lifeform, a new species in and of itself?

It is not clear why one should definitively choose between the two, but returning to Genet's exploration of 'methodical disintegration' – which, upon closer inspection, reveals itself as a subtle yet significant paradox – allows us to lean away from organization and towards a fragmentary formlessness. With the essay broken up not only in the presentation of its form but also through its multiple voices, one is rebuffed from reading Genet in line with Lopate's reading of the personal essayist, where the essayist, after revealing 'a humanity enlarged by complexity', then 'tries to make his many partial selves dance to the same beat – to unite, through force of voice and style, these discordant, fragmentary personae so that the reader can accept them as issuing from one coherent self'.[34] Through a self interrupted, fragmented and rendered incoherent – even disgusting – when assimilated into all of humanity, this is precisely what Genet's essay does not do. This is not Lukács's 'fragmentariness' as only the penultimate step towards a unified and aesthetic representation of life, but rather a fragmentation of life itself.[35] As Adorno notes, the essay 'thinks in fragments just as reality is fragmented'; 'discontinuity', therefore, 'is essential to the essay. Its concern is always a conflict brought into a standstill.'[36] Two fragments, even when paired up as they are in Genet's essay(s), do not and cannot make a whole. This is, then, the 'anti-systemic impulse of the essay', which 'proceeds, so to speak, methodically unmethodically' – a methodical disintegration.[37]

This paradox, perhaps unwittingly echoed in Genet's essay, is the tenet of thinking the essay and its 'heresy', expressed as early as Montaigne and Bacon; 'I speak my meaning in disjointed parts', remarks Montaigne.[38] Walter Pater, speaking of the Platonic dialectic as a(n essayistic) method of conversing with one's self, observes how 'there will always be much of accident in this essentially informal, this un-methodical, method'.[39] Adorno, as we have seen, recalls this in his belief that the essay is to be 'more dialectical than the dialectic',[40] and de Obaldia elaborates on Adorno's stance: 'the precepts of exhaustiveness, totality, and continuity are at stake, all of which the essay subverts by accentuating the part over the whole', highlighting the 'irreducibility of fragment to whole' in a revolt against the systemic, the totalitarian, the taxonomic.[41]

This is the fragmentation that may be named queerness, or, rather, that queers. Lazar claims that unconventional formatting (such as that in Genet's essay) is not enough to abate 'the essay's domestication, a false sense of formal radicalization. Merely breaking up paragraphs', he adds, 'or adding poetry to essays (Cowley did that in the mid-seventeenth century) doesn't make an essay queer or politically resistant'.[42] Leaving to one side the tenebrous issue of aesthetics (an issue important for Genet), Lazar's concern is applicable only to different degrees, depending on whether one talks of queer representation or queer subjectivity. 'Queers, you are made of pieces. Your gestures are broken', Genet tells us, and this way 'the notion of rupture appears'.[43] There may indeed be something more than superficial in the breaking of form – and so, what is ruptured? It is the subjective experience of the 'I', where the individual is posited not as something already existing to be creatively expressed in new ways (a new form of life), but rather as something always still to be created (a new lifeform) from the gaps, the margins.

Therefore, the queer essay, with its fragmentary 'I' manifested through fragmentary form and broken voices, undertakes the deconstruction of the essential without in turn making the marginal essential. This would be the essay as that which dwells in the aporetic 'nonpassage', where 'there is not even any space for an aporia determined as experience of the step or of the edge, crossing or not of some line, relation to some spatial figure of the limit.'[44] Aside from Derrida (and other thinkers often labelled as post-structuralist, here evoked in the spirit against 'exhaustiveness, totality, and continuity'),[45] one could here, if there were time, bring in Maurice Blanchot, and through his thoughts view the queer essay as the fragmentary work that 'does not realize the whole, but signifies it by suspending it, even breaking it'.[46] What is at risk here, as illuminated by Genet, is any sense of whole or continuous 'I'; the queer essay is thus a work 'in which a limit is reached', one where there is 'engender[ed] nothing'[47] – perhaps not even a new lifeform, instead keeping it always as that which is yet to be created – and where the personal voice is 'made and unmade', made only to be unmade.[48]

Atkins writes how 'the voice we hear in essays – that representation of embodied truth – *is* the experiencing, reflecting, and narrating self'.[49] In the queer essay, at least, this voice that speaks out is hollowed from any systemic or distinctive upholding of genre and gender, an engendering of nothing as sterile as Eliot's valley of death, a gap between self and voice as infinite as the one between Borges and his 'I'. This is the rupture Genet describes as 'ripping open my appearance and revealing… what? *a solid void* that kept perpetuating me' (*WRR*, 100A). As with St John the Baptist's famous reply – 'I am the voice of one calling in the wilderness', by which 'voice' is to be understood as that which annuls rather than identifies its speaker[50] – here, in the queer essay, voice is not used to imply personality but to fragment it, a voice used not as a tool of the essay's composition, but as its own de-composition, always awaiting (at) the arrival of the self.[51]

Here is an 'I' not yet a self, an 'I' that is, in effect, no one in particular at all. This hearkens back to what Lukács says of portraiture: 'the paradox of the essay is almost the same as that of the portrait', meaning that just as the portrait presses upon the looker the idea of likeness, so too does the essay embody a likeness of life, re-ordered and represented as a particular moment in space and time. It does not matter that one does not know the sitter, nor even if the sitter ever existed – 'Likeness? Of whom? Of no one, of course' – for the illusion of likeness is enough for the looker (the essay's reader) to be delivered the sensation of life. This would be, according to Lukács, 'the truth of the essay'.[52] To this, Good adds that the portraitist 'also represents his *own* likeness in his painting … In fact, we tend to identify portraits by the artist's rather than the sitter's name: a Rembrandt, rather than the particular dignitary depicted'.[53]

This fortuitous reference to Rembrandt brings us neatly back – no matter how much Genet hated neatness – to the Rembrandt of the essay. The suave version of Genet writes: 'I never asked myself who these ladies or gentlemen [of Rembrandt's paintings] were. And maybe it's this more or less clear-cut absence of the question that makes me wince? The more I looked at them, the less these portraits reminded me of anyone. Of no one' (*WRR*, 96B).

If there is in Genet's essay a 'reciprocal identification' between self and Other,[54] and if, in the queering of essentiality, this relationship collapses into one where 'self-other [is] only one, at the same time both me-or-him, and me-and-him', then the queer essay's portrait of the 'I' is indeed a painting of no *one*, and one is not delivered Lukács's truthful life but rather delivered from it (*WRR*, 99A). Good writes that, in the essay, a 'loss of self is followed by a sharpened sense of self'; here, there is no recovery possible.[55] If the Rembrandt portrait is of both the looker and the sitter, then what is Torn into Little Squares All the Same Size and Shot Down the Toilet is any individual essentiality prescribed to a self – and, with it, its categories of gender, limits, and the notion of a plurality that individuates only in order to taxonomize.

This queering of self and system is made evident, at the very least as an attempt, in several of Genet's other essays. Aside from the above, perhaps the clearest site of this is the eponymous essay 'Fragments…', in which prosaic and conversational language is interspersed with poetic and imagistic visions, fragments that 'are not extracts of a poem' but perhaps 'ought to lead to one'.[56] These are further interrupted through alternately formatted paragraphs, for no clearly discernible reason, and the section titled 'Fragments of a Second Discourse' presents to us once more pages vertically divided into two columns. This time, to the left, a conversation between two unnamed personae takes place, and to its right dense and enigmatic language very similar in tone to Genet's *Poèmes*.[57] Furthermore, these two columns are thrice bridged with text that runs across them – at times incomplete, lacking punctuation – further queering any notion of coherent self, individual voice or the idea of an essayist who wishes to communicate either a disclosure or a seeking of selfhood.

Similarly, the conversations recounted in 'The Studio of Alberto Giacometti' play not only with personality but also temporality; 'The Tightrope Walker' presents, through italicized sections, different Genets with different interests and relations; 'That Strange Word…' repeatedly breaks any sense of coherence or continuity through frequent and seemingly arbitrary page breaks.[58] Similarly blown to pieces, although this time without page breaks, 'Chartres Cathedral, A "Bird's-Eye" View' rebuffs any understanding of the 'I' that here only rarely appears, as if it were hiding.[59] As Genet says during an interview with Hubert Fichte, through his work, '[he] lose[s] more and more the sense of being "myself," the sense of the "I," and become[s] nothing but the perception of the artwork'.[60] Ultimately, the queer essay thus also queers the desire 'of the *portrayal* of the *self*, portrait-ing no one and resisting 'the importance of the individual, of the *person*' that less queer essays have endlessly sought to find or express in the wake of Montaigne.

Before concluding this chapter, let me quickly sum up. So far, the queer essay has emerged as that particular kind of essay that is aware of its marginal position and which plays with its own composition, at times toying with unreadability, whereby this is, to varying extents, linked to reflections that queer the position of subjectivity, highlighting not an 'I' that stands on centre stage but one which flits between the margins, limits and boundaries that attempt to define it. These complementary aspects manifest not only in content and form – and the essay's transgressive place in genre studies as a whole – but also through tone, where multiple variances of voice (these not necessarily attributed to different personae) are not authorially and authoritatively unified but rather shattered into fragments. The ultimate aim of this chapter, then, is to serve as invitation to begin looking towards a compendium – and not 'category' – of species that in these ways defy taxonomization.[61] At the very least, these lifeforms might offer a form of resistance, even if they try and do not succeed.

This idea of 'trying and failing', indeed, is what I here locate as being a third and here last gesture, albeit not separate from the first two, of the queer essay. We are in fact frequently reminded of the etymology of essay, from the French *essayer* meaning 'to try' or 'to attempt'.[62] The queer essay might be the enactment not of trying, but of trying and failing, or even, perhaps, of a failure to try; the essay as a trial failed or a trial failed in not even being undertaken. One need not shrink away from failure, linked as it is to the always inchoate figure of the queer; in this, we find in Judith Halberstam's study a reminder to commemorate failure, and this through what Halberstam terms 'low theory'.

Low theory, being that which 'tries to locate all the in-between spaces that save us from being snared by the hooks of hegemony', enables us to think through 'ways of being and knowing that stand outside of conventional understandings of success'.[63] Such spaces act as sites for 'the theorization of alternatives within an undisciplined zone of knowledge production', and while Halberstam mainly focuses on animated films and cartoons in order to 'open up new narrative doors', it would by no means be a stretch to see the essay form as one incarnation of such undisciplined zones.[64] In failure's associations with undoing, unworking, unbecoming and passivity, we see Genet's unravelled self as a failed entity, an entity incapable of being an 'I', failing before it can begin to try. This is not a failure glamorized by optimism or even some notions of aesthetics, or the kind of failure one is thankful for in the attribution of some development or self-betterment. At work here – if one can call it that – is a negativity, which is not to say a negative productivity. 'The logic of failure' is one that 'detach[es] queerness from the optimistic and humanistic activity of making meaning', and the queer subject is that 'who cannot speak, who refuse[s] to speak; subjects who unravel, who refuse to cohere; subjects who refuse "being" where being has already been defined as a self-activating, self-knowing, liberal subject'.[65] This would be to fail like Rembrandt, who, as Halberstam insightfully describes, 'painted out of darkness while refusing to make it recede and give way to the light'.[66]

Contrary, then, to the essay's traditional tendency towards self-disclosure, or the impulse of the essay to *mean* and *do* something, or any upholding of narrative responsibility (such as Annie Dillard's emphatic wish to 'encourage essay writers out of the closet'), the queer essay tends towards an ambiguity freed from productivity as self- and meaning-making – while also freed from being illuminated *as such* (as the indistinct, the in-between, the essentially ambiguous).[67] If paragraphs are broken up unconventionally, it is not for the sake of innovation and creation but rather destruction and failure. After all, 'failure is also unbeing, and ... these modes of unbeing and unbecoming propose a different relation to knowledge.'[68] The failed self of the queer essay is illogical and unreadable, negative in that it is neither productive content nor productively content, detached from the circumscriptions of one's own body and the body of the essay, a being of the margins.

Notes

1 Michel Foucault, *The History of Sexuality Volume I: The Will to Knowledge*, trans. Robert Hurley (London: Penguin Books, 1998), 43.
2 Tracey Chevalier, 'Editor's Note', in *Encyclopedia of the Essay*, ed. Tracey Chevalier (London: Fitzroy Dearborn, 1997), vii–viii (vii). In fairness, Chevalier does acknowledge the problematic nature of taxonomic gaps and exclusion.
3 Graham Good, 'Preface', in *Encyclopedia of the Essay*, ed. Tracey Chevalier, xix–xxi (xix).
4 Jean Genet, 'Fragments...', in *Fragments of the Artwork*, trans. Charlotte Mandell (Stanford, CA: Stanford University Press, 2003), 19–35 (23).
5 This sentiment is an echo of David Lazar's own: 'Essays on the essay never pin the essay down. A queer theoretical essay wouldn't even want to.' (David Lazar, 'Queering

the Essay', in *Occasional Desire: Essays* (Lincoln: University of Nebraska Press, 2013), 61–7 (67).)
6   Ibid., 62.
7   Ibid., 62–3.
8   Brian Blanchfield, 'On Housesitting', in *Proxies: Essays Permitting Shame, Error and Guilt, Myself the Single Source* (New York: Nightboat Books, 2017), 49–55 (52). An interview with Jill Talbot elaborates Blanchfield's link between queerness and essaying. (See ' "Queer it if you can": An Interview with Brian Blanchfield by Jill Talbot', *Essay Daily*, 28 March 2016, https://www.essaydaily.org/2016/03/queer-it-if-you-can-interview-with.html)
9   Blanchfield, 'On Housesitting', 50–1.
10 Lazar, 'Queering the Essay', 62.
11 Blanchfield, 'On Housesitting', 54.
12 Good, 'Preface', in *Encyclopedia of the Essay*, xx.
13 Theodor W. Adorno, 'The Essay as Form', trans. Bob Hullot-Kentor and Frederic Will, *New German Critique* 32 (1984): 151–71 (152).
14 Rachel Blau DuPlessis, 'From "*f*-Words: An Essay on the Essay" ', in *Essayists on the Essay: Montaigne to Our Time*, ed. Carl H. Klaus and Ned Stuckey-French (Iowa City: University of Iowa Press, 2012), 147–50 (148).
15 Réda Bensmaïa, *The Barthes Effect: The Essay as Reflective Text*, trans. Pat Fedkiew (Minneapolis: University of Minnesota Press, 1987), 92.
16 Thomas Harrison, 'Introduction', in Thomas Harrison, *Essayism: Conrad, Musil, and Pirandello* (Baltimore, MD: John Hopkins University Press, 1992), 1–18 (3).
17 Claire de Obaldia, *The Essayistic Spirit: Literature, Modern Criticism, and the Essay* (Oxford: Oxford University Press, 1995), 2.
18 G. Douglas Atkins, 'In-Betweenness: The Burden of the Essay', in *Tracing the Essay: Through Experience to Truth* (Athens: University of Georgia Press, 2005), 145–66 (147–8).
19 Ibid., 152.
20 Michel Foucault, 'Introduction', in Michel Foucault, *Herculine Barbin – Being the Recently Discovered Memoirs of a Nineteenth-Century French Hermaphrodite*, trans. Richard McDougall (New York: Vintage Books, 2010), vii–xvii (vii).
21 Adorno, 'The Essay as Form', 171.
22 Diana Fuss, 'Introduction', in *Inside/Out – Lesbian Theories, Gay Theories*, ed. Diana Fuss (New York: Routledge, 1991), 1–12 (1).
23 Adorno, 'The Essay as Form', 152.
24 Mark Kingston, 'Subversive Friendships: Foucault on Homosexuality and Social Experimentation', *Foucault Studies* 7 (2009): 7–17 (8, 10).
25 See Good, 'Preface', in *Encyclopedia of the Essay* (xix–xxi). Good elaborates further on these in the preface to his own monograph on the essay: Graham Good, 'Preface', in *The Observing Self: Rediscovering the Essay* (Oxon: Routledge, 2014), vii–xiii (ix–xii).
26 Phillip Lopate, 'Introduction', in *The Art of the Personal Essay: An Anthology*, ed. Phillip Lopate (New York: Anchor Books, 1995), xxiii–liv (xxiv). Lopate attributes the first part of this quotation to '*A Handbook of Literature* [sic]', though he seems to be referring to one of the numerous editions of *A Handbook to Literature*, such as William Harmon, *A Handbook to Literature*, 7th edn (New York: Pearson, 1996), 385.
27 Good, 'Preface', in *Encyclopedia of the Essay*, xxxii.

28 Jean Genet, 'What Remains of a Rembrandt Torn into Little Squares All the Same Size and Shot Down the Toilet', in *Fragments*, 91–102 (92*A*). Henceforth cited in text as (*WRR*, page number/s *A/B*). *A* designates the left-hand essay and *B* the right.
29 This same episode is recounted, with slightly different emphasis, in Genet's 'The Studio of Alberto Giacometti', in *Fragments*, 41–68 (49).
30 See Jacques Derrida, 'Living On', trans. James Hulbert, in *Deconstruction and Criticism*, ed. Harold Bloom, Paul de Man, et al. (New York: The Seabury Press, 1979), 75–176. Genet's essay was written in 1967. See also Samuel R. Delany's 'On the Unspeakable', a similarly formatted, and similarly queer, essay, in *Shorter Views: Queer Thoughts and the Politics of the Paraliterary* (Hanover: Wesleyan University Press, 1999), 58–66.
31 Good, *The Observing Self*, 1.
32 Lopate, 'Introduction', xxxviii.
33 György Lukács, 'On the Nature and Form of the Essay', in *Soul and Form*, trans. Anna Bostock, ed. John T. Sanders and Katie Terezakis (New York: Columbia University Press, 2010), 16–34 (23, 26). My emphasis.
34 Lopate, 'Introduction', xxvii–xxix.
35 Lukács, 'On the Nature and Form of the Essay', 33.
36 Adorno, 'The Essay as Form', 164.
37 Ibid., 160–1.
38 Michel de Montaigne, *The Complete Essays of Montaigne*, trans. Donald M. Frame (Stanford, CA: Stanford University Press, 1957), 824. For more on the history of this unmethodical looseness, see Carl H. Klaus, 'Toward a Collective Poetics of the Essay', in *Essayists on the Essay*, xv–xxvii (xvi–xvii).
39 Walter Pater, *Plato and Platonism – A Series of Lectures* (New York: Macmillan, 1983), 166.
40 Adorno, 'The Essay as Form', 166.
41 De Obaldia, *The Essayistic Spirit*, 116–17.
42 Lazar, 'Queering the Essay', 67.
43 Genet, 'Fragments', 24.
44 Jacques Derrida, *Aporias*, trans. Thomas Dutoit (Stanford, CA: Stanford University Press, 1993), 21.
45 For an astute reading of the essay form and its affinities with poststructuralist thought, see R. Lane Kauffmann, 'The Skewed Path: Essaying as Unmethodical Method', in *Essays on the Essay: Redefining the Genre*, ed. Alexander J. Butrym (Athens: University of Georgia Press, 1989), 221–40 (232–6).
46 Maurice Blanchot, 'The Athenaeum', in Maurice Blanchot, *The Infinite Conversation*, trans. Susan Hanson (Minneapolis: Minnesota University Press, 2003), 351–9 (353).
47 Maurice Blanchot, *The Book To Come*, trans. Charlotte Mandell (Stanford, CA: Stanford University Press, 2003), 109.
48 Maurice Blanchot, 'Literature and the Right to Death', trans. Lydia Davis, in Maurice Blanchot, *The Work of Fire*, trans. Charlotte Mandell (Stanford, CA: Stanford University Press, 1995), 300–44 (306). Here Blanchot's notion of *désoeuvrement* is crucial.
49 Atkins, *The Familiar* Essay, 48.
50 John 1:23.
51 For more on the relation between the corporeal essayists and their narrativized personae, see especially Klaus, xxiv–xxv.
52 Lukács, 'On the Nature and Form of the Essay', 26–7.

53 Good, *The Observing Self*, 21.
54 Ibid., 8.
55 Ibid.
56 Genet, 'Fragments…', 19.
57 Ibid., 32–5. See Jean Genet, *Poèmes* (Lyon: L'Arbalète, 1948).
58 Genet, 'The Tightrope Walker' and 'That Strange Word…', in *Fragments*, 69–83 and 103–12.
59 Genet, 'Chartres Cathedral, A "Bird's-Eye" View', in *Fragments*, 152–8.
60 Genet, 'Interview with Hubert Fichte', trans. Jeff Fort, in *Fragments*, 113–51 (118).
61 Aside from Delany, mentioned in an earlier footnote, other essays might include Jacques Derrida and Peter Eisenman, *Chora L Works*, ed. Jeffrey Kipnis and Thomas Leeser (New York: Monacelli Press, 1997); Raymond Federman, 'The Voice in the Closet/La Voix Dans Le Cabinet de Debarras' (New York: Barrytown/Station Hill Press, 1986); Francis Ponge, 'Fauna and Flora' and 'My Creative Method', in *The Voice of Things*, ed. and trans. Beth Archer (New York: McGraw-Hill, 1972), 62–7 and 81–107; Roland Barthes, *Mourning Diary*, trans. Richard Howard (New York: Hill and Wang, 2012) and *A Lover's Discourse – Fragments*, trans. Richard Howard (New York: Hill and Wang, 2001) and more.
62 A lucid examination of the word's etymology is undertaken by Jean Starobinski. See an excerpt from Starobinski's 'Can One Define the Essay?' in *Essayists on the Essay*, 110–15. On this idea of failure, Starobinski in fact comments: 'He who wants to *succeed*, doesn't he have to do more [than *try*]?' (112).
63 Judith Halberstam, *The Queer Art of Failure* (Durham, NC: Duke University Press, 2011), 2.
64 Ibid., 15, 20.
65 Ibid., 106, 126.
66 Halberstam, 'Notes', in *The Queer Art of Failure*, 189–91 (190), note 3.
67 Annie Dillard, 'Introduction', in *The Best American Essays 1988*, ed. Annie Dillard (New York: Ticknor and Fields, 1988), xiii–xxii (xiv).
68 Halberstam, *The Queer Art of Failure*, 23.

Chapter 10

THE ESSAY AND THE 'I':
ELIOT WEINBERGER'S TRANSFORMATION
OF THE AUTHORIAL SELF

Michael Askew

Perhaps the only thing all those attempting to define the essay can agree on is that it is impossible to define. The essay is an 'orchestra',[1] a 'sonnet',[2] a 'meadow',[3] a 'research tool',[4] a 'secular sermon',[5] a 'greased pig',[6] a 'verbal swarm'.[7] The essay is not a genre at all but 'a moment of writing before the genre', a 'matrix of generic possibilities'.[8] Its flexibility, its lack of boundaries, is something that is stressed again and again by commentators on the essay: it is a journey where 'everything is permitted'.[9] Cynthia Ozick calls it the 'movement of a free mind at play',[10] arguing that 'no one is freer than the essayist – free to leap out in any direction, to hop from thought to thought'.[11] The metaphor that comes up repeatedly is one of travelling, as though the boundaries of the essay were no stricter or tighter than the boundaries of the world, and all the thought, language and imagination it contains.

It seems paradoxical, then, to speak of a writer expanding the limits of the form, doing new things with the essay. If there are no limits, if its scope is infinite, then how can one expand its possibilities? How can one push boundaries that do not exist, or stretch boundaries that are infinitely malleable? And yet this is, frequently, how people have described Eliot Weinberger's work. His books are marketed as revelations, revolutions in the essay form, as a quick glance at their dust jackets attests to: these are essays to take us 'beyond the borders',[12] into 'unexplored territories',[13] in an 'ever-astonishing exploration of the essay form, opening up its possibilities, and reinvigorating it'.[14] Boundary pushing is also, quite explicitly, what Weinberger himself sets out as the goal of his writing: that is, to expand the remit of what the essay can do:

> The essay strikes me as unexplored territory in English. With a few exceptions, it is either stuck in the 18th century narrative model – now called the 'personal essay' with its various sub-genres (travel writing, personal journalism, memoir) – or in standard literary criticism… I can't understand this at all, as the essay seems to me to have unlimited potential. It doesn't need a first person;

it can stretch toward pure narrative or the prose poem or the documentary; anything is possible.[15]

Weinberger here conjures the same sense of openness and limitlessness that so many critics of the essay have celebrated in the form. Yet he suggests that, in reality, this limitless territory has remained largely 'unexplored', that the essay is 'stuck' in certain models, its 'unlimited potential' existing in theory rather than in practice. He re-establishes the essay's boundaries, only to try and break them open again.

Weinberger's comments suggest the boundaries of the essay have been conceived like the boundaries of the author's body, with most essays being written in a first-person voice, dealing with personal experiences and reflections.[16] With a few important exceptions, the essay has historically been, quite literally, self-centred: grounded in the singular voice and opinions of one particular essayist.[17] One of the radical impulses of Michel de Montaigne was his claim that his own opinions mattered, that the private thoughts running through his head as he retired in his bedchamber were worth recording for others to read. These thoughts did not need to be shaped into narratives or filtered through the self-eradicating reason of logical argument, but had value in their original, personal, unfinished, inchoate form. Michael Duszat notes how 'accounts of the essay as a genre often begin with Montaigne's instalment of the self, as both author and subject of the essay', and this trend has only increased in the last few decades, in which the 'personal essay' has become the dominant genre; it is the only kind, for example, regularly published in newspapers, in the form of 'think pieces' and 'life stories'.[18] This emphasis on the personal is, we find, corroborated in much writing on the form, which often champions the essayist's individual voice, what Duszat calls the 'essayistic I':[19] think of Virginia Woolf, for example, claiming that 'all essays begin with a capital I',[20] or Montaigne himself proudly declaring that he writes 'by my universal being, not as a grammarian, poet or jurisconsult but as Michel de Montaigne'.[21]

Weinberger's writing, specifically the strand that his main publisher, New Directions, refers to as his 'literary essays', is a direct challenge to the prominence of the 'essayistic I' in both essay practice and theory. His essays are characterized by an almost total erasure of the first-person pronoun or other markers of an authorial self. The majority of his output offers no opinions, no commentaries, no personal pronouns, no first-hand accounts or personal experiences. Characteristic essays like 'Dreams from the Holothurians',[22] 'Changs'[23] and 'Questions of Death'[24] offer apparently simple lists of facts or examples, with no attempt made to connect one fact to another, to establish any kind of causal, thematic, narrative or personal relationship between them. Yet, while rooted in fact, this work could never be mistaken for simple, factual journalism: there is too little context, too much mystery, no gesture towards, let alone semblance of, objectivity or clarity of explanation. This is not the 'impersonal fact gathering'[25] of the article, in which 'style is subordinate to subject, craft to coverage',[26] nor the narrativized fact-gathering of New Journalism. Rather, it is a different kind of essaying: one that keeps the free-associative, exploratory spirit of the essay, as well as its love of the suggestive detail, but which reimagines the relation of this movement and these details to the figure of the essayist.

In this chapter, I shall examine the position of the 'I' in Weinberger's work in an attempt to understand how the essay might be reimagined as something less centred in the self. I shall also track the influence of several poets on Weinberger's formulation of this 'I', arguing that Weinberger's partially erased self might be analogous to the 'lyric I' of a poem, to what Amy Bonnaffons calls 'the notion that a poem's speaker can transcend the boundaries of the poet's actual, historical self'.[27] By examining the influence of George Oppen, Lorine Niedecker, Charles Reznikoff and Octavio Paz on Weinberger's positioning of the self in his work, I hope to both finesse this idea of 'the lyric I' as an alternative possible centre of an essay, and to connect Weinberger's work to the rise of the so-called 'lyric essay' in writers like Annie Dillard, Anne Carson, Maggie Nelson and Claudia Rankine.[28] Shifting away from what we might call the 'essayistic I' – an 'I' which centres the essay, controlling what flows in and out of it – lyric essays move towards multiplicity and uncertainty. If the standard 'essayistic I' can be read as a clear, singular voice offering personal opinions, then the 'lyric I' is always doubling these opinions with other perspectives, leaking into and permeating the voices of others. The lyric essayist, at different moments and to different extents, cedes control of the essay: to other voices; to the natural world; to the reader; to the white space of the page; to images; or, most often and most strikingly, to language itself. In doing so, they play, in different and complex ways, with the position of the self within the essay. Weinberger, in this sense, though rarely grouped with the lyric essayists, demonstrates their particular play with the essay form.

*

An essay typically allows us to inhabit a particular mind: to follow along with the thoughts of another as though in real time, as though we are thinking with the essayist. In Weinberger's work, this inhabitation is often difficult or impossible. 'The Present', for example, scrambles the essayist's own thoughts in an ambiguous third person. The essay opens: 'Outside his window a man stood in a phone box all day, pretending to make a call. Inside his window he sat in a room on the fourth floor, typing.'[29] The semantic confusion generated by the first clause – where 'his' and 'a man' initially seem to refer to the same person, standing by a window that belongs to him – is only partially resolved as the sentence continues: we learn that they are separate people but do not learn their identities or their relation, if any. The phrase 'he sat in a room on the fourth floor, typing', followed by a section break and then a paragraph of typically Weinbergeresque prose detailing statistics from recent wars, invites us to plausibly identify the 'he' of the essay with the essayist himself.[30] Yet by framing his experiences in the third person, Weinberger inevitably introduces a degree of ambiguity when 'he' interacts with others, as when he is phoned by a friend in the essay's third section:

> They caught up on old friends. One had died from AIDS. Another had died from AIDS. One had written the screenplay for the most successful movie of the year, and was now more unbearable than before…. [One] had become

famous overnight ... Another was still making false teeth and was the same. One, previously unathletic, had suddenly taken up skiing and was working at a ski resort.[31]

Given its specificity, this conversation enforces our assumption that this is a first-hand account, told in the third person. Yet the lack of an 'essayistic I' to guide us makes it difficult to map the voice of the author onto any *single* voice or 'character' in the essay. The lack of proper nouns (which movie? which ski resort?) makes it impossible to map these details onto a specific context, despite their apparent intimacy (a death from AIDS, later a divorce and an operation); the repeated use of 'one' blurs one friend into another. We are also told nothing of the motivation behind the events – we do not know why the friend became famous, why the other friend took up skiing – meaning that they are not turned into narrative. The author – one or not one of the 'one's, a 'he' or not a 'he' – floats uncertainly in the midst of seemingly unconnected events.

As the essay advances, the identity of this 'he' becomes even more complex. When 'he' confesses to a murder, we presume our prior association, however tentative, between the 'he' and the 'author' was mistaken, though we are now even less clear who the 'he' does refer to, and how the real author, Weinberger, knows all the details of his life. Soon, details about the 'he' start to contradict each other: he is executed in Florida in 1977 and then, on the following page, he is shot dead in a hostage situation.[32] We start to realize that the 'he' is not all the same man, which re-complicates our assessment of the original 'he', the man typing by the window, who could equally be Weinberger or one of the later executed murderers. Clearly they are not all the author – we know he is not blind, we know he is not dead – yet some seem as though they must be, such is the odd specificity of their details. The author thus becomes implicit – and by extension, complicit – in all the acts described in the text: he is, at all points, unstable, both the subject and not the subject. This sense of an unstable identity is reinforced by many of the collaged anecdotes themselves, most potently the story of Hitler's double, who turns out to be Hitler himself,[33] and the story of the fake beggars who, paid to pretend to die of hunger, are paid so poorly they actually *do* die of hunger. Every identity in this text, every possible centre of self, is either erased, or else doubled and tripled, to the point where every 'self' becomes a part of every 'other'.

In addition to being blurred into other voices in the text, the essayist seems to hold no sway over the seemingly unrelated sections – on theme motels, the 'new President', sales figures for both Elvis paraphernalia and weapons, self-help books for children – that surround and collide into 'him'. Compare, for example, the apparently erroneous detail of George Bush Sr.'s practical jokes ('He liked to shake hands with a small buzzer hidden in his palm'[34]) with the use of the exact same detail in the more conventional essay 'Bush the Poet'.[35] In the latter, Bush's joking is directly linked to the inherent falseness in everything his family does, from his son's invasion of Iraq on false premises to his daughter-in-law Laura's false attribution of a poem to her husband. There is an analytical context here which allows us to both absorb the particular detail of the palm buzzer and understand the point the essayist is trying to make about it. In 'The Present', this sense of a 'point' or meaning impressed on the material by a particular mind, is absent. The lack of an authorial 'self' – what we might think of as the stabilizing sense of the essayist's personality or mind within the text – destabilizes the material, and the details skitter past. We are unable to follow the argument back to the author, for there seems to be no argument: the only context is a confusing and apparently tangential relation between the falseness and jokiness of Faith Popcorn's theme motels ('the bed was a giant sandwich and the whirlpool bath a cup of coffee') and the falseness and jokiness of the President: and, by inference, of life in America in 1989.[36] The author is decentred because everything in America seems to lack a stabilizing centre: everything is a joke. Jokes, we are reminded, are often based on double meanings, just as Bush and Popcorn are here doubled, and Hitler and 'Hitler' were doubled earlier. We might then read the earlier multiplying of the author's self, the multiple 'he' pronouns, as a kind of joke at the author's expense, one which strips the author of his power, both over the essay itself and over the events the essay describes; for action is impossible without a fixed, stable identity from which to act, yet the essay removes this.

One possible response to this lack of a stable authorial personality at the essay's centre is to read it as an invitation for the reader to bring meaning to the essay's disparate materials. Weinberger implicitly invites involvement in the things he describes by leaving the connections between these things unstated, requiring the reader to puzzle the essay out themselves. The essay thus raises questions about power, about our level of complicity in the events that happen around us, questions which come sharply into focus towards the essay's close, with its phone call (with clear echoes of the phone call at the essay's opening) from a 'dim hysterical voice' in 'another country', and its final call, smuggled in via a reference to a low-budget 1950s sci-fi film, to consider how events in the present (and 'The Present') will affect the future.[37]

And yet, the stripping away of context necessitated by Weinberger's decentring prose can also make this involvement difficult, for the essay's subjects always remain esoteric to us. Phillip Lopate notes that 'the whole modern essay tradition sprang from quotation'.[38] Such quotation, he argues, relied on the presence of a universal literary culture, one which no longer exists in our age of multiplicity. In the absence of this shared culture, essayists have fallen back on the personal to provide an alternative context: that is, the context of a conversation, of one voice speaking to another. Weinberger refuses to fall back on such a context. In fact, he does the opposite, pushing away from both himself and from any idea of a universal literary culture towards the esoteric, the undiscovered, be that in the Bhati villages of Rajasthan or behind the closed doors of the White House. We find a similar push towards the other when he describes the last meals of prisoners on death row:

> Jesse de la Rosa requested Spanish rice, refried beans, flour tortillas, T-bone steak, tea, chocolate cake, jalapeño peppers.
> Jeffrey Barney requested two boxes of Frosted Flakes and one pint of milk.
> Charles Wicker requested lettuce and tomatoes.[39]

Even though we have surface details, these last meals remain obscure to us. Weinberger manages to tell us a great deal here without really telling us anything at all. Is there any connection between the types of crimes committed and the decision to choose an extravagant last meal, as de la Rosa does, or to choose, like Barney and Wicker, something simple? Why does Stephen Morin choose 'unleavened bread': does it have some religious significance? What about the six men who we are told requested 'nothing at all': what were their reasons, and how did those reasons differ? Without understanding *why* the prisoners choose the last meals they do, the details of their meals reveal little, and we are left with a feeling of powerlessness. By removing the interpretive power of both author and reader, Weinberger stages the very powerlessness that these prisoners, in their last moments, must feel. The essay thus becomes a form of solidarity with the prisoners, while at the same time acting as a criticism of both our own inactivity, in the face of injustice, and the systems which foster such inactivity, by hiding away behind closed doors that which might inspire action.

In 'What I Heard about Iraq', this tone of powerlessness becomes the basis of a powerful indictment of passivity during the Iraq war. In their sheer volume, the repeated 'I heard' openings wear down the reader into the very submission the essay is implicitly critical of. The constant barrage of voices overwhelms us, and all the different U-turns and contradictions become easy to miss. Note how, over the first twelve pages, Colin Powell contradicts himself twice:

> I heard Colin Powell say that Saddam Hussein 'has not developed any significant capability with respect to weapons of mass destruction.'[40]
>
> I heard Colin Powell at the United Nations say: 'They can produce enough dry biological agent in a single month to kill thousands upon thousands of people. Saddam Hussein has never accounted for vast amounts of chemical weaponry: 550 artillery shells with mustard gas, 30,000 empty munitions… Every statement I make today is backed up by sources, solid sources. These are not assertions. What we're giving you are facts and conclusions based on solid intelligence.'[41]
>
> I heard Colin Powell say: 'I'm absolutely sure that there are weapons of mass destruction there and the evidence will be forthcoming. We're just getting it now.'[42]

No particular attention is drawn to Powell's flip-flops and lies here. The technique is not juxtaposition but accretion: a gradual accrual of contradictions that become almost impossible to unpick. If a startling juxtaposition jolts us into a response, then such accretion, almost overwhelming in its confusion, numbs us. The form dramatizes and embodies the very numbness that made the war possible. It becomes impossible to distinguish one voice from another:

> I heard the Vice President say: 'There's overwhelming evidence there was a connection between al-Qaeda and the Iraqi government. I am very confident there was an established relationship there.'

I heard Colin Powell say: 'Iraqi officials deny accusations of ties with al-Qaeda. These denials are simply not credible.'

I heard Condoleezza Rice say: 'There clearly are contacts between al-Qaeda and Saddam Hussein that can be documented.'[43]

The overlap between Hussein and al-Qaeda is mirrored in the overlap of the voices, all saying the same thing. Indeed, throughout the essay it is remarkable how little variation there is in tone, despite the huge variety of speakers. The implication being that if no single voice can be associated with any specific claim – that is, if no claim is attributable or verifiable – then no one is culpable for the consequences of those claims, for their fallout. The essay both mirrors this ambiguous overlap of voices and also counters it by re-establishing the specificity of each claim, attributing them to their original speakers, and thus re-establishing culpability. It thus functions both as a record of specifics, in its content, and, counterintuitively, in its form, as an exploration of the very ambiguities that led to the invasion of Iraq.

In terms of the position of the self within the essay, its movement is always a passive one, one of hearing rather than speaking or doing. Thus, though the 'I' is obviously present and visible here, the author, and any sense of the author's personality, is as absent and invisible as in 'The Present'. In 'What I Heard about Iraq', though, this absence feels self-critical. As the lies gather up, no one, including the author, speaks out against them, *speaks* against the *hearing*: thus the war, and the lies, continue. Though the essay's criticism is chiefly directed at its speakers, connecting their abuses of language in the first half of the essay to the increasing acts of violence as it continues, its author, blurred into these others by lacking a separate, clear, countering voice, becomes complicit in the violence too – as do we, as readers, engaged in the inherently passive act of reading.

Yet there is an alternative way of reading this silence, and it is one elucidated nicely by considering Weinberger's comments on the prolonged silence of George Oppen. Weinberger has cited Oppen as a rare model of successful political poetry, and his detailed familiarity with his poems[44] can be felt in several small touchstones in his work: its concern with the concrete example (as in 'Naked Mole Rats');[45] its looking outward rather than inward ("There are things / We live among, and to see them / Is to know ourselves'); its lack of transitions and frequent use of parallel cutting.[46] Yet as important as Oppen's poetry is his long period of silence, the thirty years in which he wrote nothing at all – a kind of total erasure of his poetic self – so that he could devote himself entirely to political action. In 'Oppen Then', Weinberger describes how that silence 'hung over' him and other writers, like 'the extreme act of a saint'; how Oppen 'had an aura about him, that of the honourable man trying to speak in the roar of history'.[47] That total silence – 'political and not personal, ideological and not writer's block'[48] – feels like the ideal to which Weinberger's work, at its most self-eradicating, aspires. Returning to 'What I Heard about Iraq' with this in mind, our reading is complicated. Might not the silence of the author, his refusal to speak to the lies and abuses of language his essay relentlessly records, be read as a form of silent protest? The essayist's silence, therefore, manages to simultaneously evoke passivity and a kind of peaceful resistance: it can thus be read either passively or actively, another handing over of power to the reader.

If Oppen's silence can be read as the ideal erasure of self to which Weinberger's essays aspire, then other poets provide him with models as to how to compromise, and capture an impression of this silence in his essays. One crucial influence here is Charles Reznikoff, who by Weinberger's own admittance taught him to 'compress large amounts of information into small spaces'.[49] Scott Saul describes 'Iraq' as bringing 'the archival collage method of Reznikoff to the "truth decay" of the Bush years'.[50] I would argue that there is also a tonal similarity between the two. There is something of the restlessness of a poem like 'Massacres' to 'What I Heard about Iraq'; both works witness and record, in full, the crimes of war, refusing to look away when their subject matter becomes complicated or uncomfortable. The poem, like Weinberger's essay, leaves the reader with an almost overwhelming sense of passivity as its horrors advance and multiply without comment. Its tone remains neutral ('They were told to lie down in fours / and were shot', 'Those who fell were shot', 'They shot her mother too', 'The Germans caught the children / and shot them, too') even as the reader longs for it to break from its reportage and lament, mourn, comment: that is, inject the self (and thus, perspective) into the poem.[51] Both writers' continued refusal to do so is balanced by the seriousness of their subject matter, a sense that any authorial comment could only diminish what is being said.

This tone is one we find in Lorine Niedecker too, another key influence. Her poems, Stephen Burt notes, 'take place after injustice has been done, presenting neither a struggle nor a debate but a fait accompli'.[52] The compressions, omissions and frequent use of gaps and white spaces that characterize much of her work can equally be seen in 'What I Heard about Iraq'. In 'Darwin', for example, with its 'holy / slowly / mulled over /matter',[53] the space after the various facts and quotes from Darwin's life is left for that 'mulling over':

> He was often becalmed
>   in this Port Desire by illness
>   or rested from species
> at billiard table
>
> As to Man
>   'I believe Man…
>   in the same predicament
> with other animals'[54]

The extraordinary work Darwin is doing (a 'delirium of delight'[55]) is offset here by ordinary details like the billiard table, a technique Weinberger often borrows, ending 'What I Heard about Iraq', for example, with Saddam Hussein eating 'cookies and muffins'.[56] Yet these details only reinforce the sense of enigma: the idea of Darwin playing billiards or Hussein eating cookies feels uncanny, almost unimaginable. There is a tone of lingering here ('becalmed', 'rested'; that ellipsis, like a pause for thought) and yet most of what we linger over are absences: we are not told what illness Darwin had, why he was in Port Desire, what 'predicament' he refers to. Niedecker takes the relatively ordinary details of a specific life – a place name, a billiard table – and through the use of elisions and unexpected associations makes them enigmatic. Spareness from Niedecker, abundance from Reznikoff[57] – the two qualities would appear to contradict each other, but it is in their combination that Weinberger finds his unique style. For that is how he 'compresses' so much into his essays: by giving us everything, yet stripping out all the wiring, all the connective tissue, leaving us with a kind of spare abundance.

If Niedecker and Reznikoff are the poetic models for self-erasure, then Paz is the model for Weinberger's continued bleeding of the self into others. Both Paz and Weinberger, in their attempts to see and hear everything, continually modulate the position from which they 'look' – thus the 'I' is always shifting. In Paz, this 'I' is closely related to the 'eye', a recurrent motif in his poems. Yet eyes, in Paz, cannot be entirely trusted, and frequently they have to be closed for truth to be perceived: 'with eyes closed / you light up within'.[58] Several poems imply a separation between the deceptive 'eyes' of the body and the inner 'eye' which can see:

Close your eyes and hear the light singing…
Close your eyes and open them[59]

They see with our eyes what eyes do not see[60]

My eyes without anger or pity
Look me in the eye[61]

The duality present throughout these lines, in which outer eyes look at inner eyes, or inner eyes open as outer eyes close, destabilizes any idea of the poem having a single, clear viewpoint. This dethroning of the poet's self as the poems' centre allows them to splinter into unexpected directions; scattered light is another motif, as in 'Objects and Apparitions', where 'the reflector of the inner eye / scatters the spectacle'.[62] A single viewpoint in Paz is not to be trusted – only through multiple viewpoints, multiple sets of eyes, can the truth be seen.

The influence of Paz is most keenly felt when Weinberger writes on Paz himself. In 'Paz in Asia', he notes how his poetry is characterized by 'the disappearance of the author', in favour of qualities such as 'pluralism', 'multilingualism', 'simultaneity' and an 'emphasis on relation rather than substance', creating a poetry which is 'the expression of an era, rather than an author'.[63] These ideas are borne out in the form of the essay itself, one of Weinberger's most pluralistic and divergent, with numerous shifts in tone and style. The text combines quoted passages from Paz with a fragmented history of Japanese–Mexican relations, a story about Vishnu and Narada, a long commentary on the poet Tablada, a meditation on tantric art, and an encyclopaedic account of which twentieth-century poets have visited which Asian countries – *not*, it should be noted, including an entry on Paz. Indeed, Paz is in the essay surprisingly little, and entirely absent until its third part. One way of reading this patchwork is as a formal response to Paz's call for poetry which is 'composed by the multitude, not the individual'.[64] This Whitmanesque sense of multiple authorship is furthered by the essay's references to other similarly open, democratic forms of poetry, such as *haiku*, a form always opening up to the reader, 'permanently at the verge of completion',[65] and *renga*, 'an endless series of permutations changing over time'.[66] Indeed, the essay itself could be read as an answer to Weinberger's call for a 'modern *renga*', which would be something like 'a multi-authored *Cantos*', or 'a single cell swiftly multiplying into hundreds of organisms';[67] though ironically the same could be said of the multiple voices in 'What I Heard about Iraq', itself a kind of *renga*. Democratic openness, we see, necessitates the possibility of undesired outcomes, of voices countering the author's own intruding into the space of the essay – yet it also allows for surprise and delight.

The sense of multiplicity is reinforced in the way the text's many elements are arranged using the stepped line that characterizes much of Paz's work after 'Sunstone'. Compare these lines from 'Vrindaban' to the essay itself. Paz:

> The whole universe a peacock's tail
> myriads of eyes
>   other eyes reflecting
> modulations
>   reverberations of a single eye
> a solitary sun
>   hidden
> behind its cloth of transparencies[68]

And Weinberger:

> By 1600 there is more trade across the Pacific than the Atlantic:
>   Mexican silver
> and gold, copper, chocolate, and cochineal, for
>   Asian silk, camel
> hair, mineral and vegetable inks, precious stones[69]

Paz's technique diffuses the force of the line break and spreads it across the page, so that the whole poem feels cracked and tentative, reflected further in its dispersed viewpoint through 'myriads of eyes'. Such is the effect of the frequent stop-starts in 'Paz in Asia', an essay whose subject seems to be constantly on the move. Its gaps open up like fissures, or pockets of air in a porous surface, allowing for a kind of osmosis between essay and essayist; as the essayist brings new ideas to the essay, it seems to bring new ideas back to him, an exchange much like the shipped and swapped cargo in its back and forth across the Pacific. The essay is thus not only democratically open to other voices and ideas from outside of it, it is open to ideas that bubble up unexpectedly from within it, to connections and ideas that surprise both author and reader.

I have argued that Weinberger both erases *and* doubles the self. These appear to be opposite movements, yet both occur simultaneously, and indeed the former might be read as a precursor to the latter. In removing the traditionally essayistic 'I' from its central, foundational position in the essay, a vacuum is created in which other voices can enter. These others, in fulfilling the *role* of the centring self, are doubled with the ghost of the author's original, vanished self. This is what I mean when I describe Weinberger's 'I' as 'lyric': as in the poetic models of Oppen, Niedecker, Reznikoff and Paz, Weinberger's authorial self 'transcends the boundaries of the poet's actual, historical self' to become the choral voice of a multitude.[70] The reader also becomes another one of these voices. Weinberger's lyric essays invite the reader to fill in their silences; the reader thus 'becomes a stakeholder in their meaning'.[71] It is this silence which is perhaps the most powerful tool at the lyric essayist's disposal. It is something we see in other so-called lyric essayists too: in Annie Dillard's emphasis on listening over speaking; in the importance of gaps and white spaces in the work of Anne Carson; in the continual moments of quiet that punctuate Maggie Nelson's *Bluets*, or that hover over Jenny Boully's *The Body*. Much of the power of these essayists' works comes from what is left unsaid. There is perhaps a slight irony here – that in this new, supposedly more musical, choral, noisy form of the essay, the essayist seems inclined, more than ever, to shut up and listen.

Furthermore, the ways in which essayists like Weinberger reinvent the form give us pause to rethink how we conceptualize the essay as a form always *at the limits*. I opened with the observation that a form with no clearly delineated boundaries, a form which stakes its very identity on its lack of, or continuous stretching of, its parameters, cannot meaningfully be described as evolving, or being taken to new places: to do so becomes a tautology, for to evolve and expand *is to do what the essay already does*. Yet the essay, in its restless, experimental spirit, is also liable to re-examine and re-imagine its own centre, to travel not outwards but inwards on its journey towards new forms and new ideas. In Weinberger's work, the essay folds in on itself, changing itself from the inside out by reorienting itself around something other than the traditionally essayistic 'I': in doing so, it finds a way to expand an unexpandable form.

Notes

1. Annie Dillard, 'To Fashion a Text', in *Inventing the Truth: The Art and Craft of Memoir*, ed. William Zinsser (New York: Houghton Mifflin Company, 1998), 141–62 (160).
2. John D'Agata, *The Next American Essay* (Minneapolis, MN: Graywolf Press, 2003), 75.
3. Phillip Lopate, 'What Happened to the Personal Essay?', in *Essayists on the Essay: Montaigne to Our Time*, ed. Carl H. Klaus and Ned Stuckey-French (Iowa City: University of Iowa Press, 2012), 127–36 (128).
4. André Belleau, 'Little Essayistic', in *Essayists on the Essay*, 116–19 (119).
5. William H. Gass, 'Emerson and the Essay', in *Essayists on the Essay*, 106–9 (108).
6. Edward Hoagland, 'What I Think, What I Am', in *Essayists on the Essay*, 101–3 (101).

7 Jean Starobinski, 'Can One Define the Essay?' in *Essayists on the Essay*, 110–15 (111).
8 Réda Bensmaïa, *The Barthes Effect: The Essay as Reflective Text*, trans. Pat Fedkiew (Minneapolis: University of Minnesota Press, 1987), 92.
9 Michael Hamburger, 'An Essay on the Essay', in *Art as Second Nature: Occasional Pieces* (Manchester: Carcanet New Press Ltd., 1975), 3–5 (3).
10 Cynthia Ozick, 'She: Portrait of the Essay as a Warm Body', in *Essayists on the Essay*, 151–8 (151).
11 Ibid., 155.
12 Eliot Weinberger, *Karmic Traces* (New York: New Directions, 2000), dust jacket.
13 Eliot Weinberger, *An Elemental Thing* (New York: New Directions, 2007), dust jacket.
14 Eliot Weinberger, *Oranges & Peanuts for Sale* (New York: New Directions, 2009), dust jacket.
15 Weinberger, 'In Conversation with Kent Johnson', *Jacket Magazine*, March 2002, http://jacketmagazine.com/16/johns-iv-weinb.html, accessed 24 April 2020.
16 It is perhaps no coincidence that Phillip Lopate, that recent champion of the personal essay and editor of *The Art of the Personal Essay: An Anthology from the Classical Era to the Present* (New York: First Anchor Books, 1995), also has a book of essays called *Portrait of My Body* (New York: First Anchor Books, 1996).
17 There *are* exceptions, of course. Almost from the beginning there is an alternative, Baconian lineage of essays more concerned with universal truths than personal opinions, essays which resist the personal in favour of formality, science and objectivity, a lineage that might include Samuel Johnson, Robert Boyle, José Ortega y Gasset, William Carlos Williams, Max Bense and others. Yet these essayists are still single voices speaking – they are simply speaking in public voices rather than private ones, building on the idea that the political sphere is when people become fully themselves, rather than in the private bedchamber Montaigne grants us access to. Essayists such as Weinberger, by contrast, resist both the private *and* public self.
18 Michael Duszat, *Donkeys, Spirits and Imperial Ladies: Enumeration in Eliot Weinberger's Essays* (Heidelberg: Universitätsverlag Winter, 2014), 16.
19 Ibid., 285.
20 Virginia Woolf, 'The Decay of Essay Writing', in *Selected Essays*, ed. David Bradshaw (Oxford: Oxford University Press, 2009), 3–5 (4).
21 Michel de Montaigne, 'On repenting', in *The Essays: A Selection*, trans. M. A. Screech (London: Penguin, 2004), 232–46 (233).
22 Weinberger, 'Dreams from the Holothurians', in *Outside Stories: 1987-1991* (New York: New Directions, 1992), 166–77.
23 Weinberger, 'Changs', in *An Elemental Thing*, 4–9.
24 Weinberger, 'Questions of Death', in *Oranges & Peanuts for Sale*, 159–62.
25 Lopate, 'What Happened to the Personal Essay?', 133.
26 Robert Atwan, 'Foreword', *The Best American Essays 1987*, ed. Gay Talese (New York: Ticknor & Fields, 1987), ix–xi (x).
27 Amy Bonnaffons, 'Bodies of Text: On the Lyric Essay', *The Essay Review* (2016), accessed 20 January 2020, http://theessayreview.org/bodies-of-text-on-the-lyric-essay/#
28 The key text so far on the lyric essay is John D'Agata's three-volume anthology *The Next American Essay*, which in its introductions and commentaries lays out the scope of the subgenre, albeit in a fairly polemical way heavily influenced by D'Agata's own personal views. There are also dozens of shorter pieces attempting to define the lyric essay: start with Deborah Tall and John D'Agata, 'New Terrain: The Lyric Essay',

Seneca Review 27, no. 2 (1997): 7–8 and Judith Kitchen's 'Grounding the Lyric Essay', *Fourth Genre: Explorations in Nonfiction* 13, no. 2 (2011): 115–21 for a succinct introduction.
29 Weinberger, 'The Present', in *Outside Stories*, 71–82 (71).
30 Though beyond the scope of this chapter, a fruitful comparison might be made with Claudia Rankine's recasting of personal anecdotes in the second person in *Citizen: An American Lyric* (London: Penguin Books, 2015).
31 Weinberger, *Outside Stories*, 71.
32 In a detail typical of Weinberger, we are told that the local McDonald's displayed a sign reading: 'Free Fries if he Fries' (ibid., 77).
33 This is further complicated by the fact that both 'Hitler' and 'Hitler's double', with their differing levels of relation to a real person from history, are also, in this anecdote, inventions, fictional characters in an unwritten novel described by an unnamed friend to an unnamed 'he'.
34 Weinberger, *Outside Stories*, 72.
35 Weinberger, 'Bush the Poet', in *What Happened Here: Bush Chronicles* (New York: Verso, 2006), 96–9.
36 Weinberger, 'The Present', 72.
37 Ibid., 82.
38 Lopate, 'What Happened to the Personal Essay?', 131.
39 Weinberger, 'The Present', 81.
40 Weinberger, 'What I Heard about Iraq', in *What Happened Here*, 144–82 (144).
41 Ibid., 147.
42 Ibid., 155.
43 Ibid., 148.
44 He wrote the Preface to the George Oppen, *New Collected Poems*, ed. Michael Davidson (New York: New Directions, 2008), for example.
45 Weinberger, 'Naked Mole Rats', in *Karmic Traces*, 53–5.
46 Oppen, 'Of Being Numerous', *New Collected Poems*, 163–88 (163).
47 Weinberger, 'Oppen Then', in *Oranges & Peanuts for Sale*, 3–8 (3).
48 Ibid.
49 Weinberger, Interview with Jeffrey Errington, *Quarterly Conversation*, 6 June 2011, https://web.archive.org/web/20190917080352/http://quarterlyconversation.com:80/the-eliot-weinberger-interview.
50 Scott Saul, 'Suspended Sentences', *The Nation*, 19 October 2009, 33–6 (34).
51 Charles Reznikoff, 'Massacres', in *American Poetry Since 1950: Innovators and Outsiders*, ed. Eliot Weinberger (New York: Marsilio Publishers, 1993), 40–7.
52 Stephen Burt, *Close Calls with Nonsense: Reading New Poetry* (Minneapolis, MN: Graywolf Press, 2009), 320.
53 Lorine Niedecker, 'Darwin', in *Collected Works*, ed. Jenny Penberthy (Berkeley: University of California Press, 2002), 295–304 (295).
54 Ibid.
55 Ibid.
56 Weinberger, 'What I Heard about Iraq',182.
57 Though both qualities can be found in each other's work, too, a point Weinberger makes himself in his essay 'Niedecker/Reznikoff' (*Oranges & Peanuts for Sale*, 45–9).
58 Octavio Paz, *Selected Poems*, ed. Eliot Weinberger (New York: New Directions, 1984), 75.
59 Paz, 'Native Stone', in *Selected Poems*, 4 (4).

60 Paz, 'Identical Time', in *The Collected Poems of Octavio Paz, 1957–1987: Bilingual Edition*, ed. Eliot Weinberger (New York: New Directions, 1991), 68–79 (79).
61 Paz, 'A Draft of Shadows', in *Selected Poems*, 122–38 (124).
62 Paz, 'Objects and Apparitions', in *Selected Poems*, 97–8 (98).
63 Weinberger, 'Paz in Asia', in *Outside Stories*, 17–45 (33).
64 Ibid.
65 Ibid., 32.
66 Ibid., 34.
67 Ibid.
68 Paz, 'Vrindaban', in *Selected Poems*, 58–62 (60).
69 Weinberger, 'Paz in Asia', 24–5.
70 Bonnaffons, 'Bodies of Text'.
71 Ibid.

Part III

THE ESSAY, FORM AND THE ESSAYISTIC

The chapters in this part of the volume explore different aspects of the formal characteristics of the essay. They also trace some of them in other genres, thus showing how the essayistic mode – or the essayistic 'spirit' – can transcend the limits of the essay as a genre and be a generating impulse elsewhere.

R. Eric Tippin focuses on the 'familial bond' between the essay and the aphorism. He begins by detailing the characteristics of the aphorism – its 'formal behaviours', its tension between movement and fixity, its 'particular brand of memorability' – and then proceeds by showing that to understand the aphorism is 'to understand the essay more adequately'. Through a discussion of Roland Barthes's views on aphorism, and a series of close readings of aphorisms by Francis Bacon, Zadie Smith, Oscar Wilde and others, Tippin not only shows how the aphorism and the essay are affiliated through particular relations to the authorial 'I' and through similar, though not identical, formal elements, but also suggests ways of thinking the essayistic in the aphorism and the aphoristic in the essay.

The 'familial bonds' that Jason Childs explores are those between the essay and the novel. Childs begins by trying to account for the 'contemporary enthusiasm for the essay', which he contextualizes in terms of the project of modernity and the predilection for the swerve, the protest and the marginal in contemporary literary culture. He suggests that in this context what needs to be discussed further is the way the anti-ideological rhetoric of the essay – its investment in openness and flexibility – may not be as radical as we may envisage. Indeed, it seems to cohere with 'qualities prized most today in the entrepreneurial class and the precariat alike', making the idea of 'people without qualities' a dystopian facet of contemporary reality. Childs grounds his theoretical speculation in a series of authors, including David Shields, Karl Ove Knausgaard, J. M. Coetzee, Ben Lerner and Milan Kundera, whose 'novelistic essays' or essayistic novels allow us to zoom in on 'essayism', its dialectic relation to truth in a post-truth world and its tension – perhaps as an anti-genre – with the novel.

The question of genre – its fluidity and porousness – is also central to Allen Durgin's chapter on the essayistic in Wallace Stevens's work. For Durgin, however, 'genre is ghosted by discussions of queerness'. In other words, following David Lazar, Durgin claims that there is an indissoluble and often forgotten link between genre and gender. In this chapter, this awareness is at the basis of the way Durgin explores the poetic impulse in some of Stevens's essays and the way he 'reread[s] Stevens's straight-laced poems as queer essays'. Eve Kosofsky Sedgwick's concept of 'queer performativity' is put in action to show how Stevens's work – in ways that Durgin tells us occasionally anticipate selected essays by Audre Lorde – may help us to understand the essayistic qualities of Stevens's poetry, such as its self-reflexiveness and its 'enacting' of the 'act of finding'. Like other chapters in the volume, Durgin's contribution is 'essayistic' in many ways, not only in style, but also in how it undercuts absolute categorical attributions we may wish to impose on it. Indeed, while Durgin's text deals with the essayistic 'form' of Stevens's work, it also shows how such a topic is inextricable from discussions of the self, so that this chapter could easily have been placed in the second part of this volume, which focuses on the relation between the essay and the self.

While Durgin explores the essayistic in poetry, Maria Frendo and Bob Cowser Jr extend their thinking of the essayistic even more radically as they move beyond the textual world of literature into music and film, respectively. In this respect, Frendo, in particular, operates in somewhat uncharted territory in essay studies, as there are few precedents to her discussion of essayistic musical compositions. More specifically, Frendo looks at selected 'elegiac musical essays' by Dmitri Shostakovich and Joseph Vella that commemorate historically significant events through 'inimitable' and 'recognizable' personal tones. Indeed, it is in this intersection between the private and the public, the personal and the political as well as the occasional and the durable that Frendo locates the essayistic in these musical compositions. The essay, for Frendo, is digressive and fragmentary, but it is also a form of recollection, both in the sense of it revisiting the past and in the sense of trying to gather or shore fragments against its ruins. Shostakovich's 'Babi Yar' *Symphony no. 13* and Vella's *Charlie on My Mind op. 144* and *Lament op. 103* are made of notes, not words and yet they are essayistic.

This insight helps us further discover what the essayistic may be and the ways in which it may transcend genre. Cowser's chapter does so too, but in relation to film. Unlike music, film has already attracted research focusing on the intersection between it and the essay. What Cowser adds to this, through his comparative analysis of John Hersey's well-known work of documentary literary journalism, *Hiroshima*, and Alain Resnais's film, *Hiroshima mon amour*, is an argument that relates form to the political possibilities of creative work, whether it is film or literature. Cowser argues that the preeminence of Hersey's work in its depiction of such a momentous historical 'event' may be attributable in part to the way in which Hersey attempts to arrive at 'wholeness and meaning exemplary of American Cold War confidence and complacency'. However, such an approach, Cowser continues, 'ultimately confirms more of what Americans believe about themselves than it challenges'. In doing so, it differs radically from Resnais's film, which Cowser reads as an 'essayistic counterpoint'. For Cowser, 'Corrigan's concept of *essayism*, with its focus on subjectivity and language and time as important components of knowledge, liberated as it is from the confines of genre, allows us to locate [Resnais's film] at the limits of the essay form.' This, though, does not only have formal significance, because an essayistic approach to history allows us also to 'think about a history-making (with words *and* images) characterized more and more by the curiosity and reflexivity on display therein'. In other words, a work imbibed with the essayistic spirit, like Resnais's film – an example of what Hayden White may call 'essayistic historiography' – is reflective by nature, and it encourages radical questioning rather than dogma through assuaging narrative.

Chapter 11

AT THE LIMITS OF *FIXITÉ*: THE ESSAY AND THE APHORISM

R. Eric Tippin

In his 1975, self-titled book, Roland Barthes wrote this:

> Il rôde dans ce livre un ton d'aphorisme (nous, on, toujours). Or la maxime est compromise dans une idée essentialiste de la nature humaine … c'est la plus arrogante (souvent la plus bête) des formes de langage. La raison en est, comme toujours, émotive: j'écris des maximes (ou j'en esquisse le mouvement) pour me rassurer: lorsqu'un trouble survient, je l'atténue en m'en remettant à une fixité qui me dépasse: au fond, c'est toujours comme ça: et la maxime est née. La maxime est une sorte de phrase-nom, et nommer, c'est apaiser. Ceci est au reste encore une maxime: elle atténue ma peur de paraître déplacé en écrivant des maximes.
>
> (There lurks in this book an aphoristic tone [we, people, always]. But the maxim is compromised by an essentialist idea of human nature … it is the most arrogant (often the most asinine) of the forms of language. The reason is, as always, emotional: I write aphorisms (or outline the motion/movement) to reassure myself: when a disorder occurs, I mitigate it by relying on a fixity beyond myself – basically, it's always like this – and the maxim is born. The maxim is a kind of phrase-naming, and to nominate is to placate. Even this is a maxim; writing maxims mitigates my fear of being seen as decentred.)[1]

It is a striking passage, wallowing in self-recrimination and dark ironies. It might be called a formal confession to a formal addiction in that Barthes demonstrates a hopeless inability to keep from aphorizing even as he condemns the practice as something both asinine and addictive. Indeed, he imagines the aphorism as a kind of narcotic habit picked up in back-alley encounters with philosophical foundationalists. More specifically, he makes four distinct, co-determining claims in this passage regarding the aphorism:

1. The aphorism is ideologically essentialist and therefore *arrogante* (arrogant).
2. The aphorism is therapeutic – therapy being the atmosphere of his words *émotive* (emotional), *apasier* (placate) and *atténue* (mitigate).

3. The aphorism is habit forming.
4. The aphorism lures the vulnerable through its *movement* (movement).

Barthes sees danger in aphorizing, and danger of a particular kind – namely of false security or phantom stability. His word, *déplacé*, is equivocal, meaning both inappropriate and, more literally, dis-placed. The literal reading is more suggestive. It offers a way to imagine in spatial terms the reality that the aphorism is, in Barthes's conception, veiling. The aphorism, Barthes claims, offers formal assurances of a philosophical centre of gravity, holding objects in place, keeping them from the *déplacement* Barthes understands to be a normative feature of human experience. In this false assurance lies the aphorism's danger to the writer and, presumably, to the reader.

Another easily missed, notable feature of Barthes's passage is that it appears in the form of an essay. And because Barthes the essayist cannot escape therapeutic aphorizing, even as he condemns it, he implicates not only the writing 'I' of the passage but the literary form in which the 'I' writes. At the least, his formal hypocrisy shows the essay to be an atmosphere in which the aphorism can gestate and thrive. Others have made this claim more explicitly. Brian Dillon, in *Essayism*, writes that the 'brevity of essays' has 'its formal apogee in aphorisms'.[2] Ben Grant sees not only compatibility but resemblance between the two forms, suggesting that the essay may be thought of as 'an expanded aphorism', or conversely, 'the aphorism as a miniature essay'.[3] Insofar as these claims express a general sense that the aphorism and the essay are often seen in one another's company, they are unremarkable. Essayists from Michel de Montaigne to Francis Bacon to Oscar Wilde to Susan Sontag have made the aphorism a key ingredient of their essays and in doing so have formed an associative link between the two forms. However, Dillon and Grant move beyond the incidental fact of mutual presence, positing a fraternal or genetic relationship between the two. And this assertion of shared paternity is indeed remarkable, given Barthes's suspicion of the aphorism as a foundationalist or essentialist refuge and the overwhelming agreement in essay scholarship – including scholarship by Dillon and Grant – that the essay is not a genre of metaphysical or epistemological rest or repose. In Alexander Smith's words, it is not the essayist's duty to 'build pathways through metaphysical morasses'.[4] The claim that the aphorism's function is *rassurer* (to reassure) and to act as a *fixité* (fixity) sits uncomfortably with this sentiment.

These seemingly incompatible claims require careful arbitration. To this end, this chapter expands Barthes's claim that the aphorism thinks therapeutically and allures through its *mouvement*, suggesting more precise ways of formulating this thought. It will approach the difficult question Barthes raises of whether the therapeutic and barbiturate qualities of the aphorism make it too dangerous for the sceptic-essayist to handle – whether it always already conditions an unhealthy metaphysical rest. It will ask whether the aphorism is, by necessity, epistemologically *arrogante* or whether there are deployments of the aphorism that might work against the kind of cheap certainty of conviction that Barthes fears aphoristic forms will pattern into him and his readers. This question is best answered, I argue, by returning to the idea that the essay and the aphorism have a familial bond, and are, as Grant suggests, made in one another's image. Barthes fears the aphorism's implicit, formal claim to time-vetted, universally applicable knowledge presented and understood as something both 'stead[y]' and 'whole'.[5] But the aphorism performs a kind of stress test on stable knowledge, revealing not only its strengths but its limitations. In doing so, it opens new ways of understanding the essay's relationship with *fixité*.

'Aphorism', like 'essay', can describe a number of forms and will be unwieldy unless defined. As Barthes's interchange of *maxime* and *aphorisme* hints, the aphorism exists in a constellation of similar short forms with similar claims to stable knowing: epigram, maxim, proverb, truism, saying and adage among others. Like the essay, the aphorism distinguishes itself by its special relationship with the individual author. In John Gross's words, it 'bears the stamp and style of the mind which created it'.[6] And unlike the epigram, it appears more often in prose than in poetry.[7] With this as an assumption, the aphorism will be defined here as a short statement, primarily in rhythmic prose, traceable (if not attributable) to a single author, usually in the present tense, making a strong assertion in a sonically memorable fashion.

1. *The aphorism:* Mouvement *as meaning*

A good deal of pressure rests on that word, 'memorable'. Understanding the aphorism's particular brand of memorability is vital to understanding its formal behaviour, and one way of approaching this understanding is to look at a sentence that falls short of the aphoristic and to ask why. Zadie Smith, in her essay 'Speaking in Tongues', provides an example when she writes this: 'To occupy a dream, exist in a dreamed space (conjured by both father and mother), is surely a quite different thing from simply inheriting a dream'.[8] The sentence is plausibly but not certainly aphoristic, primarily because its nesting asides and its adverbs ('surely' and 'simply') sacrifice memorability to precision and easy affability. However, if one removes these academic and conventional gestures, an aphorism emerges from the sentence: 'To occupy a dream is a quite different thing from inheriting a dream.'[9] It is tempting to claim that the change is merely quantitative: that the stripped-down sentence reveals more efficiently its propositional content – the distinction between two types of dreams – or that, in Samuel Johnson's words, 'it does not tire those whom' it does 'not happen to please.'[10] But the difference, I argue, is also qualitative. The stripped version is not simply shorter; it is more memorable, and not more memorable simply because it is shorter. The statement has a different way of making meaning; its terms of cogency have shifted. At this juncture, Barthes again becomes a useful interlocutor when he remarks that he does not only write (*écris*) an aphorism but he also sketches its movement (*j'en esquisse le mouvement*). The aphorism's appeal and its alluring danger for Barthes lie not only in its brevity and its syntactical anatomy but in its movement through semantic and sonic space. In other words, the aphoristic effect of Smith's shorter sentence is a function of its animate temporality as well as a function of its propositional and quantitative, static elements.

Another way of putting this is that the aphorism is not only propositionally comprehensible but also aesthetically comprehensible. It thinks in images and rhythmic phrases as well as syllogisms. It shapes its comprehensibility by creating pre-propositional visions of assent through an eminently recognizable, lilting, distilled, rhythmically predictable style. It casts visions of assent before asking for assent. Matthew McGlone and Jessica Tofighbakhsh's quantitative research has affirmed the point. In a study of aphorisms and their effects on readers' perception of truth content, they suggest that readers base 'their judgments of aphorism accuracy in part on the statements' prosodic qualities' and demonstrate a reliance 'on a rule of thumb in which the aesthetic qualities of a message are equated with its truth'.[11] Nietzsche, in *The Gay Science*, intuited the idea in his examination of the origins of poetry, writing that 'rhythm is a compulsion; it engenders an unconquerable desire to yield, to join in'.[12] Nietzsche's words 'join in' appeal implicitly to dance, and this appeal prefigures Barthes's concept of *mouvement*. The aphorism, it is implied, shapes its meaning by habituating its writers and readers to the *motion* of its thought before asking them to agree with the content of its thought, in a similar way that a rhythm-led song invites a bodily response to and movement with the music before any engagement with its semantic content.

One can understand how this pre-propositional, rhythmic memorability functions in the aphorism by way of another musical parallel, namely the tune. Roger Scruton defines the tune this way: 'It is bounded usually at each end, contains a distinctive and recognizable internal order and is regarded as a complete individual, to be memorized as a whole.'[13] There is that word 'whole' again. The sense of unqualified wholeness is what distinguishes the tune from other kinds of melodies (plainchant, theme). Tunes such as 'The Last Rose of Summer' are self-contained, hermetic, musical thoughts with a clear beginning and ending that the phrase moves toward – what is called the 'boundary experience'.[14] The aphorism is also a self-contained form that moves from and towards a definite boundary, more complete than the end of a clause. There is little question when 'The Last Rose of Summer' ends, and, in a similar way, there is little question when aphorisms such as this one from Francis Bacon end: 'A man that is young in years may be old in hours.'[15] While a clarifying clause may follow or a contextualizing clause precede, the statement does not create the necessity of a following clause nor show clear signs of a preceding clause. As Scruton writes of the tune, it 'resists the attempt to dissolve it in a narrative larger than itself'.[16] This rhythmic isolation caused by a strong boundary effect both increases what might be termed the digestibility of the aphorism and creates the conditions for its distinct movement.

The nature of that distinct movement can be described by a similar appeal to the tune – namely its tendency to move first away from and then back towards the tonic note. Within its clear boundaries, I suggest that the aphorism plays a short, two-part song, rising with its first claim ('To occupy a dream is a quite different thing') and falling to some rhetorical resolution or revision ('from inheriting a dream'). One can see this two-phase movement more clearly in a cross section

11. The Essay and the Aphorism

of aphorisms, taken from two very different aphorists: Francis Bacon and Oscar Wilde, essayists who represent two starkly contrasting modes of generating aphoristic meaning – one traditionally earnest and one transgressively ironic. However, both share a common rhythmic pattern:

> Man is least himself when he talks in his own person. Give him a mask, and he will tell you the truth.[17]
>
> Prosperity doth best discover vice, but adversity doth best discover virtue.[18]
>
> The more one analyses people, the more all reasons for analysis disappear.[19]
>
> A man were better relate himself to a statua or picture than to suffer his thoughts to pass in smother.[20]

Much of the rhythmic meaning in these aphorisms is wrapped up in the anticipation, not only of a boundary, but also of a response parallel that resolves both the content and completes the beat pattern. Wilde's aphoristic opening, 'The more one analyses people', carries with it a special rhythmic demand for a response and a resolution ('the more all reasons for analysis disappear'). This demand is beyond that of a normal dependent clause, because its antiphonal rhythm and aphoristic syntax hint at a swift and pleasurable movement towards a boundary. As in music, the rhythm of the phrase inflects the meaning prior to the full revelation of the phrase's content. In short, the aphoristic rhythms can begin to ghost meaning while the words themselves go by almost unnoticed, and the meaning ghosted by the form (as with the nursery rhyme, liturgy and domestic conversation) is often that of an immediate and deep familiarity and comprehensibility. When reading the work of an aphoristic essayist such as Wilde or Bacon, the reader is patterned to listen for the coming of these aphorisms. After the first word or two, one begins to expect the rhythmic move towards closure – to listen for and find pleasurable expectation in the knowledge of an approaching formal boundary.

One explanation for the narcotic effect of this familiar movement can be found in the aesthetics of memory – the positive reception of a text's rhythms working in or through a long haptic association with and repetition of that text, creating an instinctive response. Stephen Blackwood, in his book on 'poetic liturgy' in Boethius, situates such recognizable repetitions within the broader functions of repetition and memory, citing examples of the mother's heartbeat a child hears in the womb, family members' voices and familiar cadences, and even the expected 'alternation of night and day', all of which allow us to 'recognize the perception of the present as the same as the one in the past'.[21] This aesthetic of familiarity is formed, in Blackwood's words, by a 'recurring circle of sound' that acts as 'aural therapy'[22] for the 'memory', and, in certain cases – as with certain nursery rhymes – no metre and little discernible pattern of rhythm outside of a loose parallelism is required for the effect, forming aphorism out of non-aphorism, and making even the most puzzling aphorisms feel familiar, plausible and comprehensible.[23] Derek Attridge's contention that it is not 'possible to discuss rhythm without relating it to the movements of the human body' is applicable here as well.[24] The aphorism shapes its pre-propositional meaning by a *mouvement* away from and towards a distinct boundary and a two-beat rhythm, both of which make it seductively comprehensible in the way that Barthes fears.

But if Barthes is to be believed, 'seductive' is too weak a modifier for the aphorism. To return to the concept of the tune, Scruton argues that it is meant 'to be memorized as a whole' and, by implication, is something eminently memorable. However, 'memorable' too may not, after all, be forceful enough. Both the tune and the aphorism not only invite memorization but invade the memory and become impossible to extract. Listeners commonly encounter such unwelcome invasion in the world of popular music and sales jingles, an experience characterized by Theodor W. Adorno as 'displeasure in pleasure'.[25] There exists an important distinction between being memorable and being unforgettable, and both the tune and the aphorism at their most effective violate and seed their subject's memory by means of his inattentive preference for familiarly-patterned content. As Adorno remarks, 'familiarity of the piece is a surrogate for the quality ascribed to it. To like it is almost the same thing as to recognize it'.[26] The aphorism appeals in part because its appeal runs ahead of its propositional content and 'engenders an unconquerable desire' by utilizing familiar simple, oscillating and arcing rhythms, therapeutic and alluring to the unsuspecting.

2. *The aphorism in the essay*

It is here where the aphorism's danger lies for Barthes – what makes its pattern and patterning unavoidable even to writers like him, awakened to its tricks. So far, I have agreed with Barthes that the aphorism takes the form of an epistemological whole, and that it displays certain therapeutic, opioid behaviours that enhance its rhetorical appeal. However, Barthes's claims are nuanced and complicated by the relationship between the aphorism and the essay – a relationship displayed in his own remarks. Barthes's tail-chasing inability to rid himself of the aphorism in an essay denouncing the aphorism argues implicitly what this chapter argues directly: To understand the behaviours of the aphorism is to begin to understand the essay more adequately, and the first step to this understanding is observing the aphorism's behaviour *in* essays.

While, as was argued above, the aphorism is a bounded form, eminently extractable from its immediate semantic environment and in a sense portable, it does not follow that it exerts no formal influence over its syntactical environment. Indeed, as Barthes shows, the aphorism exerts a strong magnetic force over an essayistic paragraph, even one denouncing aphorisms. He expresses this in a paradox, imagining the aphorism as both a *mouvement* and a *fixité*. One can resolve the contradiction easily by an appeal to category – *mouvement* being a formal term and *fixité* being philosophical. And yet there is a formal sense in which the aphorism acts as a *fixité* – a way that reveals itself if one looks at an aphorism in the context of an essay. Earlier in this chapter, I argued that one learns to look and listen for the closing boundary of an aphorism even as it begins. The observation can be pushed further. When reading a habitual aphorizing essayist, it is possible to discern the coming of an aphorism sentences before it appears. Paragraphs that end in aphorisms often spin towards their final clause in a recognizable, centripetal pattern, crowding antitheses and parallelisms and proto-aphorisms as they near. In the essay, the aphorism's pre-propositional way-making for assent, in short, extends beyond its own rhythm and familiar syntax. It shapes its own syntactical and rhythmic environment. One can see this in the closing sentences of Bacon's essay 'Of Adversity', which culminates in the aphorism quoted above:

> Prosperity is the blessing of the Old Testament; adversity is the blessing of the New, which carrieth the greater benediction and the clearer revelation of God's favour. Yet even in the Old Testament, if you listen to David's harp, you shall hear as many hearse-like airs as carols; and the pencil of the Holy Ghost hath laboured more in describing the afflictions of Job than the felicities of Solomon. Prosperity is not without many fears and distastes, and adversity is not without comforts and hopes. We see in needleworks and embroideries, it is more pleasing to have a lively work upon a sad and solemn ground, than to have a dark and melancholy work upon a lightsome ground: judge therefore of the pleasure of the heart by the pleasure of the eye. Certainly virtue is like precious odours, most fragrant when they are incensed or crushed; for prosperity doth best discover vice, but adversity doth best discover virtue.[27]

The passage is constituted almost wholly of shadow-aphorisms that both prepare the way for and are fulfilled and completed in the final line of the passage. These shadow-aphorisms change as they grow nearer to the last, memorable parallelism. The first three are longer, made up of independent clauses, willing to keep ties with straggling asides ('which carrieth the greater benediction') and similes ('like airs as carols'). However, beginning with 'We see in needleworks', the parallelisms become dependent on conjunctions, drop all loose-thread clauses, and grow steadily shorter in length, until one reaches the dense centre of the final aphorism. All are remarkably balanced: 'Yet in the old testament...' (22 words) parallels 'and the pencil of the Holy...' (21 words); 'Prosperity is not without...' (8 words) parallels 'and adversity is not without...' (8 words). Even when he leaves behind independent clauses, and the phrases begin to compress, moving towards the final, memorable aphorism, the word counts remain balanced on either side of the conjunction: 'it is more pleasing to have a lively...' (15 words), 'than to have a dark and melancholy...' (12 words), 'Certainly virtue is like precious...' (6 words), 'most fragrant when they...' (6 words). As might be expected, the final aphorism is the most compressed and most parallel in its diction: 'prosperity doth best discover vice' (5 words); 'adversity doth best discover virtue' (5 words). In this way, I argue, the aphorism can become a *fixité* – a dense, planetary centre of gravity in a paragraph, bending the time of its orbiting prose, shaping the clauses nearest to it.

One more example is in order. Zadie Smith, in her essay, 'Speaking in Tongues', offers a different instance of the aphorism's 'formal back-pressure' and syntactical terraforming.[28] This passage ends the second section of the essay:

> Black reality has diversified. It's black people who talk like me, and black people who talk like Lil Wayne. It's black conservatives and black liberals, black sportsmen and black lawyers, black computer technicians and black ballet dancers and black truck drivers and black presidents. We're all black, and we all love to be black, and we all sing from our own hymn sheet. We're all surely black people, but we may be finally approaching a point of human history where you can't talk up or down to us anymore, but only *to* us. [Obama is] talking down to white people – how curious it sounds the other way round! In order to say such a thing, one would have to think collectively of white people, as a people of one mind who speak with one voice – a thought experiment in which we have no practice. But it's worth trying. It's only when you play the record backward that you hear the secret message.[29]

It is less clean than Bacon's steady journey towards a dense centre, but it depends upon the gravitational force of its final aphorism to hold together the passage's eclectic syntax and give it retrospective order. As with the Bacon passage, it plays with aphoristic elements and parallelisms without offering any whole aphorism ('can't talk up or down to us anymore but only *to* us'; 'a people of one mind who speak with one voice'). With the exception of her incantatory list circling the word 'black', the dashes and the adverbs disrupt rhythmic momentum and impart to her sentences the kind of diversity of voice that she values in the black community. However, the opening and closing clauses – declarative, syntactically uninterrupted, assured of their claims – serve as boundaries, providing a frame for the sentences within and keeping diversity from becoming dispersion. Tellingly, the final sentence also resonates sonically with the first in a backmasking reversal: 'Black reality' to 'record backwards'. The aphorism, here and elsewhere, not only resides in the essay but shapes the essay in which it resides. Its internal *mouvement* is complemented by an external *fixité*, and it exerts an astronomical, gravitational force on its essay's form and, by default, on its thought.

3. *The aphorism and the essay*

These observations, again, serve to confirm and extend Barthes's claim that the aphorism is a powerful formal-cum-epistemological force. This is particularly true in the context of the essay. But Barthes's fear that the aphorism is as an epistemological Trojan Horse – that its form is enacting an implicit philosophical claim regarding the nature of knowledge – that to read or write an aphorism is to be patterned into an ideology that sees the world steadily and sees it whole is, I argue, an incomplete picture. It is a picture that is revealed to be incomplete when one observes the aphorism, not simply in the essay but as a relation of the essay. I claimed near the beginning of this chapter that the bond between the aphorism and the essay is not incidental but 'genetic' – meaning that they share core, constitutive features that make them not only natural companions but blood relations. And while the two forms remain distinct – like two members of a single family – those features they do share show them to be forms that shape their meaning in a similar way – through a dialectic between *fixité* and *mouvement*, between certainty and doubt. As John Henry Newman writes in his own content-realizing aphorism, 'certitude of course is a point, but doubt is a progress'.[30] The essay and the aphorism are forms that can shape doubt out of certainty in similar ways and for reasons that are central to their formal make-up.

Perhaps most obviously, both forms have a special relationship with the first person. The aphorism, like the essay, distinguishes itself in the way it forms meaning, not only through its content but through its performing, writing 'I'. The maxim and the proverb can exist more easily in an ahistorical, disembodied state. This is not to say that the aphorism cannot mutate into a proverb or truism. Holbrook Jackson titled his 1911 book of aphorisms, *Platitudes in the Making*,[31] recognizing the tendency of popular aphorisms to lose sight of their 'I' and grow proverbial. But the byline of the aphorism is a vital part of its content, and as with the essay, when one reads an aphorism, one has a simulated sense of entering a conversation – or at least of being spoken to by an individual. And this presence of a speaking 'I' gives the aphorism an essayistic subtlety and irony unavailable to the ahistorical maxim. This 'I'-conditioned subtlety is particularly obvious in the essays of Oscar Wilde, which depend upon the wry and ironic speaker to bring off their rhetorical legerdemain. These lines close his essay, 'The Truth of Masks':

> Not that I agree with everything that I have said in this essay. There is much with which I entirely disagree. The essay simply represents an artistic standpoint, and in aesthetic criticism attitude is everything. For in art there is no such thing as a universal truth. A Truth in art is that whose contradictory is also true. And just as it is only in art-criticism, and through it, that we can apprehend the Platonic theory of ideas, so it is only in art-criticism, and through it, that we can realise Hegel's system of contraries. The truths of metaphysics are the truths of masks.[32]

Even this somewhat radical, wilful self-subversion dives in the familiar gravitational, centripetal spiral of parallelisms towards its final aphorism. It blends third-person ontological bravado ('in aesthetic criticism attitude is everything') and first-person self-doubt ('Not that I agree with everything that I have said in this essay'). He follows this with a ludicrous, tail-eating almost-aphorism that declaims its own universal ('in art there is no such thing as a universal truth'). The passage is always moving away from any point at which a reader might gain certainty from it, and by the time Wilde reaches his crowning aphorism, 'The truths of metaphysics are the truths of masks', he has already undermined his be-verb and the word 'truth' to the extent that they feel empty, even mask-like – which seems to be the point. The 'I' of 'Not that I agree …' distends over the entire passage, hollowing out its claims to universal wisdom.

This special relationship with the 'I' is not the only bonding agent between the aphorism and the essay. Their ties are strengthened by another of the aphorism's characteristics – what might be termed its formal delicacy. The aphorism requires a relatively specialized syntactical environment to survive. It is choked out by nesting asides, as was seen above, and is repelled by the past or future tenses. The aphorism requires some gesture of both present-ness and universality – or at least of wide applicability – and the past tense in particular evacuates universal claims from pronouns and be-verbs by particularizing them. The point is worth demonstrating. In *Lady Windemere's Fan*, Wilde's character, Lord Darlington, quips: 'Nowadays to be intelligible is to be found out' (1.194–5).[33] Even the 'nowadays', which is a particularizing adverb, fails to keep the statement from extending, if not into the past, into the future. However, if one reworks the statement to read, 'to be intelligible was to be found out', it remains formally pleasing but is only debatably aphoristic. A similar argument applies to the future tense and the question mark. Another way of putting this is that the aphorism has a connubial bond with the declarative present tense. As does the essay, which may deploy the past tense for paragraphs or pages, but – in a similar way to the nineteenth-century sentimental novel – the second-person present tense – the 'dear reader' – lies in reserve at all times, and the audience is dimly aware that it is present, if unseen. Even the past tense of the essay is present in the sense that its author recounts his story from the vantage of a present moment. One might even shift the metaphor and claim that, in an essay, the past tense waits on or serves the present. When Bacon opens his essay 'Of Gardens' with the past-tense sentence, 'God almighty first planted a garden', it exists to serve the next: 'And indeed it is the purest of human pleasures.'[34] Even those narrative essays such as Charles Lamb's 'Dream Children', Hilaire Belloc's 'On Mowing a Field' and Virginia Woolf's 'Flying over London' either snap to the present in the end or require a present temporality to shape their tone.

These two primary shared features, the special relationship with the speaking 'I' and the constant (if at times unseen) presence of the present tense are intimately connected. The essay's and the aphorism's speaking 'I' is, as it were, the presence of the present tense. The aphorism, like the essay, is not a set of disembodied wise concepts offered to a reader without context; it is a set of wise words *spoken* to a reader in her present moment, and in that speaking can exist the subtleties, ironies, paradoxes, mesmerisms, sarcasms and epistemological complexities of the human voice. In short, the experience that the essay and the aphorism simulate of being spoken to out of a present moment keeps the aphorism's and the essay's wisdom, even at its most ontologically unqualified, 'on edge' – unable to stabilize because born out of human mutability. So when Wilde writes, '"He who giveth away wisdom robbeth himself"',[35] the wisdom of this statement is itself, as Wilde would admit (and savour), necessarily in jeopardy. The kind of thinking, like Barthes's, that draws a direct correlation between formal rigidity and epistemological certainty assumes that the deployment of formal rigidity is univocal. In other words – it assumes that there is no room for irony in aphorizing or essaying. But those such as William Blake (with his *Proverbs of Hell*) and Wilde demonstrate that irony is a key component in aphoristic and essayistic meaning-making. They show that saying what you do not mean in a way you do not mean it is a subtle form of casting doubt, one uniquely available to the aphoristic essay. And this subtlety is made possible by the presence of a necessarily capricious speaking 'I' and a universalizing present tense.

One might reply that such an argument is easy to make about essayists like Wilde who are self-consciously transgressive and iconoclastic but difficult to make about earnest aphorizing essayists like Bacon. It might be added that while Bacon's essays come from a speaking 'I' and work within an essayistic present temporality, they seem primarily interested in forming stable, epistemological wholes – passing wisdom intact. Lydia Fakundiny, expressing a similar view, calls Bacon's 1597 edition of his *Essays*, 'barely more than ripe aphorisms stacked under headings', and she sees little alteration in the much longer 1625 edition.[36] While it is important to recognize Bacon's difference from essayists like Montaigne and Wilde, I argue that a closer look at the aphorism makes Fakundiny's censure begin to look more like praise. Fakundiny's phrase 'under headings' seems in particular to represent a larger suspicion of Bacon's Aristotelian impulse to categorize and list and his resulting pretensions to certainty and exhaustive coverage. However, in works like *De Dignitate et Augmentis Scientarum*, Bacon demonstrates a willingness to place radically contradictory aphorisms parallel to one another, or as he put it, 'the case exaggerated both ways with the utmost force of the wit ... quite beyond the truth.'[37] Here and elsewhere, Bacon seems less interested in an exhaustive certainty and more interested in what occurs when conflicting certainties meet – an experiment the aphoristic essay is uniquely equipped to perform. Moreover, Bacon's understanding of his own essays belies Fakundiny's suspicion. In an unpublished dedication to the 1612 edition of the *Essays*, he compares his essays to 'grains of salt, that will rather give you an appetite than offend you with satiety.'[38] The metaphor is characteristically suggestive and concrete, and it offers another way of understanding the aphorism's relationship to knowledge in Bacon's essays specifically and in the essay more generally. The essay, understood in light of the aphorism, is an object of appetency (one way of understanding Samuel Johnson's definition of it as something 'indigested').[39] Even Baconian lists and clean parallelisms have the deceptive rock-like solidity and independence of salt – that is to say, a fast-dissolving solidity and a highly contingent independence. Fakundiny's own gustatory metaphor, 'ripe', captures the formal maturity of Bacon's aphoristic essays, but it does not explain their sly ambivalence – their general flavour of both epistemic *fixité* and 'I'-conditioned *mouvement*. Bacon and Wilde are polar examples, but each works within this larger dialectic, showing that when the essay forms aphoristically around certainties it does not forgo its prerogative to doubt. The essay and the aphorism both evade the would-be critic who would accuse them of seeing the world steadily and seeing it whole.

Barthes's critique of the aphorism as a dangerously narcotic and therapeutic form in many ways recycles Socrates's critique of poetry that 'if you strip a poet's works of their musical colourings and take them by themselves', little of significance remains.[40] And Barthes's essayistic and aphoristic criticism of the aphorism offers a formal vision of a complex and equivocal form in a similar way that Plato's self-consciously artistic criticism of literary art nuances his claim. The aphorism and the essay can be forms of doubt as well as forms of certainty, and as has been shown, doubt formed *through* certainty. Barthes's fears of the aphorism's opioid behaviours are well founded but incomplete, because they do not take into account the family resemblance between aphorism and essay. Insofar as the essay participates in the aphoristic – in the present tense and in the presence of an 'I' – its *fixité* is pushed to and beyond its limits.

Notes

1. Roland Barthes, *Roland Barthes par Roland Barthes* (Paris: Editions du Seuil, 1975), 181 (translation mine). Barthes uses *maxime* (maxim) and *aphorisme* (aphorism) interchangeably here, but the form he describes (and practises later in the passage) aligns with my definition of the aphorism presented in this chapter.
2. Brian Dillon, *Essayism* (London: Fitzcarraldo Editions, 2017), 17.
3. Ben Grant, *The Aphorism and Other Short Forms*, The New Critical Idiom (London: Routledge, 2016), 68.
4. Alexander Smith, 'On the Writing of Essays', in *Dreamthorp: A Book of Essays Written in the Country* (London: Strathan & Co, 1863), 21–45 (25).
5. Matthew Arnold, 'To a Friend', in *Poetical Works*, ed. C. B. Tinker and H. F. Lowry (London: Oxford University Press, 1950), 2, line 12.
6. John Gross, 'Introduction', in *The Oxford Book of Aphorisms* (Oxford: Oxford University Press, 2003), vii–x (viii).
7. See Cleanth Brooks's claim that the epigram is 'a special sub-variety of poetry' in *The Well Wrought Urn: Studies in the Structure of Poetry* (London: Methuen & Co., 1968), 1; the epigram also has potentially confusing classical associations with inscription; the most exhaustive disambiguation of the various short forms can be found in Gary Saul Morson's *The Long and Short of It: From Aphorism to Novel* (Stanford, CA: University of Stanford Press, 2012).
8. Zadie Smith, 'Speaking in Tongues', *Changing My Mind: Occasional Essays* (New York: Penguin Press, 2009), 132–48 (137).
9. Excisions mine.
10. Samuel Johnson, 'Rambler No. 1', in *Selected Essays*, ed. David Womersley (London: Penguin, 2003), 3–7 (6).
11. Matthew S. McGlone and Jessica Tofighbakhsh, 'The Keats Heuristic: Rhyme as Reason in Aphorism Interpretation', *Poetics* 26 (1999): 235–44 (240).
12. Friedrich Nietzsche, *The Gay Science: With a Prelude in German Rhymes and an Appendix of Songs*, ed. Bernard Williams, trans. Josefine Nauckhoff and Adrian Del Caro (Cambridge: Cambridge University Press, 2001), 84.
13. Roger Scruton, *Music as an Art* (London: Bloomsbury Continuum, 2018), 11.
14. Ibid., 13.
15. Francis Bacon, 'Of Youth and Age', in *The Essays*, ed. John Pitcher (London: Penguin, 1985), 187–8 (187).
16. Scruton, *Music as an Art*, 16.
17. Oscar Wilde, 'The Critic as Artist', in *The Complete Works of Oscar Wilde: Historical Criticism, Intentions, The Soul of Man*, Vol. 4, ed. Josephine M. Guy (Oxford: Oxford University Press, 2007), 123–206 (185).

18 Bacon, 'Of Adversity', in *Essays*, 74–5 (75).
19 Wilde, 'The Decay of Lying', in *The Complete Works*, Vol. 4, 72–103 (80).
20 Bacon, 'Of Friendship', in *Essays*, 138–44 (142).
21 Stephen Blackwood, *The Consolation of Boethius as Poetic Liturgy* (Oxford: Oxford University Press, 2015), 160–1.
22 Ibid., 234.
23 Ibid., 236.
24 Derek Attridge, *Moving Words: Forms of English Poetry* (Oxford: Oxford University Press, 2013), 111.
25 Theodor W. Adorno, 'On the Fetish Character in Music and the Regression of Listening', in *The Culture Industry: Selected Essays on Mass Culture*, ed. J. M. Bernstein (London: Routledge, 1991), 26–52 (33).
26 Ibid., 30.
27 Bacon, 'Of Adversity', 74–5.
28 Richard A. Lanham, *Analyzing Prose* (London: Continuum, 2003), 125.
29 Smith, 'Speaking in Tongues', 142.
30 John Henry Newman, *Apologia Pro Vita Sua*, ed. David J. DeLaura (New York: W. W. Norton & Company, 1968), 168.
31 Holbrook Jackson, *Platitudes in the Making: Precepts and Advices for Gentlefolk* (London: D. J. Rider, 1911).
32 Wilde, 'The Truth of Masks', in *Complete Works*, Vol. 4, 208–28 (228).
33 Oscar Wilde, *Lady Windermere's Fan*, ed. Ian Small (London: Bloomsbury Metheun Drama, 2013), 15.
34 Bacon, 'Of Gardens', in *Essays*, 197–202 (197).
35 Oscar Wilde, 'The Teacher of Wisdom', in *The Complete Works of Oscar Wilde*: *Poems and Poems in Prose*, Vol. 1, ed. Karl Beckson and Bobby Fong (Oxford: Oxford University Press, 2000), 176–80 (177).
36 Lydia Fakundiny, *The Art of the Essay* (Boston: Houghton Mifflin, 1991), 6.
37 Francis Bacon, *De Dignitate et Augmentis Scientiarum*, in *The Works of Francis Bacon*, Vol. 9, ed. James Spedding, Robert Leslie Ellis, and Douglas Denon Heath (Cambridge: Riverside Press, 1882), 155.
38 Bacon, *Essays*, 239.
39 Johnson, 'Essay', in *Samuel Johnson's Dictionary of the English Language*, ed. Alexander Chalmers (London: Studio Editions, 1994), 247.
40 Plato, *Republic*, ed. C. D. C. Reeve, trans. G. M. A. Grube (Indianapolis, IN: Hackett, 1992), 271.

Chapter 12

ASSAYING THE NOVEL

Jason Childs

1.

'The essay occupies an odd place in the history of literature', writes Jeff Porter. 'One moment, the essay is a marginal form barely alive on the fringes of poetry and fiction, the next, the trendiest thing in town.'[1] As I write these words, the essay is trending; indeed, it may be the trendiest thing in letters. But what does it mean for a literary form to trend? On the one hand, it might only be fashion – 'mere' fashion – as Porter's phrasing seems to suggest. To be sure, some tastemakers are already declaring the essay's latest moment at an end. Yet for 'trend', the *Oxford English Dictionary* (*OED*) gives us not only 'fashion', but also less trivializing possibilities. To trend is 'to change or develop in a general direction'; or, in a definition that emphasizes the negative aspect of such a movement, 'to bend or turn away in a specified direction'.[2] There is always the possibility, then, that a trend, though perhaps appearing a relatively meaningless and temporary fluctuation, might turn out to be something less superficial. And this would appear an ambiguity especially germane to a turn that is, as Porter's reference to the essay's place in literary history suggests, a return. Might it be that the current trend towards the essay, rather than a kind of fad, is the latest episode in a long series of attempts, or another repetition of what is essentially the same attempt, to think anew something fundamental about the project *of the project* of modernity? Or to think again something about the project that modernity, on a certain conception, takes to be crucial about itself? To free us of a particular cosmological fantasy, one underpinning dominant modes of cognition, by placing a 'marginal form' at the centre of literary and cognitive activity, thereby edging cognition back into the space of the literary, while also returning something literary to cognition?

Though they are not always stated so explicitly, these possibilities are, among others, at the heart of much contemporary enthusiasm for the essay. They are certainly among those that animate some of the most exciting writing its theorists have lately produced. For example, though she is not responding explicitly to the trend I mention above, Joan Retallack would seem to have some of this is in mind when she describes the essay as a form with a unique capacity to embody a 'poetics of the swerve' – swerves being, for Retallack, 'sometimes gentle, often violent out-of-the-blue motions that cut obliquely across material and conceptual logics', providing 'opportunities to usefully rethink habits of thought' (and, moreover, to rethink of the status quo organized, the world configured, by the thought interrupted).[3] Adam Phillips similarly characterizes 'writing essays, and the literary essay as a form', as an act of 'resistance, a protest, a refusal to meet certain criteria'. The essay, he claims, is 'a disengagement from something in order to be able to engage something else'.[4] Yet such possibilities, as both writers acknowledge, are also among the longest-lived in the theory of the essay. A similar association is made, for instance, in the writings of Theodor W. Adorno and Robert Musil, for whom the essay is ideally anti-essentialist, anti-systematic, anti-ideological, free-associative. It is interesting, in view of this, that a number of the examples given by the *OED* for 'trend' as 'a bend or turn away in a specified direction' are curiously at odds with that definition: 'the Richelieu River trending southward to Lake Champlain' – this, for example, is more a turn *toward* than *away from*. Truer to that definition, writers like Retallack, Phillips, Adorno and Musil characterize the essay's dynamic with the converse weighting: that is, as highly self-conscious in its point of departure, in the point of its departure, but more or less unclear as to its destination, or even as to whether it will turn out to have one. To swerve is here to not quite know where one is heading, or perhaps to know that one is headed nowhere in particular, or to lose one's sense of what heading somewhere might mean, or to feel that one is headed *anywhere but there*, as in cases where one swerves to avoid a hazard. Before it aspires to find itself on the right side of literary history, as it were, the essay swerves as a matter of negative capability; indeed, even to think of the appeal of the essay as a kind of historical gravity exerted by a conception of the ideal or the good is perhaps to foreclose on its more radical possibilities. On this view, the anti-project of the essay is a tendency away from certainties and, indeed, away from the perceived necessity of a trajectory in conjunction with which such certainties would develop. The swerve demands a different, a broader kind of attentiveness.

Of course, one feature common to many such accounts of the essay is the contention that modernity ought itself to be properly described as a swerve – not, that is, as a stable point of arrival, but rather as an opening, a radical and ongoing process of interruption, digression and displacement, one about the essential uncertainty of which the essay reminds us. Building on the work of Bruno Latour, Mark M. Freed has observed that an insistence on the incomplete quality of modernity was at the heart of Musil's commitment to the essayistic. The kind of abeyance in which Musil's *Essayismus*, as a mode of comportment, aims to place the apparent determinations of history is a way less of rebelling against a too-rigid socio-cultural order than of accommodating oneself to a reality that never achieves a final stability. *Essayismus*, as Freed makes clear, is as much a way of living as a type of writing, one that prizes receptiveness more highly than control. With this in mind, one thing we might appreciate about Retallack's exploration of the relationship between the essay and the swerve is that she does not overstate the capacity of a given *poethics*, much less an individual work or literary artist, to actually *cause* a significant swerve. On the contrary, she acknowledges that her 'project' is, in a sense, anything but: 'I write the "project" of the [essay as] wager', she tells us, 'because I'm interested in a poetics that recognizes the degree to which the chaos of world history, of all complex systems, makes it imperative that we move away from models of cultural and political agency lodged in isolated heroic acts and simplistic notions of cause and effect.'[5] We might say that, as a negative project – a 'project', in scare quotes – the essay and the trend towards it, in the dual sense of the word, *contains* a positive one. Unlike many an avant-gardist, the essayist, on this view, is less concerned with overthrowing reality than with re-cognizing it – and always at once with recognizing something about cognition itself. The essay's role here, we might say, is one in the service of a particular brand of realism – a realism, like all realisms, founded on anti-realism:

> Naïve realisms, fantasy-driven surrealisms, faux naturalisms are the specialty of mass culture. Everything in mass culture is designed to deliver space-time in a series of shiny freeze-frames, each with its built-in strategy of persuasion. One writes essays and poetry to stay warm and active and realistically messy. Everything in mass culture is designed to deliver space-time in a continuous drone. One writes poetry and essays to disrupt that fatal momentum.[6]

To the simplifications of mass culture – to realisms obedient to a supposedly stable, pre-constituted reality – the essayist replies not with explicitly political action, at least as traditionally conceived, but with implicitly ethico-political complexity and reflexivity. This is a way of knowing that, far from being a kind of neutral spectatorship, knows itself as already a form of doing: observing one's observations, as a systems theorist might put it, is a way of modifying them, and thereby oneself, and thereby the world in which one lives and through which the consequences of one's abstentions – abstention, too, being a form of action – multiply: realism as ambivalence, ambivalence as disruption, disruption as experiment.

This kind of anti-project is arguably more ambitious than other, putatively more revolutionary literary-political programs, though it will almost certainly disappoint those bent on the latter. Rather than trying to escape from the damaged present into a utopian future, such a sensibility seeks to escape from a programmed future into an uncertain present. The essay, on this view, operates at the limits of, as Retallack puts it, 'ordinal accounts of things (including thoughts) that have already taken place'. That is to say, it works beyond known coordinates, where we don't know where we are, or when we know that where we are is somewhere we don't know; a territory in which who we are necessarily becomes a matter, reducible to neither fact nor fantasy, of 'conversational invention'.[7] Or rather, since this way of putting it risks a certain fantasy of transcendence, we could say it works upon the knownness of coordinates, works *on* their limits, revealing everywhere their impositions and impostures, their non-identity. At the limit of ordinal accounts, we find that accounts are ordinal; that is, they assay what counts, numbering and neatly ordering our priorities. The essay discovers this contingency without seeking to replace it with something less imperfect, more formal; it is the anti-formal form – casual, it doesn't cling. At a high level of abstraction, such an idea seems to be at work in Freed's argument that Musil's *Essayismus* constitutes the possibility of a 'nonmodern avant-garde',[8] breaking the dialectic of enlightenment by opting out of its fundamental terms, dropping out of its fundamentalist epistemic contracts, but as a renewed attempt to inhabit the very world these at once shape and occlude. This is a project only possible as impossible; as the inhabitation of an excluded middle; via the successful enactment of a failure.

All this being said, it seems to me that one important challenge for the contemporary study of the essay might be to think through more fully this entwinement of success and failure, and of the essay's attunement to the possibility of various swerves. We might profitably, for instance, call upon a particular kind of critical theory whose own ambivalence regarding the revolutionary efficacy of art and literature is epitomized by Adorno, though not especially pronounced in his 'The Essay as Form'. 'Realistic dissidence is the trademark of anyone who has a new idea in business', he and Max Horkheimer write in a famous chapter on 'the culture industry'.[9] I am reminded here that, reviewing David Shields's *Reality Hunger*, Curtis White asks what kind of call to arms that book might be. His answer: 'At best, it is the sort of call to arms that comes from an editor saying, "Why shouldn't we do a call to arms this season? I think it's time for that again. In the spring, of course. I don't see this as a Christmas book."'[10] Do such suspicious modes of reading, even as we seek to displace them, not call us to question, to think more dialectically about, some of the more appealing stories we tell ourselves about the anti-ideological character of the essay, the growing cultural prestige of which is indissociably connected to its commodity status and institutional bona fides? About the anti-systematic, anti-deterministic credentials of the form, a set of qualities so often celebrated that to repeat them is to risk cliché – or, worse, dogma? Openness, flexibility and provisionality, qualities of that epistemic comportment we so revere in a particular conception of the essay – are these not the qualities prized most today in the entrepreneurial class and the precariat alike? Our becoming increasingly indefinite and pragmatic, people 'without qualities', is the precondition for the very order upon which the call for essayistic irresolution is often premised. In the era of capitalism's creative turn, resistance via potentiation asymptotically approaches convergence with complicity. To trend, in short, may be unwittingly to trundle.

The post-truth condition is a tyranny of bad infinities; and this in turn provokes positivistic counter-insistences, 'reactionary allegiances and nostalgias', as Retallack puts it.[11] One can see this at work in vitriolic responses to the so-called lyric essay and its proponents. And indeed, what could appear more conventional, in the present conjuncture, than to proclaim the reality of 'alternative facts', to borrow a recent and notorious term of political art? Yet to my mind, the most interesting works of contemporary writing – which are also acts of reading – are perhaps not those that aim to resolve this dilemma, coming down on one side or the other, but rather those that unhappily embody a particular kind of ambivalence. Though they tend towards the essayistic, this tendency cannot, in such works, be understood straightforwardly as an act of protest or escape, nor in terms of a simple opposition to institutions. Another way of saying this, perhaps, would be to acknowledge that the essay's openness is always equally a matter of its closures – not just of its refusals or withdrawals, but of what is unavailable to it, impossible for it. The appeal of the essay might, on this view, be as much symptom as strategy, as much a reflection of inability as unwillingness. If this book is an attempt to think about the essay's relationship to limits, here we confront a less celebratory inflection of its generative title: where and why we find ourselves returning to the essay might have not only or even primarily to do with heroic acts of critique and dissent. The essay, as its oft-cited etymology suggests, takes place at the limits of our abilities. Michel de Montaigne's famous 'What do I know?' might be read, in this optic, as one of those shifts of consciousness described by Joseph Tabbi throughout his *Cognitive Fictions*, whereby the self-conscious interrogation of one's modes of relating becomes a way of going on when one cannot.[12] As Musil would come to argue, the essay is the domain, not of final truths – even of the final truth of the absence of final truths – but, instead, of 'partial solutions'.[13]

2.

Whatever the contemporary enthusiasm for the essay is a trend toward, it is difficult not to think of it as a swerve away from the novel. Certainly, the anti-ideological credentials of the essay are often held to inhere in its difference, its deviation, from the novel, especially from the forms of attention and selfhood, the models of action and agency, it is said to encode. Indeed, the 'death of the novel' is a key figure within numerous of the most important proclamations of the essay's current renaissance, in particular those concerning the lyric essay. *Reality Hunger*, for example, is replete with reports of Shields's own frustrations as a writer and reader of the novel, the form that sits, as he puts it, 'still (very still) at the heart of "literary culture" '.[14] 'The novel', he writes more bluntly, at another point, 'is dead'.[15] Shields is not arguing, of course, that novels are no longer being produced or that things called novels are not being bought and sold in record numbers. Instead, with something closely resembling Retallack's aversion to naïve realisms and faux naturalisms, Shields is claiming that for a writer – or reader – to pine for the pleasures of the novel today is to deny the passing of a world for which it was an authentically expressive form. The 'novel *qua* novel is a form of nostalgia',[16] he writes, a 'beautiful illusion'.[17] To insist on it in the face of – or, worse, in ignorance of – its legitimating conditions' disappearance is not only to make a mistake – to be using the wrong coordinates, to believe one is where one actually isn't – but to commit an act of violent and stupid anachronism, propping up a system, a mode of life, whose institutional, medial and ecological underpinnings, whose epistemic and ethical warrants, have disintegrated. Today, in Shields's view, that the novel continues to be widely published and read is a matter of delusion and dislocation.

Yet it is worth underlining the fact that, although Shields is making a universalizing claim about the viability of the novel, his aversion primarily stems from writer's block, subsequently explained in terms of an involuntary shift in taste, a transformed geometry of attention that makes an erstwhile, surely lingering, inclination impossible: 'Something has happened to my imagination', he writes, 'which can no longer yield to the earnest embrace of novelistic form'.[18] We find a similar formulation in what is, to my mind, a close cousin of *Reality Hunger*: Karl Ove Knausgaard's essay-novel *My Struggle*. In an interview with James Wood, Knausgaard reports that his vast autofiction proceeds from a sense that the 'traditional form of the novel' is no longer 'eloquent'.[19] Indeed, having long tried and failed to produce a third novel after his successful debut and follow-up, Knausgaard admits, in one of the many passages in *My Struggle* that he has described as essays, to having 'increasingly lost faith in literature'. Knausgaard's crisis of faith, then, like Shields's, is inextricable from a kind of blockage or inability: 'Just the thought of fiction', he writes in *A Man in Love*, 'just the thought of a fabricated character in a fabricated plot made me feel nauseous'.[20] I've chosen two notorious examples here, but one finds this very frequently in contemporary essayistic writing, and writing about writing: an insistence that the novel (often standing in for literature more broadly) is no longer available to the authentic writer or reader – that he is either unable or unwilling to participate in the institution.

Many critics are suspicious of such claims regarding literary forms, to say nothing of claims about literature in general. The literary death-notice provides us with a paradoxically stable canon, one dating back thousands of years, and it is a genre that, ironically enough, has only become more popular as, within the shifting media ecologies of our own time, its claims have become more plausible. Nonetheless, such pronouncements should perhaps not be dismissed as eagerly as they so often are. On the contrary, they might be understood as a core feature of literary discourse, a necessary part of the social construction of the literary, the history of which can be traced back at least as far as Plato's *Republic*. Writing of this tradition, William Marx tells us, in *The Hatred of Literature*, that 'anti-literature is anything but a reasonable discourse: it is a foundational scene that everyone wants to reenact at one point or another, to gain status or simply to exist'.[21] In this vein, in 1986, Wolfgang Iser argues that the 'repeated announcements of the death of literature which have punctuated the last hundred years' should be understood as 'symptoms of a malaise that affects the conceptions, functions, and applications of literature', rather than as anything to do with literature itself. It is, in such moments of apparent crisis, 'ideas entertained about literature, but not literature itself, [that] have come to an end'.[22] Of course, Iser's comments here address writers of the novel no less than its professional readers: the critical cancellation of literature can be understood as the means *par excellence* for its continuation. Perhaps no one has traditionally felt novel-nausea more keenly than the novelist. And this nausea has traditionally been cured by more novels, by more novel novels. Indeed, a more interesting reading of *Reality Hunger* becomes available if we complicate its self-description as a manifesto or lyric essay by refusing – a refusal that it seems clearly to invite – to simply accept it as the univocal statement of a thesis. As Pieter Vermeulen notes, '*Reality Hunger*'s death knell [for the novel] cannot avoid sounding a lot like a novel; indeed, the "novelistic" shape … of Shields's self-designated manifesto belies the clarity of its programmatic intent, and ends up reanimating the form it intends to bury.'²³ *My Struggle*, meanwhile, for all the renunciation of fiction and literature in the essays it contains, and for all its autobiographical references, frequently refers to itself, almost as if it can't help it, as a novel.

If these are novels, what kind of novels are they? Paradoxically – rather than siding with Vermeulen, who suggests that the novelistic residue of Shields's work dismisses its claim to be an essay, along with its claim that the essay is, in our time, superseding the novel – we might try to answer this question precisely insofar as it helps us understand something about these texts' essayism, and thereby about what an essay is or does. We can begin by turning to critical accounts that seek to problematize what Steven Moore calls the 'standard history of the novel', a history in which a very particular form of nineteenth-century realism comes to be taken as paradigmatic, the part we mistake for the whole.²⁴ Milan Kundera attempts to look beyond this paradigm – one he characterizes in terms of 'psychological realism'²⁵ and its adherence to what he calls 'the verisimilitude pact' – to an encompassing tradition, running from Cervantes to Laurence Sterne to Musil to the *nouveau romanciers*.²⁶ Kundera hopes to remind us of the importance to our properly understanding the novel of those instantiations usually relegated to its margins; indeed, of how the history of the novel properly conceived must include that of the anti-novel, the novel that refuses or finds unavailable all those supposedly essential elements whose absence the mainstream critic, as Moore depicts him, laments. This alternative tradition tends to favour innovations in form and style, digressions or dissolutions of plot, metafictional reflexivity, the puncturing of its own fictional illusions and so on. Kundera – anticipating Retallack and Shields – contends that an insistence on complexity and uncertainty amounts to resistance against the 'veritable whirlpool of reduction' by which we attempt to foreclose the radical uncertainty of modern life, attempts that issue in the simplifying forms of mass culture.²⁷ Writes Kundera: 'Every novel says to the reader: "Things are not as simple as you think." That is the novel's eternal truth'.²⁸ One thing that distinguishes Kundera's account from Moore's – and, for the present discussion, makes it the more important revisionist history – is the former's insistence upon the novel's cognitive purview. Where Moore emphasizes the importance of dazzling rhetorical performance to the authentic novel, and of the pleasure the reader takes therein, Kundera insists upon its capacity to furnish us with knowledge – a kind of knowledge that 'only the novel can discover'.²⁹ Indeed, the 'difficulty of knowing and the elusiveness of truth' are, paradoxically, the knowledge and the truth imparted by every genuine novel.³⁰ The novel, in its very deliberate deviation from received ideas, including from ideas about what counts as thinking and discovering, and what counts as a novel, finds itself thinking and discovering – and novel.

By pointing to the immanent critique that motivates the history of the authentic novel, and by, in Kundera's case, insisting on the novel as a means of cognition (rather than a narrower aesthetic pleasure), these writers draw our attention to ways in which literature and its criticism can, and perhaps essentially do, coincide. In many cases, of course, they coincide more or less implicitly or gesturally. But the tradition of metafiction to which both writers refer contains countless examples of books more explicitly about books, novels more explicitly about novels – or, perhaps more importantly here, about the impossibility of novels and the author's struggle with that impossibility. Many of these involve a self-referential dimension, one involving the text's assaying its own conditions of possibility, its own relation to questions about the nature and vocation of literature, the process of composition and its own epistemic status. Problematizing the boundary between the literary and the extraliterary, between the work's inside and its outside, such works deliberately bring about a confusion of primary and secondary, creative and critical. They make a turn away, as David Atwell puts it in reference to J. M. Coetzee's late work, from 'the nauseating business of producing verisimilitude' and towards what would usually be deemed 'second-order questions', thus rendering supposedly derivative concerns, especially 'the second reflection on one's practice', the first-order materials of the literary work.[31] In a similar vein, Julian Murphet describes Coetzee's *Diary of a Bad Year* as belonging to a class of novels that 'fail very precisely to be novels, and which elevate that failure into their *raison d'être* as texts in the first place'.[32] That failure can be understood as one attended by a similar kind of disappointment on behalf of its author as is expressed by many of the book's critics: JC, the autofictional protagonist of *Diary*, sorely laments the loss of his novelistic capacities. Far from a simple or even willed renunciation of the genre, we might understand Coetzee's abandonment of the trappings of the traditional novel, here and elsewhere, more dialectically (following Murphet) as 'a resolute fidelity to the novel as a form historically capable of truth, even if it means that, here and now, the greatest task is to dismantle that capacity from within: to disarm the novel of its history of truth, to subtract its truth-procedure from its post-mortem enactments'.[33] In *Cognitive Fictions*, Tabbi identifies numerous works exemplifying this recursive, 'essayistic' tendency within a certain strain of postmodern writing, comparing their structures to a Möbius strip. Such work was also described at length by Raymond Federman – a contemporary of the writers with whom Tabbi is concerned – in the opening essay of his collection *Critifiction*. There, Federman notes that his fellow postmodernists, among numerous writers since Proust, appear to be concerned primarily 'with the problems of writing their books, of letting the difficulties of fiction transpire in the fiction itself'.[34] 'Suddenly', he writes, 'literature becomes the explanation of why the writer cannot write, why he constantly confronts the failure of expression and communication, why he can no longer represent the world faithfully and truthfully'.[35] In this state of 'suspense', in the experience of an end without end, avers Federman, fiction becomes a 'continual probing of its own medium, but a probing that cancels, erases, abolishes whatever it discovers, whatever it formulates as it is performed'. Fiction becomes an 'act of searching (researching even) within the fiction itself for the implications of what it means to write fiction'.[36] Where it disappoints traditional expectations – those associated with the verisimilitude pact – the novel continues within the attempt to articulate, to assay, the reasons for this disappointment. One conclusion here could be that the novel at its most authentic, at least at certain moments in its history, turns into and persists within a kind of essay.

3.

Kundera goes on in *The Art of the Novel* to argue for the essay-novel, especially on the model of Musil and his contemporary Hermann Broch, as one of the liveliest avenues available to the authentic novel as he conceives of it. Yet what makes 'the *specifically novelistic essay*', the essay within the novel, a significant development in the form's history, for Kundera, is that, provisionalized by the structural irony constitutive of the novel as a form, the essay contained therein does not claim 'to bear an apodictic message', but instead 'remains hypothetical, playful, or ironic'. 'One thing is certain', he writes:

> the moment it becomes part of the novel, reflection changes its essence. Outside the novel, we're in the realm of affirmation: everyone is sure of his statements: the politician, the philosopher, the concierge. Within the universe of the novel, however, no one affirms: it is the realm of play and of hypotheses. In the novel, then, reflection is essentially inquiring, hypothetical.[37]

Of course, scholars of the essay might wonder here at whether the adjective *novelistic*, or the epistemic space Kundera wishes to claim as distinct for the novel, really brings to the essay what he suggests. As Claire de Obaldia points out, the essay, especially as conceived of within the Montaignian tradition, is already provisional and playful, already inquiring and hypothetical. It disavows 'responsibility with regard to what is after all only "tried out"' – indeed, this brings the essay, she tells us, very close to 'the "as if" of fiction'.[38] What I wish to suggest here is that even some of those most sympathetic to the close relation of essay to novel perhaps tend to overstate their separability, remaining too much in the grip of the same reified conceptions of each to which they object. Such accounts tend to imagine that the essay enters the novel at some unique moment of crisis in its history.[39] Filing the essayistic novel or the novelistic essay as a subspecies, however special, overlooks the possibility that the novel properly conceived *just is* an essay. Indeed, the term 'essayistic novel', where it is intended to 'draw attention to the distinct presence of the essay' within the novel, may be pleonastic, for the essay-novel represents '*the* novel in all its typicality'. 'From the outset, the novel is the most "naturally" essayistic genre', writes Obaldia.

> It is the baggiest, the most indeterminate, the most 'imperialistic' literary genre in that without scruple it colonizes and annexes surrounding territories. It is the most reflexive and critical in that it constantly questions its own form. The 'essayistic' thus appears simply to foreground the essence of the novel.[40]

Or, perhaps more radically, this appearance of the essayistic when other genres are at their most essential, self-conscious or artistic, undercuts the idea that the essay is best thought of as a literary form. Réda Bensmaïa argues – and Brian Dillon and Michael Hamburger have made similar observations – that 'the essay is not *a* genre like any other, and perhaps not a *genre* at all'. 'Nor', Bensmaïa goes on, is the essay a mixture of genres. It does not mix genres, it complicates them: the genres are, in a way, its (the essay's) 'fallout', the historically determined actualizations of what is potentially woven into the essay. The latter appears, then, as the moment of writing *before* the genre, before genericness – or as the matrix of all generic possibilities.[41]

It is striking how many recent texts that one might intuitively associate with either the 'post-novelistic horizon' or the essayistic trend I am trying to think about here frame themselves as pre-generic to achieve their effects, cleaving to an aesthetic of self-conscious unfinishedness, incompletion or neoteny. The pages of *Diary of a Bad Year*, for instance, are divided into three horizontal panels, the top panel containing a set of essay-like texts, many of them reflecting pessimistically on the nature and vocation of literature, the lower two containing some rather schematic narrative passages. Though clearly these parts bear upon one another in multiple ways, no guide is offered to the reader for how these strips should be assembled – implying, perhaps, that such indecision should be considered part of the work, or that in the end what is being presented does not quite add up to, hesitates to become, a literary work at all. John D'Agata's *The Lifespan of a Fact*, co-authored with Jim Fingal, likewise experiments with page layout to achieve a peculiar kind of unfinished quality. It presents a narrative essay by D'Agata, rejected by a prominent magazine because of its alleged factual inaccuracies, with the frame zoomed out to encompass, at the original text's margins, a philosophical and literary-theoretical dialogue between the writer and the fact-checker for its eventual publication by another magazine.[42] Again, then, we have here a text about a work that hesitates on the edge of becoming a work itself; a work made out of its working, out of its own process of attempting to cohere, and especially to establish its own genre, to become literature. One also thinks of examples in which unfinishedness means, as Shields puts it, 'deliberate unartiness, "raw" material, seemingly unprocessed, unfiltered, uncensored, and unprofessional'.[43] Christopher Schaberg aptly describes Maggie Nelson's self-referential *The Argonauts* as a book 'about *writing*'[44] in which 'Nelson pulls back the curtain to expose an unseemly writing process'. The result, notwithstanding its 'agile moves between high theoretical concepts and sincere personal reflection', is 'a cobbled together and sometimes capricious seeming performance – a project that disavows its own coherence, its own necessary attempt at resolution', yet one that that, by that very disavowal, raises anew 'the terms of this debate – critics versus (or qua) writers'.[45] In the critical reception of *My Struggle*, meanwhile, comparisons to Marcel Proust's *In Search of Lost Time* have been frequent; yet, as James Ley writes, 'Knausgaard's rough-hewn prose certainly has none of Proust's refined elegance of style.'[46] 'Maybe it's significant', Ben Lerner suggests, 'that *My Struggle* has six volumes while *À la recherche du temps perdu* has seven'.[47] I would say it is: by offering as something less than – something before – art, Knausgaard offers us something more, or after. 'Think of this', Sarah Manguso urges us, with respect to her fragmentary *300 Arguments*, 'as a short book, composed entirely of what I hoped would be a long book's quotable passages'.[48] In all of these examples – and one might also list here works by Lerner himself, alongside those by such writers as Gerald Murnane, Ali Smith and Geoff Dyer, among others – what comes after literature is an examination and performance of what comes before it. This lands us once more within the domain of the essay, insofar as the essay is always already the genre that is not one: the literature that is not quite or, better, not yet literature – that is literature only '*in potentia*', as Obaldia puts it.[49] Another way of putting this would be to say that these are fictions of an absence of fiction – or, more precisely, fictions of the moment before fictionality; fictions of a formless form, of form before form forms.

That they are fictions, however, we cannot doubt. That is, we would misread such authors were we to take their unartiness – to borrow Shields's term – as less than deliberate, their claims to pre-arty 'directness', or to pre-empt the mediation of the institution of literature, as heralding a genuinely new immediacy, even an immediacy of the secondary. As much is also betrayed in the unhappy consciousness typical of their autofictional protagonists, from Coetzee's feckless JC to Lerner's self-lacerating Adam Gordon to Knausgaard's struggling Karl Ove. Lamenting our 'purely fabricated world'[50] – our lifeworld and the world of the novel, woven of the same stuff – Knausgaard expresses the appeal, in *My Struggle*, of more direct modes of communication: 'The only genres I saw value in, which still conferred meaning', he writes, 'were diaries and essays, the types of literature that did not deal with narrative, that were not about anything, but just consisted of a voice, the voice of your own personality, a life, a face, a gaze you could meet.'[51] But *My Struggle*, as I have said, is an anti-novel that cannot help calling itself a novel. If literature, as I have tried to suggest, essentially involves the transcendence of literature, then to transcend transcendence by relinquishing it – by at once to aspiring to more and less than it – is not truly to escape its categorial logic, but only to displace it. The casualness attributed to the essay, its proximity to the draft and fragment, with their supposed spontaneity, has often been acknowledged as artifice. 'More often than not, the apparent informality of the essay is the result of great craft and care', writes Porter. 'That the essay seems artless is one of its great ruses.'[52] That is to say, the essay cannot escape the belatedness of all writing; it offers only, and must therefore resent in itself, the semblance of directness. In a sense, this leads us to the obvious conclusion that what contemporary writers of ambiguous essayistic texts offer, and what the present literary-theoretical preoccupation with the essay itself perhaps achieves, perhaps in spite of itself, is to expand and revitalize our sense of the literary, opening the way to livelier and more enigmatic writing and reading. On the other hand, the essay's rhetoric of scaling back on the grandiosity of the literary, its affectation of everydayness, paradoxically belies – and, by belying, seeks to navigate – an episteme in which the categories that once limited the literary have exploded, with the literary seeming ever more to encompass, even as it sinks down unremarkably into, the everyday. The post-truth era is also the post-fictional era, a context in which fictionality can no longer be taken to name a discrete imaginative domain set apart from and opposed to reality but rather suffuses it. In feigning a rejection of the fictional out of a desire to assay the real, we today confront the fact that reality is itself fictional – or, more paradoxically, the fact that 'there are no facts, only art'.[53] 'The realism of cognitive fictions, writes Tabbi, is 'of a piece with the illusory nature of cognition'.[54] To put it in Knausgaardian terms, we only ever 'combat fiction with fiction'.[55] It is here, today, that we must begin to contemplate anew the ends of the novel and the essay alike.

Notes

1. Jeff Porter, 'Introduction: A History and Poetics of the Essay', in *Understanding the Essay*, ed. Jeff Porter and Patricia Foster (Peterborough: Broadview Press, 2012), ix–xxiv (ix).
2. *Oxford English Dictionary*, 'trend'. (Oxford: Oxford University Press, 2014).
3. Joan Retallack, *The Poethical Wager* (Berkeley: University of California Press, 2003), 1.
4. Adam Phillips, *One Way and Another: New and Selected Essays* (London: Penguin Books, 2013, reprint 2018), 383.
5. Retallack, *The Poethical Wager*, 3.
6. Ibid., 5.
7. Ibid., 4.
8. Mark M. Freed, *Robert Musil and the NonModern* (London: Continuum, 2011), 113–36.
9. Theodor W. Adorno and Max Horkheimer, *Dialectic of Enlightenment*, trans. John Cumming (1944 [original German version], 1972 [translation]; New York: Verso, 1997), 120–67 (132).
10. Curtis White, 'David Shields' *Reality Hunger*: A Review in the Form of a Memoir', *electronic book review*, 10 January 2011, https://electronicbookreview.com/essay/david-shields-reality-hunger-a-manifesto-a-review-in-the-form-of-a-memoir/.
11. Retallack, *The Poethical Wager*, 3.
12. Joseph Tabbi, *Cognitive Fictions* (Minneapolis: University of Minnesota Press, 2002).
13. I am adapting this term from Musil's *Partiallösungen*, discussed in Freed, *Robert Musil and the NonModern*, 9.
14. David Shields, *Reality Hunger: A Manifesto* (New York: Vintage, 2011), 199.
15. Ibid., 114.
16. Ibid., 203.
17. Ibid., 201.
18. Ibid., 199.
19. Karl Ove Knausgaard and James Wood, 'Writing My Struggle: An Exchange', *The Paris Review*, no. 211 (2014), https://www.theparisreview.org/miscellaneous/6345/writing-emmy-struggle-em-an-exchange-james-wood-karl-ove-knausgaard.
20. Karl Ove Knausgaard, *A Man in Love: My Struggle Book 2*, trans. Don Bartlett (New York: Vintage, 2013), 446.
21. William Marx, *The Hatred of Literature*, trans. Nicholas Elliot (Cambridge, MA: Belknap Press of Harvard University Press, 2018), 4.
22. Wolfgang Iser, *Prospecting: From Reader Response to Literary Anthropology* (Baltimore, MD: Johns Hopkins University Press, 1989), 197.
23. Pieter Vermeulen, *Contemporary Literature and the End of the Novel: Creature, Affect, Form* (New York: Palgrave Macmillan, 2015), 22.
24. Steven Moore, *The Novel: An Alternative History: Beginnings to 1600* (New York: Continuum, 2010), 3.

25 Milan Kundera, *The Art of the Novel*, trans. L. Asher (London: Faber and Faber, [1986] 2005), 34.
26 Ibid., 94.
27 Ibid., 17.
28 Ibid., 18.
29 Ibid., 6.
30 Ibid., 18.
31 David Atwell, *J.M. Coetzee and the Life of Writing: Face to Face with Time* (Oxford: Oxford University Press, 2015), 212–13.
32 Julian Murphet, '*Diary of a Bad Year*: Parrhesia, Opinion and Novelistic Form', in *Strong Opinions: J.M. Coetzee and the Authority of Contemporary Fiction*, ed. Chris Danta, Sue Kossew and Julian Murphet (New York: Continuum, 2011), 63–80 (78).
33 Ibid.
34 Raymond Federman, *Critifiction: Postmodern Essays*, SUNY Series in Postmodern Culture (Albany, NY: State University of New York Press, 1993), 5.
35 Ibid., 6.
36 Ibid., 10.
37 Kundera, *The Art of the Novel*, 78.
38 Claire de Obaldia, *The Essayistic Spirit: Literature, Modern Criticism and the Essay* (Oxford: Oxford University Press, 1996), 3.
39 See Stefano Ercolino, *The Novel-Essay, 1884–1947* (New York: Palgrave Macmillan, 2014).
40 Ibid., 23.
41 Réda Bensmaïa, *The Barthes Effect: The Essay as Reflective Text* (Minnesota: University of Minnesota Press, 1987), 91–2.
42 Jim Fingal and John D'Agata, *The Lifespan of a Fact* (New York: W. W. Norton and Company, 2012)
43 Shields, *Reality Hunger*, 5.
44 Christopher Schaberg, *The Work of Literature in an Age of Post-Truth* (London: Bloomsbury, 2018), 85.
45 Ibid., 87.
46 James Ley, 'Notes on Kamp: *My Struggle* by Karl Ove Knausgaard', *Sydney Review of Books*, 20 December 2013, https://sydneyreviewofbooks.com/karl-ove-knausgaard-my-struggle-review.
47 Ben Lerner, 'Each Cornflake', *London Review of Books* 36, no. 10, 22 May 2014, https://www.lrb.co.uk/v36/n10/ben-lerner/each-cornflake.
48 Sarah Manguso, *300 Arguments* (London: Picador, 2018), 67.
49 De Obaldia, *The Essayistic Spirit*, 16–18.
50 Karl Ove Knausgaard, *A Death in the Family: My Struggle Book 1*, trans. Don Bartlett (New York: Vintage, 2013) 197.
51 Karl Ove Knausgaard, *A Man in Love: My Struggle Book 2*, trans. Don Bartlett (New York: Vintage, 2013), 497.
52 Porter, 'Introduction', xxiii.
53 Shields, *Reality Hunger*, 204.
54 Tabbi, *Cognitive Fictions*, 137.
55 Knausgaard, *A Death in the Family*, 198.

Chapter 13

WALLACE STEVENS, AUDRE LORDE AND THE QUEER PERFORMATIVITY OF THE ESSAY

Allen Durgin

In his essay, 'The Noble Rider and the Sound of Words', Wallace Stevens holds out to the reader over the course of five numbered sections the promise of discovering some immutable truth about the nature of poetry, reality and the imagination, only to slip the reader's grasp with such queer demurrals as 'these may be words'.[1] A lesson in the obvious. He offers illustrations without elaboration, baldly stating: 'This illustration must serve for all the rest'.[2] And he begins the fifth and final section of his essay with the embarrassing admission: 'Here I am, well-advanced in my paper, with everything of interest that I started out to say remaining to be said'.[3] By the time you get this far into Stevens's essay, you can be certain that Stevens is never going to get around to saying it. But he has, in fact, said it in the act of composition: in his aphoristic tendencies, his obsessional parataxis, his promiscuous citations, his repeated use of illustrations that illustrate nothing, summations that do not sum a thing.

1.

Wallace Stevens was not an essayist. He was the quintessential modernist poet, publishing only one book of prose, *The Necessary Angel: Essays on Reality and the Imagination*.[4] The essays contained within are mostly lectures, Stevens apologizing in the book's preface that 'they are not the carefully organized notes of systematic study ... they were written to be spoken and this affects their character'.[5] The critical consensus has been that the essays collected in *The Necessary Angel* leave a lot to be desired. In her authoritative biography of Stevens, Joan Richardson describes the most cited essay in the book, 'The Noble Rider and the Sound of Words', as 'a compendium of references to the texts that had touched him most in the last ten years; it was at the same time a lecture' that 'evaded and evades any definition'.[6] Sidney Feshbach explains: 'he approached writing the lecture as he would a poem'.[7] Harold Bloom, while championing Stevens as *the* American poet of the twentieth century, contemptuously dismisses the lecture as 'a disaffected essay'[8] – the adjective *disaffected* strangely conjuring up associations of rebellious youth (even though Stevens was sixty-one when he delivered the lecture) and perhaps unwittingly tapping into the word's antiquated meaning of 'regarded with aversion'.[9] But perhaps the most summary dismissal of Stevens as an essayist comes from B. J. Leggett who passes judgement on Stevens as if he were a grad student failing his orals. In Leggett's assessment, 'Stevens never mastered the rhetoric of the essay.'[10]

Only in recent years have Stevens's essays been seen in a less infantilizing light. In his 2016 article, 'Stevens' "The Figure of the Youth" as an Essay', Robert Barton takes past critics to task for assuming that 'we can get around the deceptive mastery of Stevens' poetry only by assuming that mastery is relaxed in certain other of his writings', namely in his essays.[11] The essay from *The Necessary Angel* upon which Barton builds his argument is 'The Figure of the Youth as Virile Poet'. Far from seeing the compendium of textual references within the essay as evidence of its illogical structure, Barton argues that Stevens's lecture deploys all the particular affordances of the essay genre – its evasiveness, its questioning nature, its compendium of quotations – in order to demonstrate the impossibility of arriving at any stable definition of poetry. But something strange happens in Barton's celebrating of Stevens as an essayist: the gender dynamics so prominent in both the essay and its title are rendered invisible.[12] 'The Figure of the Youth as Virile Poet' becomes in Barton '"The Figure of the Youth" as an Essay'. Not *the* essay, but *an* essay. But exactly whose essay, Stevens's or Barton's, is unclear. It is striking how thoroughly genre eclipses gender in Barton's discussion, as if he means to say, along with Stevens's titular Virile Poet: 'No longer do I believe that there is a mystic muse, sister of the Minotaur. This is another of the monsters I had for nurse, whom I have wasted.'[13] Of course, the mystic muse being banished here is none other than the Virile Poet – 'a muse of its own, still half-beast and somehow more than human, a kind of sister of the Minotaur'.[14] Barton concedes that he cannot fully account 'for the strangeness and complexity of the poetic content of this citation'; his main interest lies 'in the structural role of this citation in bringing about the conclusion of an essay that could not conclude otherwise'.[15] Stevens concludes his essay 'almost as a prose poem' in which the Virile Poet summons the once banished half-sister of the Minotaur, and yet Barton never explicitly connects this hybrid figure with the hybrid prose poem form.[16]

Barton's disinterest in the interplay between form and content seems odd when we consider that Stevens first delivered the essay at a conference held at Mount Holyoke College, one of a constellation of women's colleges in the US Northeast known as the Seven Sisters. In attendance was the renowned poet Marianne Moore. An alumnus of Bryn Mawr, another of the Seven Sisters, Moore nursed Stevens's early reputation as a poet, one of the few critics to champion his first book of poetry. Stevens eventually honoured Moore by including 'About One of Marianne Moore's Poems' as one of the seven essays collected in *The Necessary Angel*. Although the two had corresponded via letters for several years prior, the lecture at Mount Holyoke marked the occasion of their first meeting. When the lecture ends with Stevens's Virile Poet saying, 'inexplicable sister of the Minotaur, enigma and mask, … hear me and recognize me … guide me in those exchanges of speech in which your words are mine, mine yours',[17] the elusive thread of allusions winding its way through his labyrinthine logic would not have been lost on his audience, particularly Moore, who may have heard in Stevens's essay an ambivalent plea to let another sister in.[18]

Barton does not acknowledge this.[19] If for Stevens, 'the centuries have a way of being male', then for Barton, so too does the essay.[20] Barton's implicit regendering of the essay as male and masculine runs counter to scholarship that would figure the essay as feminine form.[21] At the same time, switching out gender for genre eclipses the complex relationship between the two. As David Lazar observes, 'genre and gender are indissolubly linked, etymologically intertwined ... Genre is a category after all. So is gender. And the gender category difficult to characterize by normative standards is queer. The genre category difficult or impossible to characterize, the essay, is also queer. The essay is the queer genre'.[22] In 'Queering the Essay', Lazar echoes many scholars who have written about the essay's resistance to definition, its refusal to even *be* genre:[23]

> *Queer* and *essay* are both problematic, escapable, changeable terms. Both imply resistance and transgression, definitional defiance. But there is more; for example, Judith Butler's sense of performativity and gender and performativity's importance to the constitution of gender through reiteration speak to the operation of persona in the essay ... it is never fully controlled or calibrated; it is subversive and always has been.[24]

Lazar points to the ways the essay engages in genre trouble, 'borrowing from, at times parodying, other forms, constantly creating new unstable ones'.[25] Like Stevens's Virile Poet who is half-beast, half-man, half-sister, 'essays have always indulged in hybridic behavior, transgendered'.[26]

Barton notes that Stevens confronts 'the problem that poetry is recognizable and yet indefinable', but Barton never links the question of genre to the problem of gender circulating in the piece.[27] And yet, the problem of genre in Stevens's essay uncannily anticipates what trans* writer Jack Halberstam has called 'the bathroom problem':[28] how 'we seem to have a difficult time defining masculinity' and yet 'as a society we have little trouble in recognizing it'.[29] Stevens was troubled by such instant recognition, how easily gender and genre assignment become naturalized through iteration and citation. Writing in his journal under the heading, 'Poetry and Manhood', the young Stevens protests: 'Those who say poetry is now the peculiar province of women say so because ideas about poetry are effeminate. Homer, Dante, Shakespeare, Milton, Keats, Browning, much of Tennyson – they are your man-poets'.[30]

2.

Wallace Stevens was not queer. While his poetry is notoriously evasive, difficult and hard to pin down, his sexuality is not. He married his hometown sweetheart,

Elsie, at a young age; raised a family in Hartford, Connecticut; and had a very successful career as an insurance executive. He also engendered a curiously large queer following. *The Wallace Stevens Journal* has dedicated numerous articles and special issues to Stevens's influence on such queer writers as John Ashbery, Elizabeth Bishop, Adrienne Rich and James Merrill. Eric Keenaghan has written extensively on Stevens's epistolary relationship with the gay Cuban writer José Rodríguez Feo.[31] In an instance of male parturition reminiscent of the Virile Poet, Stevens's mentoring of Rodríguez Feo resembles his own queer education under the tutelage of gay philosopher George Santayana while at Harvard. David R. Jarraway has written on Stevens's influence on more recent gay writers such as novelist Michael Cunningham and poet Mark Doty.[32] What is notable about these discussions of Stevens's queer intertextuality, besides being overwhelmingly white and male, is the almost complete lack of attention to genre.[33] Stevens's queer influences are discussed mostly in terms of thematics. This lacuna is particularly striking in Jarraway's case, given the title of his article: ' "The Novel that Took the Place of a Poem": Wallace Stevens and Queer Discourse'. Like Barton, Jarraway is punning on a Stevens title, this time 'The Poem that Took the Place of a Mountain'. But the particular novel taking the place of a poem is not Stevens's, but Cunningham's. Cunningham prefaces his first novel, *A Home at the End of the World*, with the entire text of Stevens's poem. However, in Jarraway's account, Cunningham mines Stevens not for his formal experimentations, either in his prose or his poetry, but rather for what Jarraway calls Stevens's 'poetics of androgyny', the many thematic moments in his poems where he either speaks about – or as – the figure of a woman.[34]

Similarly, Keenaghan discusses Stevens's profound influence on the construction of gay masculinity within the Cuban literary group *Orígenes*, tracing the complicated gender dynamics involved across Stevens's life, letters, adages, essays and poems. But he does so without teasing out the difference *genre* makes. Where Keenaghan comes closest to such a genre analysis is in 'A Virile Poet in the Borderlands: Wallace Stevens's Reimagining of Race and Masculinity'. In that article, Keenaghan locates 'the most potent and "virile" of Stevens's early poet-figures'[35] in the iconic female figure singing 'beyond the genius of the sea' in 'The Idea of Order at Key West'.[36] Grounding his analysis in Gloria E. Anzaldúa's concept of borderlands, Keenaghan demonstrates how Stevens deploys the affordances of verse, that is, its line breaks, to shore up his gender and racial identities within the borderlands of Florida. The singing woman's 'ability to separate herself from a racialized and embodied borderlands is visually reinforced by an amazing linear disjunction … the fractured line that syntactically and graphically segregates "her voice" from the "sky and sea" draw[ing] the reader's attention to the degree to which Stevens manages his poetic material'.[37] In doing so, 'Stevens's poetry evinces an uncertainty as to whether the racial, cultural, and even topographical likenesses between North Americans and Cubans were sufficient to forge a new sense of American poetic masculinity'.[38] Here, we see the poetic line in service of its gendered and racialized content. But Keenaghan does not address how meaning may fracture across *generic* lines. What Keenaghan leaves unsaid about the gender and racial differences figured in Anzaldúa's *Borderlands/La Frontera: The New Mestiza* is that she explores those differences through the disjunction between poetry and prose and the highly charged moments when she moves back and forth between the two.[39] Stevens himself enacts such *genre* performance in 'Three Academic Pieces', the third essay collected in *The Necessary Angel*. 'Three Academic Pieces' begins as a response to a question posed by Rodríguez Feo in one of his letters. While the first piece is written in standard academic prose, the last two are rendered in verse as if Stevens is searching, as he did in Key West, for 'ghostlier demarcations, keener sounds'.[40] In their discussion of gender, race and sexuality, Keenaghan and others never question why it is in Stevens 'that prose should wear a poem's guise at last'.[41]

3.

The criticism diverges. Some celebrate Stevens as an essayist; others as Wallace the queer-friendly ghost. Whereas queerness disappears in discussions of genre, genre is ghosted by discussions of queerness, and this strange transposition takes place over time. Jarraway and Keenaghan are writing about Stevens's queer intertextuality in the late 1990s and early 2000s; Barton and the few others attending to Stevens's essays are doing so only within the last decade. We could caption this shift in scholarship as 'The Essay that Took the Place of Queer.' But I am wary of the collapsing of queer into the essay, both in Stevens criticism and in scholarship on the essay. First, it seems to make impossible any discussion of Stevens's own potential queerness. For all his 'poetics of androgyny' and queer intertextuality, Stevens's unassailable heterosexuality and stable gender identity is as presumed in Jarraway and Keenaghan as it is in Barton. Second, I am concerned with fetishizing the motives attributed to both queerness as an identity/non-identity and the essay as a genre/non-genre. In criticism, both get discussed primarily in terms of *limitlessness, infinity, constant change, endlessness* and above all *transgression* and *subversion*. These may be words …

But they are the same words used to describe late capitalism, a point made salient by queer theorist Eve Kosofsky Sedgwick, who cautions against framing gender performativity only in terms of *transgression*, lest 'like good late-capitalist consumers, we persuade ourselves that deciding what we like or don't like about what's happening is the same thing as actually intervening in its production'.[42] She sees such 'dreary and routine forms of good dog/bad dog criticism' in 'the uses [some] scholars [try] to make of performativity as they think they are understanding it from Judith Butler … straining [their] eyes to ascertain whether particular performances (e.g. of drag) are really *parodic and subversive* (e.g. of gender essentialism) or just *uphold the status quo*. The bottom line is generally the same: kinda subversive, kinda hegemonic'.[43] Lisa M. Steinman observes such myopia happening in 'some of the more acrimonious arguments about Stevens and the feminine'[44] as critics strain to ascertain whether Stevens's gendered figures are sexist or subversive. In his own use of Butler, Lazar falls into a similar trap, interpreting the performativity of the essay as subverting, parodying, exposing the hegemony. But he still 'worr[ies] about the essay's domestication, a false sense of formal radicalization'[45] – echoing Sedgwick's concern over the 'sadly premature domestication of [Butler's] conceptual tool'.[46]

To assay more interesting relations to Butler's conceptual tool, Sedgwick coins the term *queer performativity*. Her case study is novelist Henry James, whose staid persona and serpentine prose rivals Stevens's. Sedgwick does not argue that the novelist is gay, 'though [she] certainly [doesn't] want, either, to make him sound as if he *isn't* gay'.[47] Instead, she reads the prefaces to James's New York Edition (a collection of his revised earlier works) for what she calls his 'queer performativity' – a strategy for dealing with the shame and life-threatening depression he suffered due to his perceived failures as a writer. Sedgwick's work on James is instructive for how we might approach both Stevens and the essay. Not only do James's 'prefaces have affinities with Stevens' own essays, with some of Stevens' poems about the poetic process, and even with Stevens' long, careful explications of his poems in the *Letters*',[48] but they are, according to Lazar, models of queer essaying:

> Are essayists queer? Yes, or they have been, I'd argue, because along with the great motto of the essay, Montaigne's 'Que sais-je'... I've always thought the other great line that spoke to the heart of the essay ... comes in fiction, in Henry James's *The Art of Fiction*, when he urges us to 'Try and be one of the people on whom nothing is lost'.[49]

In trying to be one of those people on whom nothing is lost, I propose that our failure to recognize Stevens as either an accomplished essayist or as anything other than straight stems from reading his poetry 'straight'. Elizabeth Bishop famously said of Stevens's poetry: 'I dislike the way he occasionally seems to make blank verse *moo*'[50] – what critic Angus Cleghorn has characterized as 'his comparatively staid, mechanical-bull blank verse'.[51] But Bishop's *moo* is not simply formalist critique; it also castrates his 'mechanical-bull' verse by conjuring the figure of 'a woman, regarded as misguided or incompetent' as in *silly moo* or *stupid moo*.[52]

In order to bridge this apparent gap between gender and genre in Stevens criticism, and at the same time maintain a space between *queer* and the *essay*, I want to reread Stevens's straight-laced poems as queer essays. Reading Stevens's poems alongside Audre Lorde's *Sister Outsider: Essays and Speeches*, we shall see that Stevens's poems embody a queer performativity of the essay, one centred not on subversion, but on survival. We will come to some understanding of how poetry written over half a century ago by a heterosexual, white, cis-male insurance executive can open up queer histories of the essay as well as how reading poems as queer essays might, in the words of Stevens's *Noble Rider*, 'help people to live their lives'.[53] To heed Barton's parting call: 'if after all Stevens considered himself more of a poet than an essayist, the task left for us is still to revisit his poems ... If the essays have been read *qua* poems so far, what will happen when we read the poems *qua* essays?'[54]

4.

Writing in 1959, Newton P. Stallknecht opines: 'we find in Stevens the heart of a romantic pantheist and an intellect inclined toward the caution of a modern positivist. Like Emerson he is a Plotinus-Montaigne, once inspired and skeptical and as a result capable of a subtle and ironical self-criticism.'[55] A Montaignian spirit imbues Stevens's poetry. The titles of many of his poems, in fact, announce themselves *as* essays. 'Of Bright & Blue Birds & the Gala Son'; 'Of Heaven Considered as a Tomb'; 'Of the Surface of Things'; 'On an Old Horn'; 'On the Adequacy of Landscape'; 'On the Ferry'; 'On the Road Home'; 'On the Way to the Bus' – all would find a welcome home in the table of contents of *Essais*. Just as Montaigne's titles reflect 'the range of "topics" available to the essay … from the most serious to the most trivial',[56] so too do the titles of Stevens's poems, from the mundaneness 'Of Hartford in a Purple Light' in *Parts of a World* to the metaphysics 'Of Ideal Time and Choice' at the end of 'Three Academic Pieces'. This essayistic signposting is one that Stevens maintained throughout his poetic career, from 'Of the Manner of Addressing Clouds' in his first book of poetry to the posthumously published 'Of Mere Being' – the last poem he wrote before his death.

In many ways, Stevens's approach to poetry resembles Montaigne's essaying: 'his poetic practice had been to read parts of a book in philosophy or aesthetics and to extract some proposition that interested him to be used for thinking through an aesthetic problem in terms of his daily experience and for expressing in words his "thoughts and feelings." '[57] His occasional mooing notwithstanding, Bishop, in a letter to Marianne Moore, praised Stevens's writing:

> what strikes me as so wonderful … is that it is such a display of ideas at work – making poetry, the poetry making them, etc. That, it seems to me, is the way a poet should think, and it should be a lesson to his thicker-witted opponents and critics, who read or write all their ideas in bad prose and give nothing in the way of poetry.[58]

'Of Modern Poetry' begins: 'The poem of the mind in the act of finding.'[59] Like Montaigne before him, Stevens not only thematizes 'the act of finding', he enacts it. Take, for instance, this key moment in 'The Idea of Order at Key West':

> Whose spirit is this? we said, because we knew
> It was the spirit that we sought and knew
> That we should ask this often as she sang[60]

As Steinman observes, 'the speaker listening to the woman who sings by the ocean implies that certainty is not what the poem celebrates … The enjambments in these lines first suggest and then, after each line break, overturn the suggestion that knowledge should be authoritative rather than a matter of seeking and questioning'.[61] Stevens's enjambments enact the knowing uncertainty (i.e. we knew that we didn't know) that characterizes the essay as a genre, but in a way that prose cannot. Enjambment not only subverts the line that came before, it also allows it to stand, permitting contradictory propositions on both sides of the line break to remain true: it was indeed the spirit they sought and knew *and* it was the question they should keep asking. This matter of seeking and questioning leads us to sense the 'essayistic spirit' in Stevens's poems. Claire de Obaldia distinguishes between essay as genre and essay as mode. Essay as genre, associated with the English tradition stemming from Francis Bacon, admits to some fixity as a recognizable genre, 'one in which the sceptical element does not lead so insistently to the renewed questioning of the genre as a genre'.[62] Essay as mode, on the other hand, is more fluid, 'the more elusive essayistic mode or "spirit" privileged by the etymological meaning of the word … remain[ing] more directly based on the "Montaignian" essay'.[63] She characterizes the essayistic spirit 'as an attitude (the open-ended dimension of the form)' that can travel into other genres.[64] For instance, 'the presence of locatable essayistic material in the novel goes hand in hand with a generalized "self-essaying" or essayistic attitude, that is, with a blatant reflection or "philosophizing" on the conditions of its realization'.[65] At the same time, the essayistic spirit is what leads to the essay being understood as '*not yet* literature'[66] or the 'not-yet-written':[67] 'the prevalence of the etymological sense of "rehearsal" results in the displacement of the noun "the essay" – which denotes a genre in its own right – by the verb "to essay", which denotes a relationship of transitivity and dependence. Thus, the idea of the essay "preparing for the novel" or conversely of the novel trying itself out in the essay.'[68] This 'sense of rehearsal' is what relegates the essay to the margins of literature and associates it with extra-literary elements such as titles and prefaces. The marginalization of the essay is 'reinforced by the genre's tendency to be published (often retrospectively) in the peritextual form of the preface (Barthes's, for example) in the same way that prefaces are sometimes retrospectively published as essays (Henry James's, for example)'.[69]

It is this 'not-yet-written' nature of the essay that gives Stevens's poems their essayistic quality. Recall that Cunningham prefaces his novel with the complete text of Stevens's 'The Poem that Took the Place of a Mountain'. Jarraway, in turn, 'give[s] the complete text of Stevens's poem … as a means of summarizing the plot of *A Home at the End of the World*, for it does seem that the three parts of Cunningham's novel roughly approximate, in more expanded form, the kind of brief narrative that Stevens's own poem is unfolding'.[70] By positioning Stevens's poem as preface and outline, Cunningham and Jarraway unwittingly foreground its essayistic nature. Stevens's poem, like the essay, as de Obaldia tells us, 'stands for the body of the author's ideas that have yet to be "fleshed out". And this fleshing out is exactly what the novel prospectively provides, by presenting the idea(s) in the form of a continuous plot and substantial characters ready to act them out'.[71] Stevens would position his own poetry in a similar manner. For instance, his 'Notes Toward a Supreme Fiction' are just that – notes or prefaces to a literature that is not yet written. His poems are merely attempts – essays – at a supreme fiction.[72]

The essayistic quality of Stevens's poetry becomes even more pronounced when we turn to 'Chocorua to Its Neighbor'. According to Roy Harvey Pearce,

Stevens's poem glosses Henry James's description of Mount Chocorua in *The American Scene*, a collection of his travel essays. In such a reading, 'Chocorua to Its Neighbor' becomes a poem that took the place of an essay that took the place of a mountain. This vertiginous mise en abyme mimics the self-referentiality of the poem itself, harkening back to 'the kind of criticism advocated by Oscar Wilde', to use de Obaldia's formulation, 'one in which "the critic occupies the same relation to the work of art that he criticizes as the artist does to the visible world of form and colour".[73] While local lore tells the story of Chief Chocorua who, caught in a blood feud with white settlers, cursed the land before leaping from the mountaintop to his death, it is James, Pearce argues, who is the hero of Stevens's poem.[74] The hero is adumbrated in the fifth stanza:

> He was a shell of dark blue glass, or ice,
> Or air collected in a deep essay,
> Or light embodied, or almost, a flash
> On more than muscular shoulders, arms and chest,
> Blue's last transparence as it turned to black,[75]

Stevens's poem is akin to the philosophical essayism of György Lukács and Theodor W. Adorno. According to Lazar, 'the best theories of the essay – by Lukács, Adorno, Montaigne, Emerson, DuPlessis – turn in on themselves, lose argumentative coherence in the direction of passionate, expansive thinking about the essay'.[76] Similarly, Stevens's poems are about poetry itself. As 'The Man with the Blue Guitar' instructs us, 'poetry is the subject of the poem.'[77] Stevens's poetry is a piece of modern criticism, a contemporary of Benjamin, a precursor of Barthes. Thus, his poems paradoxically realize his own prediction that 'the best poetry will be rhetorical criticism' – a criticism that both attends to rhetoric and is itself rhetorical, the performance of a question.[78] When in his search for 'ghostlier demarcations', Stevens asks, 'Whose spirit is this?' we might well answer, 'The essayistic.'

5.

Here, we are, well-advanced in this essay, with everything of interest that we started out to say remaining to be said. Stevens's essayistic poetry – 'a kind of sister of the Minotaur' –embodies the hybridity that characterizes the essay as a queer genre. But Lazar cautions us:

> Merely breaking up paragraphs or adding poetry to essays (Cowley did that in the mid-seventeenth century) doesn't make an essay queer or politically resistant once that becomes one of the old bags of essay tricks that all beginning essayists must practice to construct barricades to the paragraph, within whose contours Lamb, Woolf, Baldwin … Montaigne, wrote such wild, fascinating, queer words.[79]

For Lazar, the queer performativity of the essay lies in its ability to resist appropriation into 'more conventional genres, like poetry'.[80] Seen in such a light, Stevens's essayistic poetry would seem old hat.

But the queerness of essayistic poetry rests not in its novelty but in its necessity. Gender and genre may be intricately intertwined, but as poet and essayist Audre Lorde reminds us in *Sister Outsider: Essays and Speeches*, 'the form our creativity takes is often a class issue':

> Recently a women's magazine collective made the decision for one issue to print only prose, saying poetry was a less 'rigorous' or 'serious' art form …writing a novel on tight finances, I came to appreciate the enormous differences in the material demands between poetry and prose … A room of one's own may be a necessity for writing prose, but so are reams of paper, a typewriter, and plenty of time.[81]

Lorde summons the ghost of Virginia Woolf as both novelist and essayist in order to reclaim poetry as the prose of the oppressed, 'the major voice of poor, working class, and Colored women'.[82] It is the marginalia of the marginalized, the affordance of poetry over prose: 'Of all the art forms, poetry is the most economical. It is the one which is the most secret, which requires the least physical labor, the least material, and the one which can be done between shifts, in the hospital pantry, on the subway, and on scraps of surplus paper.'[83]

Stevens kept his poetry writing 'a great secret'[84] and 'led a double life as a successful Surety and Fidelity Claims lawyer'.[85] He composed his poems 'on slips of paper in the morning while walking to his office'[86] or 'on the way to the bus'.[87] In drawing these comparisons, I do not want to suggest, in the words of Lorde, 'a homogeneity of experience covered by the word *sisterhood* that does not in fact exist'.[88] After all, Lorde was a self-described 'forty-nine-year-old Black lesbian feminist socialist mother of two, including one boy, and a member of an interracial couple'.[89] Stevens, whose writing peddled in racist tropes, was in many respects the very embodiment of what Lorde calls 'a *mythical norm*' – 'white, thin, male, young, heterosexual, christian, and financially secure'.[90] But one of the many affordances of Lorde's essay 'Age, Race, Class, and Sex: Women Redefining Difference' is an understanding that Stevens could never attain such a mythical norm. As Lorde explains, 'each one of us within our hearts knows "that is not me"'.[91] This mythical norm is not just mythical for those like Lorde whose identities were so far from it, but even for those like Stevens whose identities were so close. Myths exist in minds and imagined places, places where Stevens could not secure sure footing. Questions of gender and genre were live ones for him, not abstractions. As Keenaghan argues with regards to Stevens's correspondences with Rodríguez Feo, 'Stevens's work evinces his attempts to read self and nation more completely and dynamically *through* difference, rather than just defined against it.'[92]

Lorde begins her essay cautioning us that 'much of Western European history conditions us to see human differences in simplistic opposition to each other'[93] and begins her conclusion by urging us to develop 'new patterns of relating across difference'.⁹⁴ She develops that new pattern through a break in genre. Like Stevens in 'Three Academic Pieces', Lorde craftily ends her essay in *Sister Outsider* with poetry. In a footnote, she indicates that the lines are taken from an unpublished poem titled 'Outlines'. Both the footnote and the title index the poem's essayistic spirit. Whether the poem is Lorde's or one rejected by the women's magazine collective – or both – remains unclear. Regardless, smuggling in verse at the essay's close circumvents 'the master's tools'.⁹⁵ The inclusion of verse, however, does not arise from a desire to be subversive in and of itself, but as a necessary expression of self. For Lorde, as for Stevens, the motive behind essayistic poetry has less to do with answering the Montaignian question, *What do I know*? and more to do with responding to the pressing question, *How do I live*? To marginalized subjects such as trans people and/or people of colour who may not have a room of their own, who may simply be trying to walk down the street or enter a public restroom without risk of arrest or violence, the attribution of subversion does not necessarily help them live their lives. What appears to be subversion of gender and genre is an attempt at survival for both.

Reading Stevens's essayistic poems through the intersectional prism of Lorde helps us map alternative histories of the essay, particularly with regards to race. Rachel Galvin has noted that 'a broad, comparative study of Stevens's relationship to race has yet to be written'.⁹⁶ Instead, she finds its outline in the poetry of Olive Senior and Terrance Hayes, whose enjambed lines grant him 'a capacity for love without/forgiveness'.⁹⁷ Essays on Stevens may be essayistic poems themselves. 'For Black and white, old and young, lesbian and heterosexual women alike', as Lorde tells us, 'this can mean new paths to our survival.'⁹⁸ Mount Chocorua may be the highest peak in White Mountain National Forest, but its neighbour, The Three Sisters, also speaks. Lorde's essayistic poem could be read as an outline of Stevens's own – one sister saying to the other:

> *We have chosen each other*
> *and the edge of each others battles*
> *the war is the same*
> *if we lose*
> *someday women's blood will congeal*
> *upon a dead planet*
> *if we win*
> *there is no telling*
> *we seek beyond history*
> *for a new and more possible meeting.*⁹⁹

Notes

1   Wallace Stevens, *Wallace Stevens: Collected Poetry and Prose* (New York: Library of America, 1997), 647.
2   Ibid., 662.

3 Ibid., 659.
4 Wallace Stevens, *The Necessary Angel: Essays on Reality and the Imagination* (New York: Alfred A. Knopf, 1951). All citations in this chapter to Stevens's work refer to *Wallace Stevens: Collected Poetry and Prose* for ease of reference.
5 Stevens, *Wallace Stevens*, 639.
6 Joan Richardson, *Wallace Stevens: The Later Years, 1923–1955* (New York: William Morrow, 1988), 180.
7 Sidney Feshbach, 'The Structural Modes of Wallace Stevens' "The Noble Rider and the Sound of Words"', *The Wallace Stevens Journal* 28, no. 1 (2004): 81–100 (81).
8 Harold Bloom, *Wallace Stevens: The Poems of Our Climate* (Ithaca, NY: Cornell University Press, 1977), 172.
9 Oxford Dictionaries, s.v. 'disaffected', 30 August 2019. www.oxforddictionaries.com/definition/english/disaffected
10 B. J. Leggett, *Wallace Stevens and Poetic Theory: Conceiving the Supreme Fiction* (Chapel Hill, NC: University of North Carolina Press, 1987), 11.
11 Robert Barton, 'Stevens' "The Figure of the Youth" as an Essay', *The Wallace Stevens Journal* 40, no. 2 (2016): 172–84 (172–3).
12 For criticism analysing the complicated gender dynamics in Stevens's essay, see Jacqueline Vaught Brogan, ' "Sister of the Minotaur": Sexism and Stevens', in *Wallace Stevens and the Feminine*, ed. Melita Shaum (Tuscaloosa: University of Alabama Press, 1993), 3–22.
13 Stevens, *Wallace Stevens*, 680.
14 Ibid., 675.
15 Barton, 'Stevens' "The Figure of the Youth" as an Essay', 181.
16 Edward Ragg, 'Apophatic Auden, Abstract Stevens: From Kierkegaard to Cézanne in "The Sea and the Mirror" and "The Figure of the Youth as Virile Poet"', *The Wallace Stevens Journal* 37, no. 2 (2013): 199–223 (219).
17 Stevens, *Wallace Stevens*, 685.
18 For Moore's recollection of the lecture, see Marianne Moore, 'On Wallace Stevens', *The New York Review of Books*, 25 June 1964, https://www.nybooks.com/articles/1964/06/25/on-wallace-stevens/.
19 In a footnote, Barton directs the reader to Edward Ragg's *Wallace Stevens and The Aesthetics of Abstraction* (Cambridge: Cambridge University Press, 2010): 'for a reading of this extraordinary passage that focuses on its indebtedness to the myth of the Minotaur and Nieztschean undertones' (183). However, as Ragg's title suggests, what gets abstracted *out* of Ragg's reading are the gender implications of Stevens's use of the Minotaur myth.
20 Stevens, *Wallace Stevens*, 675.
21 See Jenny Spinner, 'Introduction: Omission and Erasure', in *Of Women and the Essay: An Anthology from 1655 to 2000*, ed. Jenny Spinner (Athens: University of Georgia Press, 2018), 1–34; Rachel Blau DuPlessis, 'f-Words: An Essay on the Essay', *American Literature* 68, no. 1 (1996): 15–45; Nancy Mairs, 'Essaying the Feminine: From Montaigne to Kristeva', in *Voice Lessons: On Becoming a (Woman) Writer* (Boston: Beacon Press, 1994), 71–87.
22 David Lazar, 'Queering the Essay', in *Occasional Desire: Essays* (Lincoln: University of Nebraska Press, 2013), 61–7 (61).
23 For other writers who explicitly discuss the connection between the essay as a genre and the category of queer, see Ned Stuckey-French, 'Our Queer Little Hybrid Thing', *Assay: A Journal of Nonfiction Studies* 1, no. 1 (2014), https://www.assayjournal.

com/ned-stuckey-french-our-queer-little-hybrid-thing-11.html; Francesca Rendle-Short, 'Essay (queer). The. Essay. Queer. And. All. That.', *Text* 39 (2017), http://www.textjournal.com.au/speciss/issue39/RendleShort.pdf; Todd W. Reeser, 'Queer Energy and the Indeterminate Object of Desire in Montaigne's "On Some Verses of Virgil"', *Journal for Early Modern Cultural Studies* 16, no. 4 (2016): 38–71.
24 Lazar, 'Queering the Essay', 63.
25 Ibid., 64.
26 Ibid., 66.
27 Barton, 'Stevens' "The Figure of the Youth" as an Essay', 177.
28 Jack Halberstam, *Female Masculinity* (Durham, NC: Duke University Press, 1998), 22.
29 Ibid., 1.
30 Wallace Stevens, *Letters of Wallace Stevens* (Berkeley: University of California Press, 1996), 26.
31 Eric Keenaghan, 'Wallace Stevens' Influence on the Construction of Gay Masculinity by the Cuban *Orígenes* Group', *The Wallace Stevens Journal* 24, no. 2 (2000): 187–207.
32 David R. Jarraway, '"Both Sides and Neither": Stevens, Santayana, and the Aestheticism of Androgyny', *The Wallace Stevens Journal* 30, no. 2 (2006): 210–25; David R. Jarraway, 'Doty, Deleuze, and "Distance": The Stevens Intertext', *The Wallace Stevens Journal* 28, no. 2 (2004): 285–94; David R. Jarraway, '"The Novel that Took the Place of a Poem": Wallace Stevens and Queer Discourse', *English Studies in Canada* 22, no. 4 (1996): 377–97.
33 One notable exception is Angus Cleghorn, 'Moving the "Moo" from Stevensian Blank Verse: Elizabeth Bishop's Use of Prose', in *Poetry and Poetics after Wallace Stevens*, ed. Bart Eeckhout and Lisa Goldfarb (London: Bloomsbury Academic, 2017), 57–72. Cleghorn refers to Bishop's prose-poem hybrid as gendered poetry but does so in service of a heteronormative reading of Bishop.
34 David R. Jarraway, '"Creatures of the Rainbow": Wallace Stevens, Mark Doty, and the Poetics of Androgyny', *Mosaic: An Interdisciplinary Critical Journal* 30, no. 3 (1997): 169–83 (182).
35 Eric Keenaghan, 'A Virile Poet in the Borderlands: Wallace Stevens's Reimagining of Race and Masculinity', *Modernism/modernity* 9, no. 3 (2002): 439–62 (457).
36 Stevens, *Wallace Stevens*, 105.
37 Keenaghan, 'A Virile Poet in the Borderlands', 456–7.
38 Ibid., 458.
39 Gloria E. Anzaldúa, *Borderlands/La Frontera: The New Mestiza* (San Francisco, CA: Aunt Lute Book Company, 1987).
40 Stevens, *Wallace Stevens*, 106.
41 Ibid., 29.
42 Eve Kosofsky Sedgwick, 'Queer Performativity: Henry James's *The Art of the Novel*', *GLQ: A Journal of Lesbian and Gay Studies* 1, no. 1 (1993): 1–16 (15).
43 Ibid.
44 Lisa M. Steinman, 'The Feminine', in *Wallace Stevens in Context*, ed. Glen MacLeod (Cambridge: Cambridge University Press, 2017), 344–52 (345).
45 Lazar, 'Queering the Essay', 67.
46 Sedgwick, 'Queer Performativity: Henry James's *The Art of the Novel*', 15.
47 Ibid., 11.
48 Glen MacLeod, 'Wallace Stevens and Henry James: The New York Connection', *The Wallace Stevens Journal* 34, no. 1 (2010): 3–14 (7).
49 Lazar, 'Queering the Essay', 66.

50 Elizabeth Bishop, *Elizabeth Bishop: Poems, Prose, and Letters*, ed. Robert Giroux and Lloyd Schwartz (New York: Library of America, 2008), 740.
51 Cleghorn, 'Moving the "Moo" from Stevensian Blank Verse: Elizabeth Bishop's Use of Prose', 59.
52 *Oxford Dictionaries*, s.v. 'moo', 20 January 2020, www.oxforddictionaries.com/definition/english/moo.
53 Stevens, *Wallace Stevens*, 661.
54 Barton, 'Stevens' "The Figure of the Youth" as an Essay', 182.
55 Newton P. Stallknecht, 'Absence in Reality: A Study in the Epistemology of the Blue Guitar', *Kenyon Review* 21, no. 4 (1959): 545–62 (547).
56 Claire de Obaldia, *The Essayistic Spirit: Literature, Modern Criticism, and the Essay* (Oxford: Oxford University Press, 1995), 2.
57 Feshbach, 'The Structural Modes of Wallace Stevens', 81.
58 Bishop, *Elizabeth Bishop: Poems, Prose, and Letters*, 740.
59 Stevens, *Wallace Stevens*, 218.
60 Ibid., 105.
61 Steinman, 'The Feminine', 349–50.
62 De Obaldia, *The Essayistic Spirit*, 37.
63 Ibid.
64 Ibid.
65 Ibid., 21.
66 Ibid., 16.
67 Ibid., 18.
68 Ibid., 17.
69 Ibid., 20.
70 Jarraway, ' "The Novel that Took the Place of a Poem": Wallace Stevens and Queer Discourse', 379.
71 De Obaldia, *The Essayistic Spirit*, 19.
72 Stevens, *Wallace Stevens*, 329–52.
73 De Obaldia, *The Essayistic Spirit*, 11. For the Oscar Wilde quote, see 'The Critic as Artist: Part I', in *Plays, Prose Writings and Poems* (New York: Alfred A. Knopf, 1930), 1–31 (24–5).
74 Roy Harvey Pearce, *Gesta Humanorum: Studies in the Historicist Mode* (Columbia: University of Missouri Press, 1987), 132–47.
75 Stevens, *Wallace Stevens*, 264.
76 Lazar, 'Queering the Essay', 64.
77 Stevens, *Wallace Stevens*, 144.
78 These words from Stevens's journal of 1899 preface Susan Sontag's essay 'Writing Itself: On Roland Barthes', in *Where the Stress Falls* (New York: Picador, 2002), 63–88 (63).
79 Lazar, 'Queering the Essay', 67.
80 Ibid., 66.
81 Audre Lorde, *Sister Outsider: Essays and Speeches* (Berkeley, CA: Crossing Press, 2007), 116.
82 Ibid.
83 Ibid.
84 Stevens, *Letters*, 180.
85 Susan Howe, *Debths* (New York: New Directions, 2017), 10.

86 Peter Schjeldahl, 'Insurance Man: The Life and Art of Wallace Stevens', *The New Yorker*, 2 May 2016, 75.
87 Stevens, *Wallace Stevens*, 472.
88 Lorde, *Sister Outsider*, 116.
89 Ibid., 114.
90 Ibid., 116.
91 Ibid.
92 Eric Keenaghan, *Queering Cold War Poetry: Ethics of Vulnerability in Cuba and the United States* (Columbus: Ohio State University Press, 2008), 37.
93 Lorde, *Sister Outsider*, 114.
94 Ibid., 123.
95 Ibid.
96 Rachel Galvin, 'Race', in *Wallace Stevens in Context*, ed. Glen MacLeod (Cambridge: Cambridge University Press, 2017), 286–96 (288).
97 Rachel Galvin, '"This Song Is for My Foe": Olive Senior and Terrance Hayes Rewrite Stevens', in *Poetry and Poetics after Wallace Stevens*, ed. Bart Eeckhout and Lisa Goldfarb (London: Bloomsbury Academic, 2017), 229–43 (238).
98 Lorde, *Sister Outsider*, 123.
99 Ibid. Italics in original.

Chapter 14

TRANSGRESSION AS TRANSCENDENCE:
ESSAYISTIC POETICS IN SELECTED WORKS BY
DMITRI SHOSTAKOVICH AND JOSEPH VELLA

Maria Frendo

Forsam et haec olim meminisse juvabit.[1]
[Perhaps even this distress it will some day be a joy to recall.]

– Virgil, *Aeneid*

1.

I remember referring to this line from the *Aeneid* when, as a student preparing to take my Advanced Level examination in Latin, I would be asked to write an essay on an aspect of Virgil's epic. There was something about the word 'essay' that made me nervous, perhaps because in my schooldays it was used as a synonym for 'homework'. Virgil's line can be read to fit any distressing situation, and writing an essay on the *Aeneid* was one such moment for me at that time. Now, (im)matured into middle age, the word 'essay' has not quite shrugged off the connotations it already had then with the improvisatory.

For someone with an interest in music, the word 'improvisatory' immediately allies itself to jazz and its unpredictable yet compelling rhythms – largely displaced and syncopated; those rhythms that will not stay still, will not be told what to do or where to go. Imparting a quasi-chaotic sense, these rhythms can be accused of all imaginable vices but one: they will never cause one to be bored.

Jazz rhythms seem to have emerged as a reaction to the predictability of traditional versification. The randomness, the seemingly unstructured patterns, which become the yardstick by which poetry started to be measured: it was all there, in jazz rhythms. There is never a dull moment with jazz rhythms. (On the ramifications of dullness Alexander Pope had already launched the project with *The Dunciad*, lest we forget.[2]) They are natural rhythms dictating the pace at which the poet directs his syntax and the musician his phrases. The art of these improvisatory rhythms appears to be grounded in the illusion (or is it 'affectation or celebration'?) of its artlessness.[3] The issue here centres on what is expressed as well as how this is expressed, by the composer/writer, with the concomitant notion that because an essay essentially expresses personal ideas in a voice that is the artist's own then it is also lacking in rhetoric and is therefore artless. Perhaps it is this 'artlessness' that raises these rhythms to an art form. 'Ars est celare artem.'[4] The iconoclastic becomes the new iconography.

These ideas about jazz rhythms can also be accommodated to the 'essay' genre. The personal essay, especially, refutes convention. It follows a route it chooses for itself; it can dislocate its ideas out of traditional structures with the consequence that syncopated thoughts sweep across its texture, and the unpredictability of its trajectories can only be regarded quizzically, at worst, capricious, at best. This is also some of the criticism levelled at the genre. Samuel Johnson writes in 1755 that the essay is 'a loose sally of the mind; an irregular undigested piece; not a regularly and orderly composition'.[5] Uncharacteristically, Joseph Addison agrees with Johnson when he comments on 'the wildness of these compositions that go by the name of essays'.[6] Yet, it is to this 'chartered libertine', to use Alexander Smith's words, that we owe a debt of gratitude, for the essayist's capriciousness is one that allows us to engage with a private sphere through his/her work which other genres may not always be inclined to accept.[7] The essay resists precise definition, and in Theodor W. Adorno's 'The Essay as Form', there is the indication that the genre is one that is in a perpetual possibility of shaping – hence the use of the word 'Form' also implying 'forming'.[8]

2.

From my standpoint as someone interested in literature and music, an essay means a work that meets not only a literary challenge but an artistic one as well, an endeavour that shows 'individual talent', style and craft, which goes beyond the broadsheets or the magazine. It does not only speak for itself but about itself. Like the lyric, the personal essay belongs to the literature of self-expression. Dmitri Shostakovich and Joseph Vella, two composers from very different backgrounds, wrote elegiac (musical) essays which are historically placed within the time and events they are commemorating. Their personal tone is as recognisable as it is inimitable. Yet, specifically because the works I shall be discussing are products of events which happened on a particular date at a particular time, they have the power to resonate beyond the confines that created them. To quote Adorno, these essays do not seek to 'filter the eternal out of the transitory ... [but] to make the transitory eternal'.[9]

In Shostakovich's and Vella's works of this nature, there is a sense of the artist reaching back to a transgressive past in order to transcend it through art. Only through words (I should say notes) can some meaning be given to this effort at recollection. This recollecting is not only a mnemonic effort at remembering, but also an attempt at putting things together again, re-collecting, re-membering what T. S. Eliot calls 'fragments ... shored up against ... ruins'.[10] It adheres to what

Walter Pater calls 'this unmethodical method'[11] in his comments on the essay style, a method that permits 'digression and promiscuous meanderings'.[12] Artists, casting and recasting as they do, illustrate the validity of this travelling back. It is the act of memorializing which leads Eliot to turn to Pound to help edit and transform the manuscript of *The Waste Land* rather than abandon it. Even Wordsworth's late sonnet, 'Mutability', deprecates 'yesterday':

> which royally did wear
> His crown of weeds, but could not even sustain
> Some casual shout that broke the silent air,
> Or the unimaginable touch of Time.[13]

Yet, that glorious phrase 'the unimaginable touch of Time' Wordsworth reclaims from an abandoned poem. Like Wordsworth and Eliot, Shostakovich and Vella are much possessed by time, loss and reminiscence. Shostakovich is also, in Eliot's phrase about Webster, 'much possessed by death, / And saw the skull beneath the skin'.[14] In dramatizing the time rather than just fearing it, Shostakovich makes the time imaginable; no wonder he is everywhere memorably found remembering. This comment warrants some clarification. The 'Babi Yar' *Symphony no. 13* discussed in this chapter makes use of words, and this helps the listeners shape their understanding.[15] In an art form (music) that is fundamentally non-referential, the setting of a text to music arrests the fleeting movement so natural to sound. Music seeks to elicit the tone and mood inherent in the text and is always subservient to it. In this way, time becomes a fixed point, no longer fleeting and ephemeral. Words and musical sound become inseparable, and coalesce in an attempt to produce an indefinite meaning.

The two Vella works chosen for discussion are *Lament op. 103* (written in three hours on the tragic news of the terrorist attack on the Twin Towers on 11 September 2001),[16] and *Charlie on my Mind op. 144* (inspired by yet another terrorist attack, this time on the Charlie Hebdo Headquarters in Paris on 7 January 2015).[17] The musical language here is abstract in that there is no text which is set. There is an impressionistic flow of ideas, giving a sensation of movement in a state of stasis. Clarity is enhanced by a rich harmonic complex and what matters is participation in an experience concentrated on the reception of sound and silence. By the end, one feels that 'music has reached a place not yet visited by sound'.[18]

3.

At this stage I feel I should justify a couple of points. My enduring interest in literature and music lies behind the choice of this chapter's subject matter. I discuss musical works which have been selected, after careful deliberation, for qualities or properties that I believe could be termed essayistic. These works were composed as a direct result of catastrophe, hence the personal voice emerging there. They can be labelled 'elegies', even if the term is loosely applied. As I try to argue, there is certainly pain, rage, remorse, the occasional wistful reminiscence, commemoration – qualities one associates with the elegy or the elegiac essay. Moving from the particular to the universal is also a trait that the works under discussion share with the essay. Again, this is a point that is discussed in more detail throughout the chapter. Also, given the randomness of some ideas foregrounded in the chosen works, the reader will hopefully associate these with digressions (I try to consolidate this point at the end of my chapter). Digressions do not occur for their own sake but, to use Lopate's words, 'must wander off the point to fulfil it'.[19] In this manner, digressions become focal points in the work and illuminate it with purpose and vigour.

There are other musical elegies that could have been examined (Beethoven's 2nd movement, 'Marcia Funebre', from the *Eroica Symphony* comes to mind, among others). I chose three twentieth- and twenty-first-century works because of their proximity to our condition today, works that are the result of war and terrorism. I focus on Shostakovich mainly because of the polemical stance critics take in his regard, and Vella because he comes from my home town of Victoria, Gozo (Malta). The latter does not have the international profile the former has, but his music is no less valid.

The dearth of critical reference with regard to the essayistic in musical works is due to a largely under-commented aspect of comparative study. This has substantiated the challenges I faced, ones I am sure I have not always overcome.

4.

By 1961, Shostakovich (1906–1975) was firmly established as the Soviet Union's most distinguished composer. He was their most important cultural representative on both national and international platforms, travelling to America as a member of official and cultural delegations. Under considerable pressure, he formally joined the Communist Party in 1960. Despite the undeniable advantages this brought him professionally, it also caused him deep distress, for, as we read in *Henry V*, 'every subject's duty is the King's, but every subject's soul is his own'.[20] Yet, paradoxically, it was this difficult period in Shostakovich's career that led to the creation of a few of his greatest works. Most remarkably of all, in joining forces with the younger generation as represented by the poet Yevgeny Yevtushenko, he proved to be as eloquent a spokesman for the 1960s as he had been for the 1930s and 1940s.

No other musical work from this period has achieved more lasting status than Shostakovich's *Symphony no. 13*, entitled 'Babi Yar'. A long-standing critic of Soviet anti-Semitism, Shostakovich was instantly attracted to the humanitarian ethos of Babi Yar, the place that had witnessed the massacre of Ukrainian Jews by the Nazis and local Ukrainian collaborators in 1941. At the time of the *Symphony*'s publication, a massive engineering project was under way to fill in the ravine where the bodies of the massacred Jews lay. Khrushchev's administration went to extraordinary lengths to ensure all evidence of the massacre was obliterated, eventually building a road over it. In the words of Richard Davenport-Hines, 'the best-organized and most productive Stalinist industry was the falsification of history'.[21]

The poem's opening line, 'There is no monument above Babi Yar',[22] points an accusing finger at the officials responsible: no memorial was put there until 1966 – and this was repeatedly removed by the authorities. A permanent memorial was only erected at the site in 1991. Yet, perhaps, the most enduring testament has been the *Symphony*, composed in 1962, at the height of another war, this time the Cold War. This work is an essay on anti-Semitism which does not resort to eloquence for its tone but to rage and disgust. What Turgenev and Orwell attained with their political essays, Shostakovich achieved with his 'Babi Yar' *Symphony*, as I try to show at the end of Sections 5 and 6.

Initially, Shostakovich intended to set only Yevtushenko's poem 'Babi Yar' to music. However, when the poet himself gave Shostakovich a volume of his works, the composer chose three more, namely, 'Humour', 'In the Store', and 'A Career'. Another poem, entitled 'Fears', was commissioned by Shostakovich, who warmed to its message and included it in the *Symphony*. These five poems became the titles of the five movements in the *Symphony*. The *Symphony*'s closing line, 'I'll follow my career in such a way that I'm not following it!'[23] carries special resonance for Shostakovich himself, one, I feel, Julian Barnes picks subtly on in his novel *The Noise of Time*.[24] Although Shostakovich had first alluded to creative immortality as far back as 1937 with his *Symphony no. 5*, the related idea of remaining true to one's own conscience in the face of official tyranny was a favourite theme of the composer's late period, here explicitly stated for the first time.

5.

A comment on this matter is apt, I feel. Shostakovich is, arguably, one of the most vilified of twentieth-century composers. While colleagues such as Stravinsky and Prokofiev fled Soviet Russia, Shostakovich could not abandon his home country. His was a crisis brought about by love of country and equally powerful revulsion of Communism. The fact that he joined the Communist Party, albeit reluctantly, was interpreted by many to reflect his sympathies for the regime. In fact, he was officially denounced for his alleged Soviet loyalty in 1936. It can be argued that his *Symphony no. 5* (1937) is a response to this denouement, not least for the fact that a telling quotation (an intertextual echo) can be heard in this *Symphony*'s last movement, one that takes the listener to an earlier Shostakovich work, a song, significantly called 'Rebirth', on a text by Pushkin. More specifically, the fragment that is heard in this movement is the one that in the song accompanies the words 'An artist-barbarian ... Blackens over the painting of a genius.'[25] At this point, the entire stanza is worth quoting:

An artist-barbarian with a drowsy brush
Blackens over the painting of a genius

> And senselessly draws on top of it
> His own illegitimate designs.
> But over the years the foreign paint
> Flakes away like old scales,
> And the genius's work appears again
> Before us in its former beauty.
> Thus do delusions vanish
> From my worried soul,
> And in their place visions arise
> Of pure, original days.[26]

Many have identified the 'artist-barbarian' as Stalin and the 'genius' Shostakovich. Julian Barnes picks up on this point in his novel, and the irony is not lost on those who can read the story behind this reference in Barnes's work. At one point, Barnes asks 'Could irony protect his music?' Barnes argues that insofar that music remains a secret language it would allow the composer to 'smuggle things past the wrong ears'.[27] It is the height of espionage, after all. The devil is in the detail, and the detail here is the title of the poem, 'Rebirth', a renaissance after the ravages of Communism when 'visions arise / Of pure, original days'.

Taste and judgement, more or less comfortable in the presence of Shakespeare or Milton, are challenged by novelty. Moving away from musical elegy as process, Shostakovich writes musical elegy as event. This happens when artists write as a direct result of an event, generally a tragic one, which makes a lasting impact on them. For instance, just to mention one example, a contemporary American composer, William Finn, wrote his song cycle *Elegies* after the 11 September 2001 tragedy. In such moments, the composer's own personal voice is nowhere more pronounced. Here, it is tone that triumphs not sense. True to the essay form, the 'Babi Yar' *Symphony* is that work in which the writer's own private thoughts on a subject are as captivating as the subject itself; here, Shostakovich looks for the larger theme that an isolated event leads him to, when the craft and balancing of material uncovers a keen sense of a subject's true complexity. So, as event rather than commentary, this essay's musical resonance lies beyond any programme.

6.

On the surface, 'Babi Yar' conforms to the personal essay's poetics of randomness, intuited rather than studied ideas, and general structural looseness. Cast in five distinct movements, with an all-male choir and a bass solo, this unusual form has given much space for generic speculation: some have called it a cantata, others a choral symphony in the style of Beethoven's 9th, others an oratorio. Alternatively, read as an essay on anti-Semitism, the retrospective glance of the essayist comes naturally to a composer blessed with a historical awareness.

14. Transgression as Transcendence 219

Shostakovich sets his first movement on Yevtushenko's vernacular poem 'Babi Yar' in an episodic manner, with three major dramatic sequences recounting the Dreyfus Affair, the Bialystok Pogrom and Anne Frank's capture and death. The episodic structure allies itself almost too comfortably with that of the personal essay: the music occasionally bursts into hymn-like flourishes before disintegrating into the cacophony so typical of the fragmentary style of the modernist artist. Shostakovich mobilises imposing brooding paragraphs, balancing anguish and parody equitably. Like all grand narratives, this one relies on a character with compelling defects. That character is Shostakovich's own not that of a functionary like Khrennikov, who, Barnes tells us, 'had an average ear for music, but perfect pitch [only] when it came to power'.[28]

It is never easy to speak of the dead; it is even more difficult to speak for them. In the case of Shostakovich we have the added problem that even in his life, the composer could not speak for himself because history, in the shape of Stalin, forbade him to do so. We like to say that music speaks; but what makes music's language universal is its reticence and abstraction, its non-referentiality. The grand narrative of 'Babi Yar' is unadorned, the horror of which it speaks plainer still. This latter idea is profoundly disturbing, for man-made horror is intended to stand out as a spectacular event (think of the Twin Towers tragedy, for instance). Its lack of proportion classifies it as unspeakable, for what has happened cannot be accommodated within the boundaries set by language. Translating this plainness into the sublime through musical transcription helps the composer and the sensitive listener to tune in to its uniqueness, to render it special as an event an artist would be inspired by.

The composer's tone of ironic self-effacement could hammer a horseshoe; the hell it creates is a hostile universe that negates the possibility of prayer. In the best traditions of the essayistic, 'Babi Yar' rouses, rallies, eulogises and commemorates. There is neither escapism nor inauthentic consolation. It is an essay that speaks of pain, fear, and desolation, its language both plain-spoken and outspoken.[29]

The *Symphony* is only just into its stride when certain phrases, although perfectly at home in themselves, gain significance in their association with other phrases. Theme, craft and location insist on coalescing. The 'Babi Yar' communicates the straightforward event of death; victory is only attained in looking death in the face. Yeats's resolution of loss and remorse in what he calls 'terrible beauty' comes to mind here, but in utterly un-Yeatsian and emphatically Shostakovich's personal voice.[30]

One could ask whether in this *Symphony* the theme is not as developed, confirmed, varied and contrasted as the object of meditation in a sequence of philosophical ideas. Shostakovich scholars, foremost among whom is Elizabeth Wilson, assuming a more holistic position, have perennially heard the form, content, and process of his works to be unified in the expression of a new underlying idea.[31] However, it is rather difficult to follow the strands of the multiple fragments generally found in Shostakovich's works, so powerful is the illusion of cohesive selfhood he portrays in the voice he projects. Yet, the 'Babi Yar' *Symphony* gives him away, for the illusion here is ripped to shreds by a voice speaking out in brutal, naked honesty.

This should not be interpreted as belittling the previous or the later *Symphonies*, but the 'Babi Yar' rather dwarfs everything in its boldness of conception, breadth of execution, and intensity of political statement. In a well-established tradition of political essays, the 'Babi Yar' ranks among the finest. Shostakovich arguably never again approaches this feat of fiery imagination. He writes greater works after the 'Babi Yar' but he never again reacts so powerfully against the world. Every component is unusual and novel but singularly appropriate for his purpose, which is not the 'cult of personality' but that of a far-reaching prerogative: standing up to evil. Detractors have branded the 'Babi Yar' vulgar; those who resonate with history acknowledge it as a twentieth-century essay on 'de vulgari eloquentia'.

7.

Another artist who ranks as a sophisticated essayist through his musical works is Joseph Vella (1942–2018): conductor, researcher, university professor and, above all, a humanist. His works are wide-ranging and all-encompassing; among the multiple genres one finds elegies, works inspired by tragedy and grief.[32]

The alliance of music and mourning is culturally acceptable, and this rather strange alliance between grief and musical ingenuity exacerbates the deeper dialectical tension that music is an art of expression without the capacity to say denotatively what is being expressed:[33] it is transgressive with regard to any one specific meaning. Unlike words, which may have a precise dictionary meaning, music does not 'mean'. In a sense, music is about itself, and this is the intrinsic tragedy of musical eloquence. Thus, the more melancholic the music the more it approximates meta-music, imprisoned in itself, contemplating its own nature, grieving the loss of its object. Like the personal essay, musical elegy enacts the processes and possibilities of thought and self-disclosure in a distinctive personal style, with a content that is generally imperishable.

Contrary to the self-assured tone one might hear in the personal essay, the tone one discerns in Vella's elegies is fundamentally understated and non-dramatic. Perhaps this is one rare instance where the personal essayist is also a reliable narrator: the composer lets the work do the talking rather than lays down instructions on how it ought to be understood. The 'I' doubting its own sincerity becomes doubly sincere, gaining in the process a double-edged, unassailable authority. True to the anti-rhetorical tendencies of the personal essay, Vella makes his point not by resorting to rhetorical flourishes but very much inside and with the music he is creating. His is a tone given to simplicity and complexity at the same time, achieving a subtlety reminiscent of the type Yeats achieves in 'The Circus Animals' Desertion'.[34] One senses that these works are not really about the problems of good and evil, although they are inspired by that binary, as is also the case with the 'Babi Yar'. As Claire de Obaldia puts it, the essay embraces 'a split between the "I" and the world ... between art and philosophy, when all relationships are destroyed and reflected upon'.[35]

Unlike Shostakovich's, these works are essays of quiet persuasion. The musical language implemented transcends dialectical tensions. The inner turmoil in the man is expressed in exquisite serenity, the type which is not associated with a resolve to die or accept death, or with an irony in the face of implacable odds typical of Poulenc or Richard Strauss, or even Shostakovich, for that matter, but is often simply enigmatic, discernible in phrases which have a tranquil, even idyllic tone. Dystopia (the event that inspired the work) is challenged by utopia (the composer's musical language) and wisdom is imparted through the personal voice of the composer.[36] To sensitize public opinion, the particular experience is shared universally, proclaiming concepts and feelings that everyone recognizes and shares.

Although certainly denser, terser in structure and less harmonious than a couple of earlier Vella works, these compositions are to the same degree more subjective, more autonomous and spontaneous even though they are inspired by tragedy. The often-noted abbreviation in Vella's style aims not so much to purify the musical language of its phrases as to free this musical syntax from the illusion of subjective control.[37] Vella is a master of narrative economy who tends to work metonymically, and the listener is asked to grasp at phrases or parts thereof intuitively rather than consciously. Here, concept replaces narrative, and the sporadic leitmotifs serve both a structural and a thematic purpose.

In this way, the words of Adorno on Beethoven, namely, 'the emancipated phrase, released from the dynamic flow, speaks for itself', can be applied to Vella's method.[38] This happens, however, only for the moment when subjectivity, withdrawing, passes through 'the emancipated phrase' and strongly illuminates it with its purpose. Hence the subtle crescendos and diminuendos which, seemingly independent of the musical form, often shake this same structure to its foundations by the intensity of their tone. This tone seems to be controlled by an internal dimmer-switch that can transform a phrase as short as four or five notes from a diaphanous murmur into a searchlight flame.

8.

Similar to the 'Babi Yar', in these works, particularly in *Charlie on my Mind, op. 144*, there is shock, of course; there is also pain, as the composer himself attests in an interview given to French radio when recording this work in Paris.[39] Additionally, there is a continual endeavour to speak honestly, one that is central to the raison d'être of the personal essay.[40] While Shostakovich attains this sincerity through irony, Vella does it by transcending the confines the musical language imposes on him and focuses mainly on the process of writing. As György Lukács puts it: 'The essay is a judgement, but the essential, the value-determining thing about it is not the verdict ... but the process of judging.'[41]

In this sense, Vella no longer draws together the soundscape, now silent and disenchanted, into an image. In *op. 103*, especially, he floods the work with a light empowered by the subjective voice, and this in turn strikes the frame of the essay's structure in breaking free. The extremes resorted to are strictly technical: on the one hand there are phrases in unison which do not necessarily engage in narrative; on the other hand, there is polyphony soaring above that unison. It is the personal voice which compels the extremes to come together within the moment, 'charging the compressed counterpoint with its tensions, disintegrating and escaping it in the unison, leaving in its wake the naked tone'.[42] Thus, contrary to expectation, the elegiac phrase disconcerts, destabilises, dis-consoles. It offers no comfort. It is set in place as a monument to what has been, a monument in which 'subjectivity is [now] petrified'.[43]

Death-as-caesura, understood as Kristeva means it in her analysis of Holbein's dead Christ, is the abrupt stop which characterizes these musical essays perhaps more than any other feature.[44] It constitutes those tenuous moments of breaking free by suspending meaning.[45] The emerging sound is non-sound, silence; the work is now deserted. The ineffable dominates and inexpressibility becomes a potent force. Only then is the next phrase added, after the gap (the caesura) has spoken through its silence, finding its place by fleeing subjectivity and forging links with what has gone before. A secret is shared between these links, and this can be purified only by the new tone they now form together. This seemingly random concatenation of ideas is emblematic of the essayistic. It informs the contradiction whereby these 'transgressive' essays can be called both subjective and objective. The fragmented soundscape is objective, while the personal voice in which alone it echoes is subjective. Vella does not bring about a harmonious synthesis. As a dissociative power the composer dissolves them in time, perhaps to safeguard them for timeless realms. That which is not updated endures beyond the confines of history.

Typical of the personal essay form, the ideas latent in these two Vella works are flexible and adaptable. They can travel, creating new associations in different contexts, conforming to Michel de Montaigne's comment on the essay that 'all subjects are linked with one other'.[46] True to the essayistic style, this seemingly random wandering could be termed digressive (or transgressive), but these digressions (or transgressions) exist to further affirm a point not to negate it, as I discuss earlier in this essay. They create a context which adds layers of meaning to the original statement. As they do in Montaigne, among others, they serve as both a structural and a thematic anacrusis.

Vella is the master of the slow movement, much like Haydn is of his. In the works mentioned in this essay, one hears a nobility of tone that rises above the horror that inspired the work. Written in the composer's idiosyncratic style, this personal voice, however, transcends its own subjectivity and becomes the listener's own voice almost through ventriloquism.

In these works, the composer avoids the more robust instruments such as heavy brass and percussion, and instead concentrates on the upper ranges of the instrumental spectrum with his use of a string ensemble (*Lament*), and cornet

14. Transgression as Transcendence 223

and string quartet (*Charlie on my Mind*). Dissonance and clashes of the 2nd and 7th intervals find dissolution rather than resolution. Vella does not choose to defy the odds stacked against humanity but opts to transcend these through the use of a voice that tragedy does not recognize. The association of ideas, made valid through fragmentation, allows opposites to coalesce harmoniously. In the composer's understated tone, these essays of quiet persuasion, as I refer to them earlier, reassure without coercion. They state through indirection and allow the listener to participate in the production of meaning.

9.

'The essay shies away from the violence of dogma.'[47] Grief has a habit of bringing diverse people together in a collective communion with loss. This shared experience, albeit particular, becomes universal, a compelling alternative to philosophical discourse or dogma. It is un-categorical and non-fanatic. In Vella's elegiac essays, the musical language confounds expectation by implementing an ethereal tone which exudes the serenity that has been ruptured by the atrocity that ripped it apart. It is audible virtue out of which emerges peace.

Motifs found in these works are rendered with the character of a thesis, that is, an idea capable of changing the world, an unprecedented free act. Technically, this requires extreme dynamic intensity: sound is no mere sensuous attribute but is the condition of something spiritual, of structural meaning. Melody can hardly be heard and understood as organised syntax at all, but as a complex of meanings. In true essayistic style, melody makes itself present sporadically, sometimes in combination with other melodies or fragments thereof. A point is made through repetition, modified variation, inversion. This is done with a sense of gusto, almost, an occasion for flair or talent to assert itself. The difficulty in listening to these pieces is of a higher order – it concerns form. Form is not attained through the evolving variation of core motifs, but accumulated additively from sections usually imitative among themselves. There is a subtle firmness and a courteous civility of tone here.

These musical essays are characterized by understatement. The shattered unity, the transgression, is transcended through a metonymic process which is achieved by the abrupt, unmediated juxtaposing of clear themes supported by complex counterpoint. The rift between the two turns 'the impossibility of aesthetic harmony into aesthetic content,'[48] failure in the highest sense into a yardstick of success. Reaching 'the quiet limit of the world', the composer's understatement is the metaphor of severance.[49] Reading the boundary of the insignificant, this quiet, disenchanted sadness is an essayistic art of utmost elegance and sobriety.

'Genius ... enables one to find out ideas for a given concept, and, besides, to hit upon the expression for them by means of which the subjective mental condition induced by the ideas as the concomitant of a concept may be communicated to others.'[50] In these elegiac essays, Vella's genius manifests itself, among others, in a tone of sincerity devoid of irony, unlike in Shostakovich. In both, however, there is unity of purpose: sound takes precedence over sense. After all, the elegiac musical essays I have touched upon are inspired by an attack on sense. While Shostakovich burdens his work with the unbearable weight of loss, Vella forces upon his the weightlessness of human grief. Finally, because a controlled aesthetic is at work here, the musical essay seems to stand aside: it renounces claims to metaphysical statement and it pliantly, agreeably and immediately appeals to an ear surprised, perplexed even, by the music's lack of complaint. As such, in the history of the contemporary essay, these works are themselves catastrophes, dare I say as much as the tragic events that brought them about in the first place.

10.

The trepidation I always felt about writing essays lingers. Virgil's line set at the start of this essay still resonates in my conclusion, but the meaning it now takes is perhaps more far-reaching. Tragedy is always shocking; but it could just be possible to take something good out of the art that is inspired by them. It is the essayist (the artist) who presses a relentless kind of quest for intimacy of relationship with the various particular realities of experience, not with the 'light that never was on land and sea', but with the concrete actualities of the world; with the unique historical event, with the unrepeatable personal encounters and with all the rich singularity that belongs to ideas in their intractable specificity.[51] In this regard, it is the artist who is the 'genuine representative of the poetic principle'.[52]

The legend surrounding the works I have touched upon is a legacy that is, to date, un-negotiated. It is overwrought with unease, whether this is detachment or eagerness. Either way, Shostakovich's 'Babi Yar' and Vella's elegies are essays that, like the rhythms of genius, will 'not go gentle into that good night'.[53] They will resound within and beyond the noise of time. 'Ars longa, vita brevis'.[54]

Notes

1 Virgil, *Aeneid*, ed. J. Henderson, trans. H. R. Fairclough (Cambridge, MA: Loeb Classical Library (Harvard University Press), 1999), 1.5.203.
2 Alexander Pope, *The Dunciad in Four Books*, ed. V. Rumbold (London: Routledge, 2009), 6–68.
3 I would like to thank my colleague, Ivan Callus, for suggesting this.
4 'The technique of art is to conceal art.' Attributed to both Ovid and Tibullo, but the source is unknown.
5 Samuel Johnson, *Johnson's Dictionary: A Modern Selection*, ed. E. L. McAdam and George Milne (London: Franklin Classics, 1963), 167.
6 Joseph Addison, 'No. 476. Friday, September 5', in Joseph Addison and Richard Steele, *The Spectator with Sketches of the Lives of the Authors, and Index and Explanatory Notes*, Vol. 10 (Philadelphia: James Crissy, 1841), 7–10 (7).

7   Alexander Smith, 'From "On the Writing of Essays"', in *Essayists on the Essay: Montaigne to Our Time*, ed. Carl H. Klaus and Ned Stuckey-French (Iowa City: University of Iowa Press, 2012), 25–8 (25).
8   Theodor W. Adorno, 'The Essay as Form', trans. Bob Hullot-Kentor and Frederic Will, *New German Critique*, no. 32 (Spring–Summer, 1984), 151–71.
9   Adorno, 'The Essay as Form', 159.
10 T. S. Eliot, *The Waste Land*, in *Collected Poems 1909–1962* (London: Faber and Faber Ltd, 1974), 61–86 (79).
11 Walter Pater, *Appreciations: With an Essay on Style* (Charleston, SC: Nabu Press, 2010), 52.
12 Phillip Lopate, ed. 'Introduction', in *The Art of the Personal Essay: An Anthology from the Classical Era to the Present* (New York: Anchor Books, 1995), xxiii–liv (xxxvii).
13 William Wordsworth, 'Mutability', in *The Collected Poems of William Wordsworth*, ed. Antonia Till (Herts, UK: Wordsworth Editions, 1998), 991.
14 T.S. Eliot, 'Whispers of Immortality', in *Collected Poems 1909–1962*, 55–56 (55).
15 Dmitri Shostakovich, *Symphony no. 13 in Bb Minor, op. 113 'Babi Yar'*, with bass soloist Sergei Aleksashkin, Symphonieorchester und Chor des Bayerischen Rundfunks, conducted by Mariss Jansons (Munich: Warner Classics, 2005), CD.
16 *Lament op. 103*, on *Joseph Vella Chamber Works, Vol. 9: Music for String Orchestra*, recorded 2011 by the Sofia Philharmonic Orchestra and the Malta Philharmonic Orchestra. Digital Magic, 2011, compact disc. Also available as 'Joseph Vella – Lament' (video, 10:37). From its performance at St George's Basilica, Victoria, Gozo, on 12 July 2010. Posted on YouTube by St. George's Basilica, 11 August 2010. https://www.youtube.com/watch?v=4oQJhOmkVcA.
17 *Charlie on my Mind op. 144* was first performed by Alexis Demailly and the Urban Quartet at the Bastille Opera House, Paris, on 7 January 2016. It is available at Alex Demailly, *Fantasque*, accessed 27 March 2020, https://www.alexisdemailly.com/gb/shopping-fantasque.php. An interview with the composer, Joseph Vella, together with snippets of the piece during a CD recording session in Paris can be accessed at 'Alex Demailly – Joseph Vella – Charlie on My Mind' (Video, 2:14). Posted on YouTube by Alexis Demailly on 12 November 2016. https://www.youtube.com/watch?v=in6YiXsICb4&feature=share&fbclid=IwAR0CNKx2L_4XfiOexQ2xGrbV5XvwRhir1isQj8g6m66NnYX8UsPnF46eXH0.
18 Virginia Woolf, 'Impressions at Bayreuth', *The Times* (London), 21 August 1909, 22–3 (23).
19 Lopate, 'Introduction', xl.
20 William Shakespeare, *Henry V*, ed. T. W. Craik (London: The Arden Shakespeare, 1995), 4.1.175–7.
21 Richard Davenport-Hines, *Enemies Within* (London: William Collins, 2018), 32.
22 Yevgeny Yevtushenko, *Selected Poems*, trans. Robin Milner-Gulland and Peter Levi (London: Penguin, 2008), 68.
23 Yevtushenko, *Selected Poems*, 68.
24 Julian Barnes, *The Noise of Time* (London: Jonathan Cape, 2016)
25 Alexander Pushkin, *Pushkin Poems: A Russian Dual Language Book*, trans. Sergei Shatskiy (London: Maestro Publishing Group, 2017), 42.
26 Ibid.
27 Barnes, *The Noise of Time*, 86.
28 Ibid., 90.

29 Numerous essays inspired by tragedy have been written. Joan Didion, *Fixed Ideas America since 9/11* (New York: NYRB Classics, 2006); Rebecca Solnit, *A Paradise Built in Hell* (New York: Penguin, 2010); and John Hersey, *Hiroshima* (New York: Random House, 2011) are only three examples.
30 William Butler Yeats, 'Easter 1916', in *Yeats's Poems*, ed. A. Norman Jeffares (London: Macmillan, 1989), 287–9 (287).
31 See Elizabeth Wilson, *Shostakovich: A Life Remembered* (London: Faber and Faber, 2006); Laurel E. Fay, *Shostakovich: A Life* (New York: Oxford University Press, 2005); Stephen Johnson, *How Shostakovich Changed My Mind* (London: Notting Hill Editions, 2019).
32 For more information about Joseph Vella's works, see https://www.josephvella.com.mt
33 Edward Said, *Music at the Limits* (London: Bloomsbury, 2009), 149.
34 Yeats, 471.
35 Claire de Obaldia, *The Essayistic Spirit: Literature, Modern Criticism, and the Essay* (Oxford: Oxford University Press, 1996), 39.
36 This recalls St Paul's 'sub contraria specie' in his *Theologia crucis*, 2 Corinthians. 13:3–4 (New Jerusalem Bible), later also expounded by Luther in his theses for the Heidelberg Disputation (1518). See *Concordia: The Lutheran Confessions* (St Louis, MO.: Concordia Publishing House, 2007). I thank my brother, George, for discussing this with me.
37 Albert Storace, 'Mastery of Control: Joseph Vella in Concert', *The Sunday Times of Malta*, 8 February 2004, 23.
38 Theodor W. Adorno, *Beethoven: The Philosophy of Music*, ed. Rolf Tiedemann and trans. Edmund Jephcott (Cambridge: Polity Press, 2005), 18.
39 See endnote 17 above.
40 Katharine Fullerton Gerould writes: 'The essayist, whatever the limitations of his intelligence, is bound over to be honest; the propagandist is always dishonest.' ('An Essay on Essays', in *Essayists on the Essay: Montaigne to Our Time*, ed. Carl .H. Klaus and Ned Stuckey-French (Iowa City: University of Iowa Press, 2012), 61–4 (64)).
41 György Lukács, *Soul and Form*, trans. Anna Bostock (London: Merlin Press, 1974), 18.
42 Adorno, *Beethoven: The Philosophy of Music*, 126.
43 Ibid.
44 Julia Kristeva, *Black Sun: Depression and Melancholia* (New York: Columbia University Press, 1989), 105–38.
45 Adorno, among others, makes this point clearly in 'The Essay as Form', writing that 'Discontinuity is essential to the essay' (164).
46 Michel de Montaigne, 'On Some Verses of Virgil', in *The Art of the Personal Essay*, 58–112 (93).
47 Adorno, 'The Essay as Form', 158.
48 Max Paddison, *Adorno's Aesthetics of Music* (Cambridge: Cambridge University Press), 239.
49 Alfred Tennyson, 'Tithonus', in *Tennyson: Poems and Plays*, ed. Thomas Herbert Warren (Oxford: Oxford University Press, 1975), 90–1 (90).
50 Immanuel Kant, *The Critique of Judgement*, trans. James Creed Meredith (New York: Dover Publications [1790] 2005), 68.
51 William Wordsworth, 'Nature and the Poet', in *The Collected Poems of William Wordsworth*, 602.
52 Lukács, *Soul and Form*, 19.

53 Dylan Thomas, 'Do Not Go Gentle into That Good Night', in *Dylan Thomas: Collected Poems* (London: Orion Publishing Co., 2005), 42.
54 Hippocrates of Cos, *The Aphorisms of Hippocrates: and the Sentences of Celsus with Explanations and References in Physics and Philosophy*, trans. C. F. Sprengell (Kessinger Publishing: Whitefish MT, 2010), 4. This epitaph is inscribed on the tomb of Sir Christopher Wren in St Paul's Cathedral, London.

Chapter 15

HERSEY, RESNAIS AND REPRESENTING HIROSHIMA: TOWARDS AN ESSAYISTIC HISTORIOGRAPHY

Bob Cowser Jr

> The poem of the mind in the act of finding
> What will suffice. It has not always had
> To find: the scene was set; it repeated what
> Was in the script.
>   Then the theatre was changed
> To something else. Its past was a souvenir.
> – Wallace Stevens (1923), 'Of Modern Poetry'[1]

War is cultural crisis and brings about a concomitant crisis in artistic representation, the post-apocalyptic moment calling for new articulations of reality. 'The scene was set', as Stevens explains above, then the theatre is 'changed / to something else'. Every war assaults our sensibilities with new atrocities, and the Second World War's concentration camps and atomic weapons had changed Stevens's theatre again, as it were.

Since its publication a little more than a year after an American bomber dropped the first atomic weapon on the Japanese city of Hiroshima, John Hersey's account of the attack has dominated literary-historical discourse on the subject. Constituting the entire editorial contents of the *New Yorker* magazine issue dated 31 August 1946 (something the magazine has never repeated) and published by Alfred A. Knopf shortly thereafter, *Hiroshima* has enjoyed near-immediate canonical status, and Hersey himself is considered the earliest practitioner of what Tom Wolfe would call in 1973, 'The New Journalism', his meticulous reporting and revolutionary narrative methods having become stock-in-trade strategies for literary nonfiction writers.[2]

Thirteen years later in 1959, French documentary film director Alain Resnais released his own 'account' of the Hiroshima bombing, *Hiroshima mon amour*, itself one of the most important films of French New Wave Cinema.[3] In 1950 Resnais had made with Paul Éluard a film about Picasso's *Guernica*,[4] the painter's furious response to the Nazi bombing of that city, and had collaborated with the poet Jean Cayrol, a Holocaust survivor, on a conventional short documentary film commemorating the tenth anniversary of the liberation of German concentration camps, 1956's *Nuit et brouillard* (Night and Fog).[5] But *Hiroshima mon amour*, scripted by Marguerite Duras, was a feature-length film, and while it included documentary footage Resnais shot in the city, the Duras script centres, if that is the word for a film so unconventionally structured, on what Roland Barthes might call a 'lover's discourse',[6] a fictional dialogue between a Japanese architect whose family had been killed by the bomb while he was away fighting for the empire and a French actress who'd suffered her own wartime trauma in the French city of Nevers and has now come to Hiroshima to star in a film about the atomic bombing.

Both Hersey and Resnais worried the horrors of atomic fallout were un-representable. Theodor W. Adorno had famously asserted that to write poetry after Auschwitz would be barbaric, and Resnais had made *Night and Fog* reluctantly.[7] 'What hope de we really have', reads narrator Michel Bouquet from the Cayrol script, 'of capturing this reality?'[8] Film theorist Timothy Corrigan says that in 1945 and the years shortly after there was, in particular, a mistrust of documentary forms following a war in which propaganda films were presented as fact.[9] I will argue that Hersey's and Resnais's respective artistic innovations and departures are responses to this anxiety, this crisis in representation, the product of each artist's search for 'what will suffice', for sufficient forms and innovations within form.

And yet the responses are divergent: for all of Hersey's celebrated innovations and the continuing influence of his text, I believe *Hiroshima* ultimately represents a retreat into conventional, realistic forms and orthodox conservative, even coercive, historiographical practice. The Resnais film, on the other hand, is postmodern, post-historical. Though not entirely non-fictional – Hersey himself would say the film's incorporation of the fictional lover's discourse is a violation of journalism's most sacred prohibition against invention, the sort of thing 'Mr. Straight-Arrow' abhorred – I want to be even more specific and call the film *essayistic*: dynamic, subversive, multi-modal, polyvalent. Drawing on the work of meta-historian Hayden White and others, I will consider the consequences of Hersey's method and make the case for the essayistic spirit that invigorates that Resnais film, what we might call an example of an 'essayistic historiography or historiophoty', which may avail an audience of more of what Adorno calls in 'The Essay as Form' a 'whole truth' which transcends rigid formal compartmentalizations.[10] The 'essay's innermost formal law', Adorno reminds us, 'is heresy'.[11]

1. 'A work of sustained silence'

Hersey, born in China to American missionaries and later educated at Hotchkiss and Yale, returned to Asia as a journalist covering the Second World War in the Pacific Theatre, travelling eventually to Japan to report on the atomic bombing of Hiroshima. Discourse about the bomb had to that point featured a sci-fi fascination with the technology and ingenuity – the US government had employed *New Yorker* science writer William Laurence to focus reporting on the science of the Manhattan project and even eyewitness accounts observed a certain grammar: the fiery ball, mushroom cloud, the column of smoke, and so on still associated with the event. Despite the fascination with technology, all was designed to make Hiroshima seem like other conventional bombings (Pearl Harbor, London, Dresden). Officials repressed stories of human suffering. Textual discussion of injuries and after effects was acceptable, but images were not.[12]

Patrick Sharp says it was at this point that Hersey's book intervened, against the grain of prevailing discourses of technology and nationalism.[13] Hersey believed he saw a story no one else had yet seen, the human story, and told Harold Ross at *The New Yorker*, who had commissioned his Hiroshima reporting, that he planned to 'write about what happened not to buildings but to human beings'.[14] Media depictions of the Japanese had been sensational and racist, even after the bombing and amid the joy at the end of the war.[15] Furthermore that he planned to employ a novelist's techniques to do so – 'the things we remember are emotions and impressions and illusions and images and characters: the elements of fiction', he would say later.[16]

At first structuring the book had stymied Hersey – he 'cast about for a way to find a form'.[17] Someone had sent him Thornton Wilder's Pulitzer prize-winning novel, *The Bridge of San Luis Rey*, which he read during an illness aboard an American destroyer making passage from China to Hong Kong, and he decided to borrow its structure wholesale, the interrelationship of characters faced with disaster (in Wilder's case the collapse of a Peruvian bridge in 1714).[18] Hersey's biographer Jeremy Treglown writes that even before he started researching, Hersey had 'more or less decided on Wilder's device of focusing on half a dozen people, introducing others through them', and that this 'gave the narrative focus and coherence while also, through human interconnection and sheer coincidences, threw into relief the smallness of the community afflicted by so vast and mysterious a destructive force'.[19]

Hersey was determined to deliver the subjective experience of Japanese survivors while maintaining his own journalistic distance, obscuring himself. He hoped to establish his journalistic objectivity, Bret Schulte says, in two ways: 'a neutral recitation of facts' and 'a reporter's integrity, in other words, presenting a story in a way that is fair, with balance given to opposing sides'.[20] It's a highly Positivist (read: American) approach: all you can really know about an experience is what your senses tell you. Christian Kriticos identifies an 'air of neutrality' signalled even by Hersey's title. The piece 'was not to be a clear-cut damnation of the bombing quoting facts and figures about casualties and the decimation of infrastructure', writes Kriticos, but a 'declaration of the human aspect, somehow so often ignored in the nuclear debate'.[21] Readers are left to make their own judgements.

Yet Hersey still hoped to access the 'literary' via his prose style. Nineteenth-century American historiographical practice, like prudent American journalism, had eschewed poetics in the name of truth and the strict recitation of facts. Nicholas Lemann calls Hersey's narrative stance in the piece 'an unadorned, omniscient third-person voice', but it was still a departure from the magazine's usual point of view: the editorial 'we', or a generalizing preamble – that put a measure of distance between the reader and the material.[22] Lemann says Hersey obliterated that distance, bringing the reader close to the scene via description. Roger Angell called it in a 1995 retrospective of *Hiroshima* a 'work of sustained silence … prose so stripped of mannerism, sentimentality, and even minimal emphasis as to place each reader alone within scenes laid bare of all but pain'.[23] Schulte agrees: 'Despite … Hersey's talent for chilling images, *Hiroshima* is nearly devoid of emotion. Hersey gives no analysis and largely abstains from indulging his subjectivity.'[24] Cloaked thus in what would have been accepted in 1946 as journalistic dispassion, Hersey considered himself ethically unimpeachable, closely guarding himself and his masterwork from attack for the rest of his life. His influence has been immense: 'today when you read an artful, unsentimental magazine article about grunts in a firefight or cruising down an IED-infested street', writes historian Dan Gerstle, 'you are reading Hersey's journalistic patrimony'.[25]

There has been criticism of Hersey's descriptions. Yuko Shibata believes that his use of established Waste Land tropes and figurative language in general to describe the Hiroshima ground zero swerves from literalness of expression and deflects attention from states of affairs about which it purports to speak (i.e. 'the real'). 'Figuration produces stylization, which directs attention to the author and his or her creative talent', Shibata claims, 'and produces a perspective on the referent of the utterance, but in featuring one particular perspective, it closes off others … reduces or obscures certain aspects of events'.[26] We don't really see Hiroshima, in other words, only metaphor: the Waste Land, ourselves.

But perhaps more problematic is his wholesale, hermit crab-like adoption of Wilder's novel structure. Meta-historian Hayden White says that his narrativizing of history or emplotment might not, on its face, seem controversial.[27] 'Narrative is a manner of speaking as universal as language itself', White explains, 'and narrative is a mode of verbal representation so seemingly natural to human consciousness that to suggest it is a problem might well appear pedantic'.[28] White quotes Barthes describing narrative as a metacode translatable without fundamental damage, a practical human universal capable of transmitting transcultural messages about the nature of reality.[29] It purports to translate narrative into structures that are generally human-specific rather than culture-specific. The appeal of conventional narrative historical discourse, writes White, is that 'it makes the real desirable … by its imposition, upon events that are represented as real, of the formal coherency that stories possess'.[30] Even something as previously unimaginable as the A-bomb. White says the value attached to narrativity in representing real events arises out of a cultural desire to have real events display coherence, integrity, fullness, and closure, driven by the desire for a moral meaning, so that this meaning might replace the fantasies of emptiness and frustrated desire that 'inhabit our nightmares about the destructive power of time'.[31] Unlike essays (and essay films), writes Dutch photographer Taco Hidde Bakker, which inquire, experiment, and consider the self in its relation to the outside world, 'stories chiefly answer archetypes, and therefore could be recounted and are universally translatable'.[32]

But this narrative wholeness can only be imaginary. Does the world ever present itself in well-made stories, White asks, or is life mere sequences of beginnings that terminate but never end? To insist on coherence and meaning and closure, says White, is to 'deprive history of the kind of meaninglessness which alone can goad the moral sense of living human beings to make their lives different for themselves and their children'.[33] White contends that, no matter a writer's efforts at maintaining neutrality and objectivity, storytelling becomes a problem when instead of 'revealing the true essence of past reality, historical narrative imposes a mythic structure on the events it purports to describe', one freighted with the invisible assumptions and biases of the storyteller and his culture. Hersey claims not to indulge his subjectivity, but Schulte says he does not manage to reflect on or problematize it either; he 'not only obscures his own point of view, he obscures his country's'.[34] 'American points of view – that the bomb was fitting retribution for the attack on Pearl Harbor and/or was a swift and justifiably powerful end to Japanese aggression – are not only absent in *Hiroshima*, they are countermanded by that very absence.'[35]

If, as writing teachers are wont to say, constructing narrative is merely a matter of deciding what to leave in and what to leave out, Yuko Shibata speaks a word for what gets left out, goes unrepresented, is silenced in a narrativizing project like Hersey's.[36] While Patrick Sharp praises Hersey's use of modernist tropes and fictional structures, Shibata suggests these strategies are problematic solutions to what is the bombing's fundamental resistance to historicization as what Hayden White would have called a 'modernist event'. (To be classed a 'modernist' for Hayden White, events must have been impossible without technology, must call into question existing Western categories and conventions, and must resist historicization.)[37] And beyond these obscuring tropes, Shibata notes that *Hiroshima* contains remarkably few direct quotations from Hersey's six protagonists, that he seems uninterested in 'retrieving the *hibakusha*'s [atomic survivor's] voice, although it is questionable to assume the transparency of voice within narratives'; 'this[marginalization]' she writes, 'may be considered colonial'.[38] 'Narrative structures arise to make sense of new technologies,'[39] according to Sharp, but Shibata laments that Hersey, though faced with unprecedented events, does little to challenge the limits of representation. She fears what she terms the 'compartmentalization of knowledge' – the fact that it's exactly Hersey's familiar form, history-as-novel, that gives his narrative authority, and that audiences who only encounter his narratization are susceptible to its subtle coercion.[40] The presentation of Hiroshima as spectacle is not only a way to remove the reader from political responsibility, but these representational strategies also dispel the ghost that haunts the American psyche, serving as an 'apparatus of psychological deterrent'.[41]

2. 'You saw nothing at Hiroshima'

It was not only military technology that has bewildered us in the mid-twentieth century, claims Bakker; it has been the advent of and advances in technology as well.[42] Like nineteenth-century historians, Hersey clung to the faith that historical written discourse could 'transfer the phenomenal word into the verbal without loss or distortion'.[43] But 'notions about history, narrativity and chronology have been thrown into confusion since the invention of the mechanical recording of images and sounds', Bakker says.[44] 'To "describe" an event with a mechanical apparatus differs essentially from describing it with a pen.'[45] Bakker points to Czech philosopher Vilém Flusser's articulation of the period since the invention of photography – and presumably the moving image – as the '"post-historical" era':

> In historical time the written and printed word dominates. Historical consciousness requires literacy. In the post-historical era the technical image dominates, undermining linear consciousness. Flusser talks about post-historical magic, how technical images based on mathematics (photography, film) replace text. As history was a struggle against idolatry, post-history is a struggle against so-called 'textolatry'.[46]

It is possible, then, to think of Hersey's *Hiroshima* as a historical response to a post-historical (Flusser) or modern (White) event, a conservative return to old forms and images, a clutching after Stevens's souvenirs. The hegemony of Hersey's narrative is an example of Flusser's 'textolatry', whereby a traditional 'image' (the Wilder novel, the Waste Land tropes, for example) 'instead of *representing* the world', as audiences believe it does, *obscures* it, 'until human beings' lives become a function of the images they create'.[47] Human beings cease to decode the images but merely worship them – idolatry/textolatry.

I want to offer *Hiroshima mon amour*, then, as a post-historical subversive text, part of the struggle *against* textolatry, what we might even think of as an example of an 'essayistic historiography' which acknowledges *through its form* the changed theatre of the post-atomic reality. In 1988's 'Historiography and Historiophoty', White concedes as obvious the fact that 'cinema and video are better suited to the actual representation of certain kinds of historical phenomena – landscape, scene, atmosphere, complex events such as wars, battles, crowds and emotions', but echoes the worries of Robert Rosenstone that perhaps these image-based discourses (historiophoty) cannot adequately convey 'the complex, qualified, and critical dimensions of historical thinking about events' commonly thought of as lending any account of the past its certification.[48] My claim here is that the multi-modal essayism of Resnais's film makes some progress towards solving this dilemma. His essay film risks what Adorno calls 'the violence that image and concept ... do to one another'.[49]

Timothy Corrigan offers a definition of the essayistic in the introduction to his study *The Essay Film* which is useful here:

> the essayistic acts out a performative presentation of self as a kind of self-negation in which narrative or experimental structures are subsumed within the process of thinking through a public experience. In this larger sense, the essay film becomes most important in pinpointing a practice that renegotiates assumptions about

documentary objectivity, narrative epistemology, and authorial expressivity within the determining context of the unstable heterogeneity of time and place.[50]

Structures are not borrowed or reified but 'subsumed' within the thinking process of a guiding subjective consciousness (or perhaps in the case of the Resnais film, a pair of consciousnesses in dialogue).

Film theorist Hunter Vaughan says that *Hiroshima mon amour* is an example of Resnais's systematic subversion of what he calls 'classical cinema', wherein – and here he is quoting David Bordwell – ' "cause-effect logic and narrative parallelism generate a narrative which projects its action through psychologically-defined, goal oriented characters" ',[51] a fair characterization of Wilder's and Hersey's realist aesthetics, as well. *Hiroshima mon amour*, on the other hand, Vaughan says, confronts directly the 'problem of representation: spoken representation as communication between two people and, also, cultural representation as a discourse on history and the present'.[52] The film dramatizes this encounter between fictional selves (Lui and Elle) and the historic event, what Corrigan calls 'a personal point of view as a public experience'.[53] The film's dialogue represents a challenge to the orthodoxy of documentary objectivity – the Japanese architect tells his French actress lover, 'You saw nothing of Hiroshima, nothing' (*Tu n'a rien vu á Hiroshima, rien*).[54] But this is an articulation of the filmmaker's anxiety as well: what could his camera 'see' here? And how could he and Duras represent the devastation to an audience in America, even in war-torn Europe? 'What did Hiroshima mean to you, in France?' the architect asks the actress as they stand together on a balcony after lovemaking. 'The end of the war', she replies.[55]

Vaughan says Resnais was actively engaged in historiography, at least in its subversion, that all of Resnais's films from the 1960s conceive of history and memory as some form of 'linguistically paralyzed sublime in which the ability to name or to conjure images through words is constantly frustrated', and there is 'uncertainty, ambiguity and a polyvalence in his signifying systems that frustrates the straightforward production of denotative meaning, not to mention audiences'.[56] He continues:

> Directing this reflection toward contemporary geopolitical problems, as well as questions of how culture constructs history out of such problems, Resnais's films … are uniquely engaged with history as a process of representation, combining international events with the problem of recording, representing, and preserving history between individuals.[57]

After months of filming yet another realistic documentary, a kind of sequel to *Night and Fog*, Resnais abandoned the documentary genre, deeming it an inadequate form through which to represent such a traumatic event. For Resnais, according to Sarah French,

> the magnitude of the devastation in Hiroshima not only defied comprehension but also exceeded the limits of filmic representation. [His] decision [to

abandon the documentary] highlights the moral and ethical risks inherent in reconstructing historical trauma through the medium of realist cinema, a genre that traditionally purports to invest its depictions of the past with authenticity. The documentary form would imply a 'truthful' and unmediated representation of the past, which in the case of the Hiroshima bombings was considered unachievable.[58]

We hear French's (or Resnais's) subtle impeachment of projects like Hersey's and their purported authenticity (the straight-arrow accuracy and objectivity of his reporting). I think here also of *Let Us Now Praise Famous Men*,[59] the James Agee/ Walker Evans prose/image collaboration (which enjoys a place beside Hersey's book in the American Literary Nonfiction pantheon) in which Agee 'is often rueful that he cannot communicate through words with the unmediated directness that he attributes to the camera'.[60]

Resnais finds himself at the limits of classical or realistic documentary film but rather than reach back with *Hiroshima mon amour*, he combines his documentary footage (real footage of post-apocalyptic Hiroshima, so that his text does, in fact, represent the world in way that Hersey's figurative language cannot) with a fictional narrative set in the city of Hiroshima (and presented as a dialogue between characters) that Sarah French says would 'incorporate the partial memory of the atomic bombing while focussing upon an individual experience of trauma'.[61]

Duras provides a screenplay as opaque as it is lyrical, at once personal and public, with characters both French and Japanese, and French says the film's shift from historical event to personal memory is 'reflective of a broader cultural interest in using memory as a counter-discourse to normative historiography', precursor to the 'memory boom' or preoccupation with memory discourse in postmodern culture and history-making of the 1980s, which actually privilege subjective remembering.[62] (Barthes's *Camera Lucida* comes to mind, an inquiry into the nature and essence of photography which is 'disrupted' by a eulogy for his mother).[63] Bakker says it is 'exactly in this vast borderland between the world of facts (observations, products of recording equipment) and of the fictional (thoughts, associations, distorted memories), that the essayistic mode offers ample freedom to makers as well as the public'.[64] 'In essays – written, spoken, visual, or a combination thereof', Bakker writes, 'one is allowed to wander, to take steps back, to jump forward ... Essays are not driven by character-formation or a plot. They offer room for contemplation and consumption at one's own pace.'[65]

Because of the centrality of editing and montage to the works of both Resnais and Soviet filmmaker Sergei Eisenstein, the two are frequently compared, but, Vaughan says 'no two filmmakers ... could have more dissimilar philosophical functions for editing':

> Whereas Eisenstein uses montage as a means for guaranteeing the spectator's interpretation of a film, for producing specific meaning through the signification of a monolithic transcendental subject, Resnais's use of montage offers a completely different connotative meaning. Contrary to Eisenstein's precise and

certain worldview, Resnais's films aim for uncertainty, a poly-valent signified produced through a dialogic system of reference, leaving the image in a state of ambiguity and the spectator in a position of critical awareness.[66]

Hersey aimed (no pun intended) like Eisenstein at producing a specific meaning in readers. And though pious and noble and exceedingly earnest, the aim still lays him open to charges of sentimentality and its subtle coercions. Hersey the journalist is committed to making a record of life in Hiroshima *as it was lived* and claims to absent himself from the scene, his consciousness merely the recording and organizing instrument, but Resnais is fascinated by life *as it was lived AND imagined.*[67] The Resnais film mimes not the world but the mind in the act of apprehending the world, embracing rather than attempting to eschew subjectivity, dramatizing the relationship between subjective experience and the self's existence as objects in a larger world, interrogating that encounter. Vaughan's description of the film seems to echo Corrigan's definition of the essayistic: 'a kind of encounter between the self and the public domain, an encounter that measures the limits and possibilities of each as a conceptual activity', a 'renegotiation of assumptions'.[68] The film places its own interiority in question 'through the disintegration of narrative agency as a singular and coherent figure' – two protagonists presented in dialogue – and 'through the exploration of the margins of temporality and history' – non-linear and perhaps even non-narrative text.[69]

3. 'Sleepless but thankful'

'How did Hersey', marvels friendly biographer Treglown, 'not Japanese, not an eyewitness, not a scientist, come to be the first person to communicate the experience to a global audience?'[70] His question is fawningly rhetorical, but the answer is quite simple, if cynical: cultural hegemony/imperialism.

It is perhaps a significant question how much culture and/or nationality influenced the divergent responses of these artists to the bombing; as Neil Badmington suggests, also elsewhere in this volume, perhaps 'form follows history and nation'.[71] It *is* tempting to imagine Hersey as the Graham Greene character Pyle from *The Quiet American*, 'impregnably armored by his good intentions and his ignorance'.[72] 'I wish sometimes you had a few bad motives, you might understand a little more about human beings', Greene, no fan of American foreign policy, has British journalist Fowler say to Pyle.[73] Hersey's came by the rectitude honestly. Lemann explains:

> Like many élite Wasps who came of age in the early decades of the twentieth century ... Hersey started out in a deeply religious world and became essentially secular in the course of his life. It's not that the religious impulse left him; rather, he transferred it to his writing and to his myriad civic activities, all of which had a strong quality of moral preachment.[74]

While the primacy of Hersey's *Hiroshima* certainly owes in part to the fact that occupying US forces censored all other accounts of the bombing, I would suggest its pre-eminence owes as much to Hersey's reaching back to embrace an orthodox narrative structure, which offered even its highbrow audience a wholeness and meaning exemplary of American Cold War confidence and complacency. Hersey's *Hiroshima* ultimately confirms more of what Americans believe about themselves than it challenges, eradicating the lack of security Adorno says 'the norm of established thought fears like death'.[75] Esteemed *New Yorker* editor Elaine White, whom Hersey had never met, wrote to thank him for 'an amazing piece of reporting' that has left her 'sleepless but thankful', and that her husband, E. B. White, felt the same way.[76]

Against all this certainty, I have set the Resnais film, as essayistic counterpoint. It is hardly perfect: Resnais and Duras were not eyewitnesses either, not Japanese, and in her 2018 book-length post-colonial analysis, *Producing Hiroshima and Nagasaki*, Yuko Shibata discusses the many blind spots in the film, the subconscious influence of the French colonial imagination.[77] But I have tried to limit myself primarily to a discussion of form(s), their limits and opportunities. Corrigan's concept of *essayism*, with its focus on subjectivity and language and time as important components of knowledge, liberated as it is from the confines of genre, allows us to locate at the limits of the essay form a remarkable film like *Hiroshima mon amour*, and to begin to think about a history-making (with words *and* images) characterized more and more by the curiosity and reflexivity on display therein, so that we are a people more reflective by nature, seeking texts that invite us into the process of decoding and making meaning rather than venerating the old texts and images, Stevens's mere souvenirs.

Notes

1. Wallace Stevens, 'Of Modern Poetry', in *The Collected Poems of Wallace Stevens: The Corrected Edition*, ed. John N. Serio and Chris Beyers (New York: Penguin, 2015), 254–5 (254).
2. Tom Wolfe, *The New Journalism* (New York: Harper and Row, 1973).
3. *Hiroshima mon amour*, directed by Alain Resnais (France: Argos Films, [1959] 2003), DVD.
4. Pablo Picasso, *Picasso – Guernica (4-Fold)* (London: Scala, 2003).
5. *Nuit et brouillard* (Night and Fog), directed by Alain Resnais (Paris: Como Films, Argos Films & Cocinor, [1956] 2003), DVD.
6. Roland Barthes, *A Lover's Discourse: Fragments*, trans. R. Howard (New York: Hill and Wang, 1977).
7. Theodor W. Adorno, 'Cultural Criticism and Society', in *Prisms: Essays in Cultural Criticism and Society*, Studies in Contemporary German Thought, trans. Samuel Weber and Sherry Weber (Boston: Massachusetts Institute of Technology, 1981), 17–35 (34).
8. Night and Fog, directed by Alain Resnais.
9. Avneet Randhawa, Interview with Timothy Corrigan on 'The Past, Present and Future of Documentary Cinema', *34th Street*, 17

January 2018, https://www.34st.com/article/2018/01/the-past-present-and-future-of-documentary-cinema-timothy-corrigan.
10 Theodor W. Adorno, 'The Essay as Form', in *Notes to Literature*, Vol. 1, ed. Ralf Tiedemann, trans. Shierry Weber Nicholsen (New York: Columbia University Press, 1991), 3–23 (7).
11 Ibid., 23.
12 Patrick Sharp, 'From Yellow Peril to Japanese Wasteland: John Hersey's "Hiroshima"', *Twentieth Century Literature* 46, no. 4 (2000): 434–52 (444).
13 Ibid., 435.
14 Ibid., 436.
15 Ibid.
16 John Hersey, 'The Novel of Contemporary History', *The Atlantic Monthly* November 1949, 80–5 (81).
17 Patrick Sharp, 'From Yellow Peril to Japanese Wasteland: John Hersey's HIROSHIMA', 436.
18 Ibid., 437.
19 Jeremy Treglown, *Mr. Straight-Arrow: The Career of John Hersey, Author of* Hiroshima (New York: Farrar, Strauss and Giroux, 2019), 134.
20 Bret Schulte, 'Analysing Literary Journalism: Twentieth Century Stories: Objectivity and Authority in Wilkerson and Hersey', *Current Narratives* 1, no. 4 (2014): 3–16 (4).
21 Christian Kriticos, 'An Invitation to Hesitate: John Hersey's *Hiroshima* at 70', *themillions*, 31 August 2016, https://themillions.com/2016/08/invitation-hesitate-john-herseys-hiroshima.html.
22 Nicholas Lemann, 'John Hersey and the Art of Fact', *The New Yorker*, 29 April 2019, https://www.newyorker.com/magazine/2019/04/29/john-hersey-and-the-art-of-fact.
23 Roger Angell, 'Hersey and History', *The New Yorker*, 31 July 1995, https://www.newyorker.com/magazine/1995/07/31/hersey-and-history.
24 Schulte, 'Analysing Literary Journalism', 6.
25 Dan Gerstle, 'John Hersey and Hiroshima', *Dissent* 59, no. 2 (2012): 90–4 (90–1).
26 Yuko Shibata, 'Dissociative Entanglement: US–Japan Atomic Bomb Discourses by John Hersey and Nagai Takashi', *Inter-Asia Cultural Studies* 13, no. 1 (2012): 122–37 (124).
27 Hayden White, 'The Question of Narrative in Contemporary Historical Theory', *History and Theory* 23, no. 1 (1984): 1–33 (1).
28 Ibid., 1.
29 Roland Barthes, 'Introduction to the Structural Analysis of Narrative', in *Image, Music, Text*, trans. Stephen Heath (New York: Fontana Press, 1977), 79–124 (79).
30 Hayden White, *The Content of the Form: Narrative Discourse and Historical Representation* (Baltimore, MD: Johns Hopkins University Press, 1990), 113.
31 Ibid., 120.
32 Taco Hidde Bakker, 'Telling Images and Silent Stories: Narrativity and Photography in the Post-historical Age', in *On the Move: Storytelling in Contemporary Photography and Graphic Design* (Stedelijk Museum Amsterdam, 2014), 66–73 (69). Exhibition Catalogue.
33 White, *The Content of the Form*, 131–2.
34 Schulte, 'Analysing Literary Journalism', 9.
35 Ibid.
36 Shibata, 'Dissociative Entanglement: US–Japan Atomic Bomb Discourses by John Hersey and Nagai Takashi', 124.

37. White, 'The Question of Narrative in Contemporary Historical Theory'.
38. Shibata, 'Dissociative Entanglement: US–Japan Atomic Bomb Discourses by John Hersey and Nagai Takashi', 127.
39. Sharp, 'From Yellow Peril to Japanese Wasteland: John Hersey's HIROSHIMA', 436.
40. Ibid., 437.
41. Ibid.
42. Bakker, 'Telling Images and Silent Stories', 66.
43. Ibid., 67.
44. Ibid.
45. Ibid.
46. Bakker, 'Telling Images and Silent Stories', 67. The term 'textolatory' is from Vilém Flusser, *Towards a Philosophy of Photography* (London: Reaktion Books, 2000), 10.
47. Ibid., 10. Emphasis mine.
48. Hayden White, 'Historiography and Historiophoty', *The American Historical Review* 93, no. 5 (1988): 1193–9 (1193).
49. Adorno, 'The Essay as Form', 8.
50. Timothy Corrigan, *The Essay Film: From Montaigne, After Marker* (Oxford: Oxford University Press, 2011), 6.
51. Hunter Vaughan, *Where Film Meets Philosophy: Godard, Resnais, and Experiments in Cinematic Thinking* (New York: Columbia University Press, 2013), 144. The quote is from David Bordwell, *Poetics of Cinema* (New York: Routledge, 2008), 152.
52. Vaughan, *Where Film Meets Philosophy*, 147.
53. Corrigan, *The Essay Film: From Montaigne, After Marker*, 6.
54. Marguerite Duras, *Hiroshima Mon Amour: A Screenplay by Marguerite Duras for the Film by Alain Resnais*, trans. Richard Seaver (New York: Grove Press, 1961), 15.
55. Ibid.
56. Vaughan, *Where Film Meets Philosophy*, 149.
57. Ibid.
58. Sarah French, 'From History to Memory: Alain Resnais' and Marguerite Duras' *Hiroshima mon Amour*', *Electronic Melbourne Art Journal* 3 (2008): 1–13 (1), https://emajartjournal.files.wordpress.com/2012/08/french.pdf
59. James Agee and Walker Evans, *Let Us Now Praise Famous Men: The American Classic, in Words and Photographs, of Three Tenant Families in the Deep South* (Boston: Houghton Mifflin Harcourt [1941] 2001).
60. Vera Rule, 'Dispatches from the Dust Bowl', *The Guardian*, 18 August 2001, https://www.theguardian.com/books/2001/aug/18/historybooks.highereducation
61. French, 'From History to Memory', 1.
62. Ibid., 2.
63. Roland Barthes, *Camera Lucida: Reflections on Photography*, trans. Richard Howard (New York: Hill and Wang, 1980).
64. Bakker, 'Telling Images and Silent Stories', 69.
65. Ibid.
66. Vaughan, *Where Film Meets Philosophy*, 141.
67. Ibid., 142.
68. Timothy Corrigan, 'Essayism and Contemporary Film Narrative', Keynote Lecture presented at the *World Cinema and the Essay Film: International Conference at the University of Reading, UK*, 1 May 2015, http://blogs.reading.ac.uk/cfac/files/2015/03/Timothy-Corrigan-Keynote.pdf
69. Corrigan, 'Essayism and Contemporary Film Narrative'.

70 Treglown, *Mr. Straight-Arrow*, 126.
71 Please see Chapter 3, pp. 49–50.
72 Graham Greene, *The Quiet American* (New York: Penguin Books, 2002), 34.
73 Ibid., 46.
74 Treglown, *Mr. Straight-Arrow*, 120.
75 Adorno, 'The Essay as Form', 7.
76 Treglown, *Mr. Straight-Arrow*, 125–6.
77 Yuko Shibata, *Producing Hiroshima and Nagasaki: Literature, Film, and Transnational Politics* (Hilo: University of Hawaii Press, 2018).

SUGGESTED READING AROUND *THE ESSAY AT THE LIMITS*

Each of the chapters in this volume includes its own references, and the range of sources mentioned and discussed is both eclectic and extensive. However, the following list includes some of the seminal books and essays that contributors in this volume return to repeatedly. These texts may therefore be recommended to those readers who would like to read further around the main theoretical and critical issues raised by *The Essay at the Limits*.

Adorno, Theodor W., 'The Essay as Form', trans. Bob Hullot-Kentor and Frederic Will, *New German Critique* 32 (Spring–Summer, 1984): 151–71.
Atkins, G. Douglas, *Tracing the Essay: Through Experience to Truth*. Athens: University of Georgia Press, 2005.
Barthes, Roland, *Roland Barthes by Roland Barthes*, trans. Richard Howard. New York: Hill and Wang, 2010.
Bensmaïa, Réda, *The Barthes Effect: The Essay as Reflective Text*, trans. Pat Fedkiew. Minneapolis: University of Minnesota Press, 1987.
Butrym, Alexander J. (ed.), *Essays on the Essay: Redefining the Genre*. Athens: University of Georgia Press, 1989.
De Obaldia, Claire, *The Essayistic Spirit: Literature, Modern Criticism, and the Essay*. Oxford: Clarendon Press, 1995.
Dillon, Brian, *Essayism*. London: Fitzcarraldo Editions, 2017.
DuPlessis, Rachel Blau, 'f-Words: An Essay on the Essay', *American Literature* 68, no. 1 (1996): 15–45.
Good, Graham, *The Observing Self: Rediscovering the Essay*. London: Routledge, 1988.
Klaus, Carl H., and Ned Stuckey-French (eds), *Essayists on the Essay: Montaigne to Our Time*. Iowa City: University of Iowa Press, 2012.
Lazar, David, 'Queering the Essay', in *Occasional Desire: Essays*. Lincoln: University of Nebraska Press, 2013, 61–7.

INDEX

Addison, Joseph 99, 113, 120
Adorno, Theodor W. 23–33, 43, 54, 173–4, 186
Alexander, Michelle 67–8
aphorism
   Bacon and 172–80
   Barthes on 169–71, 174–6, 179–80
   definition 171
   and essay 169–80
   as *fixité* 174–80
   and the 'I' 170, 177–80
   and memorability 171–4
   as movement 171–4
   Smith and 171, 176
   and tone 99, 105, 169
   Wilde and 177–80
Appiah, Kwame Anthony 64, 68–71, 73
argument
   in essays 63, 105, 120, 125–33, 152, 155
Arnold, Matthew 105–6, 139–43
Atkins, G. Douglas 4, 125–8, 131, 140, 143
attitude
   essayistic 6–7, 12, 41–2, 73, 100–4, 204
Atwan, Robert 3, 12, 44

Bacon, Francis 4–5, 8–10, 64–5, 78–9, 172–9
Baldwin, James 64, 71–2
Barnes, Julian 217–19
Barthes, Roland 7–10, 49–58, 169–80, 232
Bensmaïa, Réda 7–10, 54–5, 128, 139, 191–2
Blanchfield, Brian 138–9
Blanchot, Maurice 9, 43, 103–7, 143
boundaries (*see also* limits *and* transgression)
   aphoristic 172–6
   definitional 1
   generic 10, 12, 23, 112, 151–2
   queer 138–40
   self 70, 73, 138, 152–3, 161

   subject and object 23, 145
   thinking 6, 104
Burdick, Anne and Janet Sarbanes, *TRINA: A Design Fiction* 77–89

canon (*see also* tradition) 78, 102, 111
Cavell, Stanley 24–6
Coates, Ta-Nehisi 69, 71–3
Coetzee, J. M. 190, 193
convention (*see also* genre) 2, 10, 230–2
   questioning of 6, 54, 81, 206, 214
conversational essay 2, 98–9, 120, 141, 144, 155, 177
Coover, Robert 77, 85
Corrigan, Timothy 234–8

De Obaldia, Claire 10–11, 40, 42–3, 143, 191, 204
death of literary forms (*see also* end of literature) 11, 44, 187–8
definitions of the essay 3, 179, 183–4, 234
   and queer essay 137–8
   resistance to 3, 38, 199, 214
Derrida, Jacques 9–10, 97, 101, 106–7, 143
digital essayism 77–89
Dillon, Brian 67, 100, 104–7, 170
Du Bois, W. E. B. 64–6, 71

Eliot, T. S. 42, 103, 144, 214–15
Emerson, Ralph Waldo 9, 67, 78, 81–3
end of literature 77, 84–6
epistemology 23–6, 43, 174, 176–9
epistolary essay (*see also* letters) 5, 112
essay (*see also* definitions of the essay)
   craft 4, 113, 193, 214
   death of 11
   experimentation in 2, 11, 28, 161, 179, 185, 192, 234
   formal 9
   and ideas 3, 5–9, 13, 63–74, 105, 127, 160, 203, 214–24

indefinability 13, 38, 139
indeterminacy 1, 31, 138–40, 191
marginal 44, 139–40, 145, 183, 204
origins 3–5, 8
possibilitarian 11, 125–6
process 1, 4, 7, 11, 28, 30, 32, 190, 192, 218
rebirths 11–12
unmethodical (*see also* veering) 6, 8, 23, 215
essay film 229–38
essay of demand 127–32
essayism 20–1, 44, 46, 165, 189, 205
  Barthes 50
  Corrigan 238
  digital 77–89
  Dillon, *Essayism* 104, 170
  multi-modal 234
  Musil, *essayismus* 40, 89, 184, 186
essayistic 46, 55, 67, 69, 104, 106, 165–7, 186, 234
  aesthetic 78–82
  aphorism 177–80
  form 41, 78
  historiography 229–38
  'I' 152–61
  mode 2–13
  music 215–24
  novel 190–4
  poetry 203–7
  possibilitarian 125–7
  style 19, 133, 139
  style of demand 127–33
  writing in philosophy 24–31
experience 4, 64, 68, 113
  collective 64–5
  and fragmented subject 143
  phenomenal experience 23–33
  personal 5, 65, 70, 72, 152–3, 231
  sensed / sensuous 41, 126, 132, 231
  shareable 2, 74, 206, 215, 221–4, 234–7

failure
  anti-project 185–6, 190
  in queer essay 138, 145–6
familiar 1–2, 6, 9
first person (*see also* identity, personality *and* self) 28, 69, 177
  aphorism 177

erasure of 152
form (*see also* limits) 1–13, 165–7
  in Adorno 43, 54, 186, 214, 230
  aphoristic 169–80
  in Barthes 55–6, 170
  and concepts 26–7
  and experience 25–6, 64
  formlessness 142
  incompleteness 67
  literary 1–2, 38, 128, 188, 191
  in Lukács 39–43, 142
  and mode 10–11
  openness 25, 29, 125, 152, 204
  and philosophy 23–4
  and queer essay 138–46
  self-reflexive 2, 70
  in Weinberger 161
Fowler, Alastair 10–12
fragment 42–3, 193, 217
  Romantic 42
fragmentary 9, 41, 43, 94, 142–3, 192, 219

gender 82, 94, 113–21, 200–2
  and genre 138–40, 144, 198–9, 206–7
Genet, Jean 137–46
genre 2–13, 101, 104, 152, 170, 190–3, 198
  a-generic 8–10, 139
  anti-genre 2, 8–10, 142, 165, 199
  before genre 151
  essay as dead genre 12–13
  and gender 114, 120, 138–40, 144, 199–207
  limits 8–11, 23, 78, 238
  and mode 10–13, 204
  origins 4, 6, 152
  queer 137–40, 199–202, 205–6
Good, Graham 2, 11, 68, 142, 144

Hamburger, Michael 3, 12
Haywood, Eliza 112–13, 116, 118
Hazlitt, William 3–4, 6–7
Hersey, John 229–38
history of the essay 112–21, 183, 224
Hume, David 25, 28, 32, 120
Husserl, Edmund 29–30

identity
  Appiah on 69–71
  Coates on 71–3

non-identity of concept to content 31–3
personal 93–4, 139–41
queer 201
Weinberger and 154–5
writing as constitutive of 28

Johnson, Samuel 7, 97–101, 214

Knausgaard, Karl Ove 188, 192–4
Korhonen, Kuisma 128, 131
Kundera, Milan 189–91

Lazar, David 138–9, 143, 199,
    201–2, 205–6
Lee, Vernon 125–33
Lerner, Ben 192–3
letters (*see also* epistolary) 5, 111,
    114–19, 202
limits (*see also* boundaries) 1–13, 23, 140,
    142, 151, 185–7
  of action 127
  of form 161
  gender-based 94
  medial 78–9
  publishing 112
  queer 140, 142–5
  of representation 233–8
  of sympathy 129
  of thinking 65–6
literary (*see also* end of literature) 37–46,
    183–94, 231
  approaches to text 24
  criticism 97, 99–102, 106
  culture 155
  essay as 1–3, 63–4, 94
  history 11, 82, 87, 138–9
  humanities 80, 84
  renewal 77
  reputation 113–16
Lopate, Phillip 4, 7, 141–2
Lorde, Audre 206–7
Lukács, György 26–7, 29, 39–43, 142, 144
lyric essay 81, 186–8
  Weinberger and 153–61

mode 10–11, 204, 236
  of being 26–9
  and genre 10–13, 204
modernity 45, 77, 101, 165, 183–4

Montagu, Lady Mary Wortley 114–19
Montaigne, Michel de 1–12, 25, 28, 55,
    63–5, 79, 99, 106, 112–13, 143,
    152, 203
Murray, Judith Sargent 113–17
music essay (*see also* essayistic
    music) 213–24
Musil, Robert 11, 40, 89, 184–7

narrative 77, 85, 89, 151–2, 232–8
  essay 178, 192
  novel 45, 77
  relation to essay 187–94, 204
  rise of the 114
  sentimental 178
  structure 231–2

objectivity 30–1, 44, 233–6
  and subjectivity 26–9
occasionalism 27, 41–6
Orwell, George 64, 128
Ozick, Cynthia 6, 12, 129, 151

pacifist essay 127–9, 133
Paz, Octavio 159–61
periodical essay 111–21, 137
persona 87, 101, 111–14, 142, 145
personality 93, 101, 103, 130, 141,
    144–5, 155–7
persuasion 102, 120, 126–33, 185, 221–3
phenomenology 23–33, 106
philosophy 21–32
poetics 32, 88–9, 183–4, 200–1
poetry 12, 41–2, 128, 143, 157–61, 185
  and Stevens's essayism 197–207
polemical (*see also* political) 9, 129,
    133, 216
political (*see also* polemical) 12–13, 64–71,
    101, 104, 127–33, 157, 185–6, 217–20
Pope, Alexander 99–100
post-literary (*see also* literary) 37–46
post-truth 12, 39, 64, 74, 165, 186, 193
protest 64, 105, 157, 165, 185, 186
public intellectuals 66–74, 127
publishing
  opportunities for women essayists
    112, 115

queer essay 137–46, 197–207

reading
    aphorism 172-3, 177-8
    the essay 1-4, 7, 63-74, 94, 126, 141-2, 155-8, 186
    as production of meaning 161, 233, 237
    public 64, 112-20
    as theme in *TRINA: A Design Fiction* 85-6
    tone 102
Resnais, Alain 229-38
Retallack, Joan 183-9
rhetoric 126, 132, 205, 214
rhetorical forms and strategies 6-10, 64, 73, 113, 117-20, 126-7, 205, 220
Romanticism 42-6
Russell, David 125-8

Said, Edward 66-7, 73
Saussure, Ferdinand de 50-5
scepticism 8, 24-6, 29
Sedgwick, Eve Kosofsky 201-2
self
    beyond gender 138-46
    and the other 126
    relation to world 68, 232, 237
    as subject of essay 2, 9, 152
    and Weinberger 153-61
semiology 50-8
Seneca 5
Shields, David 12, 186-93
Shostakovich, Dmitri 213-24
Smith, Zadie 171, 176
Solnit, Rebecca 7-9, 12
Sontag, Susan 65, 104
spirit of the essay (*see also* possibilitarian essay) 12, 104, 161, 204-5, 207, 230
    exploratory 6-7, 11, 152
Steele, Richard 98, 113, 120
style 32, 40, 223
    Bacon 4, 8, 10
    conversational 2
    difference from tone 97, 99, 100, 103
    Johnson 7
    Knausgaard 192
    Montaigne 8, 10
    possibilitarian 126, 133
    relational 129
    Vella 221-2
    Weinberger 159
subjectivity 9, 19, 23, 26-9, 44-6, 221-2, 232, 235-7

and objectivity 26-9
queer 138-45
subjective generality 44
swerve (*see also* veering) 2, 5-8, 183-7
Swift, Jonathan 99, 100

tact 126, 131
things/objects in the essay 19, 23-33, 41, 52-7, 126, 142, 155, 170
third person voice 103, 153-4, 177, 231-2
tradition 1-2, 8-9, 189
    Barthes and literary 49-50
    Baconian 204
    essay 55, 64, 77, 82, 87, 97, 137-40
    Montaignian 191
    political essay 220
tragedy 65, 218-24
transcendence 31, 44, 81, 193, 214, 221-3
transgression 1-2, 23, 78, 138-40, 201, 214, 220, 222-3
truth (*see also* post-truth)
    contested 9, 64-5, 74, 125, 129, 133
    essay as embodiment of 24-31, 140, 143-4
    essay as pursuit of 4, 24-31, 55, 159, 189, 231
    shareable 74

veering (*see also* swerve) 6-9
Vella, Joseph 213-24
voice 8-9, 113, 141, 193, 206, 231-3
    in music essays 215, 218-23
    personal 141-4, 152, 214
    public 113-16
    plurality 28-9, 125-6, 145
    in queer essay 143-4
    Seneca 5
    and tone 98-9, 103
    voice-over 78, 82-5
    Weinberger 152-61
    of women essayists 113-19

Wallace, David Foster 7
Weinberger, Eliot 151-61
White, Hayden 230-3
Wilde, Oscar 173, 177-9
Wollstonecraft, Mary 116-19
Woolf, Virginia 12, 63-4, 93, 114-15, 125-6, 128, 206

Yevtushenko, Yevgeny 216-17